D0679784

Meramec Library
St. Louis Community College
11333 Big Bend Blvd.
Kirkwood, MO 63122-5799
314-984-7797

7/01

Stand-up Comedy in Theory, or, Abjection in America

St. Louis Community College
at Meramec
Library

New Americanists   *A series edited by Donald E. Pease*

Stand-up Comedy in Theory, or, Abjection in America

John Limon

Duke University Press *Durham and London 2000*

The chapter "Analytic of the Ridiculous" is based on an
essay that first appeared in *Raritan: A Quarterly Review*
14, no. 3 (winter 1997).
The chapter "Journey to the End of the Night" is based on
an essay that first appeared in *Jx: A Journal in Culture and
Criticism* 1, no. 1 (autumn 1996).
The chapter "Nectarines" is based on an essay that first
appeared in the *Yale Journal of Criticism* 10, no. 1
(spring 1997).

© 2000 Duke University Press
All rights reserved
Printed in the United States of America on acid-free paper ♾
Typeset in Melior by Tseng Information Systems, Inc.
Library of Congress Cataloging-in-Publication Data
appear on the last printed page of this book.

Contents

Introduction: Approximations, Apologies, Acknowledgments

It was once my pretense that I was using stand-up comedy to write cultural history; the book I had in mind would have been thin as cultural history, but in any case I did not write it. The book I have written does not exploit stand-up but attempts to provide it with a theory—or a first approximation of one. It would be gratifying to imagine that the theory will contribute to some future cultural history, probably not written by me.

Here is a first glimpse of the cultural-historical data I hope this theory will eventually clarify. Around 1960, Jewish heterosexual men formed the pool of American citizens that produced most American stand-up comedians. According to one guess, 80 percent of nationally known stand-ups at the time were Jewish men; that they were Jewish men is more verifiable than that they were heterosexual, though that was the universal understanding.[1]

There are, of course, many ways to look at this, but it is easier to begin by specifying how not to look at it. I do not infer from their prevalence in stand-up that Jewish heterosexual men were, in 1960, the funniest people in America. That would be impossible to substantiate; it is impossible to be lucid about what that would even mean. However, I do not want to reduce Jewish stand-up dominance to a merely institutional fact, as if to say that just as many Methodist women were very funny but were simply not given the same breaks by the stand-up establishment as Jewish men. That many comedy sites were owned by Jews is of course true—but this would be a cultural and historical fact to be explained, not entirely dissimilar from the one that occupies us at the beginning of this study. Furthermore, the fact that Jews owned and operated many nightclubs did not entail the prevalence of Jewish popular singers, nor did it force Ed Sullivan and Steve Allen to promote Jewish comedians before a national audience.

These antithetical hypotheses—that Jewish men were the funniest Americans or that Jewish male comedians were simply preferred by Jewish male comedy impresarios—fail for the same reason: humor is (I shall say more about this) unfalsifiable and incorrigible. If there were comedy audiences (at the Grand Ole Opry or the Apollo, say) who had non-Jewish comedic preferences, they had a right to them. If, on the other hand, the general American public wanted Jewish male comedians above all, for reasons we should be able to reconstruct, then male Jews were the best ones for the job. The cultural fact I want to isolate as my starting point is the connection between being a Jewish heterosexual man in America in 1960 and making one sort of living.

The job was, I take it, to provide humor of a certain kind in a certain setting. Not the humor of the dozens, for example, or of camp. And so I began with what seemed to me a promising aperçu: the tense intimacy of national stand-up comedy as it was practiced in 1960 and the suburban moment of modern American culture. Lenny Bruce provided one take on suburbanization. From the far reaches of Long Island, he came to New York City to learn how to be a Jewish comedian, and his humor was an affront to suburbia on behalf of hip urbanites and suburbanites alike. The comedy of Mel Brooks and Carl Reiner was another take. Carl Reiner was the suburbanizer (he would set his humor commuting to New Rochelle for *The Dick Van Dyke Show*) in loving proximity to Mel Brooks's weird Englishing of urban *Yiddishkeit*. The suburbanizing Jew and the citifying Middle American (whose prime comedy habitat was the late-night New York talk show: Jack Paar of Michigan, Johnny Carson of Iowa and Nebraska, Dick Cavett of Nebraska, David Letterman of Indiana) together formed the chiasmus of our postwar national humor. "National" is key: Judaism on *The Tonight Show* was a contribution to nation rebuilding on the suburban model as a turn from Zionism and Marxism. Freud's joke theory, which centers on the covering up of laughter's sources in aggression and sex, has at least the merit of elucidating the suburban moment of American comedy and culture, if suburbs grew on the energy of the same concealments.

This is not by any means the whole story of Jewish stand-up success, but it is the cultural part of the story that first occurred to me, and I still vouch for it. It is the basis of the structure of this book: three essays on Jewish stand-up as it flourished for several years before 1960 and a few years after (first on Lenny Bruce, second on Mel Brooks and Carl Reiner, third on Mike Nichols and Elaine May), three essays on stand-up in its wake (first on David Letterman, second on Richard Pryor, third on Ellen DeGeneres and Paula Poundstone). I was not trying to locate and analyze the most influential post–World War II American stand-up comedians (where is Mort Sahl? Woody Allen? Lily Tomlin? George Carlin?) or the funniest ones (where are Jonathan Winters, Buddy Hackett, Robin Williams, and Steve Martin?). I am not, for the purposes of this book, interested in the brilliant Jewish stand-ups of the present. I confess that I only chose to write about comedians who seemed essential to my story.

Its outline is this: America, between 1960 and the millennium, in a process that began around the ascension of Johnny Carson or the Kennedy assassination, comedified.[2] Stand-up was once a field given over to a certain subsection of a certain ethnicity. By now, roughly speaking, all America is the pool for national stand-up comedy. So, in the second half of my book, I needed to examine comedians who were not Jewish, or not male, or not heterosexual, or not any of these.

The problem, from the cultural studies point of view, is that the end of my narrative had plenty of potential exemplars to support my argument, but no moral. I was quite sure that what I was describing was not reducible to a triumph of multicultural inclusiveness. That is no doubt a part of the significance of the plot. But what would it mean to add that society has taken to its heart such distinctly non-Jewish comedians as Steve Martin, Robin Williams, and David Letterman? (Would it signal a recentering or decentering of WASP culture in America? Comedy exists to upset such primer anthropology.) I seemed to need some cultural fact equal and opposite to suburbanization for the story of stand-up's post–high Jewish continuation, but I could not think of one that did not seem to me banal or prophetic or false.

It was at this impasse that the project turned theoretical rather than cultural. But it happens, I think, that you can get back to the cultural after all. This remains to be seen; in what is left of this introduction, I make a few theoretical suggestions, with the hope that it is possible to find in stand-up theory per se some indication at least of how the comedification of America might be explained.

As I wrote these essays, over time, abjection became my master theme. I mean by abjection two things. First, I mean by it what everybody means by it: abasement, groveling prostration. Second, I mean by it what Julia Kristeva means: a psychic worrying of those aspects of oneself that one cannot be rid of, that seem, but are not quite, alienable—for example, blood, urine, feces, nails, and the corpse.[3] The "abject," in Kristeva's term of art, indicates what cannot be subject or object to you; but I came to realize that that was also the essence of abjection as it is commonly understood. When you feel abject, you feel as if there were something miring your life, some skin that cannot be sloughed, some role (because "abject" always, in a way, describes how you *act*) that has become your only character. Abjection is self-typecasting.

The one-sentence version of the theory of this book would state the claim that what is stood up in stand-up comedy is abjection. Stand-up makes vertical (or ventral) what should be horizontal (or dorsal). I had not quite seen this definition at the time of the Lenny Bruce essay, but it was lurking there, and I want to leave that essay as originally written because I still like the way it formulates the issue. The conclusion of the Bruce essay is that "stand-up is the resurrection of your father as your child," which approaches the same point from another angle. What I took as the essential Lenny Bruce moment is the joke (if that is what it is) that concludes "I am going to piss on you" and provokes, at one performance, seventeen seconds of boisterous laughter. What struck me is how phallically aggressive Bruce was able to make this infantile threat, so that he appeared to the audience as punishing father and naughty son in rapid oscillation, just as his audience had to vibrate (this vibration seems to me the essence of laughter) between terrorized child and permissive parent. The abject gets erected and mobilized in the place of the phallus. To "stand up" abjection is simultaneously to erect it and miss one's date with it: comedy is a way of avowing and disavowing abjection, as fetishism is a way of avowing and disavow-

4

ing castration. Fetishism is a way of standing up the inevitability of loss; stand-up is a way of standing up the inevitability of return.

Abjection becomes an explicitly key term in my final three chapters. I begin the second half of the book with David Letterman—that I place Letterman before Pryor is one sign that the book purports to be theoretical rather than historical. Letterman's abjection takes its essential American form in an abstract repudiation of the body (which is mechanized) and its distanced and displaced return: the body declares its inalienability only by way of disposable interviewees like Eddie Murphy or Madonna. The late-night New York City talk show puts American abjection on national display before the abject watchers of TV. The structure of the show is chiasmic: the hick visitor in New York is the "host" of the show, and the city kid (which is how we identify Jackie Mason when he is interviewed by Jack Paar, Don Rickles when he is interviewed by Johnny Carson, and Eddie Murphy or Madonna when they are interviewed by Letterman, regardless of actual origins) is his "guest." The crossing is what is most lovable in America, though its mode of mechanical abstraction predicts virtual reality.

David Letterman takes the legacy of Lenny Bruce one way, Richard Pryor the other. Letterman rediscovers the fuel of paternal aggression in Bruce's filial abjection; Pryor finds in Bruce's excremental regression to infancy the possibility of forestalling abjection altogether. Pryor's refusal of the usual stand-up posture—the standing up of abjection—is the result, I think, of his self-identification in an abjected race. He is not the sufferer of abjection, he *is* the abjection, the body that is repudiated yet keeps returning. He allows the body to speak regardless of his own self-interest; when it returns in the form of a heart attack, he falls to the floor, sacrificing the stand-up posture literally. Pryor's purpose is to find the Rabelaisian comedy of this radical leveling.

That sounds like a climactic sentence, but it could not represent the climax of *this* book, which must come to a triumph of abjection or betray its subject. The issue of homosexuality in comedy is first raised in my Carl Reiner/Mel Brooks chapter; the subject of women in comedy, in my chapter on Mike Nichols and Elaine May; they return in tandem in my final chapter on Ellen DeGeneres and Paula Poundstone. These motives return in the way of the abject: as the alienable that keeps not being alienated. We might have expected female strategies parallel to Pryor's, but we do not get them. Standing up abjection turns out to be the mode of DeGeneres and Poundstone's familiar, mainstream appeal, though it is in the event so self-denying an appeal that it allows them to escape from audience view altogether. The final paradox is that their strategy of evasion by way of vertical abjection is not so much a peculiar female use of stand-up as it is a brilliant redeployment of what all stand-ups do. Stand-up itself has the structure of abjection insofar as comedians are not allowed to be either natural or artificial. (Are they themselves or acting? Are they in costume?) Reality keeps returning to stand-up performance, but the deepest desire of stand-ups is to be, with respect to their lives, unencumbered. All a stand-up's life feels abject to him or her, and stand-ups try to escape it by living it as an act.

On the back cover of Ellen DeGeneres's book, *My Point . . . And I Do Have One,* is a portrait of the comedian as chameleon. (She is dressed in white and sitting in the corner of a white room, her head bowed and her cropped hair facing forward.) *This* is where a book on stand-up needs to end. Her desire to escape has gone as far as it can—she is trying to dissolve herself in her environment. But if she were to succeed, it would be the end of stand-up begun by sitting down. The desire is for such a rampant, couchant, disembodied whiteness that it seems a fitting complement of Pryor's incorporated blackness. American abjectness taken to its extreme is a craving for abstraction.

I am, throughout these essays, impressed by the beautiful abstract geometry of stand-up. I treat this at the beginning of my essay on Bruce, and again at some length in my essay on Brooks and Reiner and at points thereafter. The appeal of comedy for me is akin to the appeal of math, except that the formal abstraction of a gag retains as its subject matter the pollution of the liminal, so that Mel Brooks's ur-joke is a logical deduction from a rotten nectarine. This is another way of putting the abjection theme, but it is also another way of putting the relevance of stand-up to the suburbanization theme, to which I can now return, with a revised understanding of it.

I said that for the suburban moment of American culture, half-suburbanized Jewish comedians, whose joke work was the structural equivalent of a suburban commute, were the desired thing; what was desired, more generally, however, was an updating of the destiny of American abjection, and it has become increasingly unclear, in this introduction, that Jewish male heterosexuals ever had it all to themselves. The solution to the paradox is how thoroughly Jewish male heterosexual comedians in 1960 were female, homosexual, black, and Christianizing.

Mike Nichols and Elaine May were enough, by themselves, to upset traditional gender categories. The cliché that stand-up was so macho that a female comedian (or comedienne, as she would have been called) had to be a hag was definitively falsified by May. (Phyllis Diller had gone so far as to phallicize or bewitch herself to make it in the world of high-gag comedy.) But the fact that May did not disguise her femininity—though it came in various guises—was compatible with the fact that she was the stronger presence of the team and often *played* rather daunting characters, as if they were roles. She was the sublime in human form. In his more oppressed moments, Nichols, both playing and inhabiting the weaker position, would cry or allow his voice to break like Shelley Berman's; at such moments, it was unclear where femininity, in Jewish comedy, would land.

In my essay on Carl Reiner and Mel Brooks, I make much of the homosexuality buried in their homosocial act. Thus queer theory comes up for the first time in the book, but not the last. It comes up in the first place because stand-up has been traditionally (this has changed) an affair of male comedians and male audiences (some of that erotics informs the relationship of Brooks and Reiner, with Reiner representing the audience's love). Freud, I think, was wrong to have assumed that what we now call homosociality is in joking only a detouring of normal heterosexuality, conceived of as competitive and sexually aggressive. The homosociality, as Eve Sedgwick would have it, defines the heterosexuality. But the subject of homosexuality lingers in my book, because the frontal macho of the stand-up position needs, somehow or other, to be paradoxical to be funny.

And what modern Jewish comedian is not in an important way already a black comedian? There was stand-up comedy before 1966, but that is when the term came into existence,[4] and what seems to have been established over the decade before it was named was the contribution of jazz improvisation to how comedians thought of themselves. Lenny Bruce placed himself directly in the jazz tradition; Nichols and May improvised to music; Mel Brooks's obsession with blackness came out explicitly in *Blazing Saddles*. Here Michael Rogin is helpful: the Jewish approach to white America —as in *The Jazz Singer*—was made through blackface.

It was made, in sum, through the black body, the homosexual body, and the female body. "Through" them means "by way of abjecting" them. These bodies—I think this is a cliché I can rely on—signify the body itself. On behalf of the American suburb, heretofore Protestant, Jewish comedians took the body and turned it into a gag, which is not the same as expressing it or repressing it. It is abstracting what is the essence of the concrete. (I invert the view of Schopenhauer, who thought of laughter as the revenge of the sensuous on the conceptual.) Meanwhile, comedians like Johnny Carson and David Letterman brought their honed talent for abstraction—in their heads, jokes become jokes about jokes—to the city in search of the bodies their minds had thrown off; they found there an abjection that was peculiarly congenial and complementary.

This is all to say that it was misguided to look for a cause of the Jewish stand-up dominance of 1960 and another cause for the full comedification of America ever since. The hypothesis is that the Jewish comedians of 1960 stood up precisely at the place where body was idealized and materiality abstracted—which after World War II was preeminently defined as a point between New York City (or Chicago) and its suburbs. A century before, the place for it was Concord; American Jewish stand-up seems to me a moment of American cultural history, or the Puritan wing of that history, whose central figure may be Thoreau, abject comedian before the letter. That some of what Jewish comedians usurped has leaked back into the mainstream or into other tributaries is only the result of a law of nature, for which this book finds evidence. A theory of stand-up is a theory of what to do with your abjection; at a moment of cultural history when abjection is startlingly pervasive, for reasons that a cultural historian ought to be commissioned to discover, stand-up inherits its highest aspiration.

Two further comments on the writing of this book. First: I wrote several of these chapters as freestanding essays. At some point, early on, I began to sense their coherence, and I have tried to assimilate them as much as I can. But the Lenny Bruce chapter began as an essay for a volume on expressions of outrage at works of art, and retains marks of that purpose. Other chapters show signs of transitory interests.

Second, and more interestingly: my sense of how to write about stand-up altered over time. The first two essays I wrote, which happen to be the first two essays of this book, were on Lenny Bruce and the team of Brooks and Reiner. In both, I keep circling paradigmatic moments of their respective oeuvres: the urinating threat in Bruce and the nectarine dithyramb in Reiner/Brooks. I was determined to study only the most inexplicable jokes, reversing the technique of previous joke theorists. I was also desperate. I had little idea, and still have little idea, how to write about the form of a stand-up routine. I am afraid that by the third essay I wrote, on David Letterman, I was so resolved not to cling to another synecdoche that I almost never mention anything funny Letterman has ever said. This seems justifiable in retrospect, since it is in the nature of Letterman's work that no single moment of his career could be brilliantly exemplary (his distinction is in the hegemony of unchanging attitude); but the absence of jokes from that essay feels odd. I knew, by the time of my Pryor piece, that I had to discuss the form of a performance.

I got lucky. The Pryor performance in question had a peculiar climax, so that it was possible to see the unity of the concert. The climax—or, really, the anticlimax—was not exactly a punch line, which simplified things: the problem with seeing a stand-up performance (five or twenty or ninety minutes) as a single aesthetic object is that stand-up is dominated by miniclimaxes—the series of punch lines—that are not readily convertible into straight lines for a metaclimax or punch line of the whole. (In the case of Pryor's anticlimax, literally about the relief of sex without ejaculation, closure is provided by the release from that intermittent pressure.) I had, therefore, established no general procedure by my Pryor analysis, and the two subsequent essays that I wrote, on Poundstone and DeGeneres and Nichols/May, make no extended allusions to the subject of aesthetic form, except insofar as I theorize in both essays the meaning of anticlimax itself. It may be that an art reliant on short bursts for its structure needs a full-blown theory of anticlimax to elucidate the unity of its form; nevertheless, I am unable to venture one here.

The one advantage of writing this book piecemeal is that the chapters have acquired separate readerships. I have received very useful advice and encouragement from these readers: Steve Tifft, Anita Sokolsky, Chris Pye, Karen Swann, Regina Kunzel, Rachana Kamtekar, Jana Sawicki, Maud Ellmann, Bob Bell, Larry Graver, Shawn Rosenheim, Cassandra Cleghorn, Jim Shepard, D. L. Smith, Frederick Crews, Lynn Wardley, Warner Berthoff, Bill Brown, Joanna Spiro and Sarah Winter (on behalf of the editorial board of the *Yale Journal of Criticism*), Jay Watson (and an anonymous reader at *Journal X*), and especially Frances Restuccia. Emma Limon makes an uncredited cameo appearance at a key point. I would like to thank Maureen Mills and Ellen Ginsburg at Home Box Office for archival help; the *Yale Journal of Criticism, Journal X,* and *Raritan* for permission to use material that first appeared in their pages; and Williams College, which supported this work by many generosities. For support and advice at Duke University Press, I am grateful to Sharon Parks Torian, Paula Dragosh, and Reynolds Smith; thanks to Donald Pease for expediting things there; I am also indebted to its three anonymous reviewers. I am slightly too late in dedicating this book to my father, Albert H. (Bob) Sands (1925–1999).

nrage: A Lenny Bruce Joke and the Topography of Stand-Up

Three theorems survey stand-up comedy as an absolute or ideal genre. In each one, "you" is second-person plural: you, the audience.

1. If you think something is funny, it is. You may be (collectively) puzzled by your amusement or disapprove of it, but you cannot be wrong about it. This means three things. First, individual reservations are irrelevant: any member of the audience who is unamused by a generally well-received joke should be regarded as merely deflecting the group response, which is still single-minded and unimpeachable. Second, individual recantations are invalid. An individual may suspect that what he or she called love was lust or loneliness, or that suffering was self-pity. But the collective experience of humor, like the personal experience of pain, fills its moment and perishes; reflection misprizes it of necessity. (Laughter may be the so-

cial equivalent of pain, the *group* incorrigible.) Third, you cannot be retro-actively disabused by a critic. To criticize a joke is to miss it, because the joke, as Freud demonstrates, is, in the first instance, an escape from criticism to a prior happiness.[1]

The incorrigibility of your response is peculiar to comedy among all forms of art. You may wrongly think a symphony, for example, is beautiful when you have been seduced by the loveliness of the evening or the lyric athleticism of the conductor. Stand-up is uniquely audience-dependent for its value because joking is, essentially, (1) a social phenomenon (no audience, no joke, Freud noted, observing that an untransmitted joke is not, structurally, a joke [*SE*, 431]), and (2) a fully embedded phenomenon. The particularities of the relationship of joke teller and audience do not make the joke seem more or less funny; they make the joke more or less funny.

Because it is plausible to assert that an audience is wrong about, say, an opera (critics will judge) or a novel (posterity will judge), opera and literature can stake claims to seriousness. To be serious means to despise the audience—to reserve the right of appeal to a higher jurisdiction. But we can say about a stand-up audience's laughter what Freud says about the unconscious: there is "no process that resembles 'judging'" in its vicinity (*SE*, 175).

2. A joke is funny if and only if you laugh at it. This theorem quarantines comedy not from the serious, but from the humorous in all nonspecific settings. If you laugh at a rude gesture in a tennis match or at a caesura of prosaic commentary during a poetry reading, you are laughing from relief; you may laugh at a presidential witticism out of respect. But laughter at a stand-up routine signifies that the joke is funny, and the joke cannot be funny without it. A joke at which the audience smiles or nods its approbation is a failed joke; a joke at which the audience laughs is a good joke in proportion to its laughter. Perhaps, say, a comedian has been so successful (in his routine, in his career) that your laughter is indiscriminate. This behavior only indicates that you are the sort of audience inclined to find humor (not every audience is this unresentful) where it knows it to have passed before.

An individual has the right to say: I am certain (I remember) that I did not experience joke *x* as funny, but I was laughing along with the audience. There are studies on the subject: laughing is only mildly correlated with the experience of humor, more strongly among women, less strongly among men.[2] The audience itself cannot claim this.

3. Your laughter is the single end of stand-up. Theorem number 2 distinguishes stand-up from the generally and informally humorous (the audi-

ence of which has not assembled for the sake of laughing); this theorem distinguishes stand-up from all other particular and formal settings of humor. Stand-up comedy does not require plot, closure, or point. Jokes may be as short as ingenuity allows, and there need not be anything *but* jokes. Constant, unanimous laughter is the limit case. Any comedian is free, of course, to thematize or editorialize or beautify, but in these respects, he or she has in mind extrinsic models. I am demarcating *absolute* stand-up.

It is simple to intuit in this ideal structure (the audience cannot err, it cannot feign, it cannot be misled) why comedians might, above all other artists and entertainers, hate their audiences; but the most comprehensive way to put the matter is that they hate their audiences because they are not, as performers, entirely distinct from them. Audiences turn their jokes into jokes, as if the comedian had not quite thought or expressed a joke until the audience thinks or expresses it. Stand-up is all supplement. Freud describes in the teller-told exchange a system of transitive inhibitions (*SE,* 150–51), but I am noting a formal as much as a psychological relation. Laughter is more than the value of a routine; more than a determinant of the routine (its rhythm influencing the comedian's timing or its volume his direction); it is the arteries and veins of the routine's circulation.[3]

In this light, it is hard to fathom how a stand-up performance can be outrageous, that is to say (etymologically) outré, outside the circle. In stand-up as opposed to all other modes of art and entertainment, there is only the circle. The audience cannot be wrong or lie because it cannot reflect or judge: you can fail to see the joke, but so long as you see it, it is yours. That syndrome is itself sufficiently outrageous; but then it is the syndrome and not the joke that creates the emotion, and we can infer that every joke emits its own outraged aura. Even in the case of Lenny Bruce, the outrageous comedian par excellence, the most that can be granted is that outrage is the aura of the circulating comedy, which is why it has never been decided whether the condition of "outrage," an inevitable term in all discussions of Bruce, is better attributed to Bruce or his audience.[4]

Absolute stand-up, so defined, is akin to Clausewitz's "absolute war": the shared object is perfect devastation. Absolute war is unlike all actual wars; real wars continue policy by other means, so that perfect devastation is never necessary or desirable. To conceive of absolute war is to measure ordinary armed belligerence by its lapse from an atemporal, geometric ideal. Absolute stand-up is a cognate notion insofar as the mathematical aspect of comedy, noted by many commentators but rarely elaborated, is the result of its pursuit of an apocalyptic technique. In the distance that an actual stand-up situation strays from the absolute, we may register the irruptions of alien impulses—we can quantify, for one thing, the interference of audience outrage.

Let us give it a try. To what variety of audience is the following Lenny Bruce quatrain a joke? That is: what variety of audience would cocreate the following Lenny Bruce quatrain *as* a joke? What variety of audience would find the quatrain outrageous—in other words, not a bad joke but a nonjoke?

> If you've, er, [pause]
> Ever seen this bit before, I want you to tell me.
> Stop me if you've seen it. [long pause]
> I'm going to piss on you.[5]

How is it possible for us (not part of the scene) to guess? The routine is so perfectly focused here as a joke (setup, delay, punch line) that it is worth pondering why, in that case, it is hard to ascertain if a joke is what we are examining. The form, according to the terms of the cognitive joke theorists, is perfect: the incongruity of the last line is at the same time a novel resolution of narrative tension. Cognitive joke theorists argue that all a joke's humor is in what Freud calls the "joke work"; the joke work here is crystalline, a rarity in a Lenny Bruce routine, so long as (a single hesitation) the punch line makes, in an unanticipated context, some sense.[6]

Freud believes, on the other hand, that in all "tendentious" jokes there is, underneath the joke work, a repressed content, unhumorous but willing to be humored, which is either aggressive or sexual. On Freud's account, we never know exactly why we laugh because we cannot estimate how much of our laughter disguises satisfactions that are distinctly unfunny. Given that "sexual" means "excremental/sexual" (*SE*, 96–98), Bruce's joke, if that is what it is, is almost too obliging a Freudian specimen: sexual and excremental and aggressive at once, almost literally exhibitionistic and almost immediately hostile where the usual joke's exhibitionism is displaced (*SE*, 143) and its hostility is triangulated (*SE*, 100).

Joke analysts and psychoanalysts are easily amused (they laugh at anything); so are, to widen the radius one more notch, joke anthropologists. Bruce, let us say, or let *them* say, is a "sacred clown," a "ceremonial buffoon": "Ritual humor is characterized by purposeful verbal and nonverbal behavior by individuals and groups in which persons of high status and authority, foreigners, and rituals and ceremonies are parodied, sexual activities are simulated in an exaggerated manner, and simulated defecation and urination are carried out with scatological overtones."[7] The point is how easy it is to refer behavior to a humor theory without quite knowing whether it is funny. As the canniest of all joke anthropologists, Mary

Douglas, puts it: "When people throw excrement at one another whenever they meet, either verbally or actually, can this be interpreted as a case of wit, or merely written down as a case of throwing excrement?"[8]

What begins to appear is that Bruce's quatrain is a tour de force of meta-humor, a play on all such comic hermeneutics. It says: for once my joke will have a perfect shape, so perfect you will comprehend the weirdness of getting aggression and excretion into form. The repressed content will be so near the surface that you will not be able to calibrate whether it is repressed or unleashed. The ritual nature of the performance will be its tired justification: "Let me do a few talk bits," Bruce tells the audience he has told prior audiences; "No," he reports that prior audiences have always responded, "piss on us first and then do the rest of it." This does not, however, settle the matter of whether anyone will laugh, which is to say that a metajoke is not necessarily even a joke.

In Australia, at any rate, it was no joke. Bruce managed, in the first half of his first show on the continent, to scandalize his audience sufficiently that four women walked out. This galled Bruce, so he told the joke immediately after intermission, in the following version: "I'm going to do something that's never been done before in a nightclub—I'm going to *piss* on you." To which the verdict, Albert Goldman reports, was negative: "The audience cowered. A few masochistic giggles were the only response. Some people thought Lenny was mad. Some thought he needed a fix. Some thought he was being deliberately outrageous because he wanted the engagement canceled." The audience could not see how to take the threat as a joke, but Goldman adds, knowingly, that "the line was 'material,' something he'd said before and would say again. It was intended as a sick joke, an attention-grabber, a Joe Ancis fantasy on the relations between performers and audiences. None of these meanings registered with the Australians."

Was it the Australians' fault? Goldman seems to think so. But if the joke is a comment on performer-audience relations, it is critical to observe with some precision what is happening between them. What appears to be happening, generally, is that Bruce and his Australian audience are failing to compose a comedy circle at all. Bruce's jokes are not bombing so much as not becoming jokes in the first place. I wonder about the accuracy of Goldman's reminder that what Bruce told the Australians was a standard bit. My only contribution to what Goldman knows almost everything about is that the bit, in the version I have heard, is exactly opposite to the Australian routine. In the setup I have transcribed, public urination is a ritual that Bruce is tired of celebrating; in Australia, it is a nightclub novelty. For that reason, the "joke" in Australia has precious little joke work. Urinating on an audience may be a surprise to them, but that urinating on an audience is a surprise is no surprise.

Bruce does not abandon his stand-up duties entirely: he makes a stab at pretending that the Australian audience will find his offensiveness delightfully unusual. But the joke can only be funny as a revelation of what an audience secretly desires, and there is no evidence that the audience in Australia secretly hoped to share the element of Bruce's abjection. The joke that Bruce and his American audience share is that the latter demands to be abject, demands, by such treatment, to be outraged, which is to say, if I may pronounce the too evident paradox, demands not to be outraged.

I cannot remember if Bruce's urinating routine ever seemed funny to me, but for twenty-five years (since I first heard it on a record) I have carried around in my memory the reaction of an American audience to the joke as I have transcribed it. Again:

> If you've, er, [pause]
> Ever seen this bit before, I want you to tell me.
> Stop me if you've seen it. [long pause]
> I'm going to piss on you.

Here is the punch line that tops the punch line: Bruce waits after his announcement, and for a half second a fraction of the audience rumbles, followed—so closely that the first stage is easy to miss—by seventeen seconds of unanimous laughter, accompanied by the sound of one or two people clapping though not applauding: adding the percussion to their laughter, as if it were not possible to laugh sharply enough. Goldman reports that Bruce could ignite an amazing laugh; all I can say is that I have not often experienced it. *This* response would be a revelation, except that jokes depend on a ratio of manifesting and concealing. Consider that two seconds of laughter is respectable; four seconds greets the best joke of a standard *Tonight Show* monologue. To get a laugh up to six seconds—an extraordinary occasion—you generally need two distinct waves of laughter, as in the case of jokes that are immediately funny and funnier (they are usually self-reflexive) upon reprocessing.

It was, technically, a better joke in America than in Australia. It is almost precise to say that only in America was it a joke. But that brute fact does not account for fifteen of the seventeen seconds. Nor does the laughter ever seem to wane and wax; everyone laughs unanimously at high volume throughout. There are no hints that the joke is being milked during that time by gestures. Twice, Bruce attempts to calm the uproar to finish the bit. At long last, he succeeds, though the magic has drained out. He tries

16

to make it clear, as if to himself, what the joke is, or to repeat it, to make sure everyone else knows. But everyone, for seventeen seconds, has been perfectly aware what the joke is.

The looming questions are these: why in America as opposed to Australia is the Bruce threat a joke (why, in the first half second of response, can you almost literally hear the joke work working), and why, after the minimum two seconds of laughter activated by the joke work, is there an additional quarter of a minute of hilarity that begins to suggest hysteria? The first clue comes from a sentence I have not explicated in Goldman's analysis of the Australian disaster: "It was intended as . . . a Joe Ancis fantasy on the relations between performers and audiences."

Joe Ancis was once, in several authoritative opinions, the funniest man in America, though he could never perform on stage. On frequent occasions in the late forties, at Hanson's luncheonette on Broadway, Ancis would improvise monologues before professional comics, among whom his greatest disciple was Bruce. According to Goldman's history, the main line of Jewish American stand-up passed through Ancis at Hanson's. Ancis would come into the luncheonette and insult the clientele of Jewish comedians—witheringly, unstoppably, profanely. Here is how Goldman describes the reaction.

> You're caught in this terrible double-bind. You're loving it! It's killing you!

You're in love with your own death. But you die, apparently, into your assassin, like the son into his consubstantial father:

> Doing his famous Spritz with the absolute freedom and self-indulgence and private craziness that you can only get into when you have a listener who is practically another part of your own head, Joe paced the room as nervously as *der Führer* in his bunker. Interior monologue, free association, stream of consciousness—these are the fancy words for the Spritz. (*LB*, 105–9)

The Spritz is where privacy is shared, and bunkers are freedom, and Jews are Nazis, and hatred is beloved. Inclusion repels; repression liberates; aggression bonds. "Stream of consciousness" is accurate, if interiors are exterior, because a "spritz" is a Yiddish spray. "I am going to piss on you" is not merely *a* Joe Ancis fantasy on the relation of audience to performer, it is *the* Joe Ancis fantasy, the thematization of his form. To feel the joke's aggression without positing an ulterior motive for it—in this aptitude the American audience is superior to the Australian—is precisely to get the joke, which is the mechanism by which aggression bonds. If the best jokes are metajokes, this joke's superiority derives from its reflection not just on itself but on every joke: the failure of comedian and audience to separate into subject and object produces the emblem of abjection and confluence. (When what seems to be a preamble *to* the joke—"If you've ever seen this bit before, I want you to tell me"—is revised as the setup *of* the joke, the formal politeness of the occasion is folded into the sordid violence of it.) The reward is a quarter of a minute of laughter that, after two seconds, is provoked and reprovoked by the laughter itself: what the audience is finding funny is that it finds this funny.

Only in America did this sort of resentment metamorphose—and it did so regularly—into this sort of consent. The *explanandum* is that scenes like the following never took place in America.

> From the second night on [of Bruce's London performances], the fist fights and walkouts were numerous and celebrated. Yevgeny Yevtushenko, John Osborne and Penelope Gilliat walked. Siobhan McKenna, the well-known stage and screen actress, went further. She appeared one evening with a party of eight, including her escort, a nineteen-year-old photographer. The party was loud and hecklish until they decided to walk out in the middle because of "extreme boredom." Peter Cook [of *Beyond the Fringe*] took the trouble to thank them for finally leaving, causing Miss McKenna's escort to grab Cook by his tie and punch his face. Holding his bloodied head, Cook accused Miss McKenna of scratching him. The belligerent actress strode around the downstairs bar, proclaiming in Gaelic bellows, "These hands are clean. They are Irish hands and they are clean." Cook replied, "This is a British face and it is bleeding!" (*LB,* 361)

Though I admire the local ingenuity required to transform Lenny Bruce into an item of antagonism between the British and the Irish, with Bruce in the camp of the beleaguered oppressor, I am not claiming that politics has intruded into the entertainment. Clearly, politics *becomes* the entertainment. The donnybrook staged here is not so much between Ireland and England as between McKenna's hygienic melodrama, her soap opera, and Cook's comedy, in which Bruce's various discharges are transformed into a martyr's blood. When I wonder why scenes like this never occurred in America, I mean only to ask about the facility with which American outrage got trumped by the joke.

Bruce offended Americans, of course, but outside of journalists (outraged to energize their prose), the only expressions of American outrage were on the part of the legal system, a delegation of moral authority that astounded Englishmen who saw Bruce in the United States. "The words themselves were perhaps less significant," said Brian Glanville, "than the fact that they brought absolutely no protest. Nobody shouted, nobody walked out, let alone threw things" (*LB*, 360). According to Goldman, no member of an American audience ever brought a complaint against Bruce, though he was arrested for obscenity in New York, Chicago, and up and down California. I have tried to define stand-up as a formal phenomenon; now I am trying to describe the cycle of stand-up that began after World War II as a cultural phenomenon. The key to the connection is the geometry of the postwar American suburb.

The clue is what suburbs were invented to leave behind; the clue leads, revealingly, to "Jokes and Their Relation to the Unconscious," specifically to a joke of Heine's—very similar to one of Bruce's—that Freud analyzes twice. Actually, when Freud first turns to it, he is laboring a point concerning the relation of jokes and analogies. Perhaps the "joke," which contrasts Protestant and Catholic clergymen but may have been nondenominationally offensive, is more accurately taxonomized as a witty conceit:

> A catholic cleric behaves rather like a clerk with a post in a large business house. The Church, the big firm, of which the Pope is head, gives him a fixed job and, in return, a fixed salary. He works lazily, as everyone does who is not working for his own profit, who has numerous colleagues and can easily escape notice in the bustle of a large concern. . . . A protestant cleric, on the other hand, is in every case his own principal and carries on the business of religion for his own profit. He does not, like his catholic fellow-traders, carry on a wholesale business but only retail. And since he must himself manage it alone, he cannot be lazy. (*SE*, 87)

But then, at the beginning of his discussion of tendentious jokes, placed as if by coincidence immediately after the discussion of analogies, Freud returns to Heine: "When at the end of my last chapter I wrote down Heine's comparison of a catholic priest to an employee in a wholesale business and of a protestant one to a retail merchant, I was aware of an inhibition which was trying to induce me not to make use of the analogy. I told myself that among my readers there would probably be a few who felt respect not only for religion but for its governors and assistants" (*SE*, 90). The question is why, in that case, Freud felt obliged to use the Heine example; evidently, he slipped in the tendentiousness of the joke under cover of a discussion of joke work, exactly the way a comedian slips in tendentiousness under the cover of the joke work itself. Like all tellers of jokes, on his analysis, Freud needed his joke without knowing why.

At his late Berkeley concert, Bruce tendered the joke in précis form: "Catholicism is like Howard Johnson, and what they lease is their franchises."[9] Bruce's literalization of the conceit is probably his best-known routine, "Religions, Inc.," which begins with talk—among Billy Graham, Oral Roberts, other religious superstars, and a Madison Avenue advertising executive—about religious novelties that are expected to sell (cocktail napkins, for one thing, bearing the slogan, "Another martini for Mother Cabrini"), moves on to a worried discussion about how to keep the religion business free of the critical moral issues of the day, and ends with desultory small talk between the advertising executive and the pope, calling by phone. All we hear is the adman's end:

> And thanks for the pepperoni. . . . Billy [Graham] wants to know if you'll get him a deal on one of those Dago sports cars. . . . When are you coming to the coast? . . . I can get you on the Sullivan show the 19th. . . . Wear the big ring. . . . Oh, did you see Spellman on Stars of Jazz? . . . Okay, sweetie, yeah, you cool it, too.[10]

Comedically speaking, this does not seem to be arriving much of anywhere. I have, however, left off the final line, which converts all of the foregoing into setup. "No," the agent reassures the pope, "nobody knows you're Jewish." (Big, explosive laugh.) This may seem like a desperate absurdity, a reach for a cheap surprise to end the routine, until you realize, as the audience did at once, that it transforms the skit. No longer anti-Christian, the joke is suddenly anti-Semitic. Or, rather, it allows a moment of anti-Semitism as a stage toward a more general misanthropy, so that the anti-Semitism makes ludicrous its own exclusiveness.[11] (Jews are not particularly venal, because everyone is as venal as a Jew.) It is commonly observed that Bruce portrays the world as show business; the emphasis is equally on the show and the business. Catholic and Protestant celebrities are in religion for the money because TV Christians are secretly show biz Jews.

Return to the Heine/Freud joke—why does Freud need to tell it, even though, as (first) an illustration of a minor technical point, it does not seem half worth the risk of outraging his Christian audience? Does Freud know the real tendency of his tendentiousness? An oddity of "Jokes and Their Relation to the Unconscious" is that it identifies business as the essence not of religion but of jokes as thoroughly as Bergson makes mechanization the essence of the comic. One indication is the proliferation of matchmaker jokes. When Freud discusses sophistical humor, he writes as if slightly, but only slightly, puzzled by what is his second set of matchmaker jokes: "It may be due to no more than a whim of chance that all the examples that I shall bring forward of this new group are once more *Schadchen* stories" (*SE*, 64). Freud returns to *Schadchen* stories a third time, later on, as examples of good jokes all the better for partaking of the "forbidden." This means that the object of the humor, ostensibly the matchmaker sharper, is really the daughter-unloading parents and wife-shoppers (*SE*, 106–7). It is the business instinct, not as focused and stigmatized in the matchmaker but as pervasive in society, that is the hidden incendiary point of the subgenre.

Freud has himself, in fact, been describing the workings of the unconscious as business dealings, in terms, when it comes to jokes, of expenditures and savings. At long last the figure becomes explicit:

> I may perhaps venture on a comparison between psychical economy and a business enterprise. So long as the turnover in the business is very small, the important thing is that outlay in general shall be kept low and administrative costs restricted to the minimum. . . . Later, when the business has expanded, the importance of the administrative cost diminishes; the height reached by the amount of expenditure is no longer of significance provided that the turnover and profits can be sufficiently increased. . . . Nevertheless it would be wrong to assume that when expenditure was absolutely great there would be no room left for the tendency to economy. The mind of the manager, if it is inclined to economy, will now turn to economy over details. . . . In a quite analogous fashion, in our complex psychical business too, economy in detail remains a source of pleasure. (*SE*, 156–57)

It might be possible to treat "Jokes" as a joke; at any rate, the Heine example has taught us to see the semblance of a joke in a conceit. If the Heine joke is that religion is a business, if the *Schadchen* joke is that love is a business, the Freudian joke is that jokes are a business. Freud allows Heine to make the point that religion is like a business for Christians; the *Schadchen* stories submit love to Jewish business instincts; but the *Schadchen* stories are pervasive in "Jokes" not, Freud implies, because he or his people are drawn to them generally, but because the penetral of tendentious jokes is less likely to be sex or savagery and more likely to be sales, if what is on the mind of the jokester unconscious is the hope of a bargain. (The metajoke of Freud's book is the disguising of a lengthy Jewish joke as psychoanalysis.)

This is a set of moves that Bruce makes more concisely—with the economy of a joke—by making a punch line of the pope's Jewishness, that is, of everyone's hidden Jewishness.

Bruce was born a suburban, almost a rural, Jew, and came to New York from remote Long Island—to which many Jews after World War II were fleeing New York[12]—to learn at the feet of Joe Ancis what it meant to be a Jewish comedian (*LB*, 75). It meant, in short, to be from the City, and to cherish all the City's techniques for making money off of sex, celebrity, credulity, art, despair, whatever. (The highlight of Bruce's failed film about New York was the flea circus at Hubert's Museum [*LB*, 231–33].) It meant to think of civilization as a scam, and of scams, which Bruce liked to invent, as the paradigm of wit. (A scam is an inverse, absolute bargain: something for nothing.) Bruce's working hypothesis that a scam is the soul of wit would seem to take literally Freud's point that the unconscious finds in jokes a psychic bargain; his donnée that a scam is the essence of civilization would seem to literalize and radicalize Heine's point that religion operates like a business. What Bruce wants to make audible, in a voice that fails to distinguish the con artist and the prophet, is the collapse of sacredness into profanity.

It was Bruce's ambition to inhabit without hypocrisy this abject world whose coming he had announced. The British and Australian audiences who chose not to dwell in it with him—who registered this choice by not getting the joke—were not acting incomprehensibly or irrationally. But to assert that American audiences, on the other hand, got the joke is not to claim that they were more sympathetic to the project: in the 1950s, it was the ambition only of Bruce among American Jews to return from the suburbs to the ethnic city. (Bruce, like Fanny Brice—could he have named himself after her?—had to memorize the little Yiddish he dropped into his act).[13] The flight from the city was an escape for American Jews, as it was a century earlier for American Protestants (around the time our native traditions of humor arose), from the industrialization that was the context of Bergson's comic and the business—not to mention sex and aggression in unholy conjunction with business—that was the basis of Freud's jokes. The flight from industry and business and money and filth—the flight, in sum, to suburban civility, the essence of which is the treatment of the fount or funding of cleanliness as excrement—is not exactly a flight from jokes but, more exactly, a flight from the power of jokes, their tendentious origins. This is what American audiences were trying to effect.

The first defense against Bruce—not participating in the transmuting of his offensiveness into humor—is to treat his act, in effect, as pure urban squalor. To get the joke, however, is not to join Bruce in his wallowing; it is to revel in the transformative power of joke work, like the transformative power of money. The joke work does not annihilate the abandoned repulsiveness of the city. It commutes it on behalf of a commuting society, which endeavors, for the sake of lawns and laundered cash, to leave behind profanity and, in the process, also the sacred. Thus society has enacted its abjection, and Bruce is its returning filth, alienable, like the tendentious meaning of jokes, but not quite alienated.

The audience—by means of its laughter, by means of its metalaughter—comes together as a community, under this pressure, to assert its right not to do community work. (It demands to be outraged in order not to be outraged.) Joke work does the work of suburbanization, since the moral method of suburbia is to note, collect, yet trivialize all offenses. This is not to say, according to M. P. Baumgartner, that suburban provocations are trivial per se, rather that they "appear trivial to an observer precisely because their victims react with such restraint"—they laugh them off, in other words.[14] Suburbanites, like stand-up audiences, effect the lightness of their being.

Why should the law in that case be moved to action? It would seem to have prosecuted Bruce on nobody's behalf.[15] The only answer is that the law acted on its own behalf, precisely because it represented no one. In 1964, while one of Bruce's obscenity trials was in progress, the Supreme Court ruled that "contemporary community standards" of decency could not refer to a particular community, but would have to refer, since a constitutional right was in question, to the nation. This is not to imagine, of course, that there *were* no subnational communities. Nevertheless, the Supreme Court established that the law could posit a fictional community for the purpose of being outraged by obscenity, in the absence of a real community that had the constitutional authority to do so, and the question is: why bother? If there is no real outraged community whose outrage legally counts, why pretend there is? Insofar as national restoration after World War II might have involved fashioning just such a fictional community, outrage might have defined it; but another America was being fabricated, and its principal was not the community but the audience, which means not outrage but entertainment. I have defined artistic seriousness as recourse to retroactive judgment, and in what remains of this essay I want to show that that capacity for judging is precisely what the laughter of audiences puts in jeopardy for the legal system. The discussion will eventually produce the last clue to the entertainment value of the urination joke.

I cannot come close to reproducing or even mapping the miasma of

Bruce's trials and hearings and legal negotiations. I want only to discuss perhaps the most bizarre legal moment out of many. A prosecuting attorney named Albert Wollenberg Jr., in the San Francisco trial, found himself obsessed with disputing the humorous content of a particularly graphic word from one of Bruce's routines, which I, pure child of the fifties and suburban diaspora, shall refuse for this chapter to write, but which Bruce, in a later routine, replaced with "blah blah blah," as I shall here. On the stand was Lou Gottlieb, a San Francisco jazz critic, folksinger, and hip intellectual, and the testimony went as follows:

> Wollenberg: You say that the main theme of Mr. Bruce is to get laughter.
> Gottlieb: That is the professional comedian's duty.
> Wollenberg: I see. And do you see anything funny in the word [blah blah blah]?
> Gottlieb: To answer that question "yes" or "no" is impossible, Your Honor.
> Judge Horn: You may answer it "yes" or "no" and then explain your answer.
> Gottlieb: I found it extremely unfunny as presented by Mr. Wollenberg, I must say.
> Judge Horn: All right, wait a minute, wait a minute! (*LB*, 352)

The moment is loony—it is difficult to avoid the sensation that the trial is enacting a Lenny Bruce routine, and when Bruce in fact turned it into a routine, the joke was how often the judge and prosecutor, like F. Lee Bailey with his "N" word, contrived excuses for pronouncing "blah blah blah." Wollenberg's hapless premise is that the obscene word cannot have a function in a funny routine because the word is not itself funny. This is puzzling, but we can divine what prompts Wollenberg to this paralogism. If the audience laughs, Wollenberg must believe, then either the performance is, so to speak, *above* obscenity (it has artistic merit), or it is *other than* obscenity (an amused audience is not a prurient one). The problem, however, is not merely that Wollenberg did not need to grant either of these points. It may even be the case that Wollenberg made his own job more difficult by not acknowledging that the converse is more plausible: that if Bruce's diction is not funny, conceivably it is serious; aesthetic or political impulses may determine his vulgarity. An obscene comedian may use a dirty word for a laugh, but why should a comedian choose *not* to be funny?

It does not become evident why Wollenberg must of necessity pursue this dangerous line, in fact, until Gottlieb makes his joke, and Judge Horn suppresses the courtroom auditors', now suddenly the courtroom audience's, laughter. The inevitability of the tactic is not visible until Gottlieb displays its disastrous consequences, the disaster being that the law has itself become part of the comedy. Gottlieb makes horribly manifest the reciprocal clarity of the duel that had, I think, enticed Wollenberg. Since humor is context-dependent, the law seeks to take its elements out of context, which is both a desperate and a plausible strategy, since retroactive judgment must be context-free. Gottlieb, after resisting this strategy for a moment, proves that the endeavor itself makes the law comic, which is to say that contextual flatfootedness is precisely the job qualification of the straight man. We can infer that nothing less than humor itself is on trial, and that the parry works to put judgment itself on stage. Wollenberg denies that Lenny Bruce's obscene word is funny, and Horn cannot admit that Wollenberg has unwittingly provided useful empirical evidence that, in the perfectly supplied comic context, it is, because they sense that in laughter's presence there can be "no process that resembles judging."

This would be the simple closure of the essay, if it were only the case that Gottlieb functioned as Bruce's surrogate, that he was making Bruce's point, that Bruce was in his own act looking to unleash the humor of dirtiness that sanctimony itself produced. That, however, would turn Bruce's comedy absolute, and the interest of Bruce's case from the theoretical view is that the ideal structure of comedy—expressed in Gottlieb's phrase as the "professional comedian's duty"—always frustrated his efforts to be outrageous. Bruce was an indulged son whose biography as a comedian reads like a vain attempt not to overthrow the law but, by threatening it, to bring it into play. Bruce's pathetic letter to his father, written when Bruce was about forty, apparently about to go to jail for narcotics, tells half the truth. "Dear Father," it begins. "This is the story of a boy and his father who spoiled him." Bruce goes on to sketch a melodrama in which the spoiled boy ascends from brat to thief to murderer until he is caught and sentenced to die. The final words of the letter are spoken not by his alter ego but by Bruce (the shocking pronoun shift veils the penal anticlimax): "I'm going to jail tomorrow because you spoiled me" (*LB*, 87–88).

The letter is misleading. Its ostensible point is that an indulged son believes he deserves pleasure without labor, so turns to crime, which eventually fails to pay. Yet the interest of the story is that every filial outrage ("I don't want this cheap old bike") inspires nothing in the father except a patience that is not so much forgiving (it does not recognize the outrage to forgive it) as disengaged. ("Alright [*sic*], my son, I'll work 24 hours a day and get you a nice one.") The spoiled son turns to crime not for its promise of unearned satisfactions, but because only the law—in the world of sub-urban fatherhood—is capable of antagonism. Bruce does not want something for nothing, the motive of the thief and, taken to absolute ideals, of the businessman and comedian. He wants something at any cost, or, rather, he wants cost itself. The son's last gesture toward his father is made on the way to the electric chair: "Come here father, I want to whisper something to you." The formality of "father" adumbrates a confession, but the son bites off his father's ear. The son's violence both precludes hearing and is a liter-alization of metaphors of being heard: the father lends his son an ear; the son chews his father's ear off.

On the other hand, judges hear evidence and grant hearings. So Bruce turned every judge into a father, and every legal performance into an op-portunity to seduce and poison the paternal ear. "I so desperately want your respect," Bruce says to a Judge Murtagh, and Goldman comments: "It was an oedipal nightmare, the whole scene—Lenny back again in his child-hood, pleading, cajoling, placating, trying desperately to avert the punish-ment meted out by his sternly disciplinarian father" (*LB,* 490–91). I gather, however, that the father was not disciplinarian enough; the impulse was as self-incriminating as self-serving. What behavior would have been better calculated to *preclude* respect?

A paradox turned up by joke research is that

> early attempts to seek attention, affection, and emotional support from adults, along with frequent requests for help on tasks and recognition seeking for achievement-related behaviors were . . . positively related to frequency of humor-related behaviors for both sexes. . . . Thus, in spite of their dominating and generally assertive style of interaction with peers, young humorists had a history of being especially sensi-tive to adult reactions and appeared to gear much of their behavior to getting some kind of positive reaction from adults. This was accom-panied (among boys) by a tendency to be highly conforming to adult demands.[16]

Stand-up, this suggests, begins with aggression toward an audience in order to submit that aggression to the law, which it hopes to mollify. The progress is to convert Audience to Law for the purpose of winning the Law back as Audience. I intend this description as formal and generic: what is being negotiated is the terms on which the stand-up setting will be orga-nized. (If Law is convened to be expelled, then we *have,* in absolute terms, a stand-up setting.) The comedian works from above his audience (audi-ence seated, comedian doing "stand-up"); he looks down on them as upon children and lectures them. But they make his jokes into jokes, or refuse to, by a reaction that is more final, less appealable, than a judgment. He wishes to humiliate them and they submit; but they think he is childish for craving their unchallengeable approval so desperately, and he knows this. There are child singers, child dancers, child actors, but no child stand-ups: an actual child would block this vacillating infantalism.[17]

My natural father was born around the same time as Lenny Bruce; he was suburban and spoiled; he was wild (he subscribed to *Mad Magazine* in the fifties, when suburban lawlessness had to be sublimated as crazy humor); he died, about to move the family closer to the factory where he worked, at around the same age as Lenny Bruce. When it became conscious to me that I was identifying Lenny Bruce with my father, I found myself combing for evidence in Bruce's features; only momentarily did it come to me that I had selected the police photograph of Lenny Bruce dead.

My daughter was born in 1990, a few years after Herbert Blau's daughter, invoked at the beginning of his book, *The Audience*. Blau tells us that she "expects an audience under any circumstances," adding that "a lingering question of the book, indebted to her, has to do with why, as one grows older, that simple expectation shouldn't continue to be so."[18] My daughter is already too old now to assume my constant attention. Laughter is the best she can get out of me: not continuous absorption, but perfect invaluable absorption for the length of the joke and response. When I try to transform myself from Audience to Law, the crisis of suburban parenthood, next to impossible now in America-the-audience, I do so by withholding laughter, since all her outrages, by the logic of the naive, are comic. "The naïve (in speech) agrees with jokes as regards wording and content: it brings about a misuse of words, a piece of nonsense, or a piece of smut" (*SE*, 185). Only one person (not in speech) has ever urinated on me; I laughed. She did not pay for her outrage. Her crime, by an alchemical plea bargain, paid.

I have tried to infer what is most abject in comedy (the city and its commercial filth, the body and its excrement) from its angelic geometry (the theorems of the indivisibility of performer and audience), and this is the largest tenet of the Euclidean faith: from two points (comedian and crowd) of the stand-up circle diametrically opposed, stand-up is the resurrection of your father as your child.

2

Nectarines: Carl Reiner and Mel Brooks

For many of the many of us who were coming into or passing through ado-
lescence at the beginning of the sixties, Carl Reiner and Mel Brooks were
an initiation; Reiner's extemporaneous interviews with the 2000 Year Old
Man and other Brooks characters were a shibboleth of comic sensibility,
when comic sensibility was *most* of sensibility.[1] Johnny Carson was a similar case to a lesser degree. No one doubted that Carson's jokes were an
evolutionary advance on Bob Hope's, and it was a revelation that the approach to and retreat from jokes could be funnier than punch lines. But
Carson still worked within or, more impressively, around the edifice of the
joke. What Brooks did with Reiner was create humor whose syntax no one
could parse. Years later, nostalgic fans of academic persuasion could satisfy

themselves that the humor of Brooks and Reiner fit none of the paradigms erected by joke analysts.

As an experiment, ask anyone who can recite the classic Brooks-Reiner routines, and who once thought of humor as a sign of grace, to identify the defining passage of all "The 2000 Year Old Man" records. Here is the consensus answer. Reiner says, "I think most people would be interested in leading a long and fruitful life." Brooks answers (before Reiner has formulated a question):

> Fruit is good, you mention fruit. Fruit kept me going 140 years when I was on a very strict diet.
>
> Mainly nectarines—I love that fruit. Half a peach, half a plum, so it's a hell of a fruit. [big laugh]
>
> Not too hot, not too cold, you know, just nice. [halcyon moment]
>
> Even a rotten one is good [big laugh]—that's how much I love them. I'd rather have a rotten nectarine than a fine plum, what do you think of that? [big, startled laugh]

"The 2000 Year Old Man" is one of the classic bits of the first era of contemporary stand-up—which is one of the most powerful if least investigated forms of postmodernist expression[2]–and the essence of contemporary stand-up is inexplicable, context- and comedian-specific, humor, not the Bob Hope joke, expropriable by Milton Berle, dear to joke analysts. Nevertheless, if Mel Brooks, along with Lenny Bruce and a few others, is a harbinger of postmodern comedy, insofar as he does not deal in gags, still it is the case that comedy cannot be formless, since comedy is deformity that is self-measuring.[3] Thus the nectarine, not because it is rotten but because its decadence is contemplated and desired by a brilliantly formal mind, can serve as the emblem of the comedy of our time.

Brooks begins with a pun on "fruitful" that is so weak as not to be a pun at all, but rather a literalization; to put it precisely, it is a weak pun whose humor is that it counterindicates a literal rather than punning disposition. This is followed by an attempt to loop the newly literalized issue of fruit back to the general theme of the sketch, since there is a modicum, maybe, of humor purely in the longevity ("Fruit kept me going 140 years") of a peculiar diet. Brooks is waiting for his inspiration; when it comes, it is revolutionary. "Mainly nectarines," he cries, suddenly invigorated. "I love that fruit. Half a peach, half a plum, so it's a hell of a fruit." What revolutionary thing, exactly, has happened?

First, it flashes on Brooks that something about the nectarine once felt as uncanny as a dream to him (I divine this): to be in the presence of the mongrel fruit was to be in the neighborhood of a mystery, arithmetically apprehensible yet ontologically obscure. What occurs to Brooks, in the moment that is granted an improvising comedian to make a decision, is that still to be charged as an adult by the childhood equivalent of Pythagorean knowledge would be funny, slightly more so if the adult is two thousand years from his nonage. "So it's a hell of a fruit" caps this impulse of the bit. "Hell of a" insists on the language of hoary appreciation ("helluva" might better capture the flatness of expression) in the transfiguring presence of a really childish enthusiasm, partly sensuous and partly taxonomic.

Note that "half a peach, half a plum, so it's a hell of a fruit" also takes the form of a fractured, fractional computation. And justifying the pronouncement is a piece of deduction. Vaguely in the background is some dubious major premise: sums of positives are positive.

The point is that taxonomy, syllogism, and ratio have been deployed on behalf of an irrational craving; you feel restored to the moment of gathering adulthood when corporeal pleasures were enhanced by the allure of esoteric rationales. Thereupon Brooks tries this measured discrimination: "Not too cold, not too hot, you know, just nice." This is not very funny, though it is sweet. The joke on moderation—the joke that extravagance here takes the *form* of moderation—is easier to admire than laugh at; the temperateness of nectarines, as opposed to their tempered parentage, is not an important datum for children or, therefore, memory for adults. There is, I believe, *some* humor in this respite. I find myself pleased to register that "just nice" replaces "just right" in the evocation of "Goldilocks." "Just nice" has the feel of off-English, the language of first-generation immigrants telling fables to their grandchildren, with the result that the structure "not extreme, not extreme, perfect mean" is nudged from dead center. Still, the balance of this line is mainly set up for the final extravagance.

> Even a rotten one is good—that's how much I love them. I'd rather have a rotten nectarine than a fine plum, what do you think of that?

This is where the audience finds itself most inexplicably amused. But, on analysis, the methodicalness of the dithyramb is perfectly in keeping with the characteristic humor of the bit. Brooks is at this point in the midst of such a sacred remembrance that he approaches rapture.

> If I forget thee, O Jerusalem, let my right hand forget her cunning.
> If I do not remember thee, let my tongue cleave to the roof of my mouth; if I prefer not Jerusalem above my chief joy.

Both comedian and psalmist are attempting to measure the lost immeasurable. Brooks is funnier insofar as the incommensurable preference seems to demand an abstraction (Jerusalem above chief joy) but gets expressed as a seemingly unremarkable concretion (nectarine above plum) that nevertheless has, for him, equal force.

The reason that Brooks says "fine plum" and not "fine peach" is that "plum" is a funnier word to land on: its abruptness sounds right in Brooks's Yiddish accent, and brings out, by comparison, the disproportionate vigor with which Brooks enunciates the prissier "nectarine." The rottenness of the amalgamated, interpolated nectarine—pronounced with Hebraic inflection and masculine emphasis despite its Hellenic etymology and weak suffix—makes it multiply liminal, multiply irrational, multiply non-Kosher. The audience is laughing already at "fine plum," partly because "fine" replaces "ripe" (as "nice" replaced "right") barely to warp the symmetry toward Old World evaluative decisiveness, but "what do you think of that?" prolongs its delight. Brooks's recollected joy has suddenly galled him to a minor belligerence in the presence of those who are not necessarily infected by the holy contagion of his memory—

> Happy shall he be, that taketh and dasheth thy little ones against the stones

—though the joke's bathos is not merely of sacred Jerusalem and profane nectarine, but also of lost Jerusalem and available nectarine (comically revivable from nonage to dotage): a nectarine has the taste of nectar, necros + tar, a little death-conqueror, like the 2000 Year Old Man himself.

If the appeal of comedy may be traced to its imposition of geometrical perfectionism on compounded liminality (so that nonthinkers cannot enjoy comedy—"the world is . . . a tragedy to those that feel"—but mathematicians can only appreciate obvious humor), then the nectarine joke is the essence of what is funny, folly of follies. The funniest jokes are meta-jokes, so this routine ought to seem, and does to many cognoscenti seem, like the very essence of humor in its rational exorbitance, pure rottenness, immortal profanity, exalted abjection.

Nevertheless, formal considerations when they are exclusive are always an evasion, and no one will be convinced by this prolegomenon that I have captured, in terms of mathematics or the perversion of mathematics, what makes Brooks and Reiner—only them—unstealably funny. I shall not be able to manage *that,* but I can do something toward understanding the particular *appeal* of their peculiar humor.

i.

Exclusively formal considerations are an evasion: what am I (and insofar as I am accurately representing their pseudogeometry, what are Brooks and Reiner) evading? The pertinent expert here would be Eve Sedgwick who, in virtuoso readings of *Dorian Gray* and "The Beast in the Jungle," scorns the "alibi of abstraction"—the reduction of content to kitsch and the elevation of formal self-consciousness to the summit of high art—as a function of the quarantining of homosexuality from early modernism.[4] If, as I hypothesize, the attractiveness of comedy is in the disturbance of its own compulsive formalism, it ought to intrigue queer theory; if a psychological study of fifty-five leading comedians in 1975 revealed that none of them was homosexual, which cannot mean more than that none was willing to be taken as homosexual, despite the high visibility of homosexuals elsewhere in show business, then comedy is perhaps a sort of institutionalization of "The Beast in the Jungle."[5] Consider what Reiner nominates in an interview as "pure Mel." Brooks is portraying a small but undefeated Jewish wrestler, who wins his matches by shocking opponents with "soul kisses." Asked if he is a homosexual, Brooks replies, "No, I have a wife!" What is the difference between kissing her and kissing a wrestler? "My wife is the only one I know who kisses from the inside out." This bit is "pure Mel," Reiner believes, not as the rococo intertwining of latency and blatancy, not, furthermore, as having anything to do with *him,* but rather as a "joke so wild it was almost abstract."[6]

Reiner's premise that abstraction is what appears as the end result of wildness is no doubt borrowed from contemporary abstract expressionism; he might with equal justice have observed that Brooks's bit is almost abstract because it is almost geometric. Reiner wants Brooks to arrive at abstraction, but the erotics of the routine begins with it. (It is a joke so abstract, it is almost wild.) The abstraction is the one that Sedgwick herself begins with, and revolves so much that it gets conic: the triangle, René Girard's to begin with, by which Girard reduces all desire to a communion of rivals over an object regarded only secondarily.[7] Sedgwick's gambit is to link Girard's triangular desire to Gayle Rubin's triangulation of political power, which itself superimposes Lévi-Strauss on Freud;[8] thus Sedgwick has a mechanism for getting from erotics to social structure. Girard's triangle involves no exclusive determination of the sex of its three points, but Rubin attempts to demonstrate that patriarchal triangles concern the trafficking in women as tokens of male association. Sedgwick can therefore identify her feminism with her analysis of male-male relationships:

the first premise of queer theory is that male homosocial desire may be homosexual or homophobic, but that in any case it triangulates women. In this structural synthesizing dwells the theoretical possibility of representing a "homosocial" continuum from homosexuality to homophobia, with sensitivity to how the continuum is practically and politically demarcated as the telltale feature of an epoch.

It is easier, probably, to sense the presence of buried, Girardian triangles in male-female relationships than in male-male relationships, and easier in both of these than in female-female ones. In ordinary heterosexual relationships, the inferiority of the woman's position makes it simple to intuit that another passion might be stronger, because it is more mutually charged, and the omnipresence in fiercely heterosexual societies of ferocious homosocial rituals bears the intuition out. It is somewhat less clear why male homosexual relationships need to detour through women (or why they need to detour at all, unless you share Girard's monomania), though Sedgwick's observation that some patriarchal societies have been homosocial and openly homoerotic, whereas others have been homosocial and homophobic, does suggest that the same dynamic is likely to be at work. Least clear is whether lesbian relationships must be triangular, since there is no matriarchy to be kept in place by subordinating a man in a structure that is not primarily for or about him.

Some theorizing in Sedgwick's wake has been designed in part to clarify just these puzzles, for example, that of Wayne Koestenbaum (a Sedgwick admirer) and Terry Castle (a critic). If it is not obvious, in a culture where homosexuality is valued, why homosexual desire must triangulate women, nevertheless Koestenbaum brilliantly elaborates the benefits of doing so in a culture that is homophobic. Koestenbaum treats *The Waste Land,* for example, as the issue of a determined effort to manufacture and master the hysterical female body between Eliot and Pound, for the sake of keeping their literary homosociality untainted. Unless we posit that there is in some sense a hysterical female already in Eliot's homoerotic psyche, prior to its objectification for the sake of heterosexuality as *The Waste Land*—a hypothesis intimated by Koestenbaum but at best only weakly triangular in implication—then it is by a heroic, if pathological, determination that heterosexuality and patriarchy produce a detour from a relationship that was originally linear.[9] This narrative of the effortful securing of triangulated females, or their surrogates, follows quite closely, in fact, from Sedgwick's version of affective Realpolitik in, for example, Dickens.

The purpose and method of triangulation are even more peculiar in the relationships conjured by Terry Castle, who wishes to rectify the marginality of lesbianism in Sedgwick's work. First, Castle premises that the scandal lurking in patriarchal triangles is that "the two male terms might hook up directly, so to speak, replacing the heterosexual with an explicitly homosexual dyad." "Dyad" here seems only to refer to the connecting of two (of still extant three) triangular points; still, "directly" seems to dismiss, in the case of homosexuality only, the third point. "So to speak" (modifying "directly"?) reclouds the issue; but then Castle suggests that in "*lesbian* bonding . . . the two female terms indeed merge and the male term drops out."[10] Why should it not, one might muse—there is no matriarchy to prop up. This is an evolution of linear (and, depending on how seriously she means "merge," punctual) desire out of triangular desire that seems and does not seem to be descended from Sedgwick.

Heterosexuality may be read, in Koestenbaum, as the adding of a third term to homosexual dyads; homosexuality may be read, in Castle, as the subtracting of a third term from heterosexual triads. The relevance of this numerology to my concerns derives from the coincidence that the structure of a "tendentious" joke, in Freud, either begins with a heterosexual dyad (insistent man, resistant woman) and adds a third term, another man, potential rival, for the sake of civilizing the excitations of smut, or begins with a male-male dyad (powerful man, weak man) and adds a third term, again another man, for the sake of defusing aggression. Only the first case seems to require a woman; even on that model, however, the heterosexuality of the event, at any rate, drops out in upper-class joking. The female object of smut, who is supposed to be excited by it, actually cannot appear.

Thus the smutty joke repeats the form of Castle's homosexuality, triad degenerating into dyad, only one sex remaining, except that the point of the joke is ostensibly heterosexual. The aggressive joke would repeat the form of Koestenbaum's homosexuality, dyad masked by triad, except that the male-male competition that it begins with is not thought to sublimate desire.[11] All you need is the concept of homosociality to get from Freud's joke theory to queer theory. What jokes traditionally do—on Freud's hypothesis as queer theory might revise it—is insist on triangulation for the sake of masking homoerotics.

This is why homosexuals have had a difficult time making comedy as much their domain as all other aspects of show business: the skeleton of homosocial society collapses at the imputation that joking is not the civilizing of heterosexual rivalry (over women, for dominance). Joking may represent a sort of hinge in society that allows the door to swing: close it, and desire can triangulate heterosexually; open it, and desire might lineate.

I put the matter in hopelessly abstract terms—in terms of triangles and

lines, twos and threes — partly in order to arrive at Barbara Johnson's celebrated essay, "The Frame of Reference: Poe, Lacan, Derrida," an interloper
in the French theoretical rivalry (within the story and without) over "The
Purloined Letter." It would be possible to make the case — having pushed to
abstraction so pure that any unwanted content must be visibly expelled —
that homosexuality is the masked theme of that essay, that Johnson's fashioning of herself as judgmental third party of a male-male rivalry is a clever
upending of the patriarchal triangle to find humor in the homosexual panic
of Lacan and Derrida's homosocial competition for Poe.[12] What I want to
emphasize is that Derrida accuses Lacan of a reassuring commitment to
threes, as opposed to the spookily multiplied duplications of "The Purloined Letter," on behalf of an oedipal triangle the object of which, as Rubin
remarked two decades ago, is to assure the reproduction of heterosexuality. On Derrida's argument, three becomes the number of balance and
normality while, in Johnson's terms, "the numbers 2 and 4 have become
uncannily odd." This remark is in a section of her essay called — now we
are prepared to get the joke — "Odd Couples." I shall attempt to make good
on the allusion, odd enough in this rarefied setting, to popular American
comedy.

ii.

When I was a kid, comedy teams were integral to comedy, though today
they are virtually extinct. (At this juncture the essay gets slightly auto-
biographical in hopes of becoming cultural and historical.) Some comedy
teams comprised a man and a woman: Nichols and May, preeminently, or
their middlebrow equivalents, Stiller and Meara. But almost all were male-
male: Wayne and Shuster (frequently on the Ed Sullivan Show), Burns and
Schreiber (beleaguered taxi driver and barking fare), Rowan and Martin
(whose doctor routine, a staple of comedy-team humor, won me to them
in advance of their epochal TV show), Peter Cook and Dudley Moore from
Beyond the Fringe, the great Bob and Ray, the creepy Smothers Brothers,
Brooks and Reiner. Other comedy pairs — not quite stand-up teams — included Johnny Carson and Ed McMahon (starting on *The Tonight Show* in
1962) or Jerry Lewis and Dean Martin from just after the war.

My adolescent ambition, never entirely jettisoned, was to hang around
the funniest person I knew. In high school, my talent for inciting the funniest person I knew was sufficiently developed that several adults suggested
that we practice to become a professional comedy team, a suggestion no
one would offer since, let us estimate, 1973. I never knew anyone else to

confess to harboring that kind of ambition until I heard Carl Reiner admit to it. In the fifties, the funniest man in the world was Sid Caesar, to whom Reiner played second banana; starting in the late seventies, it was Steve Martin, whom Reiner directed; in between (there was some overlap, but Reiner is serially monogamous in his account), he brought Mel Brooks to comedy altitudes that, on his own, Brooks has never subsequently scaled.[13] Why were the fifties and early sixties a breeding ground—adults providing role models for kids who would grow up into a world in which there was no such role—for this strange calling?

I note that in male-male comedy teams, one partner is, insofar as we take reassurance inferring sexuality from appearance and gender, blatantly heterosexual. He is often conspicuously brawnier than his partner: Ray Goulding, Ed McMahon, Carl Reiner. He has a deeper or more even-keeled voice. He is either steadier, as if prime material for bourgeois husbandhood (Dick Smothers, Dan Rowan, Carl Reiner), or he may be flamboyantly a woman's man (Dean Martin). About the sexuality of the other member of the pair—Tom Smothers or Dick Martin or Mel Brooks or Jerry Lewis—one might believe almost anything except that his sexual life was presented to him as a no-strings inheritance.

I might mention along these lines another quasi–comedy team: Tony Randall and Jack Klugman, TV embodiment of Neil Simon's *The Odd Couple,* source of Barbara Johnson's rubric. Neil Simon was a writer for Sid Caesar along with Brooks, and *The Odd Couple* may have been inspired, Kenneth Tynan suggests, by the postconnubial housekeeping of Brooks and a friend named Speed Vogel.[14] Randall plays a photographer, an amateur interior decorator, an opera lover. Klugman, messier, cigar smoking, poker playing, writes sports. Because of marital problems, they have become roommates indefinitely, so that no third term mediates either their mutual aggressiveness or their mutual amusement (without a third term, the former is not so much the repressed of the latter as its form). It goes without saying that one is typed heterosexual, the other homosexual—what would you call such a pairing? Not straight couple; not queer couple; the third possibility, in between, sui generis, is "odd couple," pronounced oddly, on its way from spondee to dactyl, as if there were such a thing.

In comedy lingo, the sober member of the team is referred to as the "straight man." I have never heard what the other is called. In Nichols-May and Stiller-Meara, there is no invariant division of labor; in male-male teams, roles are almost always strictly defined, except that one role is unlabeled. This is the laugh that dare not speak its name.

What name would it speak if it dared? It will not divulge its sexual name, but it has spoken its racial epithet. Call Reiner not "straight man" but "interlocutor," and Brooks becomes "endman"—Bones or Tambo. What Brooks plays into, by means of his literalistic swerve on "fruitful," is the whole history of ethnic or race humor (for example, "Dutch" or "Hebe" or, as in the case of Weber and Fields, Dutch and Hebe indistinguishably), whose enduring example is the minstrel team of Huck and Jim.[15]

> "What did you speculate in, Jim?"
> "Well, fust I tackled stock."
> "What kind of stock?"
> "Why, live stock. Cattle, you know. I put ten dollars in a cow."[16]

Jim's last sentence is in 2000-Year-Old-Man rhythm, pulling up short on "cow" (cf., "I'd rather have a rotten nectarine than a fine plum"). The humor is in the arrival at the unremarkable and embodied in place of the climactic and ideal. Huck, of course, unlike Reiner, does not know better. The running joke is that even when he does, it gives him no advantage. That Solomon, for example, was "the wisest man" is known to Huck: "the widow she told me so." Huck's received wisdom, however, cannot withstand Jim's literal-minded critique—"what use is a half a chile?"—of Solomon's famous threat.[17]

In the same way, it is no benefit to Reiner (in "2000 and One") to have received, also at secondhand, the conviction of Shakespeare's literary supremacy: "It was reputed, and I guess you agree," Reiner says to Brooks, "that he was the greatest writer of all time." Brooks does not agree, going so far as to improvise an unknown play of Shakespeare's, "Queen Alexandra and Murray," as a burlesque confrontation of Elizabethan gibberish and deflationary Yinglish. It turns out, though, that Brooks does not base his condescension toward Shakespeare on the existence of this play. Shakespeare was a "cute man and a pussycat," Brooks remembers, impugning his canonicity and his heterosexuality at a stroke, but he wrote very poorly. "With an 'l' that looked like a 't.' With an 'm' you didn't know if it was an 'n.' An 'o' could be a 'p.' Every letter was cockeyed and crazy. Don't tell me he was a good writer; he had the worst penmanship I ever saw in my life."

In the Solomon colloquy, Jim is guilty of misreading, of not, more precisely, registering what he had heard as a text to be read, and Brooks is guilty of not registering what he *saw* as a text to be read. Still, the twin jokes are not entirely on them, since, for their part, Huck and Reiner are incapable of any defense at all of the virtue of the Bible and Shakespeare, as against what Jim heard and the 2000 Year Old Man saw. To be ignorant, in vernacular art, is to be clever; Brooks's failure to comprehend the two meanings of "writer"—like his reduction of the two meanings of "fruitful"—comes off as a kind of illiterate, inverse, superior pun. When Jim misses the point of the Solomon story, and Brooks misses the Shakespearean oeuvre altogether, except for one addendum, they threaten literature itself, at the source.

I infer from this vernacular canonicide that Twain and Brooks are not entirely outside the objects of their fun. If Twain begins his book with an insider's boastfulness concerning the accuracy of his ear even for slave talking, the implicit accuracy of Brooks's routine is partly in its demonstration of his inner ear for ethnic *hearing*.[18] As audience, we not only hear how the 2000 Year Old Man speaks; we hear how he hears. Like dialogue in Henry James—"The Beast in the Jungle" may be the paradigm—conversation in Brooks and Reiner proceeds by misunderstanding. In James, characters fend off the perfection of privacy by the delicacy of their misprisions; Brooks keeps his comic energy stimulated by *in*delicate approximation, by misplaced concreteness. He is in this way Schopenhauerian, since, for Schopenhauer, comedy is the revenge of the sensuous on the abstract.[19]

"I think most people would be interested in leading a long and fruitful life," prompts Reiner, and Brooks misses the pedigree of the cliché— what had he taken the biblical injunction to be fruitful and multiply to mean? From fruitfulness to fruit is one step in the specifying, from fruit to nectarines, the next. The process seems harmless. Yet what is threatening in the *content* of the comedy is its testimonial to cross-pollination, the human equivalents of which would include intermarriage and miscegenation. Could an audience in 1960 not, at least subliminally, hear in a reference to mixed fruitfulness an allusion to mixed marriage? And still more threatening is Reiner's impotence to stave off Brooks's mistake. In Brooks's (literally) immortal tribute to an (etymologically) immortal fruit is simply more verbal power than Reiner himself can muster. The weakness of the ethnic ear for English is converted into triumph.

If we leave the matter there, we will have analyzed an insurrection, however local and verbal, rather than comedy—but if comedy performs a useful task for theory it is all in the reduction to nonsense of the distinction between containment and subversion models of art. The truth is that the swerve from fruitfulness to fruit is not a complete victory for ethnic literalness and physicality, since Brooks has eschewed not merely the dead term *fruitful* but also its signified: reproductive heterosexuality. What has occurred is, in effect, the substitution of one form of (encrypted) sensuousness for another, oral for vaginal, to put the matter schematically. Thus we may decrypt in Brooks's passion for nectarines an attraction to the giddy indivisibility of prissy peach and macho plum, and to its decadent deliciousness ("even a rotten one is good"). The secret knowledge of nectarines, I guessed earlier, was part taxonomic and part sensuous; it displaces the secret knowledge of homosexuality. This knowledge, however, must remain secret, which means that to replace fruitfulness with fruit is to keep the dead language of heterosexuality buried, but to image decadent orality as the eating of nectarines is not to allow the galvanizing discourse of homosexuality to surface.

Amalgamation is threatened when any repressed ethnicity appears on stage; this is the heterosexual worry of male performance. You might have thought that the diversion from compulsory fruitfulness would only magnify audience discomfort. In fact, the two horrors cancel each other, as Leslie Fiedler demonstrated in 1960, the year of "The 2000 Year Old Man." (My assertion that sensing miscegenation in an apparently natural nostalgia would have been unavoidable in 1960 is partly based on conceiving of Fiedler as a crystallization of his era.) But the demand of American men, in the presence of their most unremitting racial and sexual anxieties, is for more than local, vacillating distraction. The interference of these anxieties always entails, as Fiedler showed, a retreat to childhood; we may infer that the privileged form of obliviousness is the joke, which in Freud begins (though it does not end) in a prolongation of lost, ludic, childhood freedom.[20]

The fact remains that we are witnessing, in the case of Brooks and Reiner, two Jews, one more suburbanized and Americanized than the other, in uxorious harmony. Male anxiety cannot utterly disappear into the joke, however abstract; it keeps reappearing, embodied or at least voiced. The result is that Brooks must do male listeners the favor of representing the very threat they wish to wish away—his humor does not so much conjure it away as quarantine it. The model here is minstrelsy as Eric Lott describes it, in which the attribution of all loose homoeroticism to the blackface performer discharges the fear of miscegenation and the fear of homosexuality at once: thus the gratification, the release, the wild laugh. "Oh, Sally is de gal for me," went the blackface song, "I would'nt hab no udder / if Sally dies to-morrow night, / I'll marry Sally's brudder."[21]

To Lott, the "joking triangle, in which white men share a dominative relationship to a black man which is based above all on looking seems . . . the northern analogue of black men on the auction block."[22] This is a racial variation on Freud's smut triangle, in which two men share a laugh over a woman, who in upper-class joking cannot be present. In the case of minstrelsy, the white men who are sharing the joke are (presumably, since the joking triangle requires a joke teller and joke recipient) the blackface comedian and his audience; the object of the joke (insofar as the relationship is based "above all on looking") is also the blackface comedian, standing in for the absent black man himself. This too has resonance in the case of Reiner-Brooks, since Brooks, though Jewish, is playing a Jew, whose old world Yiddish accent is not quite Brooks's own.

Then what of Reiner? If the joke triangle consists of 2000 Year Old Man/ Brooks/audience, the relation is already triangulated by a split within Brooks descended from the blackfaced/white virgule in minstrelsy. Why add the interlocutor, if the comedy scene is already sexually mediated? (Brooks as comedian creates homosexual or iffy characters to reassure the audience whose love—his Catskills theme concluded "And though I'm not much on looks / Please love Mel Brooks" [23]—he passionately solicits.) Or why is the interlocutor necessary if the scene is already racially mediated? (Brooks shares with the audience a laugh over the old man's nondenominational Yiddishism.) What, in short, can we intuit in Brooks and Reiner's act of the special cultural function and technique of the comedy *team?*

To approach the answer, we need to track the progress of American popular entertainment from minstrelsy to its next triumphant form, vaudeville. (Brooks's comedy is as compulsively recapitulative as *The Jazz Singer,* which, Michael Rogin observes, absorbs minstrelsy and vaudeville and silent movies into their cultural conqueror, the first talkie.[24] Brooks satirizes minstrelsy in *Blazing Saddles,* revisits the silent movie in *Silent Movie,* and imitates vaudeville largely in the form of his pairing with Reiner, himself.) Vaudeville was a kind of Taylorization and bourgeoisification of variety, formulated by its founder, B. F. Keith, with Boston rectitude in mind. Among proscribed phrases on the Keith circuit were "son of a gun" and "holly gee"; words that referred to the body in a slangy way— for example, "slob"—were forbidden. The point was certainly to allow the audience to forget that its eyes were trained on human bodies. Nor was the comedian allowed to notice individuals in the audience: Fred Allen remembered that the "Notice to Performers" hung backstage at Keith theaters enjoined comedians not to "address anyone in the audience in any manner." [25]

Of course, some comedians were solo acts and were denied by Keith prohibitions merely the comic benefits of singling out members of the audience for colloquy or vituperation. But onetime blackface performer George Burns, out of blackface, interviewed Gracie for decades, and George Jessel, blackface rinsed, talked to his imaginary mother on the phone. In their own skin, some Jewish comedians looked askance at bourgeois audiences. The turn was from the indirection of blackface to the indirection of dialogue, in which a sexless heterosexuality (with infantile wife or imaginary mother) defused the ethnic charge heretofore discharged by homosexuality.[26]

Reiner's job, we may infer, is to be vaguely heterosexual and white-*ish*—in the manner of vaudeville, to stand between, and in the manner of minstrelsy, to speak between, to interlocute—the 2000 Year Old Jewish Man and his audience of gentiles and suburbanizing Jews. Is Reiner Jewish? Yes, but it is not transparent; in some ways he himself is between Jew and gentile. (On the evidence of *Enter Laughing,* his autobiographical novel, Reiner is an almost perfectly secular Jew—he begins and ends the book trying to transform his accent into Ronald Colman's.)[27] He is one degree whiter than the interlocutor who, even in black face, was white-ish (a white trying to seem like a black trying to seem like a white). "Although he sometimes wore blackface, the interlocutor dressed with more decorum than the other actors and represented the white presence on stage. . . . He commonly spoke with a deep, resonant voice and often used standard English."[28] What is the connection of standard English and a deep, resonant voice? The audience is reassured insofar as heterosexuality and whiteness can be identified in a single speech act. Whereas Brooks quarantines all possible contagions, Reiner stands next to them, enjoying them on behalf of the audience without infection: suburbanite in commuting relationship to the dangerous (sexual, aggressive, ethnic) city he moved out of. Commuting is the structural equivalent of joke work.

I seem to have assumed the diagnostic, clairvoyant, anhedoniacal voice of much cultural criticism—but I admit to finding something extremely appealing in the uncertain position of Carl Reiner (is he gentile?) vis-à-vis Mel Brooks (is he homosexual?). If Reiner mediates Brooks and audience, it is only by representing expansive whiteness and presumptive straightness in proximity, even if not in contagious contact, with Yiddish-inflected English and something not exactly straight. Reiner, while working with Brooks, worked *for* Sid Caesar, who brought elements of *Yiddishkeit* back into popular performance in the fifties when most of Jewish culture was moving the other way;[29] Reiner's attraction to the Jewish voice he tried to abandon for Ronald Colman's—like Twain's to the black voice—permitted Brooks all the sexual latitude his comedy required. To be loved for one's voice is not exactly to be loved for one's body—at least deniability is preserved—though on records what else is there besides voice?

Comedy teams cannot enact either homosexual or homophobic homo sociality—they neither out nor closet—but the indecisiveness is powerful. The final oddity of odd couples is that the man who gets the laughs is so desirable that his partner, his straight partner, must perform his attraction to him, and Tambo (black or Jewish or not) can convert his cultural weakness into vocal mastery. The odd incongruity was the regnant comic form from the fifties to the sixties, when suburbanization—heretofore largely a prerogative of Protestant couples but now available to New Rochelle's own Carl Reiner, creator of the commuting humor of *The Dick Van Dyke Show*—provoked by way of reaction to a travesty of the Protestant couple too odd to identify and exclude. This is what is worth regretting in the passing of comedy teams.

iii.

Mel Brooks begins "2000 Years" with such a strong insistence on his progenitivity—

> I've been married several hundred times. . . .
> I have over 42,000 children—and not one comes to visit me [big laugh] in an afternoon. . . . Children, good luck to them, let them go. . . .
> But they could send a note and write, hiya Pop, how ya doin' Pop?

—that one may think of Whitman and his six apocryphal children, not to mention his litters of literary disciples. I am not foisting an anxiety on this harmless fruitfulness joke. Brooks can be acute about the use of heterosexual credentials—"I've got a wife!"—which may echo as late as 1960 from Weber's broadly ethnic, vaudevillian self-exoneration to Fields: "Dat vas no lady, dat vas my wife!" That Brooks's homosociality can look odd (which I use now as a technical term) is frequently on his mind, which explains the fact that the "2000 Years" dialogues are frequently about the discovery of an unsuspected heterosexuality. The one woman the bimillennial man remembers dating was Joan of Arc, and in an excised part of the routine Brooks recounts the moment he discovered that the soldier was a woman.[30] Brooks also remembers the discovery of heterosex in general:

> Brooks: [lamenting prehistoric ignorance]: We didn't know who was a lady. [big laugh] They was with us, but we didn't know who they were. [big laugh] We didn't know who was the ladies and who was fellas.
> Reiner: You thought they were just different types of fellas.
> Brooks: Yeah, just stronger or smaller or softer. The softer ones I think were the ladies all the time. [laugh] But a cute, fat guy—you could've mistaken him for a lady. [big laugh]
> Reiner (later): How did [the discovery of females] come to pass?

Brooks: One morning [Bernie] got up smiling. [laugh] He said, "I think there's ladies here." [laugh] . . . He went into such a story, it's hundreds of years later, I still blush.

The incipience of heterosexuality is gleefully if secondhandedly and somewhat prudishly recollected, but the peculiarity is that to recall the first moment of heterosexuality is to imply a memory (not inferred by Reiner) of an indistinct time before it. "The softer ones I think were the ladies all the time" keeps ambiguous whether heterosexuality was always implicit in the homosociality that was at first, nevertheless, untriangulated.[31]

There is, not in "2000 Years with Carl Reiner and Mel Brooks" but more than a decade later in "2000 and Thirteen," an example of what seems to be gay bashing; on the near side of Stonewall, this would seem to be purely regressive. But for the purpose of bringing out what is odd rather than odious in Brooks's homosociality, even under the pressures of 1973 that would make odiousness a tempting disguise, I would like to revert to a previous moment in the history of homophobic comedy that reads similarly.

Alone in Burguete are Jake Barnes, the wounded protagonist of *The Sun Also Rises,* and his pal Bill Gorton, pretending to be Huck and Jim, fishing. One is heterosexual but castrated. What is the other? Brett (Lady Ashley) had, in Paris, been wrinkling the corners of her eyes at Gorton, and Bill was appreciative. Yet Bill, unlike Jake, unlike Brett's own Mike, unlike the Jew Cohn, unlike the bullfighter Romero, unlike, that is, every other man and his opposite, stays unmetamorphosed by Brett's Circean witchery. I do not need to know anything about Bill's private life, or anything about the sexuality of Donald Ogden Stewart, on whom he is modeled, to conclude that what Bill Gorton signifies for Jake is homosociality, per se, undefiled, with the triangulated third term being boxers or bullfighters or bulls, but not Brett, the cynosure of most of the triangulation of the novel, who destroys rather than facilitates the homosociality of the crowd. The best answer to "what is the other?" is humorist—Gorton resembles the real-life Stewart, author of several books of humor as well as the screenplay of *The Philadelphia Story.* (In which his namesake, Jimmy Stewart, cannot make his brilliant comic performance quite charismatic enough to subdue Katherine Hepburn—he passes her in an excess of brotherly love to Cary Grant—a failure the movie is helpless to explain.) One undervalued feature of Jake Barnes's character is his expertness as straight man, his strange dedication to qualifying not as a master but as an aficionado of bull slinging.

Which is why Gorton gratefully says to him in the midst of a comic riff,

"You're a hell of a good guy, and I'm fonder of you than anybody on earth. I couldn't tell you that in New York. It'd mean I was a faggot. That was what the Civil War was about. Abraham Lincoln was a faggot. He was in love with General Grant. So was Jefferson Davis." [32]

This is ugly enough, but what is its humor? I cannot see the charge of the humor, or its discharge. Outing Lincoln and Grant and Davis does not unambiguously relieve Bill and Jake of the implication of their own angling but not triangulating homosociality, since Bill has just called attention to it. There *is* something humorous in "It'd mean I was a faggot" as opposed to "They'd say I was a faggot"—what we have here is the humor of mock unrepression as a superior form of repression. Still, I am unsure of what the contagiousness of the accusation means, or rather how it works: how did Gorton, for one thing, leap to the Civil War? The lack of a logical or paralogical step aborts the joke.

There is an unpleasant—humor-draining—sense here of a joke that can go left or straight at various forks, that might be about repression or unrepression; that might be employed to punish one's betters (like the middle-class charge of inversion against aristocrats) or to gloat in one's connection to them; that might, in Sedgwick's terms, minoritize homosexuality or universalize it; that might relieve tension or exacerbate it on behalf of some future detumescence. The joke seems out of touch with its rationale: is omitting blacks from Civil War history a symptom of the exclusion of Jews and women from Burguete, at the price (the Jew and the woman had just managed an affair) of including homosexuality? Jokes may do complicated work, but this is more a riddle in reverse, a joke that might be a straight line.

It may be almost worth complaining that the historical question I raised —what brought up the Civil War?—would be a chronic problem of Donald Ogden Stewart criticism if there were such a thing, since he wrote two books of historical raillery—*Aunt Polly's Story of Mankind* and *A Parody Outline of History*—both extremely weak in justifying their historical données.[33] In a chapter of *A Parody Outline* called "How Love Came to General Grant," Grant is described (in the manner of Harold Bell Wright) as "a man's man—a man among men." [34] There is no particular effort to pass this off as double entendre, but the parody of Wright allows Stewart to assimilate Grant's virility to Billy Budd's—Grant is a blushing, clean-living virgin—which perhaps accounts for Bill Gorton's attribution of Civil War murderousness to a rivalry over him. What Hemingway may have captured in Gorton is the difficulty, in his original, of determining whether it is heterosexual or homosexual homosociality that amused him. Stewart (if I may conflate him with Gorton) seems to resent his undying fathers either because they were too manly or not manly enough to produce adequately virile sons. The chapter of *A Parody Outline* after the one on Grant treats Custer's inadequately virile son (he leaves his wife to take up painting in Paris)—though Custer might seem to be an ambiguous image of the warrior patriarch.

In "2000 and Thirteen," Reiner asks Brooks for recollections of the great American generals.

> Reiner: General Custer.
> Brooks: A fag. [big laugh] The man was a fag. [laugh]

> Reiner: The general's a fag?
> Brooks: All generals. [laugh]
> Reiner: Now just a minute. Are you trying to prove a psychiatric point?

> Reiner: George Washington.
> Brooks: A fag—the biggest. [laugh]
> Reiner: General Eisenhower.
> Brooks: A fag. [smaller laugh]
> Reiner: General Cornwallis.
> Brooks: A fag. [diminishing laugh]
> Reiner: General Patton.
> Brooks: A big fag. [renewed laugh]
> Reiner: Can you explain that, sir? . . . We haven't any history of them being homosexuals.
> Brooks: Hey, wait a minute. Hold on. Hold on, pal. I didn't say homosexuals.
> Reiner: You said fags. You said the generals are fags.
> Brooks: Yeah, Federal Army Generals. [modest laugh] . . . I shortened things, that's all.

> Reiner (suddenly doubtful): Do you know any homosexuals?
> Brooks: Maybe Custer. [laugh] Could have been. He had a lot of hair and he liked nice horses. [big laugh] Who knows?

This is close to a duplication of the Gorton routine, but I am not sure it is precisely the same joke on historical fathers. The joke, like Gorton's, does not work; but it is a more sympathetically confused failure.

The first anomaly to notice is that the sequence does not build—it deflates. The response to each apparent outing is weaker than the last, though the reference to Patton as "a big fag" revives the laughter somewhat; the punch line, which in this case Brooks may have preconceived, is a dud. One wonders, in retrospect, why Brooks commits himself to the bit in the first place. At the punch line, when Brooks denies that he has been outing all along, the audience can only regret its previous mirth, such as it was. The final pun is not merely unhilarious per se; it also nullifies the laugh in anything before it. If the audience is chastened, it is not amused. What could be Brooks's comic intention of depressing his self-condemned audience?

The best approach to this mystery begins with the possibility that the itinerary of Brooks's joke may not be from offensiveness (fag) to offensiveness ostensibly withdrawn, along with the humor (F.A.G.), to offensiveness belatedly revived for Custer (fag?). Is it possible—grant the logical possibility for a millisecond—that at the end of a rather queasy development is a secret celebration? Or that, more plausibly, there are (humor-defusing) cross-purposes?

Focus on Sedgwick's dismay (as regards the epithet mongering of Boyd McDonald and others) that "it has at various times and for various reasons seemed to gay people that there was some liberatory potential in articulating the supposed homosexual secrets of men in power." [35] I quote Sedgwick to establish at a minimum that Brooks's joke is not necessarily on behalf of heterosexuality. Would it be heterosexuality that is served by the outing of its purest symbols? Yes and no: the answer is ambiguous because the point shifts. The audience's good humor is revived by the allegation that Patton is a "big fag," which means that it is gratified to think that behind hypermasculinity is homosexual panic (so that pacifists are actually more secure, as they like to reiterate, in their masculinity). But the routine is double jeopardized by the reaccusation that *Custer* is homosexual. I would say the audience's laughter at this last outing episode is genial—it is a sunny outing—which is supported by the fact that there is no source of humor otherwise. Custer is gay. What else is new? If this is convincing, then the audience has been seduced from the humor of exposure to the humor of assimilation, from the comedy of counteraggression to the comedy of secret sharing, from war, in effect, to camp.

Though Gorton's joke threatens to universalize homosexuality, it does not embrace it; its knowingness could not conclude in a cheerfully open-minded "Who knows?" But my interest is not so much to apportion moral blame as to put into relief Brooks's position with respect to his bit—and to explain, by this example, the efflorescence of male-male stand-up teams in the fifties to sixties and their withering by, say, 1973 at the latest, after the last full reunion of Brooks and Reiner (1973) until 1997, and after the

46

Smothers Brothers (1967–1969) and Rowan and Martin (1967–1973) had performed their definitive cultural work on TV. Prime evidence is the instabilty of Brooks's sexual stance. He is, safe to say, neither as defensively heterosexual as Gorton in Hemingway nor as offensively homosexual as Boyd McDonald in Sedgwick. I think he is careless about his position; not carefree, of course, in the midst of anxieties of every kind (there is a reason, I hope it is apparent by now, for the impossibility of fixing the exact nuance). "Insouciant" seems too studied; "contumacious" conveys an inapt awareness of subordinate status. Rebellion in America is filial, but Brooks as the 2000 Year Old Man is a coeval of the various fathers whom he outs.

In "The 2000 Year Old Man," I mean, you cannot, as in the case of Gorton, blame fathers (too macho or too sissified) for the ebbing heterosexuality of their children, because Brooks is his own ancestry; like Bruce, he contrives to be father and son at a stroke. The syndrome of *The Jazz Singer,* as complicated as it gets, is comparatively simple. Rogin shows that Al Jolson gets his taboo desires (Jewish mother and "American" girl) by the same act: murder of the Jewish patriarch. The way to American male heterosexuality is through generational conflict, which may imply assimilation and intermarriage. There are crossed wires along the way: the assumption of whiteness is predicated on the liberation of blackness; to be a jazz singer is to be a cantor in one's own way. Still, what remains simple is that the father must die. If, on the one hand, homosexuality may result if one's father is a killer (in the Custer story), and heterosexuality is earned by killing him (in the cantor story), what, on the other hand, is entailed by deathless self-fathering? Assuming the Yiddish voice may cut off the Americanized future, but it promises an oddly futureless immortality—this doubles the oxymoron of the rotten nectarine—of its own. There is in Brooks's comedy an unrelentingly omnivalent ambition: to be the American kid and his Jewish ancestry at once, father of thousands and outer of fathers.

During the course of the record in which the 2000 Year Old Man debuts, Brooks inhabits several other characters, often of uncertain and sometimes of fairly certain sexuality. He portrays Fabiola, the rock musician, whose last line to Reiner is, "It was a pleasure speaking to you—you're pretty." Later, as one of the seven original astronauts, Brooks explains to Reiner why his picture had not been on the cover of *Life* magazine. He and the other six are too ugly; the picture on *Life* is of seven models. ("They take pictures of them, so we're not ashamed for Russia to show such ugly little astronauts.") When Reiner concurs that the bogus model-astronauts are "handsome," Brooks goes further: "They're seven beautiful men. As a matter of fact, one of them is *very* beautiful." Clearly, something has happened between 1960 and 1973, so that nothing like these moments can recur, so that what does recur is an allusion to the 2000 Year Old Man's 42,000 children, reinvoked to prove that the Brooks character is a "virile human being." And the "F.A.G." joke, with its subtle grossnesses, replaces the masked self-outing that had regularly amused Brooks and his audience.

Back in 1960, you could occasionally observe, on stage, two men performing comedy. They seem to be competing for the love of their triangulated audience, yet if their intentions have ever been competitive (or if they are still competitive and repressed), nevertheless the rivalry has drawn them into an entanglement. Is it possible that the third point of the triangle can, in effect, drop out? The audience, in comedy settings, is often secretly or, on bad nights, vocally resentful of its inferior position, brutalized (the comedian wants "to kill them") and feminized (little wonder that in colloquial language, "hilarity" is confused with "hysteria"). This seems like patriarchy in miniature, yet the Brooks-Reiner audiences seem particularly genial, gratified to be on the inside of humor whose secret is hieratic, like the secret of nectarines or irrationals. In their adulation of Brooks they resemble Reiner, who laughs cheerfully throughout the albums, witnessing many of Brooks's surreal flights for the first time himself. (He is a straight man who does not remain, in the manner say of George Burns with his paralogical wife, straight.) The Brooks-Reiner audience produces only weakly a third point of the triangle: it seems merely to double and reinforce what Reiner and Brooks already do for each other.

Reiner, at times, may seem to be heckling Brooks, interrupting him, hazing him, as if the agent of an audience that wants Brooks to fail, but he is not a heckler but a secret spouse, not representing the audience in its resentment so much as in its love. He may figure, on stage, suburban fifties heterosexuality, but he is a helpmate; he only wants to abet; he wants to reflect Brooks's sudden glory. The heterosexual position (as in Hemingway, except that it is voluntary) is castrated: Reiner must curtail his own considerable talent to amuse. Brooks is irrepressible; he insists on his own desires; he is willful. The "odd" position (or the position whose paradoxicalness projects the oddity of the relationship) is dominant, as in "The Odd Couple" itself. Reiner and Brooks are engaged in a dyadic intimacy that is reciprocal, charged, self-sufficient, and full, but as a comedy team they feel the need, from time to time, to triangulate—to objectify the hysteria of—their mutual attraction.

Why are there no more comedy teams? Because now, in the two decades since "2000 and Thirteen," comedy teams would have to *declare,* as Brooks feigns declaring in his "F.A.G." bit, or else we would declare for them. Comedy teams in 1960 could not declare, and tacitly prevented, by the nature of their anomalous combination, our prurient declaring on their behalf. The range of specifications of current declarative taxonomy could not include subjunctive *oddness:* the juxtaposing of two stereotypes, heterosexual and homosexual, that might (Wayne Koestenbaum–fashion) posit a third term and heterosexualize, or might (Terry Castle–fashion) collapse into two-ness and lesbianize. A pretentious actor played by Brooks in another of the routines on their first album declares proudly, "I happen to be a lesbian." Reiner corrects him, "You mean Thespian."

A male-male comedy team is an odd couple, and an odd couple is a union that cannot declare its essence to be this or that: half a prissy peach, half a virile plum, not either, not both, not a composite, not a compromise, something other, something better than either even in decay. This irrationality veiled in the simplest of ratios, 1:1, denies the surveyability of homosocial-homosexual boundaries that, castellated, protect our patriarchy; it defies the sort of knowingness, as Sedgwick puts it, that terrorizes homosexuals and heterosexuals alike. It razes, so to speak, the question of what sort of couple counts as homosexual, insofar as it razes the newly impolite question of who counts as a Jew. (We are all Jews here, says Brooks. We are all whites here, says Reiner. Are *these* predicates exclusive?) The cultural benefit is that there are as many dangers in despising this sort of pollution, as Mary Douglas might phrase it, as in celebrating it. What version of heterosexuality would dare to include the intimate coupling of Reiner and Brooks? Which would dare to exclude it? The laughter of this abjection—this failed exclusion—is a lost charm. In theories of the homosocial continuum, it is the missing link.

In San Francisco, in the late 1970s, I swear I heard the following conversation on a talk radio station, KGO. The caller should have been Mel Brooks, much of whose work, I believe, is a meditation on the epithet in question, playing a homophobe.

> Caller: I don't know why they call themselves "gay." What's gay about them?
> Host (warily): So what do *you* call them?
> Caller: I call them fruits.[30]

i.

An Indian at the table of an Englishman in Surat, when he saw a bottle of ale opened and all the beer turned into froth and overflowing, testified his great astonishment with many exclamations. When the Englishman asked him, "What is there in this to astonish you so much?" he answered, "I am not at all astonished that it should flow out, but I do wonder how you ever got it in."[1]

This is the sound of Immanuel Kant telling a joke; and if the joke is not good, it is far and away the most amusing thing in the "Analytic of the Aesthetical Judgment." Is it sublime or is it beautiful? It is neither. It is pleasant: its primary appeal is to the body rather than the mind. Or so we are informed by a "Remark" dangling at the end of the "Analytic," a bathetic afterthought.

I find this disappointing. The joke seems to me to represent a sort of anti-sublime—which is to say that it has a sublimity of its own—since the Indian feels, in his astonishment, what he should have felt before a "lofty waterfall" (*KJ*, 125), say, rather than cascading beer. That the joke is about a perversion of sublimity does not mean, of course, that it is itself a perversion of sublimity, let alone sublime. But the joke's punch line is anticlimactic—the anecdote is a joke for just that reason—which means that we double the Indian's astonishment before an unworthy object. If there is a sublime of *bathos,* as Thomas Weiskel put it, opposite that of *hypsos,*[2] then the joke (bathetic, about bathos, bathetically placed) is a perfect specimen. Kant is resolute in not seeing this, but he persistently illustrates it. In a precritical demarcation, he writes that "nothing sinks deeper beneath the sublime than the ridiculous."[3] This formulation distinctly, if unintentionally, lends the ridiculous a sublime, even oceanic, depth.

Longinus, on the other hand, does see that the ridiculous has its own sublimity: "Ridicule is an amplification of the paltriness of things."[4] But he does not seem to mean much by this—he mentions it in passing. Nor does he show the least anxiety about the converse, more troubling to his project of aesthetic discrimination: that the sublime might also amplify the paltriness of things, and so would have its own ridiculousness. Not that the sublime is ridiculous, but that it might become ridiculous in belated imaginations—the sophistication of which comes off just as silly as Kant's Indian's naïveté—is at least the *intended* lesson of the example of Timaeus. Timaeus manages, Longinus insists, only a faux sublimity when he writes that Alexander "gained possession of the whole of Asia in fewer years than it took Isocrates to write his *Panegyric* urging war against the Persians" (*LS,* 51). Longinus proves that this encomium is just puerile by extending its logic:

> How plain it is, Timaeus, that the Lacedaemonians, thus judged, were far inferior to Isocrates in prowess, for they spent thirty years in the conquest of Messene, whereas he composed his *Panegyric* in ten.

Longinus makes a joke of the measuring of incommensurables. I wonder, however, whether his mockery betrays his own missing of the joke. The faithful stretching of Timaeus's logic (not quite to snapping) would be: "How inferior is Isocrates in prowess, for it took him a decade to compose the *Panegyric* urging war, when it took the Lacedaemonians only three to win one." That Alexander took less time conquering than Isocrates took composing is more striking than that the Lacedaemonians took somewhat more, but the tendency of the comparison would be the same. What Longinus depreciates in his analysis of Timaeus is not the sublimity but the wit, which indicates sublime respect (for Alexander) by amplifying the paltriness of someone else (Isocrates). The inference is not that measuring incommensurables is a sign of a lapse from the sublime to the ridiculous, but that it is essential to the sublime, which must always *include* the ridiculous: sublimity here is the literary (Isocrates) in ridiculous proximity to power (Alexander).

Longinus manages to make the implicit Timaean point—that sublimity is inhabited by the ridiculous—as unwittingly as Kant demonstrates that the ridiculous is sublime. Here is one of Longinus's great examples of the authentically sublime, from Homer:

> And far as a man with his eyes through the sea-line
>   haze may discern,
> On a cliff as he sitteth and gazeth away o'er the wine-
>   dark deep,
> So far at a bound do the loud-neighing steeds of the
>   Deathless leap. (*LS*, 61)

Fair enough: we recognize sublimity when we hear it. But Longinus, pushing that recognition to analysis, makes a fatal if inevitable miscue: "The sublimity is so overpowering as naturally to prompt the exclamation that if the divine steeds were to leap thus twice in succession they would pass beyond the confines of the world" (*LS*, 63). I am not quite sure, reading that appreciation, how to tell it is not ridicule. Of course, in a way I know how. Passing beyond the confines of the world is exactly what the sublime is engaged to do. If we take Longinus as he would have us, the sublime equation is $2x = \infty$. Nevertheless, there is something debasing in performing the math—any formulation is a formula—and we recall that bringing out the ridiculousness of Timaeus was accomplished by a similar mathematical analysis.

Homer, to be sure, does not involve *himself* in the nonsublimity of the ratio, as Timaeus does. The solution to Longinus's predicament would seem to be never to explicate the sublimity of the sublime; the flaw is that Longinus had to ridicule the ridiculous by contrast. The sublime must be, essentially, beyond measure. In Kant's terms (with respect to the mathematical sublime), it cannot have "an adequate standard . . . outside itself. . . . It is magnitude which is like itself alone." But Kant adds, almost immediately, that the sublime is "that in comparison with which everything else is small" (*KJ*, 109), which means that incommensurability is universally measurable, that Timaeus made no mistake, that the sublime like the ridiculous is an amplification of the paltriness of things, of all things minus one. In the comparison of the sublime and the ridiculous, therefore, the ridiculous both suffers and subverts.

Would a similar but opposite analysis bring out the sublimity of the Indian's ridiculous mistake? It is not merely that the depth of his ignorance clarifies the heights of our wisdom, on the Hobbesian theory of "sudden glory." We do feel our superiority to the Indian, but our amusement by him masks another feeling, giddier but deeper. I said before that the joke astonishes us as the Indian is astonished; I would go further now and argue that we are astonished by the same thing that astonishes him. Since a joke involves tension and release, it may be emblematized by the bottle of ale—the anecdote is as much metajoke as Homer's steeds leaping into heaven are metasublime. But a joke is more than tension and release: when people tell us jokes, our mystification lasts beyond the punch line. We feel sublime helplessness not merely for the duration of the joke's suspense, but also before a timeless power. Authentically mystifying is how the joke teller gets his fizz into the bottle. To analyze a joke—this is what a metajoke invites us to do—is to see the released froth as something prepared and stored, waiting to please us by belittling us.

On analysis, sublimity is ridiculous; on analysis, jokes are sublime. We cannot feel elevation without feeling put down, we cannot feel put down without experiencing the depths, in endless vibration. This would seem to be the experience of the sublime per se, as Kant and exegetes define it. Sublimity involves a mental "vibration . . . a quickly alternating attraction toward, and repulsion from, the same Object" (*KJ*, 120). My only quarrel with Kant and exegetes is that they do not see the humor of this oscillation, as between parental power and childish helplessness. The progression of sublime theorists Weiskel, Hertz, and Knapp represents an ever more vigilant attempt to keep the sublime unselfprotective, which may mean, as Knapp puts it, keeping sublimity from degenerating into a "satirical caricature of self-congratulation" (as it risks doing, according to Knapp, in Burke).[5] Granted that advertising one's own sublimity ("How's this for sublime!")—proclaiming one's identity with the sublime object via identity with the reason that is equal to it—is ludicrous. But there may be something ludicrous in its antithesis: "I am rent and routed by sublimity!"

Knapp does not represent the sublimist as declaiming in that way. For Knapp, the Kantian subject is prevented from falling into a "satirical caricature of self-congratulation" by his oscillation "between sympathy and irony in relation to the self's identification with truth."[6] The prevention of satire by irony is homeopathy already on the border of the comic. Lyotard's ago-nized sublimist, however, rises to a height of melodrama that could use irony: "He [the law, i.e., reason] desperately needs an imagination that is violated, exceeded, exhausted. She will die in giving birth to the sublime."[7] Instead of a healthy, appreciative imagination acknowledging its master, here is a raped imagination in fatal confinement; Knapp's self-division takes the form of self-irony, but Lyotard's takes the form of self-rape and semi-suicide. This may seem ludicrous to us, but more to the point is that it is unclear why it did not seem so to Kant. Levity is also, in Kant, a form of violent self-division.

> It is remarkable that . . . the jest must [always] contain something that is capable of deceiving for a moment. Hence, when the illusion is dissi-pated, the mind turns back to try it once again, and thus through a rapidly alternating tension and relaxation it is jerked back and put in a state of oscillation. (*KJ*, 225)

The mind is not fooled only once, externally. The mind divides internally, being fooled and fooling itself, unable to match itself, as in the case of the sublime, over and over.

How would this lead to laughter? The mental oscillation sets up a physi-cal one, "an alternating tension and relaxation of the elastic portions of our intestines, which communicates itself to the diaphragm (like that which ticklish people feel)" (*KJ*, 225–26). The Indian joke is approximately a meta-joke insofar as it is about tension and release, more exactly because it does not subside comfortably in entropy, but begins to return against time. (How do you get the bubbles rebottled?) What I do not understand, since Kant grants that "with all our thoughts is harmonically combined a movement in the organs of the body" (*KJ*, 225), is why just the joking oscillation sets the intestines throbbing. Why doesn't the sublime tickle?

ii.

In 1960, around the time Mike Nichols and Elaine May arrived at Broad-way and immortality, it was obvious to many observers, in the presence of the self-mortifying Phyllis Diller, among others, that comediennes (as they were called) had to be more or less repulsive. This turns out to be un-true, along with other clichés of the period (midwesterners were not, as it happens, too bland to be funny, nor blacks too angry, nor homosexuals too upsetting). The best mainstream female comedian of our era, Ellen DeGeneres, managed when she was still doing stand-up to neutralize the issue of attractiveness by a kind of girl-next-door transvestism. But even at the time, the stereotype had an odd corollary that should have seemed bewildering: Hollywood comic actresses, as opposed to comediennes, played off of their good looks or even, in one variation on the theme, their glamour.

What was the difference? I suppose that if you could have taken a reading of the minds of male audience members (who have traditionally determined success in comedy more powerfully than women), you would have found that the position of the female stand-up is a challenge in the first place; add sexual allure to her wit and the result would have been not the tension and release of humor, but pure exacerbation. This much of the answer probably could have reached self-consciousness, and I do not dismiss it. A comic screen actress has only mediated relations with the audience, so that however beautiful and funny she may be, someone else, Spencer Tracy or Cary Grant, say, has to deal with it. But I doubt that that could be the whole explanation, given that what the explanation explains happens not to be the case. We are considering what made audiences think Phyllis Diller had to be a hag, and what made Diller think it herself, rather than the eternal necessity of it, and the discrimination opens up the possibility that whatever everybody thought was only a sublimation of the syndrome.

One peculiarity about Diller was that, though she put herself down in typical ways, she could be threatening in just those ways. She was, in one extended bit, a dangerously typical female driver—the doubling of the bind is that the stereotype condemns modern women as too masculine and not masculine enough. Also, I can remember not following the comic drift of her relationship with her mythical husband, Fang. The confusion I felt (aged 10–13, say) was that Fang seemed a good name for *her*. In retrospect, what seems obvious is the phallic nature of her grotesque looks (Phallus Diller, she might have named herself for, as it were, the stage): sharp nose, sharp chin, ophidian hair, and infinite cigarette-holder.

What preoccupies me about stand-up—why I want to analyze it in terms of its theatrical setting, beyond the formal or psychoanalytic examination of jokes per se—is that it involves, essentially, standing up, or at least elevation. In previous chapters I have been thinking only about the paradoxes of male stand-up, which has been traditionally pretty close to a redundancy. The best guide to female stand-up may turn out to be Neil Hertz, especially in his essay, "Medusa's Head: Male Hysteria under Political Pressure."[8] Political pressure in his essay means 1789 and 1848, and aftermaths, and among the male hysterics are Burke, Hugo, and Tocqueville; they keep personifying their anxiety about political revolution and epistemological disarray in terms of a female figure who, in the emblematic rendering by Hugo, is standing up—self-destructively, exhibitionistically, defiantly—on the barricades. Phyllis Diller is a descendant of these hallucinatory Medusas, doing stand-up, creating if not hysteria then, at her best, hilarity, which may be male hysteria in spasms.

Hertz's title comes from Freud's essay (or notes) of 1922, "Medusa's Head," one peculiarity of which is that it divides in half, with two different evaluations of Medusa that seem not to be in touch. First, Freud hypothesizes that men see in Medusa's hair the mother's hair surrounding her genitals, and as usual are filled with the horror of castration; but the snakes "serve actually as a mitigation of the horror, for they replace the penis."[9] Then Freud writes, confusingly, that "this is a confirmation of the technical rule according to which a multiplication of penis symbols signifies castration." Could "signifies" be right? Only in the sense, I suppose, that relief from the threat of castration signifies castration. (Then where is the relief?) In this sense, fetishism is its own opposite: the snakes resemble the penis (unlike a fetish), and they remind men of the maternal absence (instead of blocking the memory of it); still, the result seems to be a simultaneous avowal and disavowal of castration exactly *like* fetishism.

Perhaps this reversible fetishism accounts for the apparent turn in Freud's argument, when he submits that the display of Medusa's head is used to terrify enemies. "If Medusa's head takes the place of a representation of the female genitals," Freud writes, "or rather if it isolates their horrifying effects from their pleasure-giving ones, it may be recalled that displaying the genitals is familiar in other connections as an apotropaic act." This seems wrong: the Medusa's head, I had thought, represented both the female and male genitals, both the evidence of castration and the multiplication of what had been detached, so that isolating horrible and pleasurable effects would be impossible. Evidently, however, you can aim the Medusa's head so that the horror flows outward toward one's foes but the reassurance flows inward toward oneself. Could the wind shift and the gaze drift back?

Hertz has been criticized by Knapp for finding in Kant's sublime too much comfortable self-protection and not enough self-laceration.[10] Insofar as he is concerned with Freud's Medusa essay, Hertz might have been pardoned for expressing either the comfort or the agony, since Freud's two impulses seem barely to be in contact, as if he might look up at Phyllis Diller and say, "She is hideous like a phallus so she is finally no threat" and, "She is hideous like a female so she is."

In "The Laugh of the Medusa," an essay that does not have much to do with laughter or Medusa, Hélène Cixous does at least register her scorn for Medusa in her reassuring role. "Too bad for them [men] if they fall apart upon discovering that women aren't men, or that the mother doesn't have one. But isn't this fear convenient for them?"[11] As against this emasculating but remasculating Medusa, Cixous proposes one who is "beautiful and . . . laughing." Phyllis Diller is laughing, half of what is required, but she is laughing at least in part at herself, at her ugliness, and men laugh at ugly women in relief that they are not threateningly different.[12] Suppose, on the other hand, that the female comedian, up on stage as if on the barricades, were not grotesque. Suppose, therefore, that one could not chart the direction of laughter: are we laughing at her or is she laughing at us, when we seem to be laughing together?

The vacillation is between pleasure and displeasure, as in the sublime; what Cixous opens up beyond this is a version of sublimity that takes the form of beauty as disguise. Perhaps the result is not merely a vibration of pain and pleasure but an inability to be certain of the difference, pain that feels like pleasure, antagonism that feels like harmony. Masochism would seem to be a plausible cognate, but so would tickling, to return to Kant's psychosomatics of laughter: the laughing Medusa makes her victims laugh. And we cannot decide about Mike Nichols, on stage with Elaine May, whether he is in sympathy with her humor or the victim of it. Is he the mediating figure of film comedies or merely a surrogate member of the audience, always almost overwhelmed?

iii.

I have no memory of seeing Nichols and May perform (the team disbanded when I was ten), but it is as if they were always in my mind. Now, when I think of Elaine May, I only picture photographs on album covers, some of which either have become iconic or seem so to me. In one, Richard Avedon poses her as Nefertiti.[13] In another Avedon portrait, May grins openmouthed at the camera, hair wilder than usual, at the digital melting point between Elizabeth Taylor and Lucille Ball.[14] In one picture she makes her eyes droopy and asymmetrical, perhaps for a Jewish mother avatar (*E*, inside cover). On another album, she looks rather like Imogene Coca.[15] So let us say her looks are among Liz's, Lucy's, Coca's, a Jewish mother's, and Nefertiti's. Another picture would add another identity.

Meanwhile, what is perpetually fascinating in Mike Nichols's expression is absence of same. He is so blank, he might be the nerdiest or slyest or stupidest boy in the class.

All of this makes the "Telephone" routine emblematic (*E* and *B*). Nichols plays a steadily infantilizing man in a public phone booth who has only one dime to make an important phone call; while he is asking Information for the number, the dime is collected. First, he tells the operator what has transpired—her advice is to hang up, whereupon the dime will be refunded. Nichols, his voice breaking into Shelley Berman's, replies, "No, no, it won't, operator. Listen to me! I know that sound! I've heard it all my life. I know it's in there!" The operator, who calls herself by her title, is unmoved. "Information cannot argue with a closed mind."

Nichols demands to speak to her superior: "Is there anyone else I can speak to? A human?" Information coolly responds, "You wish to talk to a human?" and connects him to the supervisor, who is the origin, in voice at least, of Lily Tomlin's "Ma Bell" character, Ernestine. The information supervisor, however, is offended at Nichols's suggestion that his dime is gone. "Bell Telephone gets millions of dimes. They wouldn't pick out your dime to steal."

When Nichols asks for the next supervisor up the line, it is Miss Jones, who sounds like Marilyn Monroe. In contact with her feminine sympathy, Nichols collapses into sobs. She whispers, with interest both maternal and seductive, "You've lost your dime." Nichols only hears the maternal, and wails, "No, she took it!"

She? Well, yes, she. Because the pay phone itself, the phone company, and all its employees have become female incarnations for Nichols. "Information" is the machine personified (which is why Nichols wants to transcend her to "someone human"); "Information Supervisor" is the company itself, indignantly taking Nichols's suggestion that his dime is gone as a libel not on the technology but on the corporation (so Information Supervisor becomes Tomlin's Ma Bell). Finally, the phone company humanizes and a female voice escapes the machine. But there is something suspicious: the voice is too female; and the economic equivalent of it is the free phone call Nichols is granted. If this female voice is all it claims to be, mother and mistress in a single presence, no losses and all gains, there is such a thing as a free lunch, civilization without neurosis, perpetual motion, immortality. Nichols dials the number that he has finally learned on no dime, rather on the promise of pure costlessness, but (punch line) the number is wrong.

The names for the May characters are "Information," "Information Supervisor," and "Miss Jones"; the name for the Nichols character is only, in my mind, Nichols. May is a perverse trinity, three people none of whom is a person, while Nichols plays a part so flayed as almost not to involve a persona. (It may be worth trying to ignore that the emblematic Nichols character is Nichols in a bit about a lost dime. Still—it certainly is Nichols who is generally at risk of being swallowed in Nichols-May routines.) May, in effect, takes on all of the dynamic sublimity of the absent, looming, soul-quivering corporation and its mathematically sublime infinitude of machines before assuming the beauty of "Miss Jones," but Miss Jones is just another manifestation of the unimaginable, and she puts Nichols out of his pain in the sense of consummating it. May is the laughing Medusa, if that implies that her implicit beauty (vox et praetera nihil) seems to do less for the masculinity of men in her range than a witch's frightfulness.

iv.

In "Disc Jockey," Mike Nichols plays a name-dropping radio personality called Jack Ego, interviewing a brainless starlet called Barbara Musk (*E*). From a formal point of view, the interest of the routine is that laughs come equally from Nichols and May: as opposed to the usual construction of comedy teams, for example Mel Brooks and Carl Reiner or Dan Rowan and Dick Martin, in which one comedian is designated straight man and the other gets the laughs, Nichols and May cannot be assigned invariant positions. In "Telephone," laughs come from both Nichols and May, but Nichols is more scored against than scoring. In "Disc Jockey," there is a breathtakingly adept switching from straight to unstraight throughout.

The structure of the bit is provided, rather rotely, by increments in the enormity of Nichols's name-dropping, which starts with Bernard Baruch, climbs through the pope, and peaks at God. Meanwhile, May stays in a single character—as opposed to "Telephone"—but the central joke of her half of the dialogue is that she is a completely stupid actress publicizing a movie called "Two Gals in Paris," in which she plays the lead, Gertrude Stein. May stays in character only because her character does not stay in character. In "Disc Jockey," May begins with "femininity"—where she ends in "Telephone"—but she is playing a draggy female playing a lesbian.

Nichols is wonderful in the routine, getting laughs often enough merely from the abrupt, nasal, subtly modulated way he terminates quanta of starlet idiocy with "Uh huh. Uh huh. How about that?" At which point he resumes name-dropping, for example, Albert Schweitzer: "I haven't seen him for a week. I think he's in Africa." Barbara Musk gamely replies: "So Al is in Africa. Well, gee, I didn't know that. . . . What is there to say about Al [pause] Schweitzer?" She stops before Schweitzer, not quite sure how to pronounce it, then pronounces the "w" as "v"; her insecurity comes out in the inflection: "Schveitz'-uh?" This is the biggest laugh in the routine, and the audience applauds. I think, however, that there is confusion mixed up in the laughter—perhaps why it turns to applause. Most obviously, the joke says: Barbara Musk is so stupid, she has never heard of Albert Schweitzer. It also says: Barbara Musk is a Hollywood starlet, but under pressure she is just a dumb girl from Brooklyn with a name change, pronouncing Schweitzer's name almost correctly only by guessing that he must be a Jew. (Her given name was conceivably Barbara Muscowitz, sometimes pronounced Muscovitz.) Here things get complicated: Elaine May is a Jew, as was Gertrude Stein, though not a dumb one.

Once again, we arrive at identity confusion. If May, in "Telephone," achieves femininity only when it comes out of a machine, in "Disc Jockey," she starts with screen-replicable femininity, but it reveals something: that the borders between Broadway star and Hollywood starlet and dumb girl from the declassed boroughs are always open. This sounds vulnerable, except that May has made the discovery (useful to Ellen DeGeneres and Paula Poundstone, q.v.) that when you are in the neighborhood of the abject, threatened by the return of sloughed skin, the best place to be is nowhere, the strongest technique to master is that of disappearing in view.

For me, the endlessly interesting moment of the bit occurs when Nichols drops the name of Bernard Baruch: "He's not like a lot of your financiers. By that I mean he's not only out for money." May replies: "I think that Bernie is a real great guy—you know?—and I mean a real great financer [rhymes with dancer]." Then Musk giggles, the short nervous giggle she deploys in the face of Nichols's barking throughout. This time the audience gets confused, and thinks that May, not Musk, is laughing, in delight over her apt mispronunciation. When audiences are on their side, they love it when comedians appreciate themselves. (It is the performative and sometimes male-male equivalent of the masculine requirement that beautiful women consider themselves, even if they modestly hide it, beautiful, to ensure that they are not witches, coldly emitting rays.) The result is that the audience's laughter swells along with May's giggle; I cannot tell if it ever realizes its mistake.

May's humor is often this sort of apparition. At the moment when she seems to humanize and appear (in this case, simply laughing with the audience), she is most efficient and evasive, the paradox of Miss Jones. Her laughter, totally knowing and controlled, like the laughing Medusa's, creates our laughter, deceived and extravagant. We grant that we are inferior to her, and though we are enjoying the experience, we are hardly (if we are men) remasculated by it. This is some other kind of pleasure.

v.

On one record, we are allowed to eavesdrop on Nichols and May working out a routine; they have decided that Nichols will play a son informing his mother of his professional ambition: to become a male nurse.[16] Something in this (it is probably obvious enough) wildly amuses Nichols, and he begins to laugh out of control. May is also amused, mainly by what is happening to Nichols. She begins to taunt him, not as the son in the skit, who would not be laughing, but as the son who is: "You're a happy boy, always smiling, always glad." Hearing her allude not to his character's determination but to his own current helplessness, and further convulsed by the representation of his hysteria as "happiness," Nichols' abjectness spirals. He gasps, "Stop it, for God's sake." May will not stop.

We arrive, evidently, at the logic of tickling, which Mary Douglas describes in her analysis of joking as a "mock attack": "The baby laughs more when it is tickled by its own mother than by a stranger."[17] It is worth observing that in "Transference," a typically knowing skit, Nichols admits to his psychiatrist, "You remind me of, well, this is crazy, you remind me of my mother," and by the end of the skit he is sobbing (*B*); she sees that he is distraught, and recommends chicken soup. In "Mother and Son," Elaine May telephones her boy, a NASA scientist, and begins: "Hello, Arthur, this is your mother. Do you remember me?" (*E*). Every attack is a mock attack, and vice versa. If I granted the Freudian premise that the unconscious is a joker, I would add that Nichols was born in Nazi Berlin, and that May's real family name is Berlin: the relation of Nichols and May is so glibly and gaily incestuous that it forestalls analysis, that we read incest as tickling.[18]

Adam Phillips has written a short essay on tickling in which he quotes a girl of eight: "When we play monsters, and mummy catches me, she never kills me, she only tickles me." It may matter, however, that the young child, or perhaps Mike Nichols in the studio, would be apt to cry out, "Stop! You're killing me!" Perhaps we might wish to consider what May does to

Nichols as a perversion of tickling, since she is not a mother playing monsters but an actress playing an authentically monstrous (Jewish) mother, whose tickling is not relief from the threat of killing but a form of assassination. I shall quote Phillips now at some length to lend further support to the hypothesis that May is tickling only by perverse metaphor.

> Through tickling, the child will be initiated in a distinctive way into the helplessness and disarray of a certain primitive kind of pleasure, dependent on the adult to hold and not to exploit the experience. And this means to stop at the blurred point, so acutely felt in tickling, at which pleasure becomes pain, and the child experiences an intensely anguished confusion; because the tickling narrative, unlike the sexual narrative, has no climax.[19]

Since May goes beyond that blurred point, we may infer that she is not so much mother as dominatrix. The problem is that I do not know how you stop at a blurred point or, rather, what a blurred point is. I hold with Euclid that if there is a blur, there is no point. You might conclude, accordingly, that the adult ought to stop before the blur, before the anguished confusion—when is that?

Phillips's ultimate assertion that tickling has no climax might seem to counter his penultimate one that there is a moment beyond which it cannot go pleasurably on. He is right, of course, both that there is a pleasure in being tickled and that it bleeds into pain. What I do not believe is that the nature of a nonclimactic narrative permits the clarity of a knowable stopping point. This is what Phillips takes into account by calling the point "blurred": it is not the point that is blurred, however, it is the whole event. "Anguished confusion" characterizes *all* of tickling (the confusion is that the anguish is mixed with pleasure). The pleasure may not always be pain but it is always becoming pain. Even the victim of tickling may not be sure when enough is enough.

Nichols and May give the impression of conducting an analysis of humor within their humor, and they are almost explicit about the centrality of tickling to their conception of it. In a skit called "Mysterioso," two spies (apparently) meet on a train. Nichols has a ticket (it turns out merely to be a laundry ticket in the weird bathos of the skit) hidden down his shirt, "over [his] clavicle." May reaches for it; tickled, he bursts out laughing (*IM*). In "Physical," more tellingly, Nichols is a patient counternamed Mr. Prober, who goes to his new female physician, counternamed Dr. Mittelschmerz, to discuss a pain low in his abdomen (*B*). He wants to describe it, she wants to look. Finally, she begins to do the probing.

May: Does this hurt? Does this hurt?

Nichols: Doc, please! No wait. Doctor, please, can you wait? [Nichols laughs hysterically, explaining:] I'm very ticklish.

[And later:]

May: This is just your stomach.

Nichols: The abdomen is very . . . [hysterical giggling]

After a while, the mood turns flirtatious: Dr. Mittelschmerz finds out that Mr. Prober is a lawyer and unmarried. From the tickling we ascend or descend to actual equality and the prospect of climactic sensuality.

That is the meta–punch line, only a mildly dissatisfying one. Generally, Nichols and May work without gags; when they feel the need to end their skits, they mainly do a perfunctory job of it. The end of the "Telephone" skit—Nichols, at long last, makes his call, but it is a wrong number—gets only a letdown laugh. The climax of "Disc Jockey"—Nichols name-drops God—provokes a big laugh, but is too mechanical and adolescent to deserve one. When Nichols and May improvise to piano music, they often simply leave it to their accompanist to cap the skit. All of which is to say that they are conducting serious explorations of the sensuous and aesthetic pleasures available in nonclimactic forms.

Noelle Oxenhandler, also writing about the sensuous pleasures legitimately available between adults and children, like Adam Phillips stresses that the nature of these pleasures will always be, so to speak, ante-anti-climactic.[20] In giving us comedy that never arrives at a punch, Nichols and May restore us to that moment when pleasures were indefinite (even jokes could be repeated indefinitely). The cost is that we cannot be assured that the pleasure and pain will meet at maximum pitch and, like particles and antiparticles, execute a mutual annihilation.

When Elaine May, as mother to budding male nurse, brings Mike Nichols to paroxysms of pain and pleasure, to groans of laughter, we can imagine Nichols craving more and no more. He splits in half: kill me, save me. He does not merely, in the way of typical enthusiasts of sublime self-division, invite the threat of death to be saved; he cries out to be saved, in part, to provoke more in the way of destruction.

vi.

The audience, meanwhile, hears all this, deeply amused of course, as if Mike Nichols, in the manner of a leading man, were in the business of keeping Elaine May's power reassuring rather than apotropaic. Somehow, however, I imagine the audience as victim, too. The reason must partly be that Nichols and May often imagine a triangulation of their relationship, and the third party may be ignored to the point of death. For example:

Nichols: Clamp.
May: You have the clamp.
Nichols: Suture.
May: You have the suture.
Nichols: Edith?
May: Yes?
Nichols: I love you.
May: Please, please.

Nichols: You turned your back at the coffee machine.
May: I did not turn my back.
Nichols: You deliberately turned your back.
May: Excuse me, the oxygen is failing.

Nichols: Well, turn it up.
May: I'm trying to.

May: Now, would you like anything else, otherwise I'd like to go.
Nichols: Go in the middle of an operation?
May: Well, I have nothing else to give you, you've got it all in the patient.

May: Now the oxygen is failing again.
Nichols: Let it fail.

Who is that patient? You might say he resembles Nichols, insofar as his life is at risk. But he is dying perhaps to free Nichols to assume his less convincing role of predator. Might the patient not be, in effect, the wounded husband? Nichols and May did many adultery sketches—in all of them, of course, spouses are voiceless, though, oddly, in some of them, they are not quite negligible, like the unconscious patient. In "Second Piano Concerto," both partners in the adultery (an English dentist and his protégée) agree that they miss the betrayed husband: "I wanted us so very much to be happy, all three of us" (B, IM).

That English adultery could be so civilized as to admit the possibility of a contented ménage à trois amuses Nichols and May, as does a kinkier French notion in a skit called "Adultery" (E). May, appalled that her husband was not, by a mistake, made party to the party, worries that "he will be so hurt, he will think we don't want him." "Adultery" consists of three national takes on the theme: Americans, it turns out, are the only ones who conceive of adultery, even if histrionically, in terms of betrayal and sin. "I'm sick, I'm physically sick with guilt," Nichols says. May emotes, "Oh God, what kind of a person must I be?" Nichols tops her in his regard for the victim of their tryst: "He's a saint. He's a saint. He's a saint. He happens to be the only saint I know."

Insofar as adultery, like jokes, triangulates a third figure who is absent and victimized, it will always be available to comedy. Nevertheless, I do not find the structural similarity so compelling as to recognize in it a complete explanation for the persistence of victimized thirds in Nichols-May routines. A couple of observations add to the sense of veiled significance here. On the personal level, everyone has wondered at the fact that Nichols and May did not marry each other. However their relationship was defined, it was extramarital. The professional corollary was that their humor could, at its most sophisticated, be so audience-oblivious (no jokes, no big finishes) that they often did without audiences altogether, and recorded in the studio, as if by assignation. These facts add up to the following hypothesis: that Nichols and May's relationship was so close as not to triangulate visibly, even though as a comedy team it was almost obliged to, but that it was an illicit relationship, such that the absent third party—audience insulted as unconscious patient or unknowing husband—was not ignored, it was betrayed. If Nichols was always in danger, in May's presence, of being swallowed, the audience's danger was abandonment.

Because American-style adultery is a concern of Nichols and May's, and because, as of 1960, sin and guilt still lingered as a part of the American conception of it, *The Scarlet Letter* must of necessity become the text of the sermon. What intrigues me (in this connection) about *The Scarlet Letter* is that, for all its gloominess, Hawthorne has trouble keeping everyone (himself, too, at odd moments) straight-faced.

> The scene was not without a mixture of awe, such as must always invest the spectacle of guilt and shame in a fellow-creature, before society shall have grown corrupt enough to smile, instead of shuddering, at it. The witnesses of Hester Prynne's disgrace had not yet passed beyond their simplicity. They were stern enough to look upon her death, had that been the sentence, without a murmur at its severity, but had none of the heartlessness of another social state, which would find only a theme for jest in an exhibition like the present.[21]

A social state such as Hawthorne's or ours, for example. Oddly enough, the scaffold is always almost hilarious. Dimmesdale, we are assured, is the least humorous man in the world: "Had he once found power to smile, and wear a face of gayety, there would have been no such man!" (*SL*, 121). Nevertheless, when he ascends the scaffold and sees the Reverend Mr. Wilson walking home at midnight, "the glimmer of this luminary suggested the above conceits to Mr. Dimmesdale [that Wilson's lantern is a halo lit by heaven, newly opened for Governor Winthrop], who smiled,—nay, almost laughed at them,–and wondered if he were going mad" (122). His mind had sought relief, apparently, "by a kind of lurid playfulness." He catches himself; but he does not cease to be funny, and when he thinks of himself standing where Hester Prynne had stood, he "burst[s] into a great peal of laughter," which is echoed by Pearl's. Suddenly, he has an audience. Throughout the scene, Pearl keeps laughing. The Comedian as the Letter A.

Up climbs Hester Prynne, and now they are on stage together. Who will be the audience? Joining Pearl in that function is none other than Roger Chillingworth, victim of the adultery, but more abandoned father than abandoned husband. That is: the relationship of Hester and Dimmesdale had been a sexual but somehow nonclimactic intercourse between mother and son; the joy had been utterly painful for Dimmesdale. Pearl represents those future generations that will find hilarity in such scenes, Chillingworth the generation of patriarchs that had not. United, they demonstrate the inseparability of the ridiculous and sublime as witnessed by the triangulated.

Thomas Weiskel's version of the sublime begins with the danger of the son before his castrating father, moves on to the danger of the son before his all-consuming mother.[22] Hawthorne would modify this—not obliged to be Freudian, he notices that in America it is fathers who worry perpetually about castration at the hands of their sons. This is Chillingworth's risk, but being swallowed is Dimmesdale's, as well as Mike Nichols's and his dime's, which means that when the minister has his delayed pre-oedipal consummation, achieving with Hester what Miss Jones only promises, it is only to be consumed. Hester is sublimity in female form, as opposed to female formlessness, which is to say that she is a beautiful Medusa. Up on the scaffold, she is a figure of femininity such as those on the barricades described by Neil Hertz, self-destructive, exhibitionistic, and defiant. Thanks to Sacvan Bercovitch, among others, we can see her precisely as a Medusa of 1848.[23] Hawthorne's hysteria is under the same political pressure.

"The scene was not without a mixture of awe"—Hester could inform us how it feels to be the sublime object. And the sublime subject: around her, in her first performance as adulterer, she sees the world as a landscape of "rigid countenances." Presumably, the men are finding reassurance as best they can in the rigidity that, Freud explains in "Medusa's Head," is both emasculated and remasculating. What if the male hysteria converted itself into hilarity? It would not be better protection for the men. It is Hester Prynne who "longed . . . to behold all those rigid countenances contorted into scornful merriment."

Hester wishes that instead of stiffening against the horror of their daughter's abandonment, like Chillingworth, her audience would vibrate, like Pearl. This is a fair précis of the essential dream of the comedian, for whom audiences sit in paternal judgment until they are successfully infantilized. "Had a roar of laughter burst from the multitude,–each man, each woman, each little shrill-voiced child, contributing their individual parts,–Hester Prynne might have repaid them all with a bitter and disdainful smile" (SL, 60). If they had turned her into an object of humor, the Puritans would have made a demonic blunder, since laughter is always reversible, a toxic cloud that can always drift back, a contagion in the presence of which no faculty, including reason, can feel its ultimate health. Their laughter would have allowed Hester to smile in return: only that lack of provocation keeps Hester from incarnating all of Cixous's prophecy *avant la lettre.* If they had laughed, the object of their ridicule would have reflected back to them their own paltriness, not their transcendent destiny. An analytic of the ridiculous would locate the sublime as one of its lesser, and most containable, aspects, a bathetic afterthought.

4

i. David Letterman

A. Intelligence

David Letterman is baffled and balked by intellection; he is heaped and tasked by it. Wherever it manifests itself, he is awestricken. Like most Americans, he is unsure where to locate it—Ted Koppel is his idea of an intellectual[1]–but wherever he finds it, he is unmoored to the point of hysteria. Disconcerted, but freed of his inhibitions by her unwittiness, he bellowed at Marilyn vos Savant: "I'm as smart as you!"

David Letterman thinks as quickly as anybody in America—as fast as William F. Buckley Jr., in one field, or Stanley Fish, in another. The conundrum that he seems to confront every day is how it is possible to think dangerously fast yet possess no ideas at all. His condition is the intellectual equivalent of priapism among mannequins. It seems to make him furious.

It makes him, also, a great comedian, since jokes are successful to the extent that they impose the form of thought on disarray. Therefore Letterman's jokes are, disproportionately, metajokes; they are about the formal intelligence with only dreck for substance.

B. Female Intelligence

What David Letterman is least able to comprehend, of all forms of mind, is a particular type of female intelligence, as manifest in such personages as Jane Pauley or Teri Garr or Helen Hunt. He told an interviewer that "there is something very appealing about smart women, intelligent women. And you can see the problem there: if they're smart enough for me to be interested, then they're not going to have anything to do with me."[2]

Letterman is apt to refer to such women as "witty." By this, I think he intuits the following. Pure comedy is Euclidean form imposed on debris. Insofar as the shape of humor is congruent with its material, on the other hand, it is wit. Of course, neither Pauley nor Garr nor Hunt is an aphorist along the lines of La Rochefoucauld or Wilde. What gives their wit its unexpected integrity is gender: their femaleness is both the substance and shape of their humor. Letterman cannot fathom this, but he adores it.

C. Speed

In his purity, in what I wish to call his abject purity, Letterman can seem like a disembodied intelligence. Women on his show may fawn on him, but when they do, Letterman is often repelled—any Letterman theory would have to begin with the national seductiveness of his encircled, beleaguered, castellated comic mind. We hear that he watches his weight to the point of anorexia (on a show he said he was 6'2", 170 lbs.); a study of the jaws of afflicted Americans would force the conclusion that anorexia is the last wilderness of American Puritanism, where will nourishes itself on its own negation, where self-abasement is the only licit form of self-fashioning, where heroic bleeding is the only sanctioned form of heroism. On *Good Morning, America*,[3] after his Academy Awards show failure, Letterman said that you learn by "ingesting the negative," which is unintentionally a bulimarexic pun (the negative once ingested, Letterman's most negative emissions are in jest).

You can conceive of Letterman almost as pure velocity. An improvising comedian has a demented time sense: the world appears to be moving too slowly for his mind. (For a great comic actor, it may seem to be moving too fast.) To the extent that time is psychological, a comedian is forced to live in concentric spheres, revolving at different rates. The scraping throws off sparks, but it makes Letterman crazy. The effort to put the two worlds in gear may involve alcohol or drugs; for Letterman, it entails speeding.

"To annihilate both space and time" was the hype of American Protestant technological millenarianism of the train and telegraph era. The dream of pure soul–or pure mind—is, at its most intense, to be everywhere at once. The mode of American apocalypse proceeded from train to telegraph (the increase in speed was a progressive animation) naturally to TV and cyber-space. TV apocalypse is the American style of abjection.

D. Car-son

The paradox is that Letterman can be the loudest American comedian since Sid Caesar. He yells a large fraction of his jokes, with a leonine roar like the start of an engine, as if his first Indiana jokes had to outshout the whole Indianapolis 500. He is also oddly physical: he does facial shtick (the old skunk eye, for example); he plays with his suit; he imposes his body even as far as the camera.

Yet all the time you feel that there is a mind at the center of all this physical demonstration, driving it like a machine, like a car, trying to assemble itself into existence as the car. The great Protestant comedians turn jokes into violent, swift, sleek, beautiful mechanisms. Johnny Carson was Letterman's predecessor in this pursuit, securing a rock-age technical perfectionism from the jazzy improvisations of his Jewish coequals, Mort Sahl, Mel Brooks, Buddy Hackett, or Lenny Bruce.[4] Carson's mind would plant itself within costumes; costumes would mortify Letterman; but Letterman's suit and his body itself, and his face itself, are contraptions, like Disney's automated presidents on steroids, like the hardware of the brilliantly improvisatory Big Blue.

Letterman's height does matter. You feel slightly disoriented and depressed when his guest is taller than he is. But I read Letterman's height, as I shall argue with respect to a peculiar moment in Céline, as pure verticality, a single ideal dimension.

E. Lettermania

Almost everyone is willing, in Letterman's presence, to play at abjection: his audience grovels in order to be part of the show and sensibility. They submit to his thinking of them as his "kids." Yet when you observe him in the company of those he respects—Pauley or Garr or Hunt (who, like mothers, are adored and unattainable by tacit consent) and Carson (among fathers)—you fantasize a similar familiarity, by which I mean that he could be, with you, similarly abject. The Letterman anecdote that any essay on him has to repeat concerns the note he passed to Teri Garr before a commercial: "I hate myself." With respect to Carson, the abjection is more balanced (you are not supposed to be the man your father was): "That's the guy. Maybe I could work at it, but I'm not the guy."[5]

The TV relationship, which the Academy Awards audience resisted, is not a collision of subjects and objects, as at the movies, but a collusion of abjects.[6] David Letterman makes our abjection visible—he puts it before the camera—but visible in a twice-disowned body, once by self-disjunction, twice by the technologies of fame; and a corollary is that exposure to the dreck of New York that Letterman loves to dwell on and in leaves us feeling almost absolved. The "abject," as Kristeva calls it, is sloughed like snakeskin and nicely retailored.

ii. Kristeva/Céline/Letterman

A. Kristevan abjection

> There looms, within abjection, one of those violent, dark revolts of being, directed against a threat that seems to emanate from an exorbitant outside or inside, ejected beyond the scope of the possible, the tolerable, the thinkable. It lies there, quite close, but it cannot be assimilated. It beseeches, worries, and fascinates desire, which, nevertheless, does not let itself be seduced. Apprehensive, desire turns aside; sickened, it rejects. A certainty protects it from the shameful—a certainty of which it is proud holds on to it. But simultaneously, just the same, that impetus, that spasm, that leap is drawn toward an elsewhere as tempting as it is condemned. Unflaggingly, like an inescapable boomerang, a vortex of summons and repulsion places the one haunted by it literally beside himself.[7]

So begins Kristeva's "Essay on Abjection," and I believe it is, so to speak, empirically correct. However you take Kristeva's neo-Freudian etiology ("abjection" is a reminiscence of the condition of the subject, unseparated from the maternal body, before it is a subject, the adult affect of which is horror of the indiscrete), it is certain that she knows how abjection is experienced. It is experienced, first of all, as a negative ecstasy—you are "literally" beside yourself. It may be summarized as your failure to know what is inside of what, to find your own synecdoche, the homunculus that stands for self. This entails a series of incongruities.

(1) "Abjection," whose attitude ought to be servile, contains within itself, as one of its phases, a "revolt." (2) The revolt is not against desire, it is by desire. This is understandable enough, except that desire's willfulness and uprightness seem oddly (for desire) puritanical. (3) If desire acts like restraint, the object of abjection—the "abject," as Kristeva calls it—must resemble, at any rate, the object of desire; one is summoned by it. Desire is pseudoconscience because abjection is pseudodesire. (4) Because desire acts like restraint, it can be a source of self-pride. But instead of "it [desire] holds on to a certainty of which it is proud," we get, "a certainty of which it [desire] is proud holds on to it." Desire feels, since it is desire, as if its power to resist comes from elsewhere; yet the feeling of self-disenfranchisement must be exactly what, in abjection, desire is resisting. If abjection is pseudodesire, desire plays the role of conscience abjectly.

This flux (or "vortex") of will and victimage—such that what is tempting is not desired, and desire in turn restrains, and desire in turn is held—seems to me exactly apt as a diagnosis of Puritanism (only in the presence of the abject will desire convert itself into conscience, surviving by self-betrayal). Yet it is safe to say that Kristeva is not the theorist to appreciate the comic possibilities of deriving uprightness from prostration.

B. Abject Histrionics

The person who is "beset by abjection" (*PH,* 1) puts on, I should think, daily infradramas, actor before audience and vice versa. You are, after all, literally beside yourself, watching your faculties—desire, for example—play unaccustomed roles, always authored by someone else. Kristeva, however, does not quite say this. Her abjected subject is caught in a vortex, is haunted; even its power to resist is merely susceptibility to sickness and repulsion; it is far more acted upon than active. Nowhere before her culminating section on Céline does Kristeva focus precisely enough on the histrionic aspect of abjection; and in the Céline passages, I think, she does not contemplate it so much as just accurately note it, the result being a desideratum for David Letterman studies.

Abjection has, in English, an uncollapsible performative dimension. All of what follows is listed in one dictionary as a single meaning of the term *abject.* "Sunk to a low condition; cast down in spirit or hope; degraded; servile; groveling; despicable; as abject posture, fortune, thoughts; base and abject flatterers." The oddity is how this meaning silently turns at "servile"; and how the theatrical dimension of the second example ("abject flatterers") is already ambiguously present in the first ("base and abject flatterers" will assume an "abject posture"); and how the apparent redundancy of adjectives in the second example ("base and abject") fudges the question of whether at the root of abject performance is abject being.

The term *abjection* itself is falsely, therefore appropriately, Latinate and upright. This would be telling if everyone who was abject were aware that he or she was "abject"—which may be the case, for all I know. There may be no abjection, which is a failure of definition, without a frustrated definitional literacy. At any rate, all those who identify themselves as abject, for example Céline, will feel the telltale self-dramatization of the word. Even if we posit a victim of abjection who is psychologically illiterate, nevertheless it may be a symptom of the ego at the edge of its defenses, scouting for even a counterproductive self-definition, that any extreme state will be enacted with hostility and lobbed like a grenade to the cheap seats.

C. Comic Abjection
Not sufficiently registering the histrionic assertiveness of abjection is not sufficiently featuring, I want to argue, the essentially comic dimension of abjection.

D. Abjection and Laughter in Kristeva
Laughter ought to have more to do with Kristeva's nosography. There are moments when its exclusion seems almost perverse. Following her initial association of the abject with unthinkable permeabilities, Kristeva specifies vaguely that it is a " 'something' that I do not recognize as a thing. A weight of meaninglessness, about which there is nothing insignificant, and which crushes me" (*PH,* 2). If it crushes her, it cannot be taken lightly; yet the presence of significance without meaning seems comic in general, and like David Letterman's comedy in particular. Its symptom is verbal speed: "The speech of the phobic adult is also characterized by extreme nimbleness. But that vertiginous skill is as if void of meaning, traveling at top speed over an untouched and untouchable abyss, of which, on occasion, only the affect shows up, giving not a sign but a signal" (41). Here the crushing weight of meaninglessness seems to take the form of Road Runner levity; surely in Kristeva's oxymoron we are approaching laughter: "But with the borderline patient, sense does not emerge out of non-sense, metaphorical or witty though it might be" (50). Not quite there, however. "On the contrary, non-sense runs through signs and sense, and the resulting manipulation of words is not intellectual play but, without any laughter, a desperate attempt to hold on to the ultimate obstacles of a pure signifier that has been abandoned by the paternal metaphor" (50–51).

Occasionally one is sure that, for Kristeva, it is simply the case that laughter palliates the abject condition. Discussing Dostoevsky's *The Possessed*, Kristeva asserts that "Verkhovensky is abject because of his clammy, cunning appeal to ideals that no longer exist, from the moment when Prohibition (call it God) is lacking. Stavrogin is perhaps less so, for his immoralism admits of laughter and refusal" (*PH*, 19). This would appear to set up a disjunction: abjection or laughter. Yet when Kristeva goes on to describe the modern world, what she finds is abjection and laughter undivided: "The worlds of illusions, now dead and buried, have given way to our dreams and deliriums if not to politics or science—the religions of modern times. Lacking illusions, lacking shelter, today's universe is divided between boredom (increasingly anguished at the prospect of losing its resources, through depletion) or (when the spark of the symbolic is maintained and desire to speak explodes) abjection and piercing laughter" (133).

Which is it: or or and? Laughter would seem to be an ambiguity within a pollution. But there is a way to be more precise about the relationship. When Kristeva defines sin as "subjectified abjection" (128), you might feel inspired to refer to laughter as "objectified abjection." Kristeva finds abjection unfunny when signifiers have been "abandoned by the paternal metaphor," when "Prohibition (call it God) is lacking," but piercingly funny "when the spark of the symbolic is maintained," which may be the difference between an enervated and an electrified absence. Maintained objectivity is funny when it "sparks," perhaps, because a joke is dreck enflamed by form, that is, by a standard it inhabits but to which it cannot aspire. Thus it becomes clear why laughter, disjoined from abjection generally, attaches to it when Kristeva comes to describe modernity: in our century, apocalyptic yet Godless, abjection is a psychopathology that happens to be realistic. When you cannot abject your abjection, according to Kristeva, as filth or sin (the God of Jews and Christians alike being dead)—when objectivity lingers in the world only as a measure of abjectivity—you laugh.

This move allows Kristeva to value Céline without embracing him: an abject person may manifest a symptom, but in an abject world, a person may be a symptom.[8] But I still do not think that Kristeva—by positing that Céline's laughter makes him a symptom of an objectively abjectifying world—has gotten his humor exactly right. She arrives at the topic at long last in the brief culminating section on Céline.

> With Céline we are elsewhere. As in apocalyptic or even prophetic utterances, he speaks out on horror. But while the former can be withstood because of a distance that allows for judging, lamenting, condemning, Céline—who speaks from within—has no threats to utter, no

morality to defend. In the name of what would he do it? So his laughter bursts out, facing abjection, and always originating at the same source, of which Freud had caught a glimpse: the gushing forth of the unconscious, the repressed, suppressed pleasure, be it sex or death. (*PH*, 205–6)

Céline is an apocalyptic writer (he maintains the spark of the symbolic) without revelations; his "language of abjection" merely "topples" into "nothing more than the effervescence of passion and language we call style" (206). The unconscious gushes so the laughter bursts so the language topples; Céline is a domino. The paradoxical willfulness of abjection drops out: some have degradedness thrust upon them. Yet even Kristeva's Céline is capable of knowing that abjection may be histrionic. The two Henrouilles women in *Journey to the End of the Night*, which should have been the name of the David Letterman show, embody in Kristeva's phrase "calculated abjection" (*PH*, 168). It does not gush, burst, or topple: it manipulates and maneuvers. Abjection may be a recrudescence of the premirror stage, but it practices before a portable mirror. (Kristeva implies at various points the relation of abjection to anorexia—food is feces in the abject ethos—but the gagging nausea she describes is not the anorexic's willful self-sculpting.)

E. Céline

What is funny about *Journey to the End of the Night*?[9] Partly its humor resides in local excesses; but the greater, antithetical joke is *Journey's* refusal to ascend or decline: its perfect horizontality. You feel mounting hysteria (under particular circumstances, a condition confusable with hilarity) or spiraling despair (plus gallows giddiness) from the book's failure to ascend or decline with you. In the first place, Bardamu seems to preserve just enough innocence—just enough vulnerability to goodness—to keep horror fresh, from World War I to Africa to New York to Detroit to the insane asylum back in France and his own old age. But even the uniformity of that movement—in which goodness is a blip—is not constant enough. Bardamu's horror is always prepared; it precedes existence. Even before the Great War, a young Bardamu describes God as "sensual" and "grunt[ing] like a pig. A pig with golden wings, who falls and falls, always belly side up, ready for caresses, that's him, our master" (*J*, 1983, 4). This God is a bourgeois even before Bardamu has the experience of impoverished resentment. Bardamu knows him by inverse empathy, because his own destiny is to fall and fall, belly-side up, ready for abjection.

"You can be a virgin in horror," Céline or Bardamu notoriously proclaims, "the same as in sex" (*J*, 1983, 9). As a matter of fact, one is never, in *Journey to the End of the Night,* a virgin in horror, if that means unacquainted with it. I call attention to the possibility that one may be "innocent . . . of Horror" (Marks's translation [*J*, 1934, 9] of "on est puceau de l'Horreur" [*VBN,* 21]), nonetheless: the point is that something in Céline takes the place of innocence, that is, the place before experience. Whatever that something is, it must have the following skewed characteristics. It must precede experience as thesis to antithesis (so that the experience of horror is recognizable); it must figure experience proleptically (so that Bardamu can recognize horror as the correlative of what horrified him even before he encountered it in World War I); it must continue during experience (so that horrors, anticipated and unending, will nevertheless stay fresh).

The trivial American name for that thing is "attitude," as when Jerry Seinfeld says that David Letterman "has a great attitude." The humor of attitude is that it judges all the time but is strictly nonjudgmental; it is not, as Kristeva says, apocalyptic or prophetic, insofar as there is no experience that precedes it to judge; and when experience does accrue, it is powerless to make a case, mocked by its own superfluity. The same attitude greets every eventuality. This is significance without meaning, intelligence without ideas: attitude is a way to be of the world but not in it. Starting with attitude means that there is nowhere for a journey to get. Bardamu arrives at horror immediately, and spends the rest of his journey—undertaken on the assumption that there is an end to the night—rediscovering it, until the peripatetic immobility abruptly shuts down.

Céline says brilliantly that "one has to be more than somewhat dead in order to be truly a wisecracker!" (quoted in *PH,* 138). Death is, technically, infinite repetition without intervals, which makes Bardamu's travels an approximation of an afterdeath experience in continuous disgust. What is the humor of this? How would *The Divine Comedy* be comedic if there were only *Inferno*? Invoking the trite term *attitude* is only meant to call attention to a quality of *Journey's* abjection: its chronic inexperience. The novel may be described as a monologue that occasionally intersects not experience or other humans but other monologues. When Bardamu, in the first chapter, describes God as a pig, he is performing at the time his poem on the subject, before the history that can only justify it.

And wherever Bardamu's monologue crosses another, there abject histrionics cross. The monologue is the privileged technique of attitude: it comes first, but it confines reality such that nothing different in kind can come second. Everything that comes keeps coming first. And attitude is abjection on a roll, abjection exuberant in its basic exhibitionism. Tania, a woman whose beloved has just died, is "intent on her tragedy, and still more intent on exhibiting it to me in full flood" (*J*, 1983, 315). In this respect, she resembles the newly blinded Robinson, who "groaned under his bandages as soon as he heard me climbing the stairs" (281). It is important to locate the performativity within abjection, not outside it and compromising it. Robinson is in fact abject—prostrate, "sunk to a low condition"—but he is also acting it. "People live from one play to the next," Bardamu says, always ready with the aphorism that is his own emblematic performance (224). Thus a "tragedy" such as Tania's feeds comedies such as Céline's: a comedy here is the continuous, endless, climaxless performance of tragedies.

When Bardamu arrives at New York, he shares a laugh—unique experience, since most communal laughter in this book is of a piece with horror, merely smut amid smuttiness—with his fellow voyagers.

> Talk of surprises! What we suddenly discovered through the fog was so amazing that at first we refused to believe it, but then, when we were face to face with it, galley slaves or not, we couldn't help laughing, seeing it right there in front of us . . .
>
> Just imagine, that city was standing absolutely erect. New York was a standing city. Of course we'd seen cities, fine ones too, and magnificent seaports. But in our part of the world cities lie along the seacoast or on rivers, they recline on the landscape, awaiting the traveler, while this American city had nothing languid about her, she stood there as stiff as a board, not seductive at all, terrifyingly stiff.
>
> We laughed like fools. You can't help laughing at a city built straight up and down like that. But we could only laugh from the neck up, because of the cold blowing in from the sea through a gray and pink mist, a brisk sharp wind that attacked our pants and the chinks in that wall, I mean the city streets, which engulfed the wind-borne clouds. (*J*, 1983, 159; Céline's ellipsis)

This is a peculiar passage. Not only does Bardamu—uncharacteristically socialized—share a laugh, but the laugh goes on and on; it is a unique moment of *helpless* laughter. Nor is it immediately explicable. What is so funny about skyscrapers?

It is almost an obvious smutty joke. The city is erect in public; it is an urban exhibitionist. But the joke is trickier than that, because the European cities that "recline on the landscape, awaiting the traveler" justify the presumption that cities are women, making the grammar of the translation appropriate, even if its biology is not: "*she* stood there as stiff as a board, not seductive at all." If the woman repossesses the phallus, which seems to be equal to converting herself into a mannequin, will this be perceived as comical by men? Not entirely: the joke is only half-funny, only funny "from the neck up," because the "sharp" wind "attacked our pants." Castration is not funny when it can be felt; it is only funny insofar as the head can be separated, for the sake of intellectual amusement, from the body that suffers it. This separation, of course, is not merely a retreat to the intellectual; it is a retreat from castration to the intellectual by means of an act of self-castration. The joke here would seem to be that joking itself is the proud reenactment of castration in order to escape it.

The wind attacks both the voyagers' pants and the chinks in the wall of the city: it is castration that one (offshore) sees erected in New York. Or not so much castration, perhaps, as abjection. In the place of the phallus is permeability rather than absence. The chinks of the skyline, Bardamu specifies, are its streets; what one sees erected vertically in New York is the evidence of its horizontality, which is the same as its unboundedness, its failure to demarcate in and out (wind attacking streets, streets absorbing clouds).

When Bardamu goes ashore, the street he walks down is Broadway—in three of the sensible four dimensions he walks by the Ed Sullivan Theater, where David Letterman performs. On Broadway, the truth of New York reveals itself to be horizontal and unbounded after all: "That street was like a dismal gash, endless, with us at the bottom of it, filling it from side to side, advancing from sorrow to sorrow, toward an end that is never in sight, the end of all the streets in the world" (*J*, 1983, 166). Broadway is abjection in the streets, abjection projected, abjection objectified (the world is abject and we are its blood), abjection as the avenue of American performance. Broadway literalizes Bardamu's apothegm: advancing "from sorrow to sorrow" is equivalent to living "from one play to the next"; thus Broadway is the emblem of the interval-less automobility of Céline's own performance. New York is always the land of the joke in Céline: below ground, where men excrete, they "laughed and joked and cheered one another on"; "the new arrivals were assailed with a thousand revolting jokes" (*J*, 1983, 169). But these are the smutty jokes that Bardamu despises. If you take New York City's abjection (blood, urine, feces) and erect it as skyscrapers or enflame it as the lights of Broadway, you get the sort of joke that Bardamu himself laughs at like a fool from the perspective of his own abject verticality: from the neck up.

One of the few uses of the term *abject* in *Journey* (in the Marks translation) is in the description of blinded, criminal Robinson, who "lay in . . . bed upstairs in an abject state of mind" (*J*, 1934, 322; "Lui, dans leur lit de la chambre d'en haut menait pas large" [*VBN*, 290]). Yet this is only a page before we are told that Robinson "groaned under his bandages as soon as he heard me climbing the stairs." Abjectness is proneness seeking an audience. Whenever there is abjectness, there is performance; whenever abjectness is proudly performed, it is comic. It is comic because it should be prone but it is upright. "I was a hundred-percent sick," says Bardamu, "I felt as if I had no further use for my legs, they just hung over the edge of my bed like unimportant and rather ridiculous objects" (*J*, 1983, 148; "commes des choses négligeables et un peu comiques" [*VBN*, 158]). What is comic is that the essence of verticality uncovers itself as the sign of a complete horizontal impotence.

Napoleon said that a heroic speech would become comic if the orator sat down while orating.[10] Céline implies the inverse: the abject monologue becomes comic when it stands up. David Letterman, stranger in New York, caffeinated when he should be sleepy, vertical when he should be supine, panning New York from the Empire State Building down, is the stand-up comedian par excellence. The gestalt of New York City—the "standing city" —talk show stand-up realizes the implicit dimension: Letterman is vertical when we are prostrate, but we take his attitude as our own. All Americans are now funny, not just Jewish comedians and gag writers straining for weekly material. (The average gag on the worst situation comedies now is funnier, judged in isolation, than the best gag on, say, *The Honeymooners;* and the terrorized look on Groucho's contestants has faded from the face of the earth.) This eventuality—the comedification of America—is the most astounding fact about the American sensibility from 1960 to 2000. Where Bardamu meets America—in the New York–illuminated night, on Broadway, at the Ed Sullivan Theater—is the stage on which, at the millennial end of his century, its abjection erects its last cross.

iii. The King of Comedy

What is the fate of abjection in Martin Scorsese's scarily intelligent film, *The King of Comedy*? It ought to be everywhere in the film, but seems to be nowhere. The pathetic comedian Rupert Pupkin (Robert DeNiro) should be abject but is utterly buoyant, directed, and simple in his psychosis. He knows where to seek the end of his night. Talk show superhost Jerry Langford (Jerry Lewis) should be symmetrically abject—if I have justified applying the term to David Letterman—but shows few signs of having any of the requisite boundaries whose permeability would horrify him. A first approximation of the psychocomic situation is that neither has abjection because they have each other. Rupert Pupkin begins the movie in an exact copy of Jerry Langford's suit, and Jerry Langford ends the movie staring at multiple images, in multiple TVs, of Rupert Pupkin. When Rupert looks at Jerry, he sees his own body thrown off and replaced by an image, out of all time and space; when Jerry looks at Pupkin, he sees at a distance his own rejected body, rejected identity, rejected home.

One of the jokes of the movie is that to all appearances Jerry Langford is the real host of *The Tonight Show* and Rupert Pupkin the pretend host, yet the film gives Jerry Lewis the opportunity to pretend to be Johnny Carson. What does it mean to conclude that Jerry Lewis is to Johnny Carson as Rupert Pupkin is to Jerry Langford? It is almost precisely true to say that what Jerry Lewis gets to pretend to be is Protestant. When I first saw *The King of Comedy,* my initial reaction was: don't they understand that Jerry Lewis cannot under any circumstances be *The Tonight Show* host? Its star must be a pseudohick with attitude arriving in New York from the heartland; he hosts Jewishness there, and the chiasmus is the genius of the genre. He cannot be a Jew himself: one has only a distant memory of the ill-conceived *Joey Bishop Show,* whose only upshot was the subsequent glory of Joey's second banana, Regis Philbin.

My second reaction, however, is that the fate of Jerry Langford's Jewishness is the fate of his abjection. Not that Jewishness is the royal road to abjection, though it is a very fine road—rather that Jerry Langford's own body is treated like pork in his desire for pure imagery. Jerry is installed, in *The King of Comedy,* in layers and corridors of Waspitude (played by Shelley Hack); like the heart of the Pentagon, he is protected from infection not by impregnable walls or a moat but by an aseptic maze. At his network office, or at his penthouse, or at his country home, Langford's life is a Nordic iceberg.

But at the moment Pupkin penetrates Langford's country home, Jewishness reappears, his own body reappears, though it is unclear at first where. The Asian butler, Jonno, summons Langford home from his golf game, whimpering over the phone, "I'm getting a heart attack, already." For the time, only the Asian is a Jew. Yet when Jerry arrives on the scene, he manages to be, for perhaps the only moment of the film, expressively Jewish himself. Jerry kicks Rupert out of the house; making the pathetically tardy inference that Jerry (at a previous encounter) had only feigned kindness, Rupert says, belligerently, "So I made a mistake." "So did Hitler," Jerry counters. This riposte, I believe, could not have been in the script—it makes too little sense. It has all the marks of what passes in Jerry Lewis's mind for a witticism: it is cruel, sharp, and fast, it has the form of a joke, but it has no humor. Does Jerry Lewis (or Jerry Langford) forget at the moment who is in power? What mistake of Hitler's is he thinking of? All that is clear is that something that has been abjected returns: what Jerry Langford expels, Jerry Lewis ingests. This is a moment of abject reorientation, only possible if abjection is the sort of rotatable axis I have described. Céline claims to be the true victim of World War II, and Heller and Roth (and the Jewish comedians of their generation) enlist themselves as Céline's truest disciples.[11]

Meanwhile, Rupert (along with his accomplice, Masha, played by Sandra Bernhard) resolutely distances himself from all the New York nobodies and crazies with whom he manifestly has everything in common. As opposed to Jerry, who in this film is never anywhere in particular, Rupert is always somewhere. His comedy routine returns compulsively to his place of origin, Clifton, New Jersey; so does Rupert, who still lives in his mother's house, not fully separated from her in the way of Kristeva's abject subjects and almost all comedians.[12] But Rupert has an insight: in the world of the media, other people may carry your body for you, like your golf clubs.

What Rupert does to Jerry is give him a body and a place. In Rupert's aura, Jerry's body turns out to be bizarrely locatable and his defenses bizarrely pregnable. In Rupert, at long last, Jerry must ruminate on what he has abjected. Rupert and Masha capture Jerry, sit him down, mummify his body; for one night he is in one home, not every home. When Jerry is ensconced in tape, the film cuts to the network office where Rupert's blackmail offer (in return for Jerry's body, he will appear on *The Jerry Langford Show*) is being mulled: "Suppose we tape him," somebody says, meaning, "suppose we agree to videotape the show with Rupert before committing ourselves to broadcasting it." The pun is really an antipun: tape locates Jerry in one chair and one body but displaces Rupert from his image. When the tape is, in fact, aired, Rupert stands proudly beside his own face; Jerry is looking at many identical images in a department store window; then Rupert's face begins to multiply across hundreds of copies of *Life, Newsweek, Rolling Stone,* and *People.* Mechanical reproduction is squared idealism: it disembodies already dislocated souls.

In fame America, you can lose your body (in images), your voice (when Jerry Langford phones the office and says that he is being held hostage, it is assumed that an impressionist is staging a gag), and your name (the movie begins with a distribution of autographs, some of them pseudonyms). Here is the logic of abjection taken to its purest joke: at the end of the night, when we are on the verge of sleep, when our bodies seem so massive that sleeping itself seems a burden, David Letterman conspires with Jerry Langford to stand up for velocity and lightness of being—all intelligence, no meaning. The dream is of a world that makes a joke of class, ethnicity, origins—of all situations. The American joke, 1960–2000, is that our abjection sees in the alienation of body, voice, and name the freedom to perform.

Scatology: Richard Pryor in Concert

i. Bathroom Humor

In *Live in Concert,* Richard Pryor appears on stage—the cliché has a mean-ing, because he is there before the audience can grasp it.[1] There has been an intermission after the Patti LaBelle warm-up, but no one intones, "Ladies and Gentlemen, Richard Pryor." So Pryor assigns himself the function of getting everyone settled. The first words of the performance are, "Wait for the people to get from the bathroom." Then: "Jesus Christ. Look at the white people rushing back."

The subject of race has been broached. Who is at risk? First, the blacks: "You niggers takin' a chance in Long Beach, Jack." But no—a Richard Pryor concert is not white country, even at the Long Beach venue. "This is the fun part for me when the white people coming back after the intermission and find that niggers stole their seats. [One of Pryor's white voices, nasal:] 'Weren't we sitting there, dear?' [Black gangster voice:] 'Well, you ain't sittin' here now, motherfucker.' "

Pryor has effectively divided the audience in half—it seems comically suicidal. Only Lenny Bruce had ever made his audience this self-conscious; but Bruce had assumed a pervasive Jewishness and maleness, so that even the audience at its most affronted was unified against him as a sort of mirror inversion. Pryor's case is a degree of complexity beyond that. The audience, apparently, will have to live as a division but laugh as a unity. And Pryor will not let the subject of racial difference go. Whites even swear badly. Another Pryor white character, head bobbing and eyes popping in a cartoon of sweaty uncool belligerence, can only manage: "Yeah, c'mon peckerhead. C'mon you fuckin' jerkoff." The lesson is that whites—including whites at a Pryor concert—cannot pretend to be black.

As a first offer in a negotiation, this is as complicated as any academic could wish. Granted that whites and blacks are attending the same concert—there may be some virtue in pausing over that simplicity. They seem to occupy the same position as subjects gazing at Richard Pryor as object. But this is not the movies, and the object is gazing back.

What he sees, first of all, is whites. Or rather: he sees—at least, imagines—whites seeing blacks. When the whites return to discover their seats occupied, they find themselves looking at proximate blacks instead of, as anticipated, a lone black man on a distant stage. This puts things in a new light. The effect of the clever little maneuver is to isolate whites against a novel unity of performer and audience. Pryor may be the comedian, but the whites provide the comedy. "This is the fun part for me," Pryor says, enjoying a rare interlude, or prelude, as spectator.

This would be involved enough even if we did not consider that the white audience—the real one imagining the imaginary one—must be enjoying the scene, too. Not merely at their own expense: this is necessarily a white audience for whom self-mockery is self-flattery. Nor is abasement, such as it is, an exclusively white amusement here. What the returning white couple finds is a cliché of black lawlessness and vulgarity. Blacks who have peaceably assembled at a concert in Long Beach have been caricatured by Pryor as outsiders who can only bully their way into the best seats at its Terrace Theatre, and they laugh at this. So do the whites.

Later in the performance, Pryor is working out the comic implications of white mechanicalness as against black coolness. Whites get snakebites in the woods, Pryor submits, because of their style, meaning their fatal lack of style. Pryor mimes walking in the woods as a white man: goofy, head lolling in the clouds. When Pryor walks as a black man, he strolls to the rhythm of nature itself. He sees the snake, says "snake" nonchalantly, and executes a small sweet dance step aside. The trope is familiar: Sinbad does a white marching band/black marching band routine toward the same laugh. Since Bergson, there has been no mystery about the comic force of human mechanization, which is to say, in this context, of whiteness, but that leaves unexplained why black nonchalance gets an equal laugh. Is Pryor saying that even coolness is a machine, mass-produced and unconscious? Does this allow whites to escape their envy by considering black rhythm as sleeker machinery, not as a natural superiority of rhythm, reflex, and soul?

Yes and no. Both blacks and whites are presented with the spectacle and cliché of blackness; but the envy does not go away for the whites in the process, nor the glee of blacks. Step one of the humor is that blacks are also machines; step two is the unanimous transvaluation of that fact: the cyborgs are smooth. If blacks according to DuBois see themselves from both inside and outside in a white culture, there is a release of tension amounting to hilarity in affirming the split. Blacks see themselves as whites see them, but they like what the whites see. Whites now see themselves from the outside as well; but they are content, for the length of the occasion, to lend their mechanical bodies to the comic machinery. At no moment are whites and blacks in Pryor's audience laughing for exactly the same reason. They laugh from different positions that go in and out of symmetry. But they all laugh.

You can be more impressed by the complexity, brilliantly marshaled by Pryor, or by the stunning final reduction. Whites and blacks laugh together and they laugh for the same duration. What could that mean?

I feel incompetent to answer, but I am interested, because comedy always produces a complicated inclusion in a way that neither American multiculturalists nor uniculturalists can theorize. The chiasmus of the talk show is less complicated than the Pryor relation. The only way I can begin to understand the nature of his inclusiveness is to begin, again, with his divisiveness. Whites are returning from the bathroom to find blacks occupying their seats. Do only whites need the bathroom? Is going to the bathroom the only thing whites do during intermissions? These questions are obtuse because the laughing audience—either at Long Beach or watching the film—has intuited the answer before the questions arise: having gone to the bathroom only exacerbates the whites' abjectness upon returning to find—does it sound like a pun?—their seats occupied. Whites forfeit their class advantages when the abject calls; they have been separated in the process, but when they return, they have been equalized.

ii. Death

A summary of the Pryor concert, which turns out to be concerted, begins this way: when his opening racial division of the audience has run its course, Pryor gets interested in animals. Mainly dogs, who mainly assume the attitudes and accents of black men. First there is the police Doberman who gives up running after a speedy black criminal, saying, "Sh-it. Motherfuck that nigger, man." Pryor has his own fierce Doberman, who shows his teeth when he is about to attack, but who supplies this warning: "This looks like I'm smilin', motherfucker? I'm about to get in your ass." He also once owned a male monkey, who stopped masturbating in humans' ears only when Pryor bought him a take-charge female monkey. When both monkeys die, a neighborhood German shepherd comforts Pryor: "What's the matter, Rich?" And takes his leave, saying, "You take care. . . . Now you know I'm gonna be chasin' you again, tomorrow?" Then Pryor considers horses, who "shit while they walk." But dogs, who "don't have no racism," go to play with a miniature horse, thinking it just a big dog, and a Great Dane brags, "I don't know what it is, but I'm gonna fuck it."

It is a remarkable development: if Pryor's first sequence on blacks and whites is a shrewd manipulation of subjectivities—bestowing and reversing and refocusing them—then this sequence grants subjectivity indiscriminately to almost everyone, almost everything. The whole world talks, especially animals, as if Pryor were inventing new folktales. And the series, which begins with canine ferocity but ends with interspecies democratic sex, seems emblematic. Oddly, the only animal that does not signify (and which has trouble with any form of intercourse) is the male monkey: he squeaks as he masturbates in everyone's ear until the new female monkey says, "Freeze," and gets him reoriented. That the male monkey is more nearly human than the other animals, and perhaps African, and adept (we would have thought) at signifying makes it alarming that he is uniquely inexpressive. A negative explanation is that the comic intention of the discourse is not to flatter our Darwinian pedigree. What remains to be analyzed is the inarticulateness of the monkey's phallic self-possession.

What follows is the tour de force of the performance, when Pryor acts out his own heart attack. "Don't breathe," his heart commands, as Pryor mimes with his hands the tightening of a vise. His heart taunts him: "You're thinking about dying, now, ain't yh? . . . You didn't think about it when you was eating all that pork!" As the heart taunts him, Pryor continues to act out the squeezing of the vise, drops to his knees, writhes on the stage. There is nothing like it in all of stand-up, which almost by definition cannot permit falling down, though Mel Brooks as the 2000 Year Old Man takes some health precaution or other "that my heart should not attack me." This suggests that interpreting a heart attack as an attack not on but by the heart may be a necessity of the comic unconscious: it is a piece of self-abjection. It comes out of the animal motif insofar as Pryor lends expressiveness to yet another heretofore mute corner of the world; but that process can only reverse the general point of the recurrent black/white theme that black soul is uniquely one with black body.

Pryor now meanders on the subject of death; he loops it to another meta-theme by noting that whites mourn softly, blacks fiercely. The black woman grieves as follows: "Waaaaaaaah! Take me God! Take me take me take me!" Mourning is, apparently, orgasmic for black women, and this tacit observation brings Pryor to the second compensatory domain of black female orgasm: whipping kids. The young Pryor uses cocaine; his grandmother wails, "Take me take me take me," whips Pryor, and advises him, "Next time you do it I'm gonna tear your ass off again!" Thus begins the auto-biographical moment of the concert, and the audience can pick up clues, though it is not easy. Apparently there is no mother on the scene; the father is initially presented as being as scary as the grandmother with respect to the general assault on Pryor's bottom. When Pryor fires the opening shot of his oedipal rebellion, "I'm not taking no more ass-whipping," the father punches him in the chest, which Pryor refers to as "my ass."

But when the subject of his father really takes over, so does a new mood. I'll return to Pryor's reminiscence of hunting with his father; suffice it now that for a long hushed moment, the father is loving and long-suffering, the woods are peaceful and holy, and Pryor is a happy, hapless child again.

The segue out—which seems to continue the theme but reverse the mood —is the observation that, in the woods, you need to be able to stare animals down; heavyweight Leon Spinks, Pryor observes, would be tough enough for nature. Then the mood rereverses: Pryor recalls his own boxing career, during which his body was constantly talking back to him. He wants to punch, but his arms say, "I ain't got nothing to do with it." He receives a blow, and his legs inform him, "Excuse me, I'm falling. I don't know about you." The pain itself signifies: "I'll be fucking with you for the next hour or so." What gains our attention is that Pryor's virtuosity at turning the world loquacious is comic insofar as it is redirected against himself. Animals talk back, his own body talks back—but the signifying monkey, who like Pryor trains its fire on ears, only goes ny-ny-ny.

Pryor's recollection of life in the ring threatens at times to turn into macho of the self-effacing variety, but finally the parody of toughness wins out and anticipates a yet more interesting self-effacement. Pryor has a little song that he sings every so often, arms akimbo like a sauntering sailor or an all-American hero, for example: "Macho man—I'll take this knife and shove it up your ass." By this point it is not shocking that masculinity is satirized as agency in events of anal penetration.

In black heterosexual lovemaking, it would seem to follow, the "woman don't have orgasms." No wonder they go in for whipping and mourning. "How was it, baby?" the black man asks the black woman. She gives him the mòɐɐ'o mòɐɐo wave with her hand—so-so at best. The black man hides his rage and shame at not satisfying her. "I ain't got no time to be sensitive cuz I'm [Pryor returns to his ditty:] macho man—I don't give a damn whether you come or not cuz I'm macho man."

In an extraordinary final move, Pryor admits that he would like to ask, "Did you come?"—which he says in a wimp-nasal voice connoting "white." Then he fantasizes letting the woman get on top, so that somehow or other it is she who has the orgasm. Final words of the concert: "She says how was it, I say ____ ." The blank is silence, but Pryor's meaning is signed by the mèzz'e mèzzo hand wobble.

In a certain way, it is the only conclusion possible: after ninety minutes of omnivalent expression, what could close the polylogue besides Pryor's own silence? And why not end the performance with a demonstration of the relief of not having to perform—of joining the judgmental audience? (The concert had begun with Pryor enjoying the opportunity of watching the whites perform.) Still, it feels very strange. The ending is structurally anticlimactic as well as sexually nonclimactic. Moreover, for an instant, Pryor has considered being a woman or a white man, or taking their positions. A performance that begins with a macho-racial verbal demarcation ends with a muted bit of imaginative role swapping.

The performance, perfectly symmetrical and rounded, has five acts. I do not mean to insult Pryor's splendid talent for improvising his direction; what is less visible is his formal sense, which is at the attacking heart of comedy. (Comedy always registers an affront to form. Repressed form returns in the split-second structure of the joke, but if a comedian like Pryor eschews jokes, it returns in larger units.) Act 1 is "A Racial Division of the Audience." Act 2 is "Animals." Act 3 is "DEATH." Act 4 is "Childhood, and Hunting with Father." Act 5 is "Machismo mocked, and Sexual Divisions Transcended." The fourth act restores Pryor to the childhood inspiration of his love of animals' expressiveness as illustrated in the second act. Act 5 divides the private world in half (men and women), as Act 1 had halved the public world (blacks and whites), though at long last divisions have been transcended. The whole play pivots at Act 3, "DEATH."

Death is the engine of Pryor's vision (he will almost get himself killed a year after this concert). Confronting it seems crucial in transporting him from apartheid to identification (1 to 5), and back from his parental failure to protect his animals (his monkeys die) to a childhood sense of harmless natural well-being (he hunts with his father but forgets the rifle), by means of a fantasy, from near the epicenter of Pryor's comic mind, of his father's death in the midst of sex (2 to 4). Black maternal sex is mourning, but black paternal sex is death itself, or, rather, black paternal death is sex itself.

Pryor seems so comfortable with the excremental vernacular and so pre-occupied with occasions when the body, neither self nor other, talks back, and so alert to occasions when it is the corpse that talks back to his body that you might be inclined to call his performance an erection, in a manner antithetical to David Letterman's, of abjectness. It does not, however, seem like that. It seems a repudiation of abjectness as a willingness to hear without rancor or prejudice one's alienable aspects making their democratic claim upon subjectivity. One needs a theory that allows potency to death and excrement as a way of defusing the explosiveness of their repression.

iii. Excremental Vision

Norman O. Brown's "excremental vision" is a heroic willingness to look at the world's waste, which the death instinct takes as its product, without flinching.[2] Of course, everyone must acknowledge the world's waste in some way, but all the difference is in what you do with your knowledge. You may sublimate it, but this is to frustrate the death drive, which has erupted with a will, in the centuries since Luther, as unleashed capital and weaponry. Or you can incorporate excrement into your vision of eternal life: this is what Luther did in his century and what psychoanalysis, freed of its misguided allegiance to sublimation, can learn from religion to do in ours.

"Scatet totus orbis"—the pretty sentiment is Luther's as quoted in Brown, though it might as well be Pryor's. In both, the excremental vision is total

(Luther thought even good works fecal, manifesting an unrelieved dirty-mindedness that in our age only a comedian might endorse); it is not subli-mated but incorporated; it acknowledges death at life's behest; it connects us to the world and its animal inhabitants rather than elevates us out of it. Add Brown's other great excrementalist—Jonathan Swift—to the mix, and you put the last feature of Pryor's excremental vision into relief:

> The real theme [of *Gulliver's Travels*]—quite obvious on a dispassion-ate reading—is the conflict between our animal body, appropriately epitomized in the anal function, and our pretentious sublimations, more specifically the pretensions of sublimated or romantic-Platonic love. (*LD*, 186)

It is probably clear what Brown would make of a performance that gam-boled in animality, wallowed in excrement, revived at the verge of death, and arrived thereby at a tribute to human intercourse unmarred by ideal-izations. Brown's paragons are "that blessed race of horses, the Houyhn-hnms . . . free from the illusions of romantic-Platonic love, or rather . . . free from love" (*LD*, 189). Recall Pryor's account of dog/miniature horse re-lations. As opposed to flies, who "don't even mess with horse shit," "dogs don't have no racism"—which suddenly means that they are not only not averse to another species but also not averse to its waste. It is with a fine display of corollary non-Platonism that the Great Dane brags, "I don't know what it is, but I am gonna fuck it."

Brown might have been enraptured if he had happened to be in the audi-ence at Long Beach that night, but there could have been a reservation. Not that Pryor was too graphic in his anal talk; only that it is uncertain where Pryor was taking it, and Brown, for all his critique of sublimation, wanted always to get somewhere with excrement. It turns out that Brown is a dual-ist despite all attempts to reconcile Eros and Thanatos; he cannot quite free himself of what sounds to a nonspecialist like sublimation. Brown values in Swift that Swift values in anality "the animal body." Yet Brown can con-demn Yahoo anality as representing "the raw core of human bestiality" (*LD*, 189).

Brown's dualism comes out, I believe, by contrast with Thoreau, though when I was in college, I understood from an aside in a lecture that you could best redeem Thoreau as proto-Brown. There was acumen in the mis-judgment, but it left in me the impression, through several decades of not actually reading *Life against Death*, that Thoreau was Brown's model. In truth, he is hardly mentioned. Here is the famous passage that Brown should have considered:

Few phenomena gave me more delight than to observe the forms which thawing sand and clay assume in flowing down the sides of a deep cut on the railroad through which I passed on my way to the village. . . . Innumerable little streams overlap and interlace with one another, exhibiting a sort of hybrid product, which obeys half way the law of currents, and half way that of vegetation. As it flows it takes the form of sappy leaves on vines, making heaps of pulpy sprays a foot or more in depth, and resembling, as you look down on them, the laciniated, lobed, and imbricated thalluses of some lichens; or you are reminded of coral, of leopards' paws or birds' feet, of brains or lungs or bowels, and excrements of all kinds.[3]

Yes, but we can see where Thoreau and Brown part company. For Thoreau considers excrement so thoroughly the clay of natural creativity here that it is uncertain it takes a nonsublimating heroism to model it. Brown wants psychoanalysis to learn from mysticism "a way out of the human neurosis into that simple health that animals enjoy, but not men" (*LD,* 311). That sounds simple enough, in the Thoreauvian way; but what Brown (not Thoreau) must confront is that presumably animals as opposed to humans have to reckon with death but not the death drive.

There is death, centrally, in Thoreau and Pryor, and even a sort of death wish, but perhaps no death drive. Corpses and excrement are not abjects for them, if abjection here means possession by the horror of death drive products and by-products, because their form of self-expression is self-distanced to begin with; they are outside themselves as the basis of their self-conceptions. They are so fully abject that nothing seems particularly abject, which is to say that, if they are obsessed with death, it is not by death as *against* life, which is also to say that their excremental vision is ecstatic but not visionary.

Can we draw a line, then, from Thoreau to Pryor as an evolutionary advance, even beyond Brown, in the expansion of excremental consciousness? No: we can draw the line but must deny the advance, because something odd has befallen the excremental vision in recent years; as a consequence, Thoreau as much as Brown needs to be repudiated as precursor.

iv. Excremental Revision

Not to make a mystery of it, the odd thing that has happened to the excremental vision is a queer thing. I have described Thoreau as if his vision were too excremental for Brown, since excrement is less incorporated into

Thoreau's world (as life must acknowledge death) than it is the essence of his world (vitality itself). Yet if Michael Warner is right about Thoreau, you should rather conclude that the latter is not excremental enough.[4] Warner's thesis is that Walden takes us not, as we had assumed, from summer to spring, but rather "from the imperative of having no waste to the imperative of enjoying one's waste." The problem is the implication that even your waste can be used, even your waste can be economized, in short, even your waste is not wasted. Warner grants that Thoreau longs "to undo the ascetic self-relation without which the notion of a self-regulating market society (in itself utopian) would be inconceivable"; but apparently Thoreau's "post-renunciatory utopia will have an asceticism of its own" ("EE," 163). The ideal of it will be purity, the elimination of waste qua waste. This amounts to a solution to Daniel Bell's cultural contradiction of capitalism, the antithetical necessities of wasting and saving. Warner's Thoreau is a (victimized) agent of capitalism's response to a threat, submitting an erotic, feminizing, excremental self dissolution to an ascetic self-regard (171).

Brown might conceivably have agreed with all this: Brown too is expert in how the excremental vision can be channeled on capitalism's behalf, and how it can be perverted, in his words, as a "magic instrument for self-expression" (*LD,* 190). I doubt you can make a simple alliance of Brown and Warner as against Thoreau, however, because what Brown manages to leave out of his discussion of the excremental vision is any explicit consideration of homosexuality. Brown is all against the repression of anality, but anal sex, in his discussion, is itself shunted.[5]

Leo Bersani, like Warner and apparently for similar reasons, seems to invoke and ignore Brown at the same time. Bersani famously wonders, "Is the rectum a grave?" and his answer is yes, and that is what is good about it.[6] What lies buried in it is "the masculine ideal (an ideal shared—differently—by men *and* women) of proud subjectivity" ("RG," 227). So Bersani shares with Brown a passion for inviting death into our lives; a sense that the self-violence of the exercise will head off the global violence of self-assertive capitalism; and an approximation of where the death instinct can be corporeally located.

I say "approximation," however, because Bersani's vision is rectal without being particularly excremental. I am afraid, therefore, that though Bersani's is more pertinently sexualized than Brown's, it actually will seem somewhat regressive to Warner insofar as it shows no marked acknowledgment of waste. "Male homosexuality," writes Bersani, "advertises the risk of the sexual itself as the risk of self-dismissal, of *losing sight* of the self, and in so doing it proposes and dangerously represents *jouissance* as a mode of ascesis" ("RG," 222). Ascesis! It is not, I grant, the same ascesis that ruins Thoreau for Warner. According to Warner's rejection of it, ascetism is not self-loss, it is self-gain. The totalities, however, are the same: you can keep yourself or give yourself away, but you are ascetic if, either way, everything is consumed.

I need to hasten back to Pryor and place him in this array of excremental and rectal visions as follows. He is Brownian in anality, animality, and thanatocentrism. He transcends Brown into the vicinity of Walden, insofar as his excremental vision does not even begin with a division of Thanatos and Eros, but finds them indivisible, for example, at the moment of his father's death. The connection to Thoreau comes out in one of the eeriest moments of the performance, which I have saved until now. Pryor is hunting with his father; suddenly, he is all piety, and it is not false. He talks, almost in a whisper, about how quiet you must be in the woods: "It's almost like you know the gods are there." The tone and sentiment seem to hover for a moment between Thoreau's and Garrison Keillor's. The audience awaits the joke. When it comes, however, it is perhaps the one moment of the concert in which there is no recognition in the audience's laughter. "Something about nature, right, makes you want to [Pryor's silence splits the infinitive] shit." The audience is smart enough not to think that Pryor has reached for a crude shock; otherwise, they do not know what to think. They do not, assuredly, surmise that in the presence of the father who would die having sex, Pryor would not see pollution in the Thoreauvian intersection of divinity and defecation.

And finally the Bersani moment: what Bersani urges the world to learn from homosexuality, as against the lessons of either orthodox masculinism or standard feminism, is the joy of the under position, if the essence of sex is the burial of subjectivity. As if to endorse this point, at what should have been the climactic moment of his concert, Pryor imagines getting under a woman—*is* he the woman? Or a man being somehow penetrated?—and the concert ends with Pryor's "self-dismissal." But I would not call the moment ascetic, exactly, because of the inextricability of Pryor's identity and his abjectness, his fashioning and publicizing of self and his wasting of self. He is the shadow capitalist, maybe the underside of Warner's Thoreau, saving and wasting, but saving what he should waste, and wasting what he should save.

The project here is to understand how Pryor gets from his first gesture of the concert—instituting a local inverse Jim Crow based on the differential need of whites and blacks to use the de facto segregated toilets—to the last, in which all membranes seem permeable in a waste-saving and self-wasting vision. Scatet totus orbis is the principle of the metabolizing of difference to sameness.

v. Oceans of Mud

It is nearly impossible, Diana Fuss demonstrates, to consider psychoanalytic identification in celebratory terms; she divides the implicit Freudian conception of it into three parts: infection (or contagion), ingestion (or cannibalism), and fall (or entropy).[7] And she can document that when the issue is cross-racial identification, culture critics duplicate the Freudian wariness. Whites may try, as Kaja Silverman writes about T. E. Lawrence, to outdo natives at their own otherness, or whites may simply be looking to sample a little transgression—Gail Ching-Liang Low observes—that keeps all social rankings intact (*IP*, 148). These two variants on ingestion, cannibalizing the natives.

The premise would seem to be that whites are always up to something, and perhaps most up to something when most sympathetic. But it would be naive not to notice that they can be out of control as well, and often enough most out of control when most up to something. Take the white response to rap: Houston Baker condemns the general white American ignorance of the phenomenon as a "willed refusal to engage a form that is preeminently young, black, and male."[8] Yet

> the paradox of this refusal . . . is an unwitting complicity in the form's influence and spread. For example, many Americans—young and old, black and white—will "hiply" boast of their children's (or some child's, perhaps a cousin's or nephew's) familiarity with rap. (*BSRA*, 62)

So whites are most willful when most unwitting, in a conspiracy with the enemy's cabal. There is a paradox at work here, Baker tells us, though he had previously warned us that it is not enough "simply to label rap a new, noisy mode of urban resistance that paradoxically appeals both to middle-class white youth and the black underclass" (*BSRA*, 61). Shall we call the syndrome a compounded rather than a simple paradox, since it is one paradox that middle-class white kids enjoy black urban art, and a second that scornful adults enjoy the first? Or shall we read Baker's hostility to labeling as a sign of his dissatisfaction with the figure of paradox itself?

Dissatisfied or not, American culture critics have a hard time avoiding the trope. Cornel West, in a conversation with Anders Stephanson, describes the dilemma of jazz artists that to "preserve a tradition from mainstream domestication and dilution," they risked losing "contact with the black masses. In this case, there was eventually a move toward 'fusion,' jazz artists attempting to produce objects intended for broader black-and-white consumption."[9] The sequential paradoxes are that to keep in contact with the undiluted black tradition, black artists began to lose contact with blacks, and that to produce a music appealing to blacks, they were forced to produce a music appealing to whites. Baker's metaparadox arises from a secret, displaced fascination of white adults for rap; West's from a hidden assimilation (whites desiring what blacks desire, then blacks desiring what whites desire in blackness) of black and white susceptibility to jazz. Paradox is the inevitable rhetoric, apparently, of unforeseen cultural permeability.

However, when his own attention turns to rap, West makes a valiant effort to transcend the language of paradox.

> Rap [West tells his interviewer] is unique because it combines the black preacher and the black music tradition, replacing the liturgical-ecclesiastical setting with the African polyrhythms of the street. A tremendous *articulateness* is syncopated with the African drumbeat, the African funk, into an American postmodern product. ("CW," 280)

At the beginning of West's statement, traditional Afro-American elements are fused: preaching and music into rap. At the end, African and American, primeval and postmodern, tribal and consumerist cultures are syncopated. There is no question of susceptibility or dilution here (identification as fall from white or black superiority, respectively). Combination is the easier trope, though its facility is deceptive: preacher and music are *combined,* but street rhythm *replaces* the church, and the *combination* of presymbolic and symbolic (music and preaching) returns as the *syncopation* of them (drumbeat and articulateness). Syncopation is the uneasier trope, but better suited to the polyrhythmic complexities of the scene.

If rap "preeminently" and jazz before its "mainstream domestication and dilution" are black, then it is paradoxical to assert that they are or should be, equally, white. Paradox is what arises in such matters when you simultaneously grant and impugn notions of cultural origination and possession. This means granting and impugning, simultaneously, the Freudian trinity of infection, ingestion, and fall. What is most admirable in Baker's decomposing of paradox and West's slide from paradox to syncopation is the struggle to transcend the conceptual hopelessness and desperateness of the figure.

Yet Ishmael Reed, in his masterpiece, *Mumbo Jumbo,* treats identification without the agony. And if he more than once remarks in that book that Freud missed an opportunity,[10] he does not mean that a mere theoretical revision on Freud's part would have changed the course of interracial politics. He only implies that another mode of identification was before Freud if meaningless to him, through which he could have provided the theory of an identification already in progress and only hysterically despised as cannibalism or contagion or chaos. What Reed is talking about, in effect, is the mode of identification of Pryor and his comedy society.

A character in *Mumbo Jumbo* named PaPa LaBas (whose hieratic status I will later summon Henry Louis Gates Jr. to explicate) "would never [Reed tells us] say 'If you've seen 1 redwood tree, you've seen them all'; rather he would reply with the African Chieftain 'I am the elephant.' . . . (*Freud would read this as 'a feeling of an indissoluble bond, of being one with the external world as a whole,'* which poor Freud 'never experienced')" (*MJ*, 45). A précis of *Mumbo Jumbo* is impossible, but suffice it here that it concerns a phenomenon called "Jes Grew," a kind of plague that from time to time infects whites with all the cultural attributes of blacks, and which nearly conquers America in the 1920s, when the novel mainly takes place, because the disease, if that is what it is, has entered America at New Orleans in that decade and headed toward Harlem in search of its "text." It is at the end of the twenties that Freud wrote, in *Civilization and Its Discontents,* that he had never had the oceanic feeling, which is to say that he missed Jes Grew, and so could not himself be the one to textualize it.[11]

My impractical question might be put this way: what would *Civilization and Its Discontents* have been like if poor Freud had himself felt what Romain Rolland wrote to tell him about? And had therefore not been inclined to dismiss it merely as a remnant in certain fixated adults of the sense of indistinction they had experienced at their mothers' breasts and hardly the source of religious sentiment in general. The story of religion for Freud is, on the contrary, the story of the infant's "helplessness and the longing for the father aroused by it" (*SE*, 72): a story, in short, of privation and not fullness.

Here is the two-minute version of the birth of civilization according to Freud. First: sexuality in the male loses its ties to periodicity. Males therefore need to keep females close at all times, and females feel the urgency of keeping their young near the reigning pertinent male—hence, families. Second: "organic periodicity," of course, persists in females (i.e., the monthly cycle), but as testimony to the transcendence of it on the part of the male, taboos on it are enforced. Third: since visual, as opposed to olfactory, stimuli are perpetually, not cyclically, available, they begin to dominate. Fourth (meanwhile): the power of olfactory stimuli has been diminished by the uprightness of humankind—this also fosters the primacy of the visible. Fifth: smelling is devalued in general; the repugnance of the menstrual smell is extended to excremental smells. Sixth: "Anal erotism, therefore, succumbs in the first instance to the 'organic repression' which paved the way to civilization" (SE, 99–100).

As a quick way of leaping to Richard Pryor, we might remark here that Freud believes he has demonstrated why humans have contempt for dogs. If it were not for their lack of olfactory shame, our contumely would be incomprehensible, in light of dogs' superior ethics (100). Of course, Pryor expresses no contempt at all for dogs, whose olfactory shamelessness is their most admirable quality, epitomized by the ecumenical Great Dane.

I have another—less hit-and-run—point in mind. Freud's theory of civilization may be loony, but what it reveals even in its looniness, as a symptom, is a hatred of body smells as a hatred of the abject, traceable to women's sexuality. In Klaus Theweleit's *Male Fantasies,* we are treated to the story of the German *Freikorps,* whose murderous hatred of Communism was only matched by their murderous hatred of women's sexuality, one metaphorized and the other metonymized as the "Red Tide."[12] The average Freikorpsman's feelings about the Red Tide are equal to the average white American's about what Ishmael Reed calls regularly in *Mumbo Jumbo* the "black mud." If the red tide—anarchy, equality, femininity—threatens the German male's view of female innocence and thus German manhood, black mud is the American threat to the Virgin Land. The red tide and the black mud are what civilization experiences on the shores of the oceanic.

In Freud, the process of civilization begins with shame, but it proceeds in guilt. Uprightness produces shame and the triumph of the visual; shame is the agent of the repression of instincts, which produces aggression; aggression turns from its first target (the father) inward, carving out the superego. The superego is the result of an "identification" with the paternal authority (SE, 129), and that identification radiates outward. So *Civilization and Its Discontents* begins by denying that religion can be traced back to the mother and originary unity, ends by associating it with an "ever increasing reinforcement of the sense of guilt" (133). Freud's favorite guilt comedian, he specifies, is Mark Twain (126).

But Pryor is not a guilt comedian—Pryor's stand-up, as for example when his heart attacks him, does not prioritize the upright and upstanding—and we can refer to him, on Reed's implicit suggestion, as an oceanic comedian on the proviso that we are talking about tides and waves of mud. Mud is the universal democratic solvent; it pollutes all distinctions between the dead and the living, whites and blacks, prehistory and modernity, the vertical and the horizontal, as in Faulkner's *As I Lay Dying*, published the same year as *Civilization and Its Discontents*. If Freud acknowledges that civilization begins with the shame of female sexuality, which is the shame of menstrual smell, he has before him another source of the oceanic besides milk. The formula for the earthier version of the oceanic would be mud = feces + mother's blood. Mud is the origin and substance of a less patriarchal religion than any that Freud considers.

> In the central ceremony of the Black Mass [Brown tells us], as the Queen of the Sabbath lay prone, "the sacred host was prepared by kneading on the buttocks a mixture of the most repulsive material, faeces, menstrual blood, urine, and offal of various kinds." (*CD,* 207)

It is a stew of abject ingredients: we infer that the comedy of Richard Pryor is based on a radical overthrowing of abjectness all at once, not standing it up, in the manner of stand-up. Pryor cannot humor abjection, in the stand-up way, because he belongs to an abjected race. The black mass, Brown tells us, mixes feces, urine, and blood: these entail the colors of the world populations, coded by "whites." A white disciplinarian in *Mumbo Jumbo* wants to win back to whiteness a white radical by pitting their race "against the Legendary Army of Marching Niggers against the Yellow Peril against the Red Man" (*MJ,* 112). Is this not a shoring of whiteness against the elements—they run together without punctuation—of the Black Mass, against feces, urine, and menses? *Mumbo Jumbo* voodoo practitioners meet leaders of the Haitian resistance to American marine imperialism in a chromatically striking shiproom: "The colors of the room are black and red, the walls are red, the floor is black. A flag hangs from the ceiling upon which has been sewn the words Vin' Bain Ding, 'Blood, Pain, Excrement'" (*MJ,* 131).[13]

In *Mumbo Jumbo* what sort of phenomenon is Jes Grew? It is a sort of falling in of individuals: "Individuality. It couldn't be herded, rounded-up; it was like crystals of winter each different from one another but in a storm going down together" (*MJ,* 140). Or it is a kind of ingestion: "Jes Grew is the boll weevil eating away at the fabric of our forms our technique our aesthetic integrity" (17). Or it is, passim, a plague, though Reed stipulates that whites "did not understand that the Jes Grew epidemic was unlike physical plagues. Actually, Jes Grew was an anti-plague. Some plagues caused the body to waste away; Jes Grew enlivened the host" (6). Jes Grew exemplifies all of Fuss's Freud's metaphors of identification, though Reed negates their negativity: it is a fall of whiteness but a fall into community, a cannibalism that resurrects the body, a plague but an antiplague. There is no positive term, apparently, for positive identification.

You could call it the oceanic feeling, but the ocean would have to be conceived of as merging with its shore. One white hysterically emotes, "The Black Tide of Mud will engulf us all" (169). There can be no sense of purification or elementality to this oceanic feeling. An overcome white "said he felt like the gut heart and lungs of Africa's interior" (5). It delivers whites not only to the heart but also the innards of darkness, a place akin to Thoreau's train bank, reminiscent of brains, lungs, and bowels, and "excrements of all kinds."

Adam was made of mud, which, according to Norman O. Brown, means he was made of feces. The connection is not drawn in *Mumbo Jumbo:* Reed is talking about contagion that does *not* cause its host "to waste away"—though, on the other hand, it causes a superabundance of enthusiasm, joy, life, wasted energy from the point of view of white technologism.[14] Kids infected by Jes Grew "want to Funky Butt and Black Bottom" (*MJ*, 21–22), but the posterior component of the phenomenon is undertheorized in *Mumbo Jumbo*. And when Henry Louis Gates takes *Mumbo Jumbo* as one of his inspirational texts in *The Signifying Monkey*, a book whose scope I shall be taking advantage of, he does not excessively care about two aspects of the phenomenon he is studying: the excrementality of the "signifying monkey" and the oceanic mud central to Reed's vision.[15] Signifying for men can be an oedipal contest (it is largely about clearing a space against authorities; in its "dozens" sub-version, it has its basis in oedipal insults). But there are other ways to take Gates's own material.

The story of the signifying monkey is persistently phallic competitive, but its language is persistently anal egalitarian. The excrementality is so pervasive that it can mean anything in a story striving, against the excremental tide, to mean one thing. One version of the signifying monkey ur-story begins this way.

> Deep down in the jungle so they say
> There's a signifying monkey down the way
> There hadn't been no disturbin' in the jungle for quite a bit,
> For up jumped the monkey in the tree one day and laughed
> "I guess I'll start some shit." (*SM*, 55)

The monkey instigates a dispute between the lion and the elephant, and part of the metacritical interest is that Gates cannot decide whether to call this agitating a "mediation," an "(anti)mediation," or an "antimediation" (56). If, in racial terms, the monkey is black and the lion is white, what would that make the elephant? Since the monkey creates a conflict between the lion and the elephant, you might look for his position in relation to theirs, i.e., they are the antagonists and he is the mediator; but the real conflict is between lion and monkey. There is some numerical or structural oddity here. We have three figures, but we do not have a Hegelian organization of them, nor is it obvious what human dialectic is being allegorized.

At any rate, "shit" means trouble at first. That is only one of its many denotations. After the lion returns to the monkey, having been thrashed by the elephant, the monkey taunts (signifies) him.

> He said, "Whup! Motherfucker, don't you roar,
> I'll jump down on the ground and beat your
>   fucking ass some more."
> Say, "While I'm swinging around in my tree,"
> say, "I ought to swing over your chickenshit head
>   and pee." (57)

Here, excrement in one of its barnyard forms equals what the lion has become as the result of physical and verbal abuse—ass whipping. He has *become* abjectness and waste, outside and in. The next lines continue the signifying.

> Say, "Everytime me and my old lady be tryin' to
>   to get a little bit,
> here you come down through the jungle with that
>   old 'Hi Ho' shit." (ibid.)

"Shit" now means false display. The monkey at this point is concerned to oppose his own phallic pursuit with the anality of the lion. But he seems to forget himself, forget that his own initial impulse was not to find a moment of private genital intercourse but to stir up some public excremental trouble. He falls from his branch, and "his ass must have hit the ground"; now vulnerable, he tries to apologize to the lion, who tells him,

> "Apologize, shit," say, "I'm gonna stop you from
>   signifyin'" (ibid.),

where "shit" expresses contempt for the gesture.

The nuances of ubiquitous excrement are not Gates's theme. But Gates traces the ancestry of the signifying monkey back to the trickster and translator between gods and humans, Esu-Elegbara (who is known "in the loa of Hoodoo in the United States" by the name of Papa LaBas, which is also the name of a character in *Mumbo Jumbo*); and the most famous Esu-Elegbara story (*SM*, 32–34) begins with a similar act of trouble—my burden is to suggest that it is not gratuitous to conceive of it as excremental trouble.

The imbroglio begins when two men vow eternal friendship but do not remember or revere Esu in the act. So trickster Esu makes a cloth cap, the right side black, the left side white. One day, as Ayodele Ogundipe retells the myth, "the two friends were out in the fields, tilling their land. One was hoeing on the right side, the other was clearing the bushes on the left. Esu came by on a horse, riding between the two men. The one on the right saw the black side of the hat. The friend on the left noticed the whiteness of Esu's cap."

They argue over it. Esu—who caused the conflict, antimediator and mediator—now comes to settle it: "Both of you are right." The lesson, according to Gates, is that there is no determinate vantage point; Esu is the patron saint of reader response. Esu reconnects the friends, but he had put them asunder in the first place; even reconciled, they seem to be united on the understanding that they will never share the same point of view. Thus, writes Gates, "what appears in a binary system to be a contradiction resolvable only by the unity of opposites is more subtly—and mysteriously—resolved by the Yoruba, in the concept central to the Ogboni secret society that 'two, it becomes three'" (37). Say that the "two" are god and man in the anecdote—and then the men divide. Unlike the three-in-one of the Trinity, we have two-thirds.

Is Gates justified in finding interpretive relativism in the Esu story? For humans there are only partial truths, but Esu knows the whole truth, though it is not simple. Item: is Gates right to believe that the conflict of leonine literalism and simian figurativeness can produce a victory of the figural? The monkey does not triumph in the end, and the elephant is beyond the battle. If we take the monkey as black and the lion as white, then not the simian but the elephantine position is equivalent to Esu's, beyond the color war.

I do not assume that the elephant's position can be our own: beyond black and white, gray. And I do not see how to inherit Esu's dislocation. But the elephant exists, even if it is not me; and the monkey, until he forgets his own essential excrementality, manages to get on his side. It is possible that remembering our own excrementality gets us on Esu's side (or sidelessness) as well. According to the Yoruba creation myth, first there was air, air enlivened to water, air and water thickened to mud. "Then the mud is given form as proto-Esu" (36). Esu is himself liminal (between gods and humans), and the mud is two transitions back (almost proto-Esu, i.e., almost almost Esu, i.e., almost almost almost a god): creation is continuous. Mud is substance and almost form, and gives rise to the form of Esu but not yet his substance. Mud, to put it yet another way, is where the world arrives at the form of Esu. It is not the abject within subjectivity; it predicts something divine beyond subjectivity. We may conceive, then, of *Mumbo Jumbo* as between the muddening Jes Grew and its eternal, absconded text. We may think of Pryor's comedy as located at the same juncture of excrement and the strictures of form: in the position of proto-Esu. It takes place, in effect, in the woods where "it's almost like you know the gods are there" and "you want to shit."

There is an audience. It is opposite—but not necessarily opposed to—the performer. It is normally the comedian's business to get everyone laughing together. But Richard Pryor comes on stage and instead of trying to make one out of two, he makes three. He wears a cap that is half black, half white, and it halves the audience: whites returning from the bathroom, blacks in their seats. It seems a misfortune for whites on the order of the morbid white fantasy in *Gravity's Rainbow* of having one's head in a toilet while being anally raped by Malcolm X. But then *The Crying of Lot 49,* whose spirit more nearly equals that of *Mumbo Jumbo* than that of any other work of recent fiction I know, becomes the analogue text: WASTE begins to spread unstoppably. We call this entropy, and Fuss mates entropy with the fall as a paradigm of identification. Jes Grew, however, is a force of negentropy, and whites and blacks come together.

The purpose of Pryor's opening is not so much to divide whites and blacks as to triangulate them. Once that occurs, they can be reunited— along with men and women at the end of the performance—on a new principle of identification. It is beyond the opposition of literal and figurative, lion and monkey (like Papa LaBas, Pryor declares, "I am the elephant"); it inserts itself between Esu's overview and the friends' resigned underview. It is where formlessness meets form, where mud adumbrates but is not yet Esu or Adam: the night, as Hegel almost scornfully said, in which all elephants are gray. Contagious laughter is the antiplague.

Pryor attempts to form a new nation on the model of a stand-up audience, as it crystallizes around a new type—or, rather, antitype—of comedian. Lenny Bruce is one precursor: David Letterman recovered the aggressiveness in Bruce's filial abjection, but Pryor recognized in the Spritz the potential for the liquidating of child into parent. The lineage can be traced to Rabelais: Gargantua's warrior mare, who "pissed so copiously that there was a flood for fifteen miles around," which has the effect of wiping out nearly an entire company of the enemy, seems a Brucean figure, and her discharge a Brucean concoction of aggression and tidal unity.[16] It is

Bakhtin of course who saw in such deluges (Pantagruel urinates another one) what we might call antiabjectness—since the aspiration is marginal joining rather than disjoining—with democratic potential for inundating social distinctions.[17] Pryor confronts a somewhat different problem—not individualism so much as groupism, a sort of gigantism, itself—so he plays not the giant but the ventriloquist, the cypher, Proteus, proto-Esu, finally the mime. He seems fluidity itself rather than its mass producer.

We get momentary views of the audience in the performance film. Whites seem to laugh differently from blacks: they thrust up their chins, a seemingly assertive gesture except that it makes vulnerable their jaws in all their glassiness. Meanwhile, blacks are laughing in the opposite direction, doubling over as if self-protectively, except that the reflex seems to register a jab in the solar plexus. The masculine metaphoric violence is justified by Pryor's occasional use of boxing as a model of comedy. But the noise produced by a Pryor audience is unifying: shrieks of laughter, mixed with clapping, hooting, and screaming, its volume intact for two to ten seconds duration. You can lose your identity in the high pitch: the embodiedness of the response to Pryor (whole body laughing) is exactly equal to its disembodiedness (whole audience laughing). Your body is not the point of distinction of ego and other; it is the point of convulsion.

Skirting, Kidding: Ellen DeGeneres and Paula Poundstone

i.

The specific benefit of laughter is obliviousness. In this respect, laughter has a strange intimacy with pain. I have argued that laughter, like pain, is incorrigible: pain is the thing about which I cannot be wrong, and laughter is the thing about which *we* cannot be wrong. Pain is also, according to Elaine Scarry, universe contracting, and so is laughter.[1] Whatever its physiological basis (e.g., the contribution of jokes to surges of salivary immunoglobulin-A), the use of laughter to combat disease must have something to do with the capacity of pain and humor for creating exclusive, hence mutually exclusive, worlds. There is at least one obvious connection between the two attributes of laughter—it is incorrigible, it is apocalyptic—that I have mentioned. It is not merely the intensity and the embodiment of laughter, but also its unfalsifiability, that obviates the world.

So I was not in the intellectual (i.e., thinking) mode when I registered that Ellen DeGeneres and Paula Poundstone were amusing me as female stand-up comedians. But this has come to seem to me a breakthrough. I have felt no resistance to appreciating the humor of women as expressed either in movies and TV or in real life—women's humor seems to me to flourish in situations either more artificial than the stand-up setting or less. Or rather, the humor of women seems to me at its best when the artificial and the authentic exchange places: when the comic actress stylizes her own nature, and when the woman in actuality naturalizes a brilliant role.

Female stand-up comedians, on the other hand, had only earned from me a grudging laugh—which, from the point of view of the purist, is equal to an easy laugh—insofar as they joked about husbands, boyfriends, commitment, airline stewardesses, and PMS. These subjects are comfortable to laugh at, for men as well as for women; a knowing distance from the joke is available to everyone, and nothing interesting transpires between performer and audience. The tension of nature and artifice is diminished rather too easily in a complete triumph of the conventional, as in ancient mother-in-law gags. But the fascination of stand-up—and its identifiability in contrast to old-style comedy of the wicked mother-in-law variety—has everything to do with its essential abjectness; all stand-ups are abject insofar as they give themselves over to the stand-up condition, which is a noncondition *between* nature and artifice. (They are neither acting nor conversing, neither in nor out of costume.) Reality itself, in the way of the abject, keeps returning to the stand-up comedian, who throws it off in the form of jokes. Obliviousness is earned from moment to moment.

When I decided to forswear that hard-earned obliviousness—when I decided to notice what was in front of me as a first step—what I noticed was that both DeGeneres and Poundstone were wearing (were they costumes?) suits.

ii.

If the end of stand-up is obliviousness, then it belongs to the genre of escapist art—what genre is that? I am not sure it has its theory yet; let me nominate Rodgers and Hammerstein as its best theorists.

This is not merely to say that their musicals are escapist, though they are. Take *The King and I:* the fantasy is that dictatorial paternalism converts to humorous pathos at the advent of a strong woman; part of the pathos is that the dictator himself is oriental and the strong woman herself is occidental, so that the sexual outcome can only be the impotence of the beautiful patriarch. Or take *The Sound of Music:* again, the benevolent dictator, Von Trapp, is humbled by a strong woman (who arrives, as in *The King and I,* apparently to put a stop to the wanton production of children). Again, the strong woman is not sexually available for conquest—she is training to be a nun. Even the context of Nazism contributes to the escapism; Von Trapp can submit to the strong woman without its signaling absolute prostration, since his softening makes credible his heroic antifascism. Yul Brynner's role splits in two (Hitler/Von Trapp) to purify the escapism, which seems to involve complete gender freedom within perfect gender conventionality.

The interest of all this for me is that Rodgers and Hammerstein knew what they were doing and hid in their escapism a profounder escape. Both *The King and I* and *The Sound of Music* have metamoments: the Family Von Trapp performs its music on stage within the musical; the concubines of the King put on a play, *Small House of Uncle Thomas* (*Uncle Tom's Cabin*), within the play. Both metaperformances mask refusals to go on performing. On behalf of the musicals of which they are emblems, they define the point of exhibition as camouflage.

In *The King and I,* a Burmese concubine, Tuptim, has been torn from her husband, Lun Tha, who lurks around the King's palace for the whole musical. Tuptim is the adapter and narrator of *Small House of Uncle Thomas,* and during the performance in front of the King and his English guests, she comes out of her own narrative for a moment almost to make explicit the relationship of her enslavement to those portrayed in her play. She is quickly returned to her play by a glare and a snap of the fingers from Brynner. This has the effect of returning *Small House of Uncle Thomas* (mounted in a slave state, in the presence of imperialists, during the American Civil War) into a demonstration of the grace and poise of enslaved concubines that the British can find charming.

The Family Von Trapp performance at the equivalent crisis of *The Sound of Music* seems harmless when the family is singing "Do, Re, Mi," but somewhat more troubling when Von Trapp sings "Edelweiss." It is a complicated selection if you think about it, though you do not: his ideal of purely white nature and nation is not so different from the Nazis'. Perhaps we are permitted to assume that this is the cleverness of Von Trapp—to sing a hymn so close to what the Nazis want to hear that they can only suspect that the natural purity of Austria makes Nazis into a stain, like Jews. Then the Family Von Trapp sings "Farewell," which had been a charming song earlier in the musical when it attenuated the withdrawal of innocents from adult worldliness; the Nazis, of course, cannot realize that it is adults who are now interested in escaping their party.

The escape in *The Sound of Music* succeeds. The escape in *The King and I* fails. The splitting of the King of Siam into Hitler and Von Trapp allows the Von Trapps to escape without implying the complete collapse of patriarchy, whose secret sweetness we have been dreamily contemplating. But the meaning of escapism is the same in both cases. The invaders miss the significance of *Small House of Uncle Thomas* in *The King and I*: in place of repudiation, they see beautifully disciplined concubinage. The invaders miss the significance of "Edelweiss" and "Farewell": in place of repudiation, they see pure whiteness and patriarchal domestic innocence. They love what they see and they are not utterly wrong, because they see nearly what we do. We enjoy both performances, also, in the way oblivious fascists and imperialists do, if the musicals work for us at all. *Small House of Uncle Thomas* is a great success, and the audience applauds heartily; so is the Von Trapp performance, which wins first prize. During the applause, the escaping slave Tuptim does not appear, and everyone is amazed. During the applause, the escaping Von Trapps do not appear, and everyone is mystified.

Above all, don't performers want our applause? Possibly not as much as the audience wants to give it. Plays occasionally finalize claims to seriousness by denying audiences the right to approve. Applause is a relief from the strain of attention; it is an explosion of consciousness that had been compressed, much like laughter. We force, thereby, our return to profane space. Performers whose aspiration is formal perfection turn out to be human after all, and we worship their superiority on condition that they turn out to be our equals. They humanize; they are reembodied; they come back to time and entropy. On the cusp is our adulation and gratitude.

Marjorie Garber has written a compendious book on transvestism, one theme of which is the essential unity of transvestism and performance in general. Transvestism is the space of (not being or having but) seeming, to resituate Lacan's trinity. In this connection, she notes that the metamoment of *South Pacific* is the cross-dressing performance of "101 Pounds of Fun." [2] This implies that the moment of applause is the antitransvestite, or call it the divesting, moment, when performers resume their profane identities, though still a moment before returning to their street clothes and natural faces. For a moment they are like stand-ups, between nature and artifice. The surprise is that that moment of abjection or return is in Rodgers and Hammerstein the moment of disembodiment or flight. The theatrical scene (literally transvestite in *Small House of Uncle Thomas*, in which all parts are played by women) is doubly false. It *seems* escapist—it seems to seem—in order to camouflage the actual escape. The escape that turns sex into seeming (that makes it possible to believe in the hidden phallus of women or the hidden emptiness of tyrants) masks the escape that eliminates bodies altogether. In the process, escape becomes the provenance of the performer, not the audience. This is akin to humor if Kant is right to consider the joke as strained attention that suddenly finds itself looking at nothing.

I want to consider escapism in reference to Ellen DeGeneres and Paula Poundstone as the evacuation of the star's body at the moment it is evoked.

iii.

Paula Poundstone, first of all. What to do with her body is one theme of her HBO performance at Harvard, and part of its form as well. A running distraction is whether she will decide to get behind her stool—her only prop or in front of it, or whether, sitting on it, she should scrunch one leg or even both her legs onto the top bar.[3] In a bit about finding herself on a one-passenger flight, Poundstone claims that the crew asked her to move for ballast. To illustrate this denigration of herself to pure mass, she removes one leg from the top rung of the stool and thrusts it out stage left.

From such discomforts, shouldn't her suit be liberating? Poundstone seems large on stage; standing above us, the stand-up comedian always seems larger than he, usually "he," is. It would be difficult for the typical stand-up comedian, even if he so desired, to disavow the phallicness of his position, and one move a female comedian, not wishing to consternate her partly or mainly male audience, might make is to play dumb, Gracie-style. Even a woman as publicly smart as Ellen DeGeneres will take up dumbness as a posture, represented as the incapacity for remembering her point. But Poundstone, attracting an audience of both sexes, sometimes mainly of women, might be able to fool with the phallic position more committedly or comfortably. And transvestism, the space, as Marjorie Garber would have it, of seeming, might for such a purpose be the best space to occupy.

So it is time—we seek all revelations of necessity at the end—for Poundstone to take her bow. We would expect this to be the divesting moment: what will Poundstone turn out to be beneath her suit? If she had been an actress, there would have been no problem. Clothed by applause, she might have chosen to stay in character or drop it. But for a comedian, neither exposing himself or herself nor quite playing a part, the moment is ontologically obscure, as in the case of Andrew Dice Clay. In Poundstone's case, her multicolored suit, over (it is revealed to us) her baggy underwear, would seem to double her comedian's position in the zone between artifice and actuality. She is already, during her act, where an actress arrives during the applause. So where, during the applause, can Poundstone go?

She ends her act, the audience cheers. Then Poundstone is gone; the Harvard Band marches on stage, playing "Ten Thousand Men of Harvard." It feels terribly abrupt. Among the things we want less of at that moment is the Harvard Band, and the one thing we want more of is Poundstone. She had been an intimate of the audience's for the length of the act: half the act was joking with selected individuals. She had become so familiar that it seems crushing to be suddenly abandoned.

Then we—video watchers—realize that Poundstone has not left us, abruptly, forever. She is in the band—she is playing the tuba. The HBO camera picks her out, but it probably takes the live audience a moment to spot her. Poundstone reappears on stage in stages—but as what? Not in her suit nor yet in her civvies, she has stuffed herself into yet another uni-sex uniform, above which we can pick out her face, somehow reminiscent of the chiseled faces of Hollywood actresses of the last black-and-white era, and the revelation of the real but partially secreted Poundstone is the revelation of a partial disguise. Finally, the camera follows Poundstone off-stage. Now she exists only for the HBO audience, not the Harvard audience. Poundstone, by herself, is actually trying to play the tuba. Is there a well-documented category of abjectness devoted to phallic flatulence? The star's body has not disappeared, exactly, but the moment of ostensible appearance has been redefined as a restaging of the complexities of escape. Seeing Poundstone again, we realize that we had not seen her yet. Her familiarity itself has been defamiliarized. If for the Von Trapps and the slave, Tuptim, the moment of applause reveals by their unavailability for it that they are now in flight, for Poundstone the moment reveals by her presence at it that she had been escaping all along.

iv.

If I may translate Lacan into less doctrinally specific language, then what he is urging about the play of "being" and "having" (being and having the phallus, to put the matter with doctrinal specificity) amounts to this. Inso-far as x is the object of y's desire, y (weaker) wants to be what x (stronger) does not have.[4] Y cannot simply have what x does not have and offer it: if it is disposable, it is precisely not what x wants. But of course y cannot *be* what x does not have, either, because what x wants is generic and complementary, and y is specific and discrete. Thus "seeming" in Lacan is a necessary third term: seeming protects having and being from reality. Y wants to seem to be what x wants to seem to have.

For Marjorie Garber, the space of seeming is the place of the transvestite, who plays phallic hide-and-seek, and Paula Poundstone and Ellen DeGeneres are both mild transvestites on stage; but my argument is that they are not so much seeming, on stage, as seeming to seem. I mean to argue that this is equal to disappearing. To get at how this works, I want to consult the locus classicus of these dialectics: Gabriel Marcel's *Being and Having: An Existentialist Diary.*[5] At first glance, Marcel's opposition of being and having would appear to share nothing with Lacan's. "Being," for one thing, is no mere gerund. What Lacan and Marcel have in common, however, is a fascination with what in human experience is detachable.

Marcel would usually say disposable, that is, under one's control, sacrificeable. The difference is that he tends not to believe in the disposability of anything important, whereas Lacan would seem to believe that detachability is the source of a thing's importance. From Marcel's view, for example, the body is not really disposable—even, paradoxically, by suicide (*BH*, 82–83). My body is mine, but it is also me. The world already fails to split into subjects and objects, without going farther into it than one's flesh (12). Corporeity is the "frontier district" between being and having (82), and pain, which drives my body into me (my body when it is in pain seems me rather than mine to the extent of the pain), is the frontier guide for conducting having into being (85, 86, 115, 144).

The project of this essay is to find in the disappearance of DeGeneres and Poundstone at the divesting moment the revelation of a technique—based in laughter as opposed to pain—for making the conversion of having into being impossible.

I want the being/having/seeming trinity to work out, in part, because the title and mantra of DeGeneres's best-selling book is *My Point . . . And I Do Have One.*[6] The joke is, of course, that she insists she has a point even as she reveals that she does not, but of course she only *seems* not to have one; the punch line is the point. That is to say that the apparently unwitting revelation of female blather is clothing for the concealed weapon, the masculine punch. But this is all to say what DeGeneres has and seems to be. Who is she?

Or who is Paula Poundstone? She seems knowable; in her stand-up routine, she speaks about herself, sometimes intimately, and asks us in the audience about ourselves. The funnier half of her Harvard concert is her extended colloquies with the audience. The open egalitarianism of the approach, however, is limited by the running gag: that this is Harvard but the audience keeps saying inane things. One student seems so unsure what she is supposed to be learning in a class that Poundstone commandeers a cellular phone to call her roommate; gradually Poundstone, by interrelating her conversations, builds up a whole little society of Harvard vacuousness. It is difficult to estimate the ratio of hostility and affability in this, which is itself part of the interest. The hostility provides the laughs, but at the same time it obscures the shift of attention from what Poundstone is and has to what the audience is and has.

Poundstone picks out an audience member: "What do you do?" she wonders. It is not unheard-of as a conversational gambit, but improvising comedians use the question so often in their routines that it gives pause. Why wedge such a dull opener into a routine that needs energizing? The answer is that there is a charge to it in the stand-up setting, because stand-ups at their deepest are in awe of the fact that people do *anything.* Stand-up, in the minds of comedians, is a way of continuing to do nothing. A precondition of the popularity of the *Seinfeld* show (on each episode of which, contrary to universal opinion, a lot actually happens) is that we concur. In the cultural imagination, stand-ups like, formerly, poets are adored for (what seems to be) their simple devotion to being. Poundstone interviews one member of the audience:

> PP: This guy here with a red tie. What do you do for a living, sir?
> RT: Engineering.
> PP: You do engineering? Where do you do your engineering at?
> RT: Mechanical engineering.
> PP: "Mechanical engineering." Can you see that's a "what" and not a "where," sir? . . . Sir, get off the script, damn it. . . . It's as if you went over it in your head before you left the house. I'll tell her "engineering" and then I'll tell her "mechanical engineering." I don't care what anybody asks me, I'm only gonna say, "mechanical engineering."

When it turns out that the mechanical engineer develops new furniture, Poundstone asks, "Somehow the chair isn't good enough anymore?" The engineer replies that he develops new chairs for prisons; this calls down a barrage of questions, the last one of which is:

> PP: What were you told before you invented your last chair?
> RT: Pricing.
> PP: Because the prisoners are cheap?

And the joke here, as I understand it, is Poundstone's suspicion that Red Tie really does nothing—he is working from a script. Similarly with the student: does she really go to Harvard? Does she actually attend classes? Why can't people account for what they do?

This means that people cannot account for how they go about being adults. Work is the successful outcome of childhood. Being turns into doing to the extent that one grows up, perhaps goes to college, and gets a job. The unfortunate corollary is that, insofar as adults identify themselves by what they do, they identify themselves by one of the most disposable of the things they have. Even a job close to one's self-definition can seem an arbitrary consequence of the transition out of childhood. Stand-up comedy, I want to hypothesize, works to protect being not by cultivating pain that drives having into being but by a reversal of all that Gabriel Marcel most cherishes: by disposing of all that can be disposed of, so that being has, to the extent possible, nothing at all to pain it.

But Poundstone makes another claim on adulthood. Here is what she has.

v.

"I have two foster daughters," says Poundstone, whereupon the subject immediately becomes clothing and gender. It is a bad time, Poundstone complains, for buying clothes for kids. She hates buying pink frilly things for girls; what is the decisive difference between boy and girl babies that requires such a dramatic distinction of outfits? Only the penis and vagina define the difference, Poundstone asserts, adding (so that we know she still is close to the infantile position she describes) that "this is only the third time in my life I ever said those words."

Does DeGeneres have a baby? Near the beginning of her recent CD, *Taste This,* DeGeneres shares some personal feelings with the audience.[7] The hard thing about the job of comedian is the traveling: three-and-a-half weeks are too long to be on the road. She is forced to ask friends to water the plants, turn on the lights, and "make sure that the mobile over the crib isn't tangled or the baby's gonna get bored. [laugh] So that's, you know, hard to impose on people. [pause] I don't have a baby; I have a mobile and a crib. [laugh] I just have 'em. I enjoy those things; I don't know why."

DeGeneres continues: "I want to have a baby. I don't want to *have* the baby. I just wanna [very fast:] have-a-baby."

She concedes that "it's a beautiful thing you end up with—I'm aware of that. But I want to have a new washer and dryer but I don't think I'd go through *that* for *that.*"

She does have a goddaughter, who is "the light of my life. She's three [pause] or five, or something. She lives clear across town—I don't have that kind of time."

What does all this baby talk amount to? The answer begins with the observation that DeGeneres and Poundstone are both forced to acknowledge parenting as the most inevitable form, for a woman, of having. On the other hand, the most inevitable form of having for a stand-up—controlling the mike, talking down to us, solely erect—is having the phallus; in Freudian terms, of course, penis envy ought to be redirected in the former direction and not the latter.[8] (Joking is an all-male sport in Freud.) This would not be worth mentioning if it were not the kind of judgment a comedy audience is conventionally as ready to make as Freud. The phallic comedian is funny on the proviso that his phallicness is merely one more encumbrance—that he is rather than has or does—but the female comedian begins by seeming to usurp the phallus. Poundstone grants the obligation of facing the problem in her depreciation of the penis as a determinant of baby clothing; the effect is to shift attention from phallus to baby without conceding that the latter is merely a surrogate of the former, and then from the baby to the baby's clothing, as a realm of perfect newfound freedom (her baby's or, by extension, her own).

DeGeneres's approach to the bind is especially subtle. Her technique, first of all, is always to seem to assert that she has children, as for example, again, in her book, when she describes her typical day: "Okay, that brings me to around six o'clock when I go pick up the kids from day care. Not my kids; I drive a van for the neighborhood moms who are busy" (MP, 171). The effect is always of un-having the baby. Babies are apparitions in De-Generes's life. They are always verbally constructed and then jokingly deconstructed: DeGeneres supposes and DeGeneres disposes.

The joke gets more complicated when DeGeneres claims not to have a baby but to have, anyway, a crib and mobile. In the CD routine, this is merely because she enjoys them. In the book version, she also wants to be prepared; she has a nurse, and "in case I decide to have a baby, it's nice to know that Bok Choy is there" (73). But even Bok Choy's function gets attached to DeGeneres's own regressive pleasure: "To keep him in practice, I have him read me a bedtime story every night and occasionally I let him burp me."

It is safe to say that self-babying is never far removed among DeGeneres's temptations; being burped by Bok Choy is as sensual a pleasure as she ever, in stand-up routines, reports. It is as if the correct outcome of penis envy for her is the subversion of Freudian/Lacanian wisdom: the phallus becomes the baby, all right, but the baby and not the phallus becomes her. (It may be worth noting that on *Ellen,* in a season devoted to the coy delay of "Ellen's" coming out as a lesbian, the only people who came out early in the season were her parents, who came out as heterosexuals, against the horror of which DeGeneres literally started babbling baby talk.) Key for my purposes is that if Poundstone discusses children produced, for her, painlessly (they are foster children), DeGeneres hovers around the painfulness in order to jettison it more imaginatively. "I don't want to *have* the baby—I just wanna have-a-baby."

Having a baby in the sense of parturition means separating from it, though having a baby, in DeGeneres's imaginary sense, means possessing it. But possessing it means possessing it as a consumer good, like a washer and dryer, which means possessing it as a disposable item. That is how, in the stand-up ethos, anything at all is possessed, so possession turns out just to mean constant separation, whenever the tour schedule demands it. Everything is always left behind, detachable, alienable. If pain, according to a Christian existentialist, forces having into being, then DeGeneres uses laughter, as the antithesis of pain, to detach being from having altogether. The end, for Marcel, is universal being, being that finds the universe increasingly indisposable to infinity. The end, for DeGeneres, is evacuated being, which finds the universe disposable down and into the body itself, as if the body were a baby one chooses not to have.

v.

It is difficult by glancing to tell the title of Ellen DeGeneres's book. In large letters, at the top, is "ELLEN"; in somewhat smaller letters, at the bottom, is "DEGENERES." In between is a picture of DeGeneres, and to the side of her face is, in somewhat smaller letters yet, "MY POINT," followed by an ellipsis, and then in quite small letters, "AND I DO HAVE ONE." It looks at first glance as if the title is "Ellen," which is of course the title of her TV show. "My Point . . . And I Do Have One" looks like the gratuitous digression—between Ellen and DeGeneres—that the asseveration itself is meant to head off.

The title phrase appears twice in the book. In the first instance of it, DeGeneres is discussing "ridiculous fears" (e.g., "Fear of combing your hair so hard your head bleeds while your date is waiting in the front room" [*MP,* 109]), which takes her to the subject of the "boogey man." Here, infantilism fails as escape, which forces DeGeneres off on a digression: "boogey men" reminds her of K.C. and the Sunshine Band and their song, which

DeGeneres "danced to . . . as much as the rest of you in 1975" (110). Then: "But I digress. My point . . . and I do have one, is that I still get scared at night. Every tiny creak, every little noise, I open my eyes wide and listen with them."

The iteration of the phrase comes in the middle of an anecdote set in Maine, which DeGeneres momentarily confuses with Montana. DeGeneres is camping when she hears "some kind of noise": "Since I'm alone in the middle of the woods, I'm a little bit scared" (145). It is, however, only a family of deer—"mother, father, and two little baby deer"—drinking from a brook; their cuteness causes DeGeneres to think, "I wish I had a gun." No: she did not have that wish or fantasy, but she did go camping in Maine. No: she never went camping in Maine, but she did spend some nights at the Hilton on Maui. Finally: "My point . . . and I do have one, is that I was being sarcastic. I don't understand hunting at all."

It is evident what causes DeGeneres to digress: fear. In the first story, the digression is away from the fear, because fear is the point. In the second story, fear is the subject of the digression (that she is scared in the woods is a baroque way to introduce her antihunting message). In both cases, the fear is of being alone in uncertainty; in both cases, DeGeneres hears a noise whose origin she cannot see. I hope it is not illicit to force the form of DeGeneres's stand-up onto the content: she digresses, she blathers to get the alien noise out of her head and her own noise substituted for it.

Terrors, by the time DeGeneres is, by calendar measure, an adult, have not been transcended but have been transformed. Once the terror has been redefined, not as natural or supernatural but as human, for example the date waiting in the parlor, aloneness becomes not the source of DeGeneres's terror but the best defense against it: she becomes the baby doe whose only hope is to avoid the ones with guns. This is a self-destructive syndrome for a performer, but a good breeding ground for escapist art. It is as if DeGeneres chatters to an audience to palliate fears whose origin is also the audience.

> Someone recently wrote a letter recently to a magazine recently (and you know it must really be recently since I've mentioned it so many times) asking, "Why does Ellen DeGeneres always wear pants and never skirts?"
>
> I'm guessing that the person who wrote that letter meant skirt, a noun signifying an article of clothing, and not skirt, a verb defined as, "to evade or elude (as a topic of conversation) by circumlocution." Because, if they mean the *verb* skirt, well, they're dead wrong. I'm always skirting. (93)

She is skirting here, in fact, with violent decisiveness: to skirt is to digress is to escape is not to explain wearing pants.

Then DeGeneres returns to the point—she wears pants because at summer camp she was "tattooed with designs of bougainvillea," which provoked an attack of bees; this "point" has the look of another skirting, unless you remember that DeGeneres had recommended explaining sex to children in terms of male bees buzzing around the queen (77). Is DeGeneres approaching a confession? For a millisecond, she seems to want to.

> All kidding aside—actually, I change my mind. I don't want to put all kidding aside. I want the kidding right there in front where we all can see it. The main point of this book is kidding. If I put all kidding aside, there would be nothing left but nonkidding, and believe me, that wouldn't make a very interesting book. (94)

In sum: DeGeneres wants to get to her "main point." She wants to put her main point, exhibitionistically, in front for all to see and not aside. Except: kidding is her point. She does not allow her kidding to revert to nonkidding the way she allows her imaginary kids to revert to nonkids. (If skirting is not having to explain not wearing skirts, kidding is not having to explain not raising kids.) Which is to say: digression itself is the point. What she does not wish to put aside is the aside. The presence she is after is disembodied and absentminded.

> It is unfair to be judged by appearances [DeGeneres continues]. Even though I don't wear skirts, I know I'm a girl. . . . I'm a person who's a woman, and I don't like dresses or panty hose or heels. I guess you could chuckle and say that I'm a woman trapped in a woman's body. But, if you did say that, nobody would know what you meant, and probably more than one person would ask you to kindly stop chuckling. (94–95)

I should probably allow DeGeneres's mot—"I'm a woman trapped in a woman's body"—to shine by its own brilliance. I want, however, to attach three addenda.

1. The witticism may represent the only moment in the book that does not feel like skirting. The meanings of the terms finally coalesce—DeGeneres does not skirt why she does not skirt.

2. But witticisms of this sort—the sort that do not skirt—are precisely what the inquisitive public is not supposed to welcome. DeGeneres does not

116

expect anyone to find humor in the horror of her perfectly fitting entrapment.

3. Skirting is refusing to put "all kidding aside." What is made visible—"right there in front where all can see it"—is evasion. Joking is the camouflaging of camouflage: what we do not see is the evacuated stage.[9]

vi.

Who is Ellen? This is the question that DeGeneres keeps posing, only to keep on posing it. The first words of the book are "Who am I?" (*MP*, 3); by the end of the book, the question seems not merely a formal device for instigating an answer. A comedian has, I have mentioned, an odd relation to his or her identity, caused by the indiscretion of role and reality, personality and character, having and being. A comedian whose name is Jerry Seinfeld playing a character named Jerry Seinfeld is perhaps the limit case. A comedian whose name is Ellen DeGeneres playing a character named Ellen Morgan in a show called *Ellen* (after the character? after the star?) comes close. This sort of imbrication is almost unheard-of in a dramatic series.[10]

I call the comedian's position abject for the following reason. A fascination with what is detachable may be fetishistic if its object is a distraction from what one fears to lose, what one fears one has never really possessed. A fascination with what is detachable may be abject if it concerns what one fears cannot be lost, what will always return. It is not anxiety about the cutting off of the penis that causes abjectness: it is anxiety that fingernails, hair, excrement, and the corpse itself will always be with you, despite all cuttings, excretings, and buryings. These are symmetrical unhappinesses in the realm of the disposable. To Lacan, one's relation to the phallus is basically fetishistic, since we choose not to face its unpossessibility. To Marcel, one's relation to the body is (this is not his term or tonality) abject, since the failure of the subject/object binarism is—in the first place—based on its undispossessibility.

In the case of comedians, the appearance of phallicism implicit in stand up itself is what makes the abjection funny. But the source of the phallus's power is, as always, its detachability: it is the detachable mike that comedians adore, which is to say that abjection produces a fetishistic relation to anything that can come off. The thing, on the other hand, that always returns to comedians is their lives, apparently, and it may seem dismaying or disgusting. The close approach of having and being seems to a comedian, as opposed to a Christian existentialist, dreadful. From what one can gather from understated autobiographical interludes of her book, DeGeneres's early life seems to have been filled with fears, self-loathings, cruelty, two-way incomprehension—and so on, the usual abject comedian's fare. She was, for one thing, "a little hefty" (*MP*, 8), and you feel that her subsequent losing of weight is tantamount to abandoning her old life. This is the extreme fantasy of disposability. (Possibly one can feel in her wish to have-a-baby without having one the shame of that old weight.) The point is to lose everything for the sake of some essence of "Ellen." [11]

So using "Ellen" as the title of her show does not seem to fictionalize its signified. It seems to protect it from attributes. The show *Ellen* was originally called *These Friends of Mine*. It seems, in retrospect, a particularly misguided title: the characters on the show who surround DeGeneres are rather uninteresting, compared for example to the Seinfeld rectangle, or even the group around Candice Bergen in *Murphy Brown* or the ensembles that supported Bob Newhart in two shows or Mary Tyler Moore. The thing to notice on the *Ellen* show is the curious Oz-ish bubble that envelops De-Generes as she interacts—charmingly, generously, on "regular" terms (it is unclear to me whether I am describing the character or the actor)—with her "friends." *These Friends of Mine* placed an awkward weight on the having mode—but being is the show's essence.

In a chapter of *My Point* called "Ellenvision," DeGeneres begins: "I feel extremely lucky to have my own TV show."

> I guess what I'm trying to say is that I'm so happy that my show is as good, and as based in reality, as it is. (59)

Are we one step behind, here? This sounds like plausibly modest gratification. Yet can DeGeneres, a plexus of insecurities, hesitations, and self-effacements, along with their compensations and overcompensations, be registering simple contentment with what she has? And whatever could "reality" mean to her in a book that mixes fantasy, invention, autobiography, opinion, and "material" (jokes without ulterior motive)? Is DeGeneres as happy with the realism of the show as she is with the realism of her next sentence?

> You wouldn't believe some of the shows that were offered me by network executives before I accepted *Ellen* (which, by the way, is named after Ellen Burstyn).

What follows is an attempt to suggest that everything DeGeneres does, including playing with coming out or actually coming out as a lesbian, is meant to protect the pure, attributeless, Ellen. That is to say that "Ellen" needs to be protected so thoroughly from the life of Ellen DeGeneres that it might as well be attached to the life of Ellen Burstyn. Poundstone's abjection is interesting, and I shall consider it briefly, but I mean to concentrate on DeGeneres's project of founding her comedy on abjection by treating all her biography as an encumbrance, by making a point of the digression between Ellen ("MY POINT . . . AND I DO HAVE ONE"—even the metapoint survives an ellipsis) and DeGeneres.

vii.

Paula Poundstone begins her HBO routine at Harvard by announcing that her body is all pain to her. "I wish I had a degenerative disease. I'm tired and achy all the time, anyway." This remark leads to a discussion of the guy in the wheelchair on Wal-Mart commercials: Poundstone begins with abjection (the mortifying body makes a nice reference to DeGeneres) and wishes not to be cured of it but to exacerbate it. She wishes to slough her body entirely. This is the context in which to locate her first conversation with a member of the audience, early in the concert.

> PP (to student): What are you studying?
> Student: Women's Studies.
> PP: So are you getting credit right now? [lots of laughter] I am, by all accounts, a woman.

That is: a woman trapped in a woman's body. Thus when Poundstone says (in dialogue with a blind man, wondering about the compensatory power of his other senses), "I don't have sex so I always assumed that I'd have expertise in another area. . . . If I played croquet I'd be really fantastic," we assume that the joke is not merely based on the *Lysistrata* protocol (frustrated sex is funnier than sex).

Poundstone is almost literally at pains in her routine to get across that "I don't have sex. I'm not intimate with people. I don't have friends." She takes her foster child to a bookstore while a reading of once-banned books is in progress; she is forced to distract the child from a passage of *Lady Chatterly's Lover* that apparently has much to do with heavy surf and sunrises. Poundstone comments: "None of it was ringing a bell. I am no expert on sex—for sure—but this was not something vaguely familiar to me." The one time she had sex that was "not totally horrible," she thought of it as at best a "freshly stirred glass of Tang."

You might sense in the judgment a description of *heterosex*: perhaps

Poundstone found sex with men so distasteful that she realized her own lesbianism. But no: "Sex has never been my area—which is good. My campaign contributions can be accepted on all quarters. I don't have that side. No one is much attracted to me and I don't care to be much attractive to anyone else." She is in fact a lesbian. She makes this last remark in a diatribe against homosexuals who aspire to donate money to Dole: how can this be? "We disapprove of our *own* lifestyle? We beat *ourselves* up in parking lots?" The way to forestall beating oneself up in parking lots is not self-approval, however; it is abjection so complete that Poundstone is disincarnated by it.

The desire, even as a joke, to have a degenerative disease is the desire not to have any body at all: to have so much pain as to finish it off. The desire not to have desire, in fact, is not the challenge so much as the essence of the joke. If joking can alleviate pain by distraction from the body, it can (the logic of joking would go) eliminate pain only by fantasizing the destruction of the body.

viii.

In DeGeneres's book, her HBO concert "One Night Stand," and her CD, there is perhaps one reference to homosexuality: in a bit about "Trivial Pursuits," she quotes the question, "What is the only animal that mates while going 80 miles per hour?" and admits that "Danny Kaye was a bad guess." Her own body only appears in her routines as something to keep covered.[12] In "One Night Stand," she is amazed by the premise of a health farm: "They want you to be naked to get rid of stress." Her CD culminates with a reflection on public toilets, which begins with the embarrassed response she gives when she has left the door unhinged and someone barges in accidentally: "That's okay." This leads to an extended fantasy on what would occur if the intruder, having taken the remark literally, returned with friends: "Get the ramrod, this one is tight."

Possibly DeGeneres's defining routine is "Scary Things." The running joke is that she keeps referring to scary things as maximally scary until she flashes on a scarier thing; then at the end the bit turns absurdist, in the manner of an Escher staircase, when the ultimately scary thing is a lamb, and DeGeneres is forced into contortions of paralogism to get the lamb to seem the ne plus ultra of frightfulness. The first scary thing is a spider in a shoe, then baby spiders in the other shoe, then a snake up the leg. (Does this seem like parenting in reverse?) Next:

You're on a beach playing frisbee with a friend or not even a friend just somebody you're attracted to and they had a frisbee. . . . And they throw the frisbee . . . and it goes into a cave and you're like spelunking into the abyss of the cave . . . and you're like, "hey, how come my frisbee feels squishy?" and all of a sudden you realize what you're squeezing is a bat.

The bat bites her on the ear, and sharks attack the blood. And next she is going to look for a "thing," to get out of a house occupied by a perverted uncle, and what she finds herself squeezing this time is the lamb.

It takes no formal training to register that the descent into the abyss followed by the squeezing of the squishy thing reads like a sexual nightmare. It all begins with a game of frisbee with someone DeGeneres is attracted to—what is the relevance of that digression? The bat cave is where the infatuation repairs after the beach.

DeGeneres goes Poundstone one extra depletion. If Poundstone has only infrequent and joyless sex, DeGeneres is almost asexual in her stand-up presentation. To say that her sexuality is of the Peter Pan variety sets off a myriad of implications in the Marjorie Garber vein: let us say that DeGeneres has one sort of sexuality submerged in one sort of presexuality.[13] She is attracted on the beach to a "they," and no doubt the "they" is a "she," but the fantasy of the bat cave sounds exactly like the sort of nightmare that Freud analyzes: it will turn out to reveal some sort of misconceived sexual disturbance in the life of the child (the bat girl) that only later will cause hysterical symptoms in light of advanced sophistication. It is unclear whether DeGeneres wants to land us, or whether she in fact manages to land herself, in the childish inconceivable trauma or in the adult revisiting and symptomizing of it. Possibly the laugh here is in the regressive ambiguity. Is knowledge of the body repressed or unlearned? Is the body itself decoded or disclaimed? Do bats and frisbees stand for birds and bees, or for something more primitive or infantile?

Where is DeGeneres heading? On the front of the book, between ELLEN and DEGENERES, there is Ellen herself, smiling at the prospective buyer or incipient reader with great gratifying normality. This picture can be described, but there is little to be gained by describing it. It is a picture of Ellen DeGeneres.

In the picture on the back, Ellen is sitting in a corner of a room. She is pulling her legs in tight against her body. One hand is around one ankle; the other hand is against the other. One knee is pulled up to the level of Ellen's bowing head; the other knee is lower. The reason one knee is higher is that Ellen has one foot up on a low parallelepiped of some kind, which she is sitting on in the corner, and the other foot on the floor. The thing she sits on in the corner is unknown to me; it is perhaps three inches high, a foot wide for sitting, two feet long, and it is snug into the corner of the wall. It has an oblong hole, maybe three inches long, in its width. An opening? An opening to a trap?

We do not see Ellen's face: she is looking straight down into the small gap behind her knees. We are faced only by her cropped hair. What on earth is she doing? First of all, she is hiding, in a childish way: by contracting her body into as tight a space as she can in the restricting corner of a room. She is attempting to make herself minuscule; she wants to be too enfolded for any assault.

Second of all, she is hiding by a less common stratagem. The wall behind her and to her side is white. The floor and box beneath her, either naturally or as the result of shadows, are white too but almost gray. The color scheme is mimicked by Ellen's clothing: whiter shirt, white but grayer pants. Her socks are white. She wears white sneakers with whitish-peachish laces. Her arms seem to be tan, probably inadvertently, and she has on rings and a bracelet, but she has her arms exposed for a purpose, and what they do is exhibit the body that is trying to furl toward the wall. Also, her head, shoulders, and the curve of her arms form a kind of zero. Her circle of hair is blond; under the circumstances, blondness reads like blandness reads like blankness, another zero, like a dumb blond stone on the ring of curving shoulders and arms. She is trying to be the room, a chameleon who works not by color but by colorlessness.

She is doing one thing more. On the front cover, she faces the camera, smiling so ingratiatingly that we seem to recognize her as the girl next door we never knew. The space between the essential "Ellen" and the histori-cal "DeGeneres" is almost entirely filled in: the comedian is merely the woman herself on stage, no more artificial than that. So what is Ellen doing on the back? She is so recessive that we do not register, at first, what she is doing with her head. She is bowing. She bows her head in shame, perhaps, having been banished to the corner for committing some indecency. She is also taking her bow, at the end of her performance. Her moment of pride is equal to her moment of shame. (She is an inverse Lenny Bruce, whose shame existed to be displayed as pride.) This is the essence of stand-up.

Ellen goes yet further inward: at the conclusion of the performance, at the divesting crisis, what we get is some hint of retransvesting (sneak-ers, pants, cropped hair) subsumed in Ellen's overwhelming desire not to be clothed at all or naked either, not sitting or standing, neither ashamed nor proud, but to be unborn, rewombed—the obvious term for her posture is fetal—like all her unhaved children. If her book were a musical—*Ellen!*—enwombed is where she would be by now. The ideal hypothesis of stand-up—that pain is shunted when abjection is stood up—has been transcended; Ellen's last hope is that if you carry abjection far enough into the infantile, all pain is consigned to an unspeakable future. But this is the end of stand-up.

Notes

Introduction

1   Steve Allen made the 80 percent estimate. I heard him make it, but I cannot footnote
    the occasion. In 1975 Samuel S. Janus conducted an extensive polling of comedians,
    interviewing 55 nationally known stand-ups (51 were men). Unfortunately, he did not
    summarize their religious affiliations, except to say that a majority were Jewish. He
    also refers to his sample as "homogeneous in terms of religion" (173), which suggests
    much more than a majority, though he notes that, as of 1975, diversity was on the in-
    crease. In 1992, Ronald L. Smith compiled a list of 138 stand-up comedians or teams
    without regard to era, though the list was heavily weighted toward the present; my
    estimate is that around 40 percent are Jewish. Although the evidence here is sketchy,
    it is clear that the percentage of Jews among nationally known stand-ups has declined
    from 1960 to 1975 to the present—possibly it has halved.

All of Janus's 55 reported themselves to be heterosexual. I do not infer from this that they were. All I need to know is the apparently unanimous sense of the importance of that presentation. Whether or not these Jewish men were heterosexual, they were heterosexual for America. See Samuel S. Janus, "The Great Comedians: Personality and Other Factors," *American Journal of Psychoanalysis* 35 (1975): 169–74; and Ronald L. Smith, *Who's Who in Comedy: Comedians, Comics, and Clowns from Vaudeville to Today's Stand-Ups* (New York: Facts on File, 1992).

2   A brief justification for thinking of the Kennedy assassination as a turning point in the history of stand-up will come in a footnote to chapter 4. The comedic moment I am beginning to describe is a function of the Eisenhower years, though for Brooks and Reiner and for Nichols and May, the fruition of their careers together seems timed to present a correlative to the election of Kennedy. Whatever it may mean, and I do not begin to speculate about it in this book, such paradigmatic Jewish comedians as Mort Sahl and Lenny Bruce felt it essential to their stand-up acts to present heterodox views of the assassination, sometimes to the detriment of humor. The history of stand-up went another way.

3   See Julia Kristeva, *Powers of Horror: An Essay on Abjection*, trans. Leon S. Roudiez (New York: Columbia University Press, 1982).

4   I have this from Robert A. Stebbins, *The Laugh-Makers: Standup Comedy as Art, Business, and Life-Style* (Montreal: McGill-Queen's University Press, 1990). Stebbins has it on the authority of *Webster's Collegiate Dictionary.* The first use in the *OED* is also from 1966.

1. Inrage: A Lenny Bruce Joke and the Topography of Stand-Up

1   See Sigmund Freud, "Jokes and Their Relation to the Unconscious" (1905), in *The Standard Edition of the Complete Psychological Works of Sigmund Freud,* trans. James Strachey (London: Hogarth Press, 1960), 8:125–27 (hereafter abbreviated *SE*).

2   See Paul E. McGhee and Jeffrey H. Goldstein, *Handbook of Humor Research,* vol. 1, *Basic Issues* (New York: Springer-Verlag, 1983); see esp. Marianne LaFrance, "Felt versus Feigned Funniness: Issues in Coding Smiling and Laughing," 1–12; and Paul E. McGhee, "The Role of Arousal and Hemispheric Lateralization in Humor," 21, 23, 28. The gender disparity comes with the following caveat: women can distinguish between their laughter and their sense of funniness if "instructed to do so" (23). My own caveat is that the book was published in 1983; conceivably, women are more suspicious of their laughter now.

3   In these three theorems, I make no attempt to distinguish contemporary stand-up (or, since stand-up was named in or around the year of Lenny Bruce's death, stand-up per se) from ancestral, vaudeville forms of comedy performance. This chapter is based on an early essay, and I saw Lenny Bruce as unusually resistant to these intimacy criteria; in fact, contemporary stand-up is generally resistant to them. Nevertheless, the audience-performer intimacy is still in place, which lends interest to the

struggle; you cannot understand contemporary stand-up abjection without acknowledging that intimacy as a first step.

4 See Albert Goldman, *Ladies and Gentlemen—Lenny Bruce!!* (New York: Random House, 1974) (hereafter abbreviated *LB*). That Bruce was outrageous was such a cliché that it annoyed Bruce (41). On the moral outrage of his audience, see 277. On his own moral outrage, see 473.

5 From the record, *To Is a Preposition, Come Is a Verb* (Douglas, 1964?). I borrow the convention of dividing the joke into breath lines from *Breaking It Up! The Best Routines of the Stand-up Comics,* ed. Ross Firestone (New York: Bantam, 1975).

6 See Jerry M. Suls, "Cognitive Processes in Humor Appreciation," in McGhee and Goldstein, *Handbook of Humor Research,* 39–57.

7 See Mahadev L. Apte, "Humor Research, Methodology, and Theory in Anthropology," in McGhee and Goldstein, *Handbook of Humor Research,* 183–212; for ritual clowning, see ibid., 188–92.

8 Mary Douglas, *Implicit Meanings: Essays in Anthropology* (London: Routledge and Kegan Paul, 1975), 92.

9 Lenny Bruce, *The Berkeley Concert* (Reprise/Warner, 1969).

10 Lenny Bruce, *The Sick Humor of Lenny Bruce* (Fantasy, 1959).

11 Cf. Carl Hill, *The Soul of Wit: Joke Theory from Grimm to Freud* (Lincoln: University of Nebraska Press, 1993), 133ff. Hill believes that modern Jewish humor began in the Enlightenment; self-mockery was part of a general critique of difference that would make possible universal rationality and assimilation for Jews. I read Hill's excellent book after writing this essay, or else I would have alluded to it more frequently.

12 See, for example, Nathan Glazer and Daniel Patrick Moynihan, *Beyond the Melting Pot: The Negroes, Puerto Ricans, Jews, Italians, and Irish of New York City,* 2d ed. (Cambridge, Mass.: MIT Press, 1970), 161.

13 That Fanny Brice had to feign her Yiddish I learned from Irving Howe, *World of Our Fathers* (New York: Harcourt Brace Jovanovich, 1976), 563.

14 M. P. Baumgartner, *The Moral Order of a Suburb* (New York: Oxford University Press, 1988), 56.

15 This is not quite true. I have described Bruce's humor as occurring at the intersection of urban *Yiddishkeit* and Protestant suburban civility, which would seem to leave Catholics out of the equation; but it is likely that much of Bruce's troubles came from Catholic indignation. Bruce speculated at his Berkeley concert that he was arrested in New York for making fun of Cardinal Spellman; Goldman produces evidence that he was arrested in Chicago for jokes about the pope (*LB,* 398–99). City Catholics, apparently, were able to make a last stand against the sort of civility that demanded Bruce's affronts. But this is perhaps a variety of not getting the joke, and the remainder of my thesis is that the law, despite its obtuseness, did.

16 See Paul E. McGhee, "Humor Development: Toward a Life Span Approach," in McGhee and Goldstein, *Handbook of Humor Research,* 123–24. See also Samuel S. Janus, "The Great Comedians: Personality and Other Factors," *American Journal of*

Psychoanalysis 35 (1975). Janus notes that the fathers of his fifty-five well-known comedians were "described for the most part as either absent, uninterested, or overtly disapproving" (171). He observes elsewhere that 80 percent of the comedians had been, at some time, in psychoanalysis, out of a need for "a power struggle with an overwhelming father" (172), and that the technique for winning the struggle was to turn the psychoanalyst from father into audience, inviting him to the show. Psychoanalysis, apparently, can replace the law as nostalgia for a never experienced, fully engaged antagonism, which the comedian wishes to charm.

17 See Janus, "Great Comedians," 173. Janus looked for successful child comedians, but found none. Also, many comedians in his study felt that being young was a comic handicap.

18 Herbert Blau, *The Audience* (Baltimore, Md.: Johns Hopkins University Press, 1990), x.

2. Nectarines: Carl Reiner and Mel Brooks

1 I shall be quoting from three records in which the character appears: *2000 Years with Carl Reiner and Mel Brooks* (World-Pacific, 1960), *2000 and One Years with Carl Reiner and Mel Brooks* (Capitol, 1961), and *2000 and Thirteen* (Warner, 1973).

2 Some good work has been done. For a poststructuralist, Freudian account of humor, see Jerry Aline Flieger, *The Purloined Punch Line: Freud, Comic Theory, and Postmodern Texts* (Baltimore, Md.: Johns Hopkins University Press, 1991); for a rival, historicizing account of Freudian humor theory, see Carl Hill, *The Soul of Wit: Joke Theory from Grimm to Freud* (Lincoln: University of Nebraska Press, 1993); on the postmodern politics of comedy, see Philip Auslander, *Presence and Resistance: Postmodernism and Cultural Politics in Contemporary American Performance* (Ann Arbor: University of Michigan Press, 1992). It would have been helpful to read Mark Simpson's "The Straight Men of Comedy," in *Because I Tell a Joke or Two: Comedy, Politics, and Social Difference,* ed. Stephen Wagg (New York: Routledge, 1998), 137–45, before writing this essay.

3 Cf. Mary Douglas, *Implicit Meanings: Essays in Anthropology* (London: Routledge and Kegan Paul, 1975), esp. the chapter "Jokes." Douglas describes a joke as a "play upon form" (92). We differ, however, when she goes on to say that the frivolity of a joke is in its "exhilarating sense of freedom from form in general." I think Douglas underestimates the formal requirements of the joke itself.

4 See Eve Kosofsky Sedgwick, *Epistemology of the Closet* (Berkeley: University of California Press, 1990), 163–67, 182–212.

5 Janus, "Great Comedians," 173. Amazingly, this study by an academic psychologist concludes that "none of this sample were homosexual," as if this could be known. The next sentence reads, "While this seems unusual for show business, it apparently reflects the situation for comedians"; note also this similar remark by a comedian named Mark Breslin, who is asked a question not about homosexuals but about

women in comedy. "Stand-up is one of the last bastions of male heterosexual machismo in show business. . . . Very few homosexual males are in stand-up comedy. This is very interesting considering there are so many in the theatre and music" (quoted in Robert A. Stebbins, *The Laugh-Makers: Standup Comedy as Art, Business, and Life-Style* [Montreal: McGill-Queen's University Press, 1990], 105).

6   Reiner is quoted in Kenneth Tynan, "Frolics and Detours of a Short Hebrew Man," *New Yorker,* 30 October 1978, 47.

7   René Girard, *Deceit, Desire, and the Novel: Self and Other in Literary Structure,* trans. Yvonne Freccero (Baltimore, Md.: Johns Hopkins University Press, 1965).

8   Eve Kosofsky Sedgwick, *Between Men: English Literature and Male Homosocial Desire* (New York: Columbia University Press, 1985), 22–27. See also Gayle Rubin, "The Traffic in Women: Notes on the 'Political Economy' of Sex," in *Toward an Anthropology of Women,* ed. Rayna R. Reiter (New York: Monthly Review Press, 1975), 157–210.

9   Wayne Koestenbaum, *Double Talk: The Erotics of Male Literary Collaboration* (New York: Routledge, 1989).

10   Terry Castle, *The Apparitional Lesbian: Female Homosexuality and Modern Culture* (New York: Columbia University Press, 1993), 66–73.

11   It should be noted for accuracy's sake that the added third party, in Freud's aggressive jokes, is male; in Koestenbaum's aggressive poetry, it is female. I assume this is because joke tellers, unlike twentieth-century poets, do not need so unsubtle a disguise for the nature of their originary, concealed dyad: the usual joke, unlike the usual poem, *is* the disguise.

12   Barbara Johnson, *The Critical Difference: Essays in the Contemporary Rhetoric of Reading* (Baltimore, Md.: Johns Hopkins University Press, 1980), 110–46. I shall now quote Johnson's quoting of "Derrida's quotation of Lacan's paraphrase of Poe's quoted narration." The passage refers to shifting triangles in the Poe story (King, Queen, Minister; police, Minister, Dupin) in which "the second [as it were, point] believ[es] itself invisible because the first has its head stuck in the ground, and all the while let[s] the third calmly pluck its rear" (115). Johnson extends this metaphor to the dyadic relationship of Derrida and Lacan, by way of a transformation of Poe's even-odd guessing game into a head-tail guessing game, thus making available a pun: "But if the complexities of these texts could be reduced to a nice combat between ostriches, a mere game of heads and tails played out to determine a 'winner,' they would have very little theoretical interest. It is, on the contrary, the way in which each mastermind avoids simply becoming the butt of his own joke that displaces the opposition in unpredictable ways and transforms the textual encounter into a source of insight" (119).

13   I apologize here for information I cannot document; I heard Reiner reveal all this far in advance of my realization that I would someday need to footnote it.

14   Tynan, "Frolics and Detours of a Short Hebrew Man," 101.

15   That Huck and Jim's routines have at least a whiff of minstrelsy about them was first broached by Ralph Ellison in his essay "Change the Joke and Slip the Yoke," reprinted

in *Shadow and Act* (New York: Random House, 1964), 45–59. For further discussions of the minstrelsy dimension of *Huckleberry Finn,* see Eric Lott, *Love and Theft: Blackface Minstrelsy and the American Working Class* (New York: Oxford University Press, 1993), esp. 31–37; and Shelley Fisher Fishkin, *Was Huck Black? Mark Twain and African-American Voices* (New York: Oxford University Press, 1993), esp. 88–92. (Fishkin agrees with D. L. Smith, among others, that Jim gets the better of Huck in the "King Sollermun" debate, 89). I have invented Huck and Jim as Reiner and Brooks's precursors on a suggestion of Bill Brown's; I have tried to historicize Reiner and Brooks's comedy on a suggestion of Brown's and the editors of the *Yale Journal of Criticism.*

16 Mark Twain, *The Adventures of Huckleberry Finn* (New York: Modern Library, 1993), 72.

17 Ibid., 118.

18 If Jim is merely a Bones or Tambo, there is little connection in this regard to the 2000-Year-Old Man. But—leaving aside disputes about the accuracy of minstrelsy dialect—I agree with almost all of Fishkin's thesis that Twain's knowledge of black dialect is an insider's knowledge.

19 See John Morreal, ed., *The Philosophy of Laughter and Humor* (Albany: State University of New York Press, 1987). This is Schopenhauer from *The World as Will and Idea:* "The cause of laughter in every case is simply the sudden perception of the incongruity between a concept and the real objects which have been thought through it in some relation, and laughter itself is just the expression of this incongruity" (Morreal, *Philosophy of Laughter and Humor,* 52).

20 Sigmund Freud, "Jokes and Their Relation to the Unconscious" (1905), vol. 8 of *The Standard Edition of the Complete Psychological Works of Sigmund Freud,* trans. James Strachey (London: Hogarth Press, 1960).

21 Lott, *Love and Theft,* 164.

22 Ibid., 163.

23 Stefan Kanfer, *A Summer World: The Attempt to Build a Jewish Eden in the Catskills, From the Days of the Ghetto to the Rise and Decline of the Borscht Belt* (New York: Farrar, Straus, Giroux, 1989), 227.

24 Michael Rogin, "Blackface, White Noise: The Jewish Jazz Singer Finds His Voice," *Critical Inquiry* 18 (1992): 417–53.

25 Charles W. Stein, ed., *American Vaudeville as Seen by Its Contemporaries* (New York: Knopf, 1984), 254.

26 Black performers, unable to revert to whiteface, could only deny themselves even such directness as vaudeville allowed. "Most Negro performers work in a cubicle," Sammy Davis Jr. wrote. "They'd run on, sing twelve songs, dance, and do jokes—but not to people. The jokes weren't done like Milton Berle was doing them, to the audience, they were done between men on stage, as if they didn't have the right to communicate with the people out front" (quoted in Mel Watkins, *On the Real Side: Laughing, Lying, and Signifying—the Underground Tradition of African-American*

Humor That Transformed American Culture, from Slavery to Richard Pryor [New York: Simon and Schuster, 1994], 372). It may be too obvious to add that Berle developed his own method of not appearing directly before his audience: his transvestism defused the usual threat.

27 Carl Reiner, *Enter Laughing* (New York: Simon and Schuster, 1958).

28 Watkins, *On the Real Side,* 90.

29 Irving Howe, *World of Our Fathers* (New York: Harcourt Brace Jovanovich, 1976), 568–69.

30 I apologize again for information recalled from preacademic days: again, it is from an interview with Reiner that I remember garnering that there is such an excised section.

31 One of Brooks's Borscht Belt routines inaugurated his devotion to the comedy of belated reorientation. Brooks himself recalls the bit as follows: "The girl and I walked out from the wings and met in the center of the stage. I said, 'I am a masochist.' She said, 'I am a sadist.' I said, 'Hit me,' and she hit me, very hard, right in the face. And I said, 'Wait a minute, wait a minute, hold it. I think I'm a sadist.' Blackout" (quoted in Kanfer, *Summer World,* 227). All of Brooks's tardy discoveries (that ladies exist, that Joan of Arc is female, that, when he is impersonating an actor, the word for his vocation is "Thespian" not "lesbian," that Reiner thinks that FAG means "fag," that the role of sadist is much preferable) are sexual misidentification jokes, with Brooks at long last resuming the male heterosexual position.

32 Ernest Hemingway, *The Sun Also Rises* (New York: Scribner's, 1970), 116.

33 Donald Ogden Stewart, *Aunt Polly's Story of Mankind* (New York: Doran, 1923); and Stewart, *A Parody Outline of History* (New York: Doran, 1921).

34 Stewart, *Parody Outline of History,* 160.

35 Sedgwick, *Epistemology of the Closet,* 244–45.

36 Brooks more than occasionally reveals that he finds something funny in the idea of fruit per se. Also: in a recent and brilliant episode of the TV sitcom *Mad About You,* Brooks, playing Paul Reiser's uncle, serves him a drink that he worries is too peachy; Reiser, obviously happy just to be in Brooks's presence, replies that it is "just nice" in tribute.

3. Analytic of the Ridiculous: Mike Nichols and Elaine May

1 Immanuel Kant, *Kant's Kritik of Judgment,* trans. J. H. Bernard (New York: Macmillan, 1892), 224 (hereafter abbreviated *KJ*).

2 See Thomas Weiskel, *The Romantic Sublime: Studies in the Structure and Psychology of Transcendence* (Baltimore, Md.: Johns Hopkins University Press, 1976), 19ff.

3 Immanuel Kant, *Observations on the Feeling of the Beautiful and Sublime,* trans. John T. Goldthwait (Berkeley: University of California Press, 1965), 83.

4 Longinus, *Longinus on the Sublime,* trans. W. Rhys Roberts (Cambridge: Cambridge University Press, 1935), 141 (hereafter abbreviated *LS*).

5 See Steven Knapp, *Personification and the Sublime: Milton to Coleridge* (Cambridge,

Mass.: Harvard University Press, 1985), 73, passim. See also Neil Hertz, *The End of the Line: Essays in Psychoanalysis and the Sublime* (New York: Columbia University Press, 1985).

6   Ibid., 82.

7   Jean-François Lyotard, *Lessons on the Analytic of the Sublime,* trans. Elizabeth Rottenberg (Stanford, Calif.: Stanford University Press, 1994), 180.

8   Hertz, *End of the Line,* 161–215.

9   Sigmund Freud, "Medusa's Head" (1922), vol. 18 of *The Standard Edition of the Complete Psychological Works of Sigmund Freud,* trans. James Strachey (London: Hogarth Press, 1955), 273–74.

10 Knapp, *Personification and the Sublime,* 77.

11 Hélène Cixous, "The Laugh of the Medusa," in *New French Feminisms: An Anthology,* ed. Elaine Marks and Isabelle de Courtivron (New York: Schocken, 1981), 255.

12 A full discussion of Phyllis Diller and sublimity would include Burke's belief that "ugliness I imagine . . . to be consistent with an idea of the sublime," if it is "united with such qualities as excite a strong terror." See Edmund Burke, *A Philosophical Enquiry into the Origin of Our Idea of the Sublime and Beautiful* (Notre Dame, Ind.: University of Notre Dame Press, 1968), 119. Kant defines the grotesque as sublimity in combination with unnaturalness (*Observations on the Feeling of the Beautiful and Sublime,* 55). Thomas Weiskel thinks that grotesquerie is the form that the sublime takes "to please us" in our post-Romantic irony (*Romantic Sublime,* 6).

13 On the back of *An Evening with Mike Nichols and Elaine May* (Mercury, 1961) (hereafter abbreviated *E*).

14 On the cover of *E* and also *The Best of Mike Nichols and Elaine May* (Mercury, 1965) (hereafter abbreviated *B*).

15 *Improvisations to Music: Mike Nichols and Elaine May* (Mercury, 1958) (hereafter abbreviated *IM*).

16 *Mike Nichols and Elaine May in Retrospect* (Mercury, 1972). Thanks to Neil Hertz for identifying this album to me.

17 Mary Douglas, *Implicit Meanings: Essays in Anthropology* (London: Routledge and Kegan Paul, 1975), 101.

18 For Nichols's biography, see H. Wayne Schuth, *Mike Nichols* (Boston: Twayne, 1978). Elaine May's father was the Yiddish actor Jack Berlin (see liner notes to *E*).

19 Adam Phillips, *On Kissing, Tickling, and Being Bored: Psychoanalytic Essays on the Unexamined Life* (Cambridge, Mass.: Harvard University Press, 1993), 10, 11.

20 Noelle Oxenhandler, "The Eros of Parenthood," *New Yorker,* 19 February 1996, 47–49.

21 Nathaniel Hawthorne, *The Scarlet Letter* (Boston: St. Martin's Press, 1991), 59–60 (hereafter abbreviated *SL*).

22 See in Weiskel, "Logic of Terror," in *Romantic Sublime,* 83–106.

23 See Sacvan Bercovitch, *The Office of the Scarlet Letter* (Baltimore, Md.: Johns Hopkins University Press, 1991).

4. Journey to the End of the Night: David Letterman with Kristeva, Céline, Scorsese

1   The *Family Feud* audience was asked in the early 1980s to "name an intellectual."
    The winners in the poll were Henry Kissinger, William F. Buckley, Jr., Joyce Brothers,
    Tony Randall, and the host of the show, Richard Dawson, himself.

2   Bill Zehme, "Letterman Lets His Guard Down," *Esquire,* December 1994, 101.

3   *Good Morning, America,* 11 May 1995.

4   Around 1974, Johnny Carson told something like the following joke about one of the
    Watergate burglars, let us say Liddy (let us guess on 15 October 1974, when Liddy
    was released on bail): "Did you see that Gordon Liddy was released from prison?
    [pause] He didn't have the right idea, though. [pause] He went home and broke into
    his house." To extrapolate the Mort Sahl joke idealized by this one, insert the word
    "own": "He went home and broke into his own house." Carson, having established
    the premise of his joke economically but deliberately, races to the punch line so as
    to arrive there a split second ahead of his audience; the final word makes an abrupt
    pop, and the audience, propelled momentarily into the silence, as if in a car that stops
    short, is jolted into laughter. Sahl arrives a split second later: the audience is alerted
    to the joke by the extra word and a facetious drawling tone in Sahl's voice (also slow-
    ing the delivery) and a wicked smile. This is partly a function of Sahl's insecurity (he
    needs to let the audience know he has amused them), but partly also a result of his
    desire to keep his audience depressed (emotionally and hierarchically low).

    If this book had remained a cultural history, I would have used Carson as the first
    term of the perfectionist moment of stand-up: Carson perfected the Mort Sahl politi-
    cal joke; George Carlin foolproofed Brucean profanity. (Later, Robin Williams would
    take the risk out of Jonathan Winters.) Dick Cavett, especially as a writer, was the per-
    fect joke perfectionist: he could write for both Sahl and Carson. Just as the Kennedy
    assassination made the Beatles in America, so it also gave impetus to Carson's reign.
    In both cases, ethnicity was subsumed, and sex and violence technologized.

5   I am not sure how everyone is in possession of the first anecdote. For the remark
    about Carson, see Fred Schruers, "Man of the Year: David Letterman," *Rolling Stone,*
    29 December 1994–12 January 1995, 32.

6   From Frankfurt to Birmingham, TV criticism has increasingly propped up its object,
    the TV audience. First proclaimed to be absorbed and catatonic, then peripatetic and
    distracted, the TV audience is now conceived of as interactive and contumacious. For
    variations on the Birmingham view, see Stuart Hall et al., eds., *Culture, Music, Lan-
    guage* (London: Hutchinson, 1980); John Fiske and John Hartley, *Reading Television*
    (New York: Methuen, 1978); Andrea L. Press, *Women Watching Television: Gender,
    Class, and Generation in the American Television Experience* (Philadelphia: Univer-
    sity of Pennsylvania Press, 1991). The point of my own essay is to explain how the TV
    audience as well as the TV star can be symmetrically and simultaneously absorbed,
    peripatetic, and interactive.

7   Julia Kristeva, *Powers of Horror: An Essay on Abjection,* trans. Leon S. Roudiez (New
    York: Columbia University Press, 1982), 1 (hereafter abbreviated *PH*).

8 For Céline as symptom in Kristeva, see Leslie Hill, "Julia Kristeva: Theorizing the Avant-Garde," in *Abjection, Melancholia, and Love: The Work of Julia Kristeva*, ed. John Fletcher and Andrew Benjamin (New York: Routledge, 1990), 137–56.

9 Louis-Ferdinand Céline, *Voyage au bout de la nuit* (Paris: Gallimard, 1954) (hereafter abbreviated *VBN*). All translations, unless otherwise stated, are from Ralph Manheim, trans., *Journey to the End of the Night* (New York: New Directions, 1983) (hereafter abbreviated *J*, 1983). Occasional reference is made to John H. P. Marks, trans., *Journey to the End of the Night* (Boston: Little, Brown, 1934) (hereafter abbreviated *J*, 1934).

10 Henri Bergson, *Laughter: An Essay on the Meaning of the Comic,* trans. Cloudesley Brereton and Fred Rothwell (New York: Macmillan, 1911), 52.

11 See "Céline, USA," a special issue of *SAQ* 93 (spring 1994). One recurring theme is the pervasive Jewishness of Céline's American audience; the phenomenon is first remarked by Morris Dickstein, "Sea Change: Céline and the Problem of Cultural Transmission," *SAQ* 93 (spring 1994): 205–24, who notes the influence of Céline on Heller, Roth, and the sick comedians.

12 See Samuel S. Janus, "The Great Comedians: Personality and Other Factors," *American Journal of Psychoanalysis* 35 (1975). Of his survey of fifty-five leading comedians, "only three . . . reported that anyone other than their mothers really understood them." Fathers were almost always absent or disapproving (171).

5. Scatology: Richard Pryor in Concert

1 I will be working from the performance film, *Richard Pryor: Live in Concert*, dir. Jeff Margolis (MPI, 1979).

2 Norman O. Brown, *Life against Death: The Psychoanalytical Meaning of History*, 2d ed. (Middletown, Conn.: Wesleyan University Press, 1985) (hereafter abbreviated *LD*).

3 Henry David Thoreau, *Walden* (New York: Norton, 1951), 324–26.

4 Michael Warner, "*Walden*'s Erotic Economy," in *Comparative American Identities: Race, Sex, and Nationality in the Modern Text*, ed. Hortense J. Spillers (New York: Routledge, 1991), 151–74 (hereafter abbreviated "EE").

5 Brown writes these words without, apparently, considering their meaning for homosexuals: "The persistently anal character of the Devil has not been emphasized enough. The color preeminently associated with the Devil is black—not because of his place of abode (a circular explanation) but because of the association of black and filth" (*Life against Death*, 207). Nor does he seem to care about their meaning for blacks.

6 Leo Bersani, "Is the Rectum a Grave?" *October* 43 (1987): 197–222 (hereafter abbreviated "RG").

7 Diana Fuss, *Identification Papers* (New York: Routledge, 1995) (hereafter abbreviated *IP*).

8 Houston A. Baker, *Black Studies, Rap, and the Academy* (Chicago: University of Chicago Press, 1993), 61 (hereafter abbreviated *BSRA*).

9 Anders Stephanson, "Interview with Cornel West," in *Universal Abandon? The Politics of Postmodernism* (Minneapolis: University of Minnesota Press, 1988), 279 (hereafter abbreviated "CW").

10 Ishmael Reed, *Mumbo Jumbo* (New York: Atheneum, 1972), 45, 209 (hereafter abbreviated *MJ*).

11 Sigmund Freud, *Civilization and Its Discontents* (1930), vol. 21 of *The Standard Edition of the Complete Psychological Works of Sigmund Freud*, trans. James Strachey (London: Hogarth Press, 1961) (hereafter abbreviated *CD*).

12 Klaus Theweleit, *Women, Floods, Bodies, History*, trans. Stephen Conway, vol. 1 of *Male Fantasies* (Minneapolis: University of Minnesota Press, 1987).

13 Cf. Klaus Theweleit, *Male Bodies: Psychoanalyzing the White Terror*, trans. Erica Carter and Chris Turner, vol. 2 of *Male Fantasies* (Minneapolis: University of Minnesota Press, 1989). Theweleit's analysis of the Nazi colors puts white into relation with the abjectness of red and black this way: "Black is the color of forbidden love between men, of a dance of death in dark, deranged ecstasy. . . . Red is female flesh wallowing in its blood; a reeking mass, severed from the man" (283).

14 Ellis Hanson critiques the metaphor of the rectum as a "'dark continent' men dare not penetrate," and quotes Randy Shilts on AIDS as a version of going native: "This was so African [Shilts writes]. Here was a man whose intestines were being sucked dry by incorrigible amebic parasites, just like some African bushman" ("Undead," in *Inside/Out: Lesbian Theories, Gay Theories*, ed. Diana Fuss [New York: Routledge, 1991], 331). Reed creates in Jes Grew an inversion of this metaphor: blacks are the origin of a *healthy* contagion whose origin is the dark continent.

15 Henry Louis Gates Jr., *The Signifying Monkey: A Theory of Afro-American Literary Criticism* (New York: Oxford University Press, 1988) (hereafter abbreviated *SM*).

16 François Rabelais, *Gargantua and Pantagruel*, trans. Burton Raffel (New York: Norton, 1990), 85.

17 Mikhail Bakhtin, *Rabelais and His World*, trans. Helene Iswoksky (Cambridge, Mass.: MIT Press, 1968). For comments on excrementality that make it distinctly the opposite of the abject (and not at all a product of the death drive), see esp. 175, 335.

6. Skirting, Kidding: Ellen DeGeneres and Paula Poundstone

1 Elaine Scarry, *The Body in Pain: The Making and Unmaking of the World* (New York: Oxford University Press, 1985).

2 Marjorie Garber, *Vested Interests: Cross-Dressing and Cultural Anxiety* (New York: HarperCollins, 1993), 121. The having/being/seeming trinity is from Jacques Lacan's essay, "The Signification of the Phallus," in *Écrits: A Selection*, trans. Alan Sheridan (New York: Norton, 1977), 281–99.

3 *Paula Poundstone Goes to Harvard*, HBO, 3 February 1996.

4 See Lacan, "Signification of the Phallus," 289: the child wishes to be the phallus in order to satisfy the mother. Also, a woman wishes to be the phallus in order to serve as "the signifier of the desire of the Other" (289–90). This amounts to self-fetishization

(290), which I translate as the frustrated willingness to be complementary and generic.

5   Gabriel Marcel, *Being and Having: An Existentialist Diary,* trans. Katherine Farrer
    (New York: Harper and Row, 1965) (hereafter abbreviated *BH*).

6   Ellen DeGeneres, *My Point . . . And I Do Have One* (New York: Bantam, 1996) (here-
    after abbreviated *MP*).

7   Ellen DeGeneres, *Taste This* (Atlantic Records, 1996).

8   Sigmund Freud, "Femininity" (1932–36), vol. 22 of *The Standard Edition of the Com-
    plete Psychological Works of Sigmund Freud,* trans. James Strachey (London: Hogarth
    Press, 1964), esp. 128–29.

9   Since Joan Riviere's influential essay, "Womanliness as a Masquerade," *International
    Journal of Psychoanalysis* 10 (1929): 303–13, it is generally appreciated that every
    woman is a woman trapped in a woman's body. This is to say that the conjunction
    of sex and gender, once the heart of the notion of naturalness, is now seen as the
    essence of artificiality. (The artificiality of that conjunction, in her essay, is exempli-
    fied by the university lecturer who jokes to maintain it [308].) For another relation-
    ship of the joke to the masquerade, see Pamela Robertson, "'The Kinda Comedy That
    Imitates Me': Mae West's Identification with the Feminist Camp," in *Camp Grounds:
    Style and Homosexuality,* ed. David Bergman (Amherst: University of Massachusetts
    Press, 1993), 156–72.

    Judith Butler, in *Bodies That Matter: On the Discursive Limits of Sex* (New York:
    Routledge, 1993), wants to understand how "normative criteria" are not "simply epis-
    temological impositions on bodies" but, rather, "specific social regulating ideals by
    which bodies are trained, shaped, and formed." That is: the woman's body is formed
    deliberately just for the purpose of the trapping of women. Camp—as Robertson ar-
    gues—may be one way to make something of the inevitability of this incarceration.
    Mainstream stand-up comedy, as performed by women, works another way: not by
    exaggerating the body as the thing a woman most definitively has, but by depreciating
    the body as the sort of having that essentially entails disposing.

10 See Susanne Langer, "The Comic Rhythm," in *Comedy: Meaning and Form,* ed. Rob-
    ert W. Corrigan (New York: Harper and Row, 1981), 67–83. Langer considers laughter
    a natural but problematic evocation of comedy (i.e., comic drama). It is problematic
    because it "appears to be a direct emotional response to persons on the stage," and
    so seduces our attention from the full, organic presentation of vital feeling (80). Thus
    she seems to be no friend of stand-up (81), which, as I argue, muddles the distinction
    of art and life altogether.

11 My conception of abjection, as usual, comes from Julia Kristeva, *Powers of Horror: An
    Essay on Abjection,* trans. Leon S. Roudiez (New York: Columbia University Press,
    1982).

    Butler, in *Bodies That Matter,* refers to the "abjected body" of the lesbian. I am not
    sure precisely what she means—more than rejected or scorned, surely. She seems
    to mean merely this when she writes that heterosexuality is "secured through the
    repudiation and abjection of homosexuality" (111)—the ambiguity is in the tension

136

of repudiation and abjection, since what is abjected cannot be repudiated. But then Butler adds that the "abjection of homosexuality can take place only through an identification with that abjection, an identification that must be disavowed." This seems accurate. In short: the lesbian body is abjected insofar as heterosexual bodies cannot get rid of it. Butler defines one goal of her study as the "reworking of abjection into political agency"—this is close to the goal of stand-up, with a different source of agency in bodies that dematerialize.

See also Elin Diamond, "The Shudder of Catharsis in Twentieth-Century Performance," in *Performativity and Performance*, ed. Andrew Parker and Eve Kosofsky Sedgwick (New York: Routledge, 1995), 152–72. The essay concerns Karen Finley's performance art, which is centered on the abject as, in Kristeva's terms, "the place where meaning collapses." According to Diamond, Finley produces—out of an indulgence in the abject—cathartic shudders, i.e., gestures at once bodily and meaningful. DeGeneres (and to a lesser extent, Poundstone) would seem to be essentially non-Finley: laughing is the strongest alternative to shuddering.

One final allusion: to Eve Kosofsky Sedgwick, *Tendencies* (Durham, N.C.: Duke University Press, 1993), esp. her essay with Michael Moon, "Divinity: A Dossier, A Performance Piece, A Little-Understood Emotion," 215–51. The essay considers "glamour" in the star Divine, defined as the interface between "abjection and defiance." This is one way of "reworking abjection," as Butler puts it; Finley would seem to be after a similar conjunction that does not accept its glamour. That DeGeneres's original abjectness centered on her fatness—which is, to Sedgwick and Moon, abjection made visible—is certainly related to her desire to perform bodilessness, sometimes by means of rather proficient physical gags, in public.

12 I am aware that DeGeneres has come out, between drafts of this essay, on and off her TV show. I am defining her mode as stand-up; she retired from stand-up, but seems to be coming out of retirement now.

13 For Garber on Peter Pan, see *Vested Interests*, 165–85. "Transgression without guilt, pain, penalty, conflict, or cost: this is what Peter Pan—and *Peter Pan*—is all about. The boy who is really a woman; the woman who is really a boy; the child who will never grow up; the colony that is only a country of the mind." The next chapter, "Cherchez La Femme," begins: "Cross-dressing is a classic strategy of disappearance in detective fiction." I want to combine effects: disappearance is the high road to transgression without pain.

Works Cited

Auslander, Philip. *Presence and Resistance: Postmodernism and Cultural Politics in Contemporary American Performance*. Ann Arbor: University of Michigan Press, 1992.

Baker, Houston A. *Black Studies, Rap, and the Academy*. Chicago: University of Chicago Press, 1993.

Bakhtin, Mikhail. *Rabelais and His World*. Trans. Helene Iswoksky. Cambridge, Mass.: MIT Press, 1968.

Baumgartner, M. P. *The Moral Order of a Suburb*. New York: Oxford University Press, 1988.

Bercovitch, Sacvan. *The Office of the Scarlet Letter*. Baltimore, Md.: Johns Hopkins University Press, 1991.

Bergson, Henri. *Laughter: An Essay on the Meaning of the Comic*. Trans. Cloudesley Brereton and Fred Rothwell. New York: Macmillan, 1911.

Bersani, Leo. "Is the Rectum a Grave?" *October* 43 (1987): 197–222.

Blau, Herbert. *The Audience*. Baltimore, Md.: Johns Hopkins University Press, 1990.

Brown, Norman O. *Life against Death: The Psychoanalytic Meaning of History*. 2d ed. Middleton, Conn.: Wesleyan University Press, 1985.

Bruce, Lenny. *The Sick Humor of Lenny Bruce*. Fantasy, 1959.

———. *To Is a Preposition, Come Is a Verb*. Douglas, 1964?

———. *The Berkeley Concert*. Reprise/Warner, 1969.

Burke, Edmund. *A Philosophical Enquiry into the Origin of Our Idea of the Sublime and Beautiful*. Notre Dame, Ind.: University of Notre Dame Press, 1968.

Butler, Judith. *Bodies That Matter: On the Discursive Limits of Sex*. New York: Routledge, 1993.

Castle, Terry. *The Apparitional Lesbian: Female Homosexuality and Modern Culture*. New York: Columbia University Press, 1993.

Céline, Louis-Ferdinand. *Voyage au bout de la nuit*. Paris: Gallimard, 1954.

Cixous, Hélène. "The Laugh of the Medusa." In *New French Feminisms: An Anthology*, ed. Elaine Marks and Isabelle de Courtivron. New York: Schocken, 1981.

DeGeneres, Ellen. *My Point . . . And I Do Have One*. New York: Bantam, 1996.

———. *Taste This*. Atlantic Records, 1996.

Diamond, Elin. "The Shudder of Catharsis in Twentieth-Century Performance." In *Performativity and Performance*, ed. Andrew Parker and Eve Kosofsky Sedgwick, 152–72. New York: Routledge, 1995.

Dickstein, Morris. "Sea Change: Céline and the Problem of Cultural Transmission." *SAQ* 93 (1994): 205–24.

Douglas, Mary. *Implicit Meanings: Essays in Anthropology*. London: Routledge and Kegan Paul, 1975.

Ellison, Ralph. *Shadow and Act*. New York: Random House, 1964.

Firestone, Ross, ed. *Breaking It Up! The Best Routines of the Stand-up Comics*. New York: Bantam, 1975.

Fishkin, Shelley Fisher. *Was Huck Black? Mark Twain and African-American Voices*. New York: Oxford University Press, 1993.

Fiske, John, and John Hartley. *Reading Television*. New York: Methuen, 1978.

Fletcher, John, and Andrew Benjamin, eds. *Abjection, Melancholia, and Love: The Work of Julia Kristeva*. New York: Routledge, 1990.

Flieger, Jerry Aline. *The Purloined Punch Line: Freud, Comic Theory, and Postmodern Texts*. Baltimore, Md.: Johns Hopkins University Press, 1991.

Freud, Sigmund. *The Standard Edition of the Complete Psychological Works of Sigmund Freud*. 24 vols. Trans. James Strachey. London: Hogarth Press, 1953–1974.

Fuss, Diana. *Identification Papers*. New York: Routledge, 1995.

Garber, Marjorie. *Vested Interests: Cross-Dressing and Cultural Anxiety*. New York: HarperCollins, 1993.

Gates, Henry Louis, Jr. *The Signifying Monkey: A Theory of Afro-American Literary Criticism*. New York: Oxford University Press, 1988.

Girard, René. *Deceit, Desire, and the Novel: Self and Other in Literary Structure.* Trans. Yvonne Freccero. Baltimore, Md.: Johns Hopkins University Press, 1965.

Glazer, Nathan, and Daniel Patrick Moynihan. *Beyond the Melting Pot: The Negroes, Puerto Ricans, Jews, Italians, and Irish of New York City.* 2d ed. Cambridge, Mass.: MIT Press, 1970.

Goldman, Albert. *Ladies and Gentlemen—Lenny Bruce!!* New York: Random House, 1974.

Hall, Stuart, et al., eds. *Culture, Music, Language.* London: Hutchinson, 1980.

Hanson, Ellis. "Undead." In *Inside/Out: Lesbian Theories, Gay Theories,* ed. Diana Fuss. New York: Routledge, 1991.

Hawthorne, Nathaniel. *The Scarlet Letter.* Boston: St. Martin's Press, 1991.

Hemingway, Ernest. *The Sun Also Rises.* New York: Scribner's, 1970.

Hertz, Neil. *The End of the Line: Essays in Psychoanalysis and the Sublime.* New York: Columbia University Press, 1985.

Hill, Carl. *The Soul of Wit: Joke Theory from Grimm to Freud.* Lincoln: University of Nebraska Press, 1993.

Howe, Irving. *World of Our Fathers.* New York: Harcourt Brace Jovanovich, 1976.

Janus, Samuel S. "The Great Comedians: Personality and Other Factors." *American Journal of Psychoanalysis* 35 (1975): 169–74.

Johnson, Barbara. *The Critical Difference: Essays in the Contemporary Rhetoric of Reading.* Baltimore, Md.: Johns Hopkins University Press, 1980.

Kanfer, Stefan. *A Summer World: The Attempt to Build a Jewish Eden in the Catskills, From the Days of the Ghetto to the Rise and Decline of the Borscht Belt.* New York: Farrar, Straus, Giroux, 1989.

Kant, Immanuel. *Kant's Kritik of Judgment.* Trans. J. H. Bernard. New York: Macmillan, 1892.

———. *Observations on the Feeling of the Beautiful and Sublime.* Trans. John T. Goldthwait. Berkeley: University of California Press, 1965.

Knapp, Steven. *Personification and the Sublime: Milton to Coleridge.* Cambridge, Mass.: Harvard University Press, 1985.

Koestenbaum, Wayne. *Double Talk: The Erotics of Male Literary Collaboration.* New York: Routledge, 1989.

Kristeva, Julia. *Powers of Horror: An Essay on Abjection.* Trans. Leon S. Roudiez. New York: Columbia University Press, 1982.

Lacan, Jacques. "The Signification of the Phallus." In *Écrits: A Selection,* trans. Alan Sheridan. New York: Norton, 1977.

Langer, Susanne. "The Comic Rhythm." In *Comedy: Meaning and Form,* ed. Robert W. Corrigan. New York: Harper and Row, 1981.

Longinus. *Longinus on the Sublime.* Trans. W. Rhys Roberts. Cambridge: Cambridge University Press, 1935.

Lott, Eric. *Love and Theft: Blackface Minstrelsy and the American Working Class.* New York: Oxford University Press, 1993.

Lyotard, Jean-François. *Lessons on the Analytic of the Sublime.* Trans. Elizabeth Rotten-
    berg. Stanford, Calif.: Stanford University Press, 1994.

Manheim, Ralph, trans. *Journey to the End of the Night.* By Louis-Ferdinand Céline. New
    York: New Directions, 1983.

Marcel, Gabriel. *Being and Having: An Existentialist Diary.* Trans. Katherine Farrer. New
    York: Harper and Row, 1965.

Marks, John H. P., trans. *Journey to the End of the Night.* By Louis-Ferdinand Céline. Bos-
    ton: Little, Brown, 1934.

McGhee, Paul E., and Jeffrey H. Goldstein. *Handbook of Humor Research.* Vol. 1, *Basic
    Issues.* New York: Springer-Verlag, 1983.

Morreal, John, ed. *The Philosophy of Laughter and Humor.* Albany: State University of
    New York Press, 1987.

Nichols, Mike, and Elaine May. *Improvisations to Music: Mike Nichols and Elaine May.*
    Mercury, 1958.

———. *An Evening with Mike Nichols and Elaine May.* Mercury, 1961.

———. *The Best of Mike Nichols and Elaine May.* Mercury, 1965.

———. *Mike Nichols and Elaine May in Retrospect.* Mercury, 1972.

Oxenhandler, Noelle. "The Eros of Parenthood." *New Yorker,* 19 February 1996, 47–49.

Phillips, Adam. *On Kissing, Tickling, and Being Bored: Psychoanalytic Essays on the Un-
    examined Life.* Cambridge, Mass.: Harvard University Press, 1993.

Poundstone, Paula. *Paula Poundstone Goes to Harvard.* HBO, 3 February 1996.

Press, Andrea L. *Women Watching Television: Gender, Class, and Generation in the
    American Television Experience.* Philadelphia: University of Pennsylvania Press,
    1991.

Pryor, Richard. *Richard Pryor: Live in Concert.* Dir. Jeff Margolis. MPI, 1979. Video-
    cassette.

Rabelais, François. *Gargantua and Pantagruel.* Trans. Burton Raffel. New York: Norton,
    1990.

Reed, Ishmael. *Mumbo Jumbo.* New York: Atheneum, 1972.

Reiner, Carl. *Enter Laughing.* New York: Simon and Schuster, 1958.

Reiner, Carl, and Mel Brooks. *2000 Years with Carl Reiner and Mel Brooks.* World-Pacific,
    1960.

———. *2000 and One Years with Carl Reiner and Mel Brooks.* Capitol, 1961.

———. *2000 and Thirteen.* Warner, 1973.

Riviere, Joan. "Womanliness as a Masquerade." *International Journal of Psychoanalysis*
    10 (1929): 303–13.

Robertson, Pamela. "'The Kinda Comedy That Imitates Me': Mae West's Identification
    with the Feminist Camp." In *Camp Grounds,* ed. David Bergman. Amherst: University
    of Massachusetts Press, 1993.

Rogin, Michael. "Blackface, White Noise: The Jewish Jazz Singer Finds His Voice." *Critical
    Inquiry* 18 (1992): 417–53.

Rubin, Gayle. "The Traffic in Women: Notes on the 'Political Economy' of Sex." In *Toward* an *Anthropology of Women,* ed. Rayna R. Reiter, 157–210. New York: Monthly Review Press, 1975.

Scarry, Elaine. *The Body in Pain: The Making and Unmaking of the World.* New York: Oxford University Press, 1985.

Schruers, Fred. "Man of the Year: David Letterman." *Rolling Stone,* 29 December 1994– 12 January 1995, 30–34, 204–5.

Schuth, H. Wayne. *Mike Nichols.* Boston: Twayne, 1978.

Sedgwick, Eve Kosofsky. *Between Men: English Literature and Male Homosocial Desire.* New York: Columbia University Press, 1985.

———. *Epistemology of the Closet.* Berkeley: University of California Press, 1990.

———. *Tendencies.* Durham, N.C.: Duke University Press, 1993.

Simpson, Mark. "The Straight Men of Comedy." In *Because I Tell a Joke or Two: Comedy, Politics, and Social Difference,* ed. Stephen Wagg. New York: Routledge, 1998.

Smith, Ronald L. *Who's Who in Comedy: Comedians, Comics, and Clowns from Vaudeville to Today's Stand-Ups.* New York: Facts on File, 1992.

Stebbins, Robert A. *The Laugh-Makers: Standup Comedy as Art, Business, and Life-Style.* Montreal: McGill-Queen's University Press, 1990.

Stein, Charles W., ed. *American Vaudeville as Seen by Its Contemporaries.* New York: Knopf, 1984.

Stephanson, Anders. "Interview with Cornel West." In *Universal Abandon? The Politics of Postmodernism,* ed. Andrew Ross. Minneapolis: University of Minnesota Press, 1988.

Stewart, Donald Ogden. *A Parody Outline of History.* New York: Doran, 1921.

———. *Aunt Polly's Story of Mankind.* New York: Doran, 1923.

Theweleit, Klaus. *Women, Floods, Bodies, History.* Trans. Stephen Conway. Vol. 1 of *Male Fantasies.* Minneapolis: University of Minnesota Press, 1987.

———. *Male Bodies: Psychoanalyzing the White Terror.* Trans. Erica Carter and Chris Turner. Vol. 2 of *Male Fantasies.* Minneapolis: University of Minnesota Press, 1989.

Thoreau, Henry David. *Walden.* New York: Norton, 1951.

Twain, Mark. *The Adventures of Huckleberry Finn.* New York: Modern Library, 1993.

Tynan, Kenneth. "Frolics and Detours of a Short Hebrew Man." *New Yorker,* 30 October 1978, 46–130.

Warner, Michael. "*Walden*'s Erotic Economy." In *Comparative American Identities: Race, Sex, and Nationality in the Modern Text,* ed. Hortense J. Spillers, 151–74. New York: Routledge, 1991.

Watkins, Mel. *On the Real Side: Laughing, Lying, and Signifying—The Underground Tradition of African-American Humor That Transformed American Culture, from Slavery to Richard Pryor.* New York: Simon and Schuster, 1994.

Weiskel, Thomas. *The Romantic Sublime: Studies in the Structure and Psychology of Transcendence.* Baltimore, Md.: Johns Hopkins University Press, 1976.

Zehme, Bill. "Letterman Lets His Guard Down." *Esquire,* December 1994, 96–102.

Index

Audiences (*continued*)
dependence on, 12; performers' relations with, 13, 15, 17–18, 26–27, 126–27 n.3, 128 n.16; TV, 71, 133 n.6; urinating on, 14–16

Aunt Polly's Story of Mankind (D. O. Stewart), 44

Avedon, Richard, 57–58

Baby-clothing joke (Poundstone), 112, 113

Baby jokes (DeGeneres), 112–14

Baker, Houston, 94, 95

Bakhtin, Mikhail, 103

Bathos/hypsos, 51

Bathroom humor, 83–86

Baumgartner, M. P., 23

"The Beast in the Jungle" (James), 38

Beatles, 133 n.4

Being/having/seeming, 109–10, 112–13, 114, 117–18

Bell, Daniel, 92

Bercovitch, Sacvan, 66

Bergen, Candice, 118

Bergson, Henri, 20, 85

Berle, Milton, 29, 130–31 n.26

Bersani, Leo, 92–93

Blackface, 7, 37–38, 39–41, 130 n.18

Black/red, significance of, 98, 135 n.13

Blacks. *See* Race

Blau, Herbert, 27

Blazing Saddles (Brooks), 7, 40

Bob and Ray, 35

Bodies, 7–8, 110, 114, 117–18, 136 n.9

Body jokes (DeGeneres), 120

Breslin, Mark, 128–29 n.5

Brice, Fanny, 22

Brooks, Mel, 6; audiences of, 48; and blackness, 7; *Blazing Saddles,* 7, 40; citifying humor of, 2–3; in comedy team, 36–37, 40–41, 46–47; on fruit, 131 n.36; heterosexuality used by, 42–43, 131 n.31; homosexuality/homosociality used by, 7, 40, 42–43, 47–48; "Huck and Jim" routine, 37–38, 129–30 n.15; influence of, 70; and Kennedy election, 126

n.2; postmodernism of, 29; and Reiner, 36; sexual misidentification jokes, 131 n.31; "Shakespeare" routine, 37–38; *Silent Movie,* 40; "2000 and Thirteen," 43, 45–46; "The 2000 Year Old Man," 28–31, 38–41, 47–48, 49, 87 (*see also* "Huck and Jim" routine); "2000 Years," 42–43; wrestler routine, 32; Yiddish accent used by, 31, 40

Brown, Norman O., 89–92, 98, 99, 134 n.5

Bruce, Lenny, 133 n.4; and audience-performer relations, 15–16, 126 n.3; background of, 22; on civilization as scam, 22; influence of, 70, 102; and jazz, 7; and Kennedy assassination, 126 n.2; obscenity arrests/trials of, 19, 23–26, 127 n.15; outrage/outrageousness of, 13, 14, 15, 18–19, 84, 127 n.4; postmodernism of, 29; "Religions, Inc.," 20, 22; spoiled-boy letter to his father, 25–26; and suburbanization, 2, 22–23; urination joke, 4, 14–18; Yiddish used by, 22

Burke, Edmund, 56, 132 n.12

Burns, George, 40

Burns, Jack, 35

Butler, Judith, 136 nn. 9, 11

Caesar, Sid, 36, 41

Cannibalism/ingestion, 94, 95–96, 98–99

Capitalism, 92

Carlin, George, 133 n.4

Carson, Johnny, 28, 35; abstraction used by, 7–8; comedians' influence, 70, 133 n.4; and Letterman, 70–71; talk show of, 2–3; Watergate joke, 133 n.4

Castle, Terry, 33–34

Castration, 56, 78, 117

Cavett, Dick, 2–3, 133 n.4

Céline, Louis-Ferdinand: abjection of, 73; audiences of, 134 n.11; influence of, 81, 134 n.11; *Journey to the End of the Night,* 75–79; Kristeva on, 74–75

Cixous, Hélène, 57

Clausewitz, Karl Marie von, 13

and funniness of jokes, 12; as goal of comedy, 12–13; incongruity as cause of, 130 n.19; incorrigibility of, 104–5; length of, 16; and obliviousness, 104–5; and oscillation, 54; and pain, 104; of women vs. men, 12, 126 n.2

Law, 25–27

Lesbianism, 33–34, 136–37 n.11

Letterman, David: abjection of, 70–71, 102; abstraction used by, 7–8; attitude of, 8, 76, 79; audiences of, 70; height of, 70; and intellectuals, 68–69; loudness of, 70; and paternal aggression, 5; talk show of, 2–3; verbal speed of, 69–70, 73, 82

Lévi-Strauss, Claude, 32

Lewis, Jerry, 35, 36, 79–81

Live in Concert (Pryor), 9, 83–89, 93–94, 97, 102–3

Longinus, 51–52

Lott, Eric, 39

Low, Gail Ching-Liang, 94

Luther, Martin, 89–90

Lyotard, Jean-François, 54

"Macho man" song (Pryor), 88

Mad About You, 131 n.36

Marcel, Gabriel, 110, 112, 114, 117

Martin, Dean, 35, 36

Martin, Dick, 35, 46–47

Martin, Steve, 36

Marx, Groucho, 79

Masochism, 57

Matchmaker jokes (*Schadchen* stories), 20–21

May, Elaine: "Adultery," 64–65; audiences of, 60–61, 65; Avedon portraits of, 57–58; career of, 54; in comedy team, 35, 36; "Disc Jockey," 59–60, 63; femininity of, 6–7, 60; and jazz, 7; Jewishness of, 60; and Kennedy election, 126 n.2; "Mother and Son," 61; "Mysterioso," 62; Nichols's tickling by, 61–63; "Physical," 62–63; relationship with Nichols, 65; "Second Piano Concerto," 64; "Tele-

phone," 58–59, 61, 63; "Transference," 61; triangulation used by, 63–64

McMahon, Ed, 35, 36

Meara, Anne, 35, 36

Mechanization, human, 84–85

Medusa, 56–57

Metajokes, 18, 31, 53, 54

Minstrelsy. *See* Blackface

Moon, Michael, 137 n.11

Moore, Dudley, 35

Moore, Mary Tyler, 118

Mother-in-law jokes, 105

"Mother and Son" (Nichols and May), 61

Mud, 97–98, 99, 101–2

Mumbo Jumbo (Reed), 95–96, 98–99, 102, 135 n.14

Murtagh, Judge, 26

My Point . . . And I Do Have One (DeGeneres), 110, 114–17, 118–19, 121–22

"Mysterioso" (Nichols and May), 62

Napoleon, 79

Nature vs. artifice, 105, 136 nn. 9–10

Nazi colors, 98, 135 n.13

Nectarine joke. *See* "The 2000 Year Old Man"

Newhart, Bob, 118

New York City, 77–78

Nichols, Mike, 6–7, 35, 57; "Adultery," 64–65; audiences of, 65; background of, 61; career, 54; in comedy team, 35, 36; "Disc Jockey," 59–60, 63; expressionlessness of, 58; and jazz, 7; and Kennedy election, 126 n.2; May's tickling of, 61–63; "Mother and Son," 61; "Mysterioso," 62; "Physical," 62–63; relationship with May, 65; "Second Piano Concerto," 64; "Telephone," 58–59, 61, 63; "Transference," 61; triangulation used by, 63–64

Obliviousness, 104–5

Obscenity laws, 23

Oceanic feeling, 96, 97–98, 99

The Odd Couple (Simon), 36

John Limon is Professor of English at Williams College.
He is the author of *Writing after War: American War Fiction
from Realism to Postmodernism* (1994) and *The Place of
Fiction in the Time of Science: A Disciplinary History
of American Writing* (1990).

Library of Congress Cataloging-in-Publication Data
Limon, John.
Stand-up comedy in theory, or, abjection in America /
John Limon.
Includes bibliographical references and index.
ISBN 0-8223-2509-8 (cloth : alk. paper)
ISBN 0-8223-2546-2 (pbk. : alk. paper)
1. Stand-up comedy.   I. Title.
PN1969.C65 L56   2000   792'.7—dc21   00-029446

St. Louis Community College
at Meramec
Library

10579783

AMRIDGE UNIVERSITY
LIBRARY

I WISH YOU DIDN'T KNOW MY NAME

Copyright © 1990 by Batfilm Productions, Inc.
All rights reserved.

Warner Books, Inc., 666 Fifth Avenue, New York, NY 10103

 A Time Warner Company

Printed in the United States of America
First printing: September 1990
10 9 8 7 6 5 4 3 2 1

LIBRARY OF CONGRESS CATALOGING-IN-PUBLICATION DATA

Launders, Michele.
    I wish you didn't know my name : the story of Michele Launders and
her daughter Lisa / Michele Launders and Penina Spiegel.
        p.   cm.
    ISBN 0-446-51587-6
        1. Adoption—New York Metropolitan Area—Corrupt practices—Case
studies.   2. Murder—New York (N.Y.)—Case studies.   3. Launders,
Michele.   4. Birthparents—New York (State)—Nassau County—
Biography.   5. Steinberg, Lisa, 1981–1987.   I. Spiegel, Penina.
II. Title.
HV875.57.N48L38   1990
364.1′523′092—dc20
    [B]   90-35547
                                                                CIP

Designed by Giorgetta Bell McRee

LIBRARY OF CONGRESS
5
AUG 27 1990
COPY
CIP

I WISH YOU DIDN'T KNOW MY NAME

The Story of Michele Launders and Her Daughter Lisa

MICHELE LAUNDERS
and PENINA SPIEGEL

WARNER BOOKS

A Time Warner Company

Southern Christian University Library
1200 Taylor Rd
Montgomery, AL 36117   6204

control 14937 record 197 disk 22

For Lisa . . .

MICHELE LAUNDERS

. . . *And for birth mothers everywhere*

PENINA SPIEGEL

I don't think there was ever a time in the writing of this book when Lisa left my mind, or Michele's. I must acknowledge here Michele Launders's honesty and courage in reliving a chapter of unrelieved torment in her life. We talked frequently of our hope that the hot white light shed on the entire subject of child abuse as a result of Lisa's death will serve to save the lives of others who might have shared her fate.

We talked also of the hopes and dreams of birth mothers. Like all birth mothers, Michele sought someone to cherish her child, to stand in her place and love her baby every day of her life. As an adoptive mother, I give thanks every day for the angel who shares my co-op, and that's why this book is dedicated in part to birth mothers, in acknowledgment of their wisdom in trying to secure for their child what they themselves cannot give.

This book was written with the encouragement and support of: Anita Launders; John Launders; Joseph Famighetti; Ed Gordon; Marian Hunter; Naomi Schwartz; Joann Davis, an editor of intelligence and integrity; and Robert Gottlieb, a staunch and loyal friend as well as agent . . .

. . . and in the hope that no child anywhere will go to bed tonight in loneliness and despair.

PENINA SPIEGEL
New York City
April 1990

Preface

$\mathscr{I}$ wish I weren't writing this book. I wish you didn't know my name. I wish nobody outside of my family and friends had heard of me. Because that would mean that my daughter was still alive.

You may know her as Lisa Steinberg, but that wasn't her name. Before I buried her, I fought to give her back her true name: Launders. That's what it said on her birth certificate. That's what I put on her gravestone.

I was nineteen when she was born, and not married. I gave her up for adoption—for many reasons, but mostly because I wanted her to have a good life, better than I could give her.

Joel Steinberg was the attorney I hired to arrange the adoption. He didn't do it. He kept her. And when she was six years, five months, and two weeks old, he killed her.

The day of her funeral I hadn't slept in a week—not since the night an assistant DA and a police detective had come to my home and told me that the little girl whose story I had been following on television was the daughter I had given up on the day she was born.

My baby was dead. Murdered.

There had never been an adoption. The doctor who was supposed to be helping me had lied. His receptionist, who'd taken me into her home, had lied. Steinberg had lied. He'd stolen my baby. Hedda

Nussbaum—a wreck of a woman, looking in her forties like a crone—what part had she played in it?

On the way to the funeral home someone turned on the TV in the limo. All the stations were carrying the broadcast live. I made them turn off the television. I couldn't watch it. I looked out the window. There were crowds lining the street. I was afraid to get out of the car. I didn't think I'd make it through all those people without my knees giving way.

I found out later there were almost a thousand people there. Most of them didn't even know Lisa. They came from all over the city, women in furs, construction workers, parents with small children, teenagers, businessmen, street people. It was very cold that morning, but that didn't stop them from standing in line for hours. They left drawings, notes, letters, poems, flowers. Even Cardinal O'Connor came, to say a silent prayer for Lisa's soul. She would have a happy life for all eternity, he said.

Lisa had been so alone in life. Now all these people were standing in the cold, just to show they cared. I didn't look at anybody as I got out of the car, but even so, I knew that many of them were crying.

The funeral home was packed. There wasn't room for another person. Somehow I got to my seat at the front . . . and there was the casket. White. Small. I was surprised at how tiny it was. But she was only a little girl. The coffin was surrounded by flowers, huge bouquets and single roses, expensive arrangements and simple offerings. They were sent by sports teams and corporations and individuals, by strangers and friends, by adults and by children. A tall candle stood at her head, and a crucifix. At the foot of her coffin an easel held the letters, notes, and cards that had been left at the doorway of the apartment building in Greenwich Village where Lisa had lived out her short span on this earth. Someone had gathered them up and brought them to the funeral home.

My mother had wanted to have the funeral at home, in Rockville Centre, Long Island, but I said no. Lisa had lived her whole life in Greenwich Village. Her little friends were there. I didn't want to shut them out. It wouldn't be fair. All the lives she touched—it would have been selfish to keep them away. I wanted everyone to have the chance to say good-bye.

That was why I had insisted on a joint Catholic/Jewish service with both a rabbi and a priest officiating. My family and I are

Catholics, but Lisa was brought up Jewish. I wanted to honor and respect what she was in life.

There were good things in her life. I wanted to concentrate on the good, bring out all the good I could find.

And I knew that in the end, she'd come home to us, to our family. This city service wasn't for me, it was for Lisa's friends and for the public. Our time would come later, when we would bring her home and lay her to rest in our family plot in Gate of Heaven Cemetery in Westchester County. There was an empty grave next to the one in which we would bury Lisa; it would not be empty for long. Lisa's great-grandmother, my beloved Nana, was literally on her deathbed; she would follow Lisa very soon. Nana had never seen this great-grandchild of hers. She had learned of her existence only days before. Yet she had asked me—directed me—to bury Lisa next to her. Lisa would not be alone for long. From that, I drew comfort.

Father O'Brien prayed: "Father, we entrust to you this child whom you loved so much in this life. Welcome her to your paradise, where there is no more sorrow, no more weeping, no more pain, but only peace and joy, for ever and ever."

Amen.

A little boy had written, "I hope all the angels watch over you."

Amen.

Rabbi Math said Kaddish, the Jewish prayer for the dead, for Lisa. Father O'Brien ended simply, "May she be with God."

All during the service, I wanted so badly to go to Lisa, but I sat in my seat until I felt I could walk the few short steps to the casket without breaking down. It was important to keep my dignity. For Lisa. I owed her that. It doesn't make sense to say I was setting an example for her. She's dead and I'll never get to teach her and guide her and help her grow up. But I didn't want to make a spectacle of myself at her funeral.

I waited till almost everyone was gone. The casket was closed. I would have liked it to be open. I never saw her when she was alive. But knowing what the Steinbergs did to her, if I'd had the coffin opened, even privately, for myself alone, the image I'd carry with me would be one of everlasting horror. The bruises where his fist had smacked into her body . . . the places where he'd punched her. The hole they'd drilled in her skull to relieve the bleeding on her brain. . . .

No. I'd rather remember her from the pictures. The police found

them in Steinberg's apartment. A detective gave them to me on the
night Steinberg was convicted for killing my daughter. He said the
police had no use for them anymore. I do. I look at those pictures
and try to imagine how she was.

I went up to her coffin. I knelt there, next to the dear body I had
never cradled in my arms.

I prayed for her soul.

I prayed for my soul. I prayed for forgiveness.

This poor tortured child. I, her mother, had delivered her into
the hands of her killers. I hoped that God had watched over her,
because I certainly hadn't.

If He had, I couldn't see it.

But I asked His blessing on her anyway.

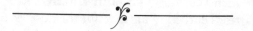

Like everyone else, I had followed the story of the child who became
known as Little Lisa on television and in the newspapers. In the
early hours of November 2, 1987, paramedics were called to the
apartment at 14 West Tenth Street where Joel Steinberg lived with
his common-law wife, Hedda Nussbaum. They found a filthy, dark-
ened apartment, without a single working light fixture. Lisa lay
naked and comatose on the couch that served as her bed; seventeen-
month-old Mitchell, tethered to a playpen, naked save for a soiled,
urine-soaked diaper, was sucking on a bottle of spoiled milk. Their
"mother," Hedda Nussbaum, limped in the shadows, hiding her
disfigured face. Steinberg explained that Lisa had choked on some
vegetables.

The paramedics were appalled. And they didn't believe him. One
of them blurted out, "Who eats vegetables at six in the morning?"

Lisa had eaten the vegetables the night before, Steinberg explained. It was then that she had choked on her own vomit and
sunk into a coma. The paramedics working over Lisa told him to
get some light in there. "Is that really important?" Steinberg asked.

He was afraid of the light. He didn't want them to *see*.

Later, police would find drug paraphernalia in the apartment,
along with quantities of cocaine and suspiciously large amounts of
cash. There were bloodstained sheets and stacks of what the news-

papers reported as "electronic equipment." I was told privately by the DA's office—it was never printed in the press—that the "electronic equipment" included an abortion suction machine.

Lisa never recovered consciousness. At four-thirty P.M. on November 4 she was declared brain-dead. The respirator was turned off the following morning at eight-forty. Her heart stopped beating fifteen minutes later.

She died from injuries to the brain arising from a blow dealt by her "adoptive father," Joel Steinberg. An autopsy showed she had been subjected to long-term abuse; her body bore the marks of multiple beatings, some fresh, some old.

Under "Cause of death" the autopsy said "Child Abuse."

The story filled front pages daily, led off every newscast. Never for one moment did I connect the unshaven, disheveled man I saw on television with the muscular, authoritative attorney I had met six and a half years earlier to arrange for the adoption of my unborn daughter.

For six and a half years I had clung to a dream, a dream that someday a young woman would knock on my door and call me by the name I had never been called: Mommy.

On the night the detective and the DA entered my house, sympathy in their eyes, the dream died and the visions of the perfect life my daughter was leading as the cherished and adored daughter of grateful adoptive parents stopped playing in my head. My daughter's life had come to an abrupt and hideous end.

When we came out of the funeral home, there was a flight of steps to walk down. I didn't remember going up them on my way in, and I was afraid I wouldn't make it without stumbling, but with the help of the two bodyguards my attorney had hired to protect me, I managed to make it across the narrow gap of sidewalk to the waiting limousine. There were even more people jamming the street. I could see them lining up and down the block. A moment of hush as Lisa's small coffin was borne out of the funeral home and set gently—far more gently than the touch she knew in life—into the flower-laden hearse.

I saw children in the crowd, Lisa's schoolmates, and I was glad I had made the funeral nearby so they could come. The other service, out in Westchester County, that would be for us, for me, for the family.

We followed the hearse bearing the little white casket out to
Gate of Heaven Cemetery. In the city there had been hundreds of
mourners; here there were less than a dozen.

The ground was frozen and slippery with ice in the biting cold.
They had a carpet down for us to walk on. I was grateful; without
it I would surely have lost my footing. A cruel wind was blowing.
The canvas awning they'd put up did little to block it.

I didn't think about the cold. I never felt it. I was thinking about
Lisa, crying for her suffering, for the years we had lost, for the sad
life and lonely death to which I had unwittingly condemned her.

I was wondering if she would ever forgive me. I knew beyond a
shadow of a doubt I would never forgive myself.

The service was short, barely nine minutes long. The priest said
the usual things they say about a young child who dies. He said
she had made a difference in her short life. He said we shouldn't
be sad. God had called her back because her work was done.

Or perhaps, the priest mused, He took her home to Him because
He could no longer bear to see her suffering.

Oh, how that hurt. Whatever the priest said next, I didn't hear.

I do remember when he turned to me and said, "Thank you,
Michele, for bringing Lisa home to us."

As the service ended, the workers and gravediggers stood in a
line near the gravesite, and they, too, bowed their heads in prayer.
Someone handed me a bouquet, and I placed it on her coffin.

It wasn't good-bye. I knew I'd be back. I knew I'd be there a lot.

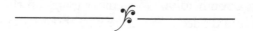

Lisa's natural father didn't attend the service. I'd like to think he
would have come were it not for the press. They had not as yet
found out the name of her biological father—and they still haven't.
I promised him I wouldn't tell, and with two exceptions, I have
kept my promise. (Even in this book, I will only use his Christian
name, not his surname, and that only because finally, after much
persuasion, I convinced him to allow me to put it on her gravestone,
so that much is public knowledge.)

I could understand his fear of exposure. I myself had tried desperately to keep my pregnancy secret from everyone, even her father.
He had known nothing until sometime after she was born, and even

then I only told him because he betrayed me and I was angry at him, and hurt.

Now the whole world—literally, for the story was covered in detail by the international press—knew about it. My most private matters were discussed by strangers. But the identity of Lisa's father—that was one secret the press had not penetrated, and I was going to do my best to see that no one ever did.

If there was scandal, I would take it upon myself.

If there was shame, I would take it upon myself.

If there was blame, it was all mine.

I was only sorry for the innocents who suffered as a result of my actions; Lisa chief among them, but my mother and grandmother as well. I had given my baby up for adoption at least in part to protect them.

But most of all, I did it for Lisa. I had wanted her to have a good life, better than I could give her. I wanted her to have two parents, parents who were married. That was important to me.

I saw my father only once that I can remember. He abandoned us when I was four years old. I didn't see him again for twenty years, until I was called to his bedside. He was dying of cancer and I was told that he wanted to see me.

"It's been a long time," he said, and two days later, he died.

He is buried somewhere in that same cemetery. I don't visit his grave. He abandoned us in life. It seems a sham to pretend that I lost something at his death.

But that was one of the main reasons I gave up my baby for adoption. I wanted her to have what I hadn't had, a laughing, loving father who'd be tender with her and take her places and wait for the moment he'd come home from work and raise her high up in his arms to touch the sky.

So maybe I missed it more than I realized.

Chapter 1

xI couldn't describe my father to you if I tried. I have no memories of him at all. Here's what I knew before I started writing this book: that my mom had been unhappy with him; that he hit her more than once or twice; that for a long time he refused to give her a divorce; that we were better off without him—a lot better off. That was all. We didn't talk about him much while I was growing up.

When Mom met Joseph Launders, she was twenty-three years old, living at home, working full-time, and studying accounting at night. Two weeks after she met him, she was ready to marry him. That amazes me because Mom is not an impulsive person. I can't picture her falling head over heels in love with anybody, but apparently she did with him. And she thought he loved her. Mom says Joseph was brilliant and glamorous and exciting, and she thought they'd have a wonderful life together. She couldn't wait to marry him. They were going to elope, but they decided to do things "right," to save for a Church wedding with all the trimmings. They didn't get married for two years. Joseph enrolled at Pace and he was a solid-A student. He was like that at everything, Mom says. Sure he drank—so did everyone. The first two years Mom knew him it didn't seem to trouble him at all. It was kind of manly to be able to knock them back, and she nursed her drinks to keep up.

They were married during school break in 1955, with, as they had wished, all the trimmings, a diamond engagement ring, a wedding in the Catholic Church, a Bermuda honeymoon. They moved into a lovely apartment in Forest Hills, Queens, and they had money in the bank; a young couple off to a good start.

One night after they'd been married about four months, Joseph didn't come home after class. By midnight Mom was worried. By one A.M. she was frantic. Two o'clock. Three o'clock.

Finally he walked in. You could tell he'd had a few drinks. He said he'd gone out with one of the instructors at Pace, a male instructor. She accepted that. What else could she do? She remembers the first time he hit her:

> *It was on a Lexington Avenue subway station, Friday night, about two in the morning. We'd been married about a year. We'd had dinner with another couple—a nice evening, I thought, and we were on our way home to Queens. It was late, the platform was deserted. We passed a ladies' room and I had to go. When I came back out—wham! Joseph punched me in the face. Out of nowhere. I wasn't expecting it. I fell back against the wall.*
>
> *"Where the hell did you go? Where were you?" He was screaming at me. He thought I'd left him.*
>
> *The next morning, Joseph asked what was the matter with my eye.*
>
> *I guess he'd had more to drink than I thought. That was my first inkling that I was in a real, honest-to-goodness trap.*
>
> *By Monday morning my eye was a blotch of yellow, black, purple. I did my hair in a kind of Veronica Lake style, a deep wave over one eye, put on a lot of makeup, and went to work. Everyone exclaimed; they thought my new hairdo was stunning.*

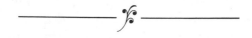

When things started to go bad in her marriage, Mom felt alone and isolated. She tried to confide in her family. They wouldn't hear of it. "What did you think marriage was going to be, a bed of roses? You're no worse off than the next one. Nobody's life is a bed of roses." They needled her about not having children. "What's the matter with you, Anita? What kind of married woman doesn't have any children?"

But Mom wasn't childless by accident. Joseph didn't want children, he didn't like them and never intended to have them. They'd cramp his lifestyle. And after she saw what their marriage was going to be like, she was the one who made sure he used contraception. She didn't want to bring children into that world either.

Mom says that after that incident in the subway, Joseph didn't hit her again for a long time. She began to think it was over and done with, a onetime thing that was best put out of mind.

Until one night Joseph came home very late. Mom waited up; she was worried, although deep down she assumed he was probably partying somewhere. "I did think he could at least have phoned to tell me he was okay," she remembers.

"I heard him come in and went to the door. His fist shot out. He punched me in the eye. A direct punch to the eye. 'Get out of my way.' Joseph staggered past me into the bedroom and went to sleep. In the morning he asked again, 'What happened to your eye?'"

Eventually, Mom remembers, there was a night when he didn't come home at all. And then those nights became a regular thing. He stayed out so much Mom began to get the feeling that he came home only as a last resort, when all the fun dried up and there was absolutely nothing else to do.

Nana would tell her, "It's up to the woman to make a marriage work. You don't have it any worse than anybody else. Keep trying. Give it time. Keep trying."

She did leave him once, but it only lasted for a weekend. By Monday morning, she was back. Everyone kept pressuring her to return. So she did what they said to do. She returned and she tried to be an "interesting wife" to my father. She cooked fancy dinners and arranged social evenings with friends. But slowly it began to dawn on her that the kind of life she was trying to lead had no appeal for him.

Both my mother and father are first-generation Americans, the children of Irish Catholic immigrants. Divorce was unheard of in their families. My mom was stuck.

When they had been married for four and a half years my mother found out she was pregnant. When she told my father, he was

Southern Christian University Library
1200 Taylor Rd
Montgomery, AL 36117

AIRRIDGE UNIVERSITY LIBRARY

furious! He ordered her to get rid of it, the sooner the better. Mom remembers, "All he kept saying was 'get an abortion, get an abortion.'"

Mom felt that abortion was murder, just as the Church taught. Besides, in those days it wasn't legal and she would have had to go to some grotesque back alley and have God-knows-who do it with a coat hanger. She resented that and she refused to do it.

My father started slacking off at work. He was put on probation and eventually fired. Mom thought he did it deliberately as a way of showing her that he meant business about the abortion.

But now that my father was out of a job, he sat around the house all day drinking coffee and reading. When that palled, he'd go off on a drinking spree with his buddies and didn't bother to come home for a week or more at a time.

They moved to a cheaper apartment, one owned by Nana and her new husband, my beloved Papa Jack. It wasn't in a residential area, so there was no one around to hear her screams at night when he slapped her around. Since it was a dead-end apartment with no back door, she was pretty much trapped there alone with him.

Despite our father's wishes, my big brother, John Emmett, was born healthy and well in April 1960. After the birth, mom went to the doctor and got fitted for a diaphragm. Still, when John was less than a year old, she found herself pregnant again, this time with me.

Her second pregnancy was not an easy time either. My father was bringing in no money, and there were nights Mom would have to return deposit bottles in order to buy supper for herself and for my brother. Still, she made preparations for the new baby as best she could. She picked out names: if she had a boy, she was going to name him Michael. If I was a girl, she planned to name me Lisa.

Chapter 2

Something was wrong with her labor; my mother knew it. She couldn't manage the breathing for natural childbirth the way she had last time. The pains weren't coming in contractions, just one big pain that didn't seem to stop. Suddenly there were a lot of people in the room. She remembers turning her head and seeing them throwing the doctor into white scrubs. She begged for gas . . . and went off into oblivion.

I was in danger. They needed someone to sign a consent form for a procedure that would save my life. They called my father and explained. Would he come down and sign?

No, he wouldn't. He was tired. He'd been out all day and he didn't feel like going out again.

The obstetrician remembered that Mom had another phone number on her chart. They called Nana. She came to the hospital and authorized whatever it was they had to do.

I was born nearly blind in one eye and Mom believes it's a result of the delayed birth. Says Mom, "They held the baby back while they were trying to get the so-called father, this biological accident of a father, to come down and give his permission for the procedure that saved her life. That's what caused her eye damage. I will never forgive him for that."

The only reason I wasn't named Lisa was because Mom felt that the name Lisa belonged to a fair-haired child. A sunny, bright-haired child. I had dark hair so she called me Michele instead. She never dreamed that there would one day be a sunny, bright-haired child who would be called Lisa, and she would be the grandchild my mother would never see.

My mother brought me home from the hospital to her mother's place. She telephoned Joseph. "Wouldn't you like to see your new baby?" she asked him. Yes, he wanted to see me. He came; he looked at me. And he left. That was it.

Mom didn't want to go back to him. But the family put pressure on her, so she did and things didn't get any better. My father ran up his bills and spent little time with us.

My brother remembers waking up in his crib and seeing our father punching Mom. He was about two years old. Our father was a big man, about six foot three or four. He towered over Mom. John knew instinctively that they weren't playing. He sensed Joseph's anger and the rage and the violence in the air.

Mom says, "At first when he hit me, I'd ask him what I had done to deserve it. He said he hit me because I had done something wrong and needed to be punished or corrected. But sometimes I'd be sitting there doing nothing at all and he'd suddenly lash out and punch me. I hadn't done anything—so he hit me for doing nothing. I began to realize it had nothing to do with me. I was just a handy way for him to release some frustration."

Eventually she had to have surgery on her eye to repair the damage Joseph had inflicted in his beatings. He hit her so many times in the same spot he destroyed the muscle in her eyelid and it drooped.

My father never hit me. I was a quiet child, so he just let me toddle around the house and didn't interfere with me one way or the other. He slapped John a few times and once he even locked him in the closet.

Sometimes when Mom would have to go someplace, she'd ask our father to watch us. As soon as she was gone, he'd lock us into the apartment and leave. I was spared a lot because I was so young. I wasn't scared. I had my big brother with me.

I don't know how Mom found the strength to get away from this man. She says she had no choice. She had to do it for our sakes, for the sake of her children.

It took her years. Her self-esteem was being ground down to nothing. Joseph kept telling her she was worthless and useless; you hear that enough and you begin to believe it. Divorce was frowned upon in our family; they wouldn't help. The priests she went to for guidance were sympathetic but basically told her that marriage was forever and she had to live with it.

She didn't get much help from the law, either. She eventually got a warrant from family court sworn out for Joseph's arrest—and the deputies who were supposed to arrest him refused to execute it. They told her she knew him better than they did, she should arrest him herself. She should handcuff him, throw him in the car, and drive them both down to the station!

Mom didn't give up. She waited for her chance. Every Wednesday night she would walk with us to the Laundromat on Myrtle Avenue, drop off our laundry, and go across the street to a diner. She wanted John and me to learn to eat in a restaurant. One Wednesday, she followed our routine and got the shopping cart, left the house with us and our laundry, and walked to Myrtle Avenue. But instead of going to the Laundromat we went to the police station. Mom presented them with the arrest warrant.

The police didn't want to get involved in a family dispute. "What do you want us to do with this?" they asked her.

"What it says on there. Arrest my husband."

"That's between you and him."

Mom wouldn't budge until they agreed to send someone out to our house. They sent four cops, two burly young ones, she remembers, and two older, presumably cooler-headed, men.

 She had to be there to identify Joseph for them. The cops came screeching up to the house. She took them up the stairs. Joseph looked past her, saw the police, and went out of his mind. He was furious that she had called the cops on him. He cursed her and physically attacked her in front of the police—they had to hold him back. He was out of jail by morning.

The only help Mom really had was from other women—an attorney, a neighbor, friends. Women helped each other; they had nobody else.

Mom remembers that she came home one evening from another fruitless meeting with the lawyer about the divorce Joseph wasn't giving her. A neighborhood girl baby-sat for us. Her mother was there because the meeting had run late. She asked Mom why she looked so bad. Mom told her that she had to make a decision about leaving Joseph.

The baby-sitter's mother said, "There's nothing to decide. Get out before he does something to you." They all knew because Joseph used to come home drunk and stand outside calling Mom filthy names and yelling at the neighbors that they had a whore living in the building.

Mom stood there, not moving. Joseph was due back any minute. He was on his way over. The woman grabbed all the pillowcases in the house and yelled at Mom to start stuffing them. They jammed what they could into those pillowcases—our clothes, Mom's clothes—with the woman yelling at her all the while, "Come on, push the stuff down! You can get more in! Jam it down!"

And that's how Mom made her escape. She left with nothing but her two kids and a bunch of pillowcases stuffed with our belongings. I was about four then, and John about five.

Mom moved us into a furnished room in Astoria, Queens. Our father kept after her, calling her constantly, alternately threatening and pleading with her to come back to him. He called her at work because Mom refused to tell him where we were living, and from then on she tried to keep our whereabouts a secret from him.

He promised to change, but she didn't believe him and she never went back. Mom says, "I had two little ones who were totally dependent on me. You have no idea how that motivates you. In my case it unleashed a tiger. I couldn't sit down and cry. I had to make a life for us."

The grounds for divorce in New York State were then very limited and Joseph refused to grant her one. Why, I don't know. Any guess is as good as the next. Perhaps he felt it represented failure, perhaps he just didn't want her to have her way. And perhaps he felt that their life together was the way marriage should be. It probably wasn't all that different from his parents' marriage. As I said, women were more powerless then, and punching your wife around a bit wasn't unusual in some circles. Certainly it was not unheard of in the Irish immigrant neighborhoods in which Joseph was raised.

Mom was awarded some minimal amount of child support by the

family court, which used to grant it in cases where the man didn't support the family, but she didn't even get that support. My father was awarded visiting rights, but he seldom came. Once, when he did, he brought us back after half an hour. "She," my father said, pointing to me, "had to go to the bathroom."

He had no idea how to take a little girl to the toilet.

Chapter 3

     I always felt I had a happy childhood. That may seem strange given the relationship between my mother and father, but you have to remember I knew nothing of that, or almost nothing; certainly the details were kept from me. My concerns were school, homework, ballet lessons.

Every weekend Mom took us someplace. It was part of her ongoing program to raise John and me to be cultured and refined young adults. Mom's penchant for self-improvement rivals that of any schoolmarm. We'd go to museums, the aquarium, or simply "get to know our neighborhood." Later, it was *Peter and the Wolf*, *The Nutcracker Suite*, Broadway shows, but while we were small it was simply outings in the surrounding area.

Eventually, our father dropped out of our lives. Apparently he moved away, first to Florida and later to California, and Mom heard from him less and less, although she never stopped worrying that he would turn up, and on some level, she never stopped being afraid of him. Wherever we moved, we either had an unlisted number or one listed under somebody else's name.

But I knew nothing of this. To me, my life seemed pleasant and ordinary. I had Mom and John, I had Nana and Papa Jack.

Growing up, I was the dutiful one. My brother was full of exuberance, always up to something. He was very different from me.

If we had to leave to go somewhere, I'd be at the door with my mittens, coat, hat, and scarf. John would be upstairs crawling around under the beds looking for his other sneaker. Probably the worst offense I committed was being late to school.

In grade school every Wednesday afternoon we went for religious instruction to Our Lady of Refuge. Afterward we went to confession. God forgive me, I used to make things up. I hadn't done anything particularly wrong, but you're in confession, you can't say, "Father, I didn't sin this week." So I'd say I stole a piece of gum or I lied to my mother or I got angry at my mother. He'd give me my four Hail Marys or whatever to say as penance and I figured I was clean. Lying in the confessional is a sin, too. I'd lied to the priest in saying I'd lied to my mother. There is a kind of logic to that, and I felt I'd satisfied everybody's requirements.

I wasn't as smart as my brother; I wasn't as creative as he was —and I wasn't in trouble all the time the way he was. I had a horror of calling attention to myself, so I avoided doing the things that made the grown-ups upset, and therefore they thought of me as a good girl. And I suppose I was.

I took ballet lessons for seven years at Miss Rickie's Dance Studio. We had recitals at Brooklyn College. Mom and Nana and Papa Jack would come. I knew Nana was proud of me, but the nice thing was I didn't have to do anything special to earn her love. I just had to *be*. She loved me just the way I was.

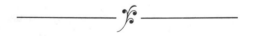

Mom worked two jobs to support us. She had her regular office job during the day, and at night she transcribed court-reporters' notes at home. She really scrimped on herself, much more so than on John and me, who always had pretty much what the other kids had. She wouldn't order coffee out at work like the others, but made her own at her desk with one of those little immerser things that heat up and a jar of instant coffee. She had always dreamed of owning a home of her own, but even after she had managed to save up the down payment, she couldn't buy a house without her husband's signature. She had worked for years to pay off his debts and his back taxes, and still, in the eyes of the law, she was not a legal entity. She was trying desperately to get a divorce from Joseph, but until they amended the divorce laws in the early seventies, she was unable to get one without his consent. Finally they changed the laws to include abandonment of minor children as grounds, and in 1971, long after any of us had seen him or heard from him, Mom and our father were finally divorced. He did not appear in court for the proceeding.

The divorce didn't seem important in our lives. What did was that when I was ten years old, we moved to Rockville Centre, to that home of our own. Mom had been unable to buy a house until she got a divorce because as a married woman she needed her husband's signature on the deed and the mortgage. I guess that gave her more years to save, because when she was finally able to do it, she did it right. The house was really nice, black and white and gray with lots of peaks and gables and columns; it looked kind of like a sea-captain's house. The house was large—a finished attic, second floor, first floor, and finished basement. There was a porch that went all the way around, steps leading down to the lawn, shrubbery and trees, and its own little walk to the street. Out back was a yard and a garage with an attached shed.

Rockville Centre was a great place to grow up, really a small town like countless others around the country. There were lots of kids on our block. There were so many kids that the Mr. Softee man took an hour to get off the block. We kids had a ball; we were in the streets every day from three-fifteen when school let out until six in the evening. And Nana and Papa Jack were right there, just a few blocks away.

I was always close to my grandmother. Nana was simply a loving presence in our lives, John's and mine. I was closer to her than John was, probably because I was a girl. I was also the good one, the one who never gave anybody any trouble.

We looked forward all week to going to Nana's on the weekend. There were other grandchildren, but they didn't live as close to Nana and Papa Jack as we did, so we got most of the cuddling and the love and the affection. Nana used to take me out on her porch at night. We'd sit in the rocking chair and watch the planes take off from JFK airport and she'd sing to me.

Nana was a jolly woman, happy and energetic, but also stern; not really stern; "solid" is the word I'm looking for. She had standards; high standards. Nana never raised her voice. You could tell when she was annoyed, but she never raised her voice. We were taught table manners. We were taught respect for our elders. We were taught not to interrupt conversations. Simple, old-fashioned values, I guess, but taught with an awful lot of love.

We'd go over to Nana's house every day after school; Mom was at work. Nana didn't allow TV during the day, but she'd take us shopping with her; whatever she was doing we did it with her. When we were playing out in the street, we always knew where to go for a hug and a kiss or a story.

When we got older, either Nana or Papa Jack would drive over to our house after school, just to see what was going on. Papa Jack would come over a lot. At least once a day. Even if he didn't stop in, he would drive by to see us playing in the street. John and I would laugh and say he was policing the block.

Our house was the hangout for all the kids, John's friends and mine. We weren't allowed to have friends over after school, but we did anyway. We'd take the pillows off the couches and lie around listening to music. Then Mom's car would pull up outside and it was like the Marx Brothers. She would walk in the front door just as the gang was flying out the back.

If I wasn't with my friends, I was on the phone with them.

I never felt I lacked for anything as a kid, never felt deprived. Whatever the other girls had, I had. Spending money, clothes, lessons. As a kid, you never realize what your parents are doing for you. All the things we had, the ballet lessons, tennis lessons, ski trips, I never asked myself where it was coming from.

In my teenage years Mom and I fought constantly. Over nothing. We were both independent, strong-minded people. We were just like two rams butting heads. There were times when I'd yell at her that I wished she were more like my friend Mary's parents—easy-going, fun-loving partying types.

I didn't realize then what a tough job she had, raising the two of us on her own.

I never thought of Mom as a battered wife. I never thought of John and me as deserted children. I didn't miss having a father. You can't miss what you never had. It wasn't as if I'd had him and he was taken away from me. He was never there. But I didn't feel anything lacking. There was always enough money for the things I wanted and needed. When I got old enough, I baby-sat to earn extra money. I'm great with kids. I love being around them, watching them laugh, watching them grow up. I was such a popular baby-sitter that I'd have three baby-sitting jobs during the day, from two till six, six till nine, and from nine to ten. On New Year's Eve I got to pick and choose whom I would baby-sit for.

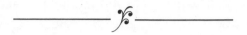

One day Mom sat down to explain the facts of life to me. I told her I knew all of that, we'd learned it in school in the sex education class she'd enrolled me in. You needed special permission from your parents for that; not all parents wanted their kids to have that kind of information. My mom did. She didn't want me to pick it up on the street. She wanted me to have it right. She always said we had more instruction in that area than she ever did.

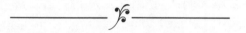

Even as a little girl, I was pretty levelheaded. I never dreamed of being something glamorous like a model or an actress when I grew up. I wanted to be a social worker. I liked finding solutions to problems, working things out, and most of all I liked helping people. I was the one the crowd brought their problems to. Mine was the shoulder they leaned on.

But by the time I graduated high school, I'd pretty much had enough of full-time school. My grades weren't good enough for college anyway, so I took a job baby-sitting full-time, Monday through Friday. I took night classes at Nassau Community College in business law, marketing, economics. My social life didn't change any when I graduated high school. I saw the same people in the same places.

Saturday afternoons the girls would wander over to somebody's house. We'd stroll around, meet up with the boys, and make the rounds. By that time lots of our friends had jobs in town, at the ice cream shop, the bagel place, the pizza place. We'd go from one to the next, have a bite at each, and of course we never paid because our friend was the one who was taking the money. Mom used to say she felt sorry for the owners.

But it was always a group thing. We didn't really "date" in the sense of going out with one person and spending an entire evening with him. Even if you were with someone in particular, there were always other people around.

One night a bunch of us were sitting around in a local bar, a place called the New Village Inn in Rockville Centre, splitting a pitcher of beer. We were celebrating something—someone's birth-day, I think. I can't remember exactly what. Four girls were at our table. Four boys were at the next. One thing led to another. We started to talk.

Maureen met Chuck that night; she married him. I met Chuck's friend Kevin. We didn't get married, but we did fall in love.

And we had a child, a beautiful little girl whom strangers would name Lisa.

Chapter 4

꒰T꒱oday when I look at pictures of Lisa, I see a lot of Kevin in her. Her blond hair and pretty features remind me of him.

Kevin was tall, very good-looking—blond hair and an athlete's body—and a star basketball player. Most star athletes are kind of pushy and showy. Kevin wasn't. He was quiet, introverted even. He was six months younger than I, and a year behind me in school. We were both seventeen. We met in the fall, at the beginning of the school year. I would turn eighteen that October, Kevin the following May. He was a senior in high school. I had just given up my baby-sitting job and started doing bookkeeping and general office work at the aluminum-mill supply firm where Mom was controller.

I liked Kevin right away. He must've liked me, too, because he didn't seem to want to leave that bar that night even though he was taking his SATs the next day. We stayed out pretty late. I didn't know if I would see him again, although I knew I wanted to.

My friend Maureen had hit it off really well with Chuck, and the next night they came over to my house. I didn't particularly want to go out, but they made a big thing about my coming along with them to the movies. When we got there, I found out why it

was so earth-shatteringly important that I go to some dumb movie
I had no desire to see.

Kevin worked there. He had a part-time job for after school and
weekends. He wanted to see me again, so he told Chuck and Chuck
told Maureen, and they dragged me over there. We saw the last
show—free, naturally, since Kevin was taking the tickets. We waited
till he got off work, then the four of us went out together. Not for
too long, just an hour or so.

Kevin had messed up on his SATs because he'd stayed out so late
the night before. He stayed out late because he hadn't wanted to
go home until I did.

We didn't give it a formal name like "going steady," but Kevin
and I became a couple and the gang knew us as that. We saw each
other as much as we could and talked on the phone constantly.
Kevin would call and tell me how crowded the theater was. If it
was busy, we'd make a date to meet after work. If not, I went to
the theater and hung around with him. The movie *1941* was playing
then. I saw it so many times I could recite the dialogue together
with the actors.

From the time I met Kevin I lost interest in anybody else. Our
feelings for each other grew more intense with time. He was always
in my mind. I'd daydream about him wherever I was, just waiting
for the next time we would be together.

Mom and John both met Kevin—he came to our house—but I
don't think they realized how much we meant to each other. We
were very much in love.

Kevin was on the baseball team as well as the basketball team.
In the dead of summer, ninety-degree heat, when other sane people
were at the beach or in their air-conditioned dens, I'd be in the
bleachers with my girlfriends yelling ourselves hoarse cheering for
our boyfriends.

Kevin's parents came to the games, too. I'd go over to say hello
and they were always nice, cordial, but there was something distant
about them. I wouldn't say they were cold, but they certainly weren't
chummy. They were private people, they kept to themselves; that
was their style. I never got to know them well.

Kevin, too, had an inner reserve. He was closed, emotionally
closed. It took a lot for him to open up, to talk about things. But
then again, I'm pretty private myself.

Kevin and Chuck were good friends and that brought Maureen and me closer. We'd known each other before, but we became really friendly when we were dating two best friends.

We did all the usual things that suburban kids do. I'd go over to Kevin's house and watch TV on his porch; he'd come over to my place and sit around. Kevin's family lived one block away from my grandparents. Some of our friends had cars, so we'd drive to this place that was a hangout for teenagers, a kind of overpass leading to the park. On a nice evening there'd be ten couples there in each other's arms.

For Christmas, our first together, Kevin gave me a necklace, a little solid-gold heart on a delicate, fine chain. Though simple and understated, it had substance to it, just the kind of thing I like. It was exquisite, really quite beautiful. I was impressed with Kevin's taste—until I saw the present Maureen got from Chuck. She got the identical necklace. I was furious and she was, too, but each of our boyfriends said that he was the one who found it first and the other copied him.

Kevin was a big Boston Red Sox fan. His favorite player was Dwight Evans. For his eighteenth birthday I went to Cosby's, a store in Manhattan's Penn Station that sold authentic sports clothing. The Long Island Rail Road was on strike, but I wasn't going to let that stop me from getting Kevin his birthday present. I dragged Maureen with me on buses and subways into the city. I bought Kevin a full Boston Red Sox outfit with Dwight Evans's name on the back of the jersey. The whole thing came to maybe a hundred dollars, but I was out of high school and working by then and could afford it.

If someone had asked me, "Are you and Kevin going to get married?" I would have said, "Not for a long time, but eventually, yes, for sure." Though we were both very young, we were definitely going to spend our lives together, that much I knew.

Actually, Kevin brought up the subject of marriage more than me. As far as I was concerned, the important thing was that we were committed to each other. When exactly we formalized it wasn't the issue with me. But Kevin used to like to dream out loud about the time when we'd be married. Once he said to me, half jokingly, "How about we skip the wedding and just live together?"

"Are you kidding!" I retorted. "Live in sin? It would break my grandmother's heart!"

I wasn't joking at all. I really thought it would. Young people never think that older people have romantic or sexual lives, especially not their parents and grandparents. We always think our parents would "just die!" if they knew what we were doing.

By the time I found out that Nana wasn't as fragile as I thought—and a lot smarter—it was too late.

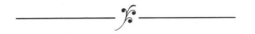

I'd never had a real boyfriend before Kevin. The most I'd done was a little kissing, nothing as serious as what we were getting into. Kevin and I were both from Catholic families. We had been taught that sex before marriage was wrong, and on some level we believed it. We put it off as long as we could, but one afternoon we were alone in my house, one thing led to another, and we wound up going all the way.

We'd been seeing each other for about seven months by then, and we'd been doing more than kissing—quite a bit more—but we'd always stopped ourselves. We didn't make a conscious decision that this time we were actually going to have sex. It just happened, without either of us knowing it was going to. It wasn't that he pressured me; he didn't. It was completely mutual. I wanted it as much as he did.

I think it was Kevin's first time, too. He was sweet, but I can't say I got much pleasure out of it that first time. I really didn't exactly know what was happening or what I was supposed to feel, and I was very, very nervous. I don't think either one of us knew exactly what was going on. We were just winging it. Those sex education classes we'd been given were mostly something to laugh at. They showed you movies and we'd sit there and giggle and make jokes about the dancing sperm. Nothing I saw or heard in class seemed to have much connection to us, Kevin and me, here and now.

Afterward, though, lying there with Kevin holding me, I was happy. I felt we were even closer now, even more committed to each other. I would never have slept with him otherwise. We weren't just "fooling around." I loved him and he loved me. Kevin was my partner in life.

I had little twinges of guilt every now and then. It was a case of having an angel on one shoulder and the devil on another. The

Church taught that what we were doing was a sin, but it felt natural, right. I liked it and didn't want to stop. So I stopped thinking about it.

I didn't tell the priest at confession, though. I don't know if Kevin did or not.

After that first time we didn't do it again for about a month. I'm not sure why. Perhaps the opportunity just didn't arise. The second time was better for me. I was able to relax and get into it a little more.

Even after that we didn't sleep together on a regular basis. Gradually our lovemaking became more frequent, but it was never an all-the-time kind of thing. I think the main reason we didn't have sex very often is that we didn't really have a place to do it. The backseat of a car is just not for me, and if we went to one or another of our houses, even if no one was home at the time, I was always afraid someone would walk in on us.

In fact, one night when Mom was away, John came home late and found Kevin and me alone in the house. John knew he'd kind of walked in on something. He glossed over it then, but the next day he told me that if there was anything sexual going on between Kevin and me, it shouldn't happen in the house.

I denied that there was "anything" going on. John wasn't completely fooled. He merely said, "Well, whatever you and Kevin are carrying on with, don't do it here."

John has told me since that he almost brought up the subject of contraception that day, but I was so defensive about the whole thing, he dropped the subject. He guessed—rightly—that I'd be angry at him for butting into my business, and he assumed that Kevin and I were smart enough to use some kind of contraception if we were active sexually.

John was wrong. Neither one of us ever mentioned birth control. It was simply too embarrassing to talk about. Sometimes Kevin had condoms with him and used them. Sometimes he didn't. I would rather have died than ask how come we weren't using a condom today. I don't think I could have said that word aloud, and I know that no power on earth could have compelled me to be the first to bring up the subject. I can still feel a kind of squirmy embarrassment at the thought: *Kevin, don't forget to bring the condoms next time.* . . . Not a chance.

The fact that I could get pregnant never once entered my mind.

I certainly knew that sex led to babies, but I never thought it would happen to me.

Why? Because I was eighteen, that's why. Teenagers always think they're invulnerable. That's why it's so hard to get them to wear seat belts and motorcycle helmets. The same thing that allows a "good kid" to take his family car out without permission, put a dent in it, and return it to the garage without mentioning it, that's what allowed me to have unprotected sex. First he doesn't think he'll have an accident, and then he doesn't think his parents will notice. He *knows* better . . . but he doesn't believe it.

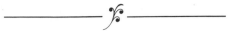

The summer of 1980 was bittersweet. Kevin and I were so in love, yet every moment we had together was colored by sadness. At the end of the summer we would be separated. Kevin was going away to college, to Mount Saint Mary's in Maryland. The mere thought of separation was torture. We spent every moment we could together, and every moment we spent together was tinged with impending loss. Kevin hated leaving me as much as I hated having him go.

And then I was faced with another, more terrible loss. In August my family was told that Nana had breast cancer. She had to have a mastectomy, but the doctors were worried that she wouldn't survive the operation since she was over eighty at the time. The thought of losing Nana scared me deep at the core—and for good reason. Nana was one of the foundations of my life.

We went to visit her in the hospital before the operation. I was frightened but I knew I had to be cheerful and optimistic as long as I was with her. When people face serious surgery, especially at her age, they need to go into it in a positive frame of mind. Everyone tried hard to put on a happy face so Nana wouldn't have the burden of trying to cheer us up. We didn't talk about her condition; in her room we spoke of other things, everyday things. But as soon as we got out to the corridor, it was a different story. There we all gave in to the worry and the fear and broke down in tears. Nana was very dear to us.

She came through the operation well. The doctors said the cancer hadn't spread as widely as they'd feared, and they thought they had gotten it all. We were all overjoyed. Soon she was back home, as active as she ever was.

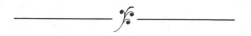

I remember the day Kevin went away. It was a beautiful day, more like fall than late August. The season must have turned early that year, because I remember the leaves were down in the park. Kevin was leaving in the late afternoon at four o'clock. We went to the park early and spent the whole day there, talking and walking around. It was really strange that the leaves had changed colors so early.

We didn't want to let go of each other. Kevin stayed with me till almost the last minute. He got home at about two minutes to four. His parents were outside the house waiting for him in the car. We kissed one last time and I watched the car drive away. I walked home with tears streaming down my face.

I had no idea that sometime in the last two weeks I had conceived a child. I was carrying Kevin's baby.

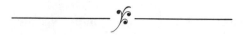

That first semester Kevin and I saw each other almost every weekend. Either he came home or I went down to his college. When we were apart, we talked at least once a day, often twice. Kevin called in the morning before class and often again in the afternoon after class. His first semester at college was rough; he had trouble connecting. He had undergone knee surgery the summer before going to college and still wore the brace from his operation. He couldn't play sports; he was homesick and lonely and generally miserable.

And I'd like to think that missing me was part of his misery. I worked in my mother's office where they had an 800 number, which I promptly gave to Kevin. I don't want to think of what their phone bill must have been.

I'm not one to write things down, such as the dates of menstrual periods. It wasn't till maybe October that the fleeting thought that I had missed a period crossed my mind. I was usually pretty regular and it seemed as if it had been a while. I don't get cramps, I'm not bedridden or anything, so there's nothing to mark the day in my mind. I can't look back and say, I missed a Monday at work because of my period, or I had wanted to go do this or that but my period started.

At the end of October I came down with the flu, or so I thought. I felt listless and tired, not really sick, but not well either. I didn't throw up, but I felt slightly nauseous all the time. I couldn't put my finger on it, but I felt different somehow, different inside.

I told my mother I had a virus. She told me to drink lots of fluids and rest. I managed to go to work, but I came straight home and got into bed with the covers over my head.

The sickness got worse and not better. One morning I got up feeling nauseous as usual, but this time the feeling grew instead of lessening until I did actually have to vomit.

I felt better for a day or two, then I threw up again in the morning. I put it down to the change of seasons. It was getting colder and it rained a lot and I thought I'd come down with a bug. Some days I'd feel okay; some days I felt achy and sick, as if I were coming down with a virus. Some days were in between. It wasn't that I felt so bad that I couldn't function; more like I was overtired.

I was up in my room the first time the thought came into my head: Maybe I'm pregnant.

Chapter 5

$\mathcal{O}$nce the thought entered my mind—once I *allowed* the thought to enter my mind—it wouldn't go away. I tried to concentrate on something else, but I couldn't shake the fear. What if I'm pregnant? Could I be pregnant? What on earth will I do?

I was putting it all together in my mind . . . feeling sick, throwing up . . . missing periods. I was pretty sure I'd missed two, maybe even three by now. I don't want to make myself sound stupid. I know as much biology as the average person. But I didn't really want to face the fact that I might be pregnant.

I didn't know what to do, so I didn't do anything. I couldn't face it, so I ignored it. It's not difficult to put something out of your mind when the alternative, acknowledging your situation, is so fundamentally terrifying.

The sickness got worse. When they call it morning sickness, they lie. I woke up nauseous and it came in waves all day long. Anything could make me sick. If I came across the wrong smell, such as from passing a deli, I was sick as a dog. I might have to throw up anytime, morning, noon, or night. But the mornings were almost a definite.

Every morning my mom has a cup of tea waiting for me when I come out of the shower. She makes it just the way I like it, milk and sugar. It's part of our morning routine. I had to drink the tea or she'd know something was wrong. I sat there and forced it down when the mere thought of it was enough to start my stomach heaving. Then I'd wait, and whichever bathroom she chose, the one upstairs or downstairs, I'd be in the other, vomiting into the toilet.

It took me half an hour to recover from that cup of tea. Mom and I drove to work together, so I had to start getting up earlier to give myself time to drink the tea, vomit it up, and recover a little.

At work I threw up immediately after lunch every day. I ate with everybody, chatted and made conversation, excused myself, went to the bathroom, and vomited. It was really an odd feeling putting food in my mouth, forcing myself to chew and swallow, praying I could hold off until I got to the bathroom.

If anybody asked, I said I was recovering from a bad bout of flu and was still a little under the weather. But nobody really noticed anything. I guess they didn't used to call me Sarah Bernhardt for nothing.

I thought of taking a home pregnancy test, but I figured it would probably tell me what I didn't want to know, so I didn't take one. As long as I wasn't absolutely sure I was pregnant, I wouldn't have to deal with it. As long as I didn't know for sure, there was still room for hope.

Until somebody told me otherwise, I could put everything that was happening down to my imagination. I thought of a thousand other things that could cause me to miss periods. I'd heard that stress did that sometimes. It could be some kind of vitamin deficiency. Maybe I was anemic. Possibly I had a cyst. Anything sounded good in comparison to being pregnant.

And then the holiday season started. It's easy to put things out of your mind when you're caught up in the holidays, family, friends, shopping. We always had a big family Thanksgiving, with all the aunts and uncles and everybody. Nana would still do all the vegetable dishes at her house and bring them over with her, and Papa Jack would always complain that she'd forgotten the particular favorite he'd been looking forward to.

Kevin had his holidays with his family and we'd meet afterward. I'd be sitting at my dining room table watching the clock, and he'd be doing the same thing at his house, waiting for a reasonable time to leave. We'd stick it out till eight, eight-thirty—fair enough since we started at one or two o'clock in the afternoon—then we'd excuse ourselves and dash out to wherever we were going to meet. We couldn't wait to see each other, and every hour we spent apart seemed wasted.

Kevin wasn't happy at college; in fact, he was miserable. He wasn't making any friends and was eager to come home.

We exchanged our gifts on Christmas Eve, just before midnight Mass. Our gifts were small ones that year. I was working but Kevin was studying full-time and I wouldn't embarrass him by giving him an expensive gift when he couldn't reciprocate. I gave him a portable radio/tape deck. He gave me a sweater and a couple of the electronic games, one football, one baseball, that were a craze that year.

As usual, there was lots of socializing, everybody visiting back and forth. I was nauseous almost all the time. I'd go out with everybody, but I'd ask Kevin to take me home early because I was always tired. Sometimes he continued on home from there, and sometimes he'd drop me at my house and go back to the party, depending on how late it was when I hit my brick wall.

That New Year's Eve, Maureen and Chuck and Kevin and I rented rooms at a Holiday Inn. All the fun and festivities helped to put my physical ailments and their possible causes out of my mind, most of the time. The worry was always there. I had trouble sleeping. It was getting harder and harder to convince myself that whatever I had was going to go away. The ringing in of the year 1981 was very much marred by my lingering feeling that I was in big trouble.

No one looking at me could have guessed I was pregnant. I carried small—even at term I had barely gained twenty pounds. I didn't start to really show until the last trimester of my pregnancy.

I thought of telling Kevin what I suspected, but I dismissed that idea almost as soon as it crossed my mind. Nobody had *told* me I was pregnant, it was only a possibility. It hadn't been confirmed by a doctor, so what was the need to say anything? I'd skipped a few periods, so what? Women skipped periods sometimes. Sure, I'd been regular until then, but maybe my body was just changing. This whole thing could be just a big false alarm and I'd get my period any day now—probably right after I told Kevin and got him all upset.

I realize now I was working so hard at hiding my pregnancy from everybody else because I was working equally hard at hiding it from myself. At this point I gave no thought of the baby inside me, of the new life growing in my womb. That came much later. Now I was focused on myself and my predicament and I could never see past that.

After New Year's I started thinking seriously about the dilemma I was in. I had pretty much run out of excuses. Okay, Michele, you're going to have to do something soon.

I went to the drugstore to buy a home pregnancy test kit—at least that was my intention. I walked up and down the aisles, picking up everything else *but* what I had come in there for. I was sure that every single person in the store was waiting to pounce the minute I put my hand on it. Never mind, I'd come back another time when the store wasn't full.

One other shopper in the store was enough for me to declare the store "full." I bought shampoo, conditioner, highlighter, hairbrushes, anything and everything. By the time I actually succeeded in snagging a home pregnancy test, we had a year's supply of toothpaste in the house.

The instructions said you had to do it in the morning, but I couldn't wait. I ran a bubble bath so I'd have an excuse to lock myself in the bathroom for a long time. I don't know why I thought anybody would care. I don't even think anybody was home. There's nothing like a guilty conscience to make you paranoid.

The test was the kind that turned color if you were pregnant and stayed clear if you weren't.

It turned pink.

I can't say I was shocked. I knew.

But still . . . this was reality staring me in the face.

I gathered up all the testing material, put it in a bag, and snuck out to the garbage can. I unwrapped the twist tie and stowed the evidence way down deep under the garbage.

Now I was really scared. As much as I tried to push the thought out of my mind, it kept coming back. I'm pregnant. I'm pregnant. What am I going to do?

I'm not opposed to abortion. One of my girlfriends had an abortion. I went with her, waited for her till it was over, and took her home. I felt then, and feel today, that it's every woman's decision to make, and since that was what she decided to do, I went along with it and tried to make it as comfortable as possible for her. I even paid for it. She was supposed to pay me back, but I don't think she ever will.

I could have asked her to return the favor and help me. I didn't.

There were any number of other people I could have gone to. I didn't.

For other people, I'm a pillar of strength. Just lean on me, I'll take care of everything. I was the "Dear Abby" for the whole gang. But when I was in trouble, the one thing I couldn't do was ask for help.

I still didn't show much—a loose shirt over jeans was enough to conceal any roundness of my tummy. I've heard of women having swollen breasts and other symptoms. I didn't. Aside from the nausea and the general blahs, I felt pretty much the same. I didn't feel the baby move until I was almost in my seventh month. If you suggest that there is some deep denial operating here, I won't argue with you, but every person is different and that's how it was with me. Perhaps it would have been better if I had shown earlier and people had guessed. As it was, I was the only one who knew for a long time.

I was panic-stricken—frightened and confused and simply unable to think. One thought stood out in the clamor that rang in my head: No one was going to know. Not my mother, not a friend, nobody.

It had crossed my mind to confide in one of my close girlfriends, maybe the one whom I'd helped with her abortion. It would probably have been more natural to tell somebody. This is not the kind of thing you usually keep completely to yourself. But I felt I couldn't trust anyone to keep a secret the way I had for my girlfriend. If I told her, she'd tell her boyfriend and he'd tell somebody else and pretty soon it wouldn't be a secret anymore.

I'd be whispered about for life: "Michele got into trouble a few years ago . . . didn't you know?"

I couldn't stand that. Call it pride if you will, but I couldn't take that kind of embarrassment. I didn't know what I was going to do or how I'd manage it, but whatever I did, I would do it on my own, me, myself, and I. That was my driving force.

Kevin was the one exception. I might have to tell Kevin, on the simple grounds of fairness. He had a right to know. But until my pregnancy was confirmed by a doctor, there was nothing to tell, was there? It would be silly to get him all worked up and then find out I had that vitamin deficiency I hoped for, wouldn't it?

My passion for secrecy would have been fine if I could have handled the situation on my own. But the same girl who had solutions for everybody else was a wet noodle for herself. I was a jellyfish. You can't ask a jellyfish to make decisions, can you?

I was frozen, unable to move in any direction.

I didn't decide *not* to have an abortion. I didn't decide anything at all. I suppose if I'd really wanted to have an abortion, I would have done something in time. I have to believe that subconsciously, I didn't want to. Otherwise there's no way to explain why I waited so long.

I knew in my heart that I had a real problem, that it wouldn't just go away, but I couldn't make myself *move*.

Every night I promised myself that in the morning I'd do *something*—what I didn't know. In the morning I'd say, "It's Wednesday, it doesn't pay to start in the middle of the week. I'll wait till Monday and then I'll definitely do something."

Monday morning I'd wake up and think, there's a whole week ahead, you have plenty of time, don't get yourself all worked up. I'll do something. This week I'll definitely do something.

Even then I still had hope that this was all some kind of silly mistake. Maybe the test was defective. I could have screwed up while doing it; I'm no lab technician. And who says they're fool-proof? Maybe I'm the fool they weren't proof against.

You know the song Mary Martin sang in *South Pacific*, the one about being a cockeyed optimist? Well, I don't consider myself a cockeyed optimist, but I do cling to hope long after somebody more rational might give up.

I know it sounds contradictory, and of course it was, but at the same time, I lay awake in bed at night trying to think of a way out. I couldn't come up with any long-term solutions, but I knew one thing that had to be done: I had to go to a doctor.

I'm not one for doctors in general. I have a strong constitution, and if I get sick, I just lie low for a few days and whatever it is goes away. I didn't have a family doctor, let alone a gynecologist. I had never been to a gynecologist; I had never had a gynecological exam.

I had been in the office of an ob/gyn only once in my life, when my girlfriend had her abortion. How she got to him, I don't know. But he was the only one I could think of.

His name was Dr. Michael Bergman.

The "if only's" that have tormented me since November 1987 start here. If only I had gone somewhere else—anywhere else. For Dr. Michael Bergman would lead me directly to Joel Steinberg, who

would steal my daughter from me and eventually kill her with his
bare hands.

It took me about three weeks after the home pregnancy test to get
up the courage to call Dr. Bergman's office. The woman on the other
end wanted to know exactly what the nature of the problem was.
I said, "I think I may be pregnant." Notice the word "think." I was
still in a state of denial, still hoping I'd come out with a prescription
for iron pills. Even a cyst would look good compared to what I
feared most. It had taken me nearly seven months to make this
phone call. I wasn't about to let go of all that denial at once.

She scheduled an immediate appointment for me, in the next day
or so. Later I would come to know that voice very well. It belonged
to Ginny Liebrader who would also be instrumental in the events
which led to my turning Lisa over to the hands of her killers.

I arrived at Dr. Bergman's office terrified, to say the least. Since
Mom and I worked in the same office, I couldn't just telephone in
to work and say I wasn't coming. I had to lie to her as well. As
soon as I came downstairs, I told her I was sick. I didn't have to
pretend much. That morning I let her see me throw up. She herself
told me to stay home from work and rest. That made me feel worse.
She loved me and cared about me and believed whatever lie I was
telling her.

As soon as Mom left for work, I dressed and went to the bank
and took out three or four hundred dollars in cash. My mom's an
accountant. What if the bank messed up on another check of mine
for some reason and she went through my checkbook, just to clear
it up? I had no idea how much a visit to a gynecologist would cost
and I just hoped I had enough.

The receptionist was sitting behind a little window. I managed
to get my name out, and to say that I had an appointment. I was
trying hard to look normal. She gave me a clipboard with a form to
fill out. One of the questions was who recommended you to this

doctor. I wrote "A friend." I didn't name names; I would never betray a confidence.

I handed Ginny back the clipboard with the forms filled out. She sent me into the bathroom for a urine test. I had no trouble urinating; I was so nervous I was glad for the opportunity.

I went back to my seat and picked up a magazine. I pretended I was reading. The waiting room was filled with women, most of them—all of them it seemed to me—pregnant.

The nurse took me into the examination room, handed me a gown, and told me to take off all my clothes. She showed me the stirrups and how to put my feet in them. I tried to keep my mind blank, totally blank. There was a mobile over the table, little silver sailboats. I concentrated on that and tried to keep my mind a million miles away.

Dr. Bergman came in and examined me—quickly, it took maybe thirty seconds at the most. I think he knew when he walked into the room, from the urine test. Almost immediately he told me to get dressed, he would see me in his office.

I don't remember getting dressed or going to his office. The next thing I remember is finding myself across the desk from him.

"Yes, you are pregnant," he said.

He asked when my last period was. I said I wasn't sure. I felt like a fool. I didn't really keep track, but it was at least four months, maybe five. I was trying hard not to cry.

Without a sonogram he couldn't be sure exactly how far along I was. I was to have one done and have the results sent to his office. But he could tell me right now that an abortion was out of the question. I didn't ask about abortion. He volunteered the information.

He glanced at the form I'd filled out. I had answered everything honestly. I smoked moderately, about half a pack a day; he said moderate smoking would be fine. I didn't drink during the pregnancy—liquor disagreed with me. My general health was great; I took no drugs of any kind, legal or otherwise.

I was nineteen years old and not married.

"What are you going to do, Michele? Do you have any plans?"

"I have no idea. No idea at all." I tried not to let him see that I was shaking.

"Do your parents know?"

"My parents are divorced. I haven't seen my father in years."

"Mother?"

"I haven't told her. I'm not going to."

"What about other relatives? Some friends, maybe?"

I blurted out, "I don't want anybody to know! There's not a soul in this world who knows except you and me."

That may have been the moment I sealed my fate, and the fate of the little girl I was carrying.

Chapter 6

Dr. Bergman instantly fell in with my desire for secrecy. He was even concerned about contacting me with the sonogram results. Was it okay to call me at home?

Not with my mother around. That's all she would have to do—pick up the phone and hear that a doctor was calling me.

How about at work? No good either. Mom and I worked together; the firm was small and friendly. If a doctor called me, the girls would be at my elbow in two seconds, and Mom would find out within three. There would be no way I could slough her off, either. Mom was a terror when she wanted to know something concerning one of her kids.

Dr. Bergman had an idea. We would decide on a phony name and he would use it when he called me! That way no one would ever catch on.

How could I have been suspicious? Just being with Dr. Bergman was somehow comforting. He was businesslike and professional, but he was kind, too; you could sense that. He was a short man with dark curly hair and beard. He looked just like the teddy bear you snuggled with when you were a kid. I thought he was helping me keep my pregnancy secret because he was such a sympathetic and understanding man.

I had no idea I was delivering myself—and my baby—into his

hands. I let him see how naive I was, how alone and desperate. If I had looked more confident, in control, as if I knew what I was doing, he never would've picked my child to hand over to Joel Steinberg. But I'm not a good liar, and anyway, I wouldn't have lied to a doctor.

I can still remember how good he made me feel. I want to believe that he didn't really have this whole thing planned out, that he was being caring and not manipulative.

Looking back, wouldn't it have been appropriate for him to encourage me to confide in *someone*? Shouldn't he have said things like, Michele, this isn't so bad. Your mom won't have a heart attack, nobody dies from this, it happens. Could you talk to an aunt, a family friend? You really don't have to go through this alone.

He never said anything like that. I thought he was going along with me, with my wishes, but it turned out he was operating for his own reasons.

I left Dr. Bergman's office with a great sense of relief. I'd been carrying this terrible secret alone for so long. At last, somebody else knew, another human being. There was someone I could sit down and talk to about it.

I kept my mind focused on the job I had to do. I had to get a sonogram. I didn't think beyond that. Beyond that lay big questions, scary questions, questions I wasn't equipped to deal with. Like, what on earth was I going to do?

Dr. Bergman hadn't told me where or how one obtained a sonogram. I assumed one did it in a hospital. But which hospital? The closest one to me was Mercy, a Catholic hospital. That was out. Too many priests and nuns walking around. I don't think I could've stood that, given the circumstances. I didn't need all those priests and nuns reminding me of words like "sin" and "out of wedlock" and "fornication."

It had to be fairly close, I couldn't go too far, but not so close that I'd run into somebody I knew and have to explain what I was doing there. I didn't think I could pass myself off as a candy striper. And if I did, with my luck whoever I ran into would see Mom that night and tell her what a charitable person I was.

Finally I called South Nassau Community Hospital and simply told the switchboard I needed a sonogram. The operator asked no questions, merely connected me to the department that did outpatient sonograms.

Time was running out. I made an appointment for as soon as they could take me, which was the day after next. Mom came home from work; I was upstairs in my room. She asked how I felt. I said, "Not good," and I wasn't lying.

My family knows when I'm sick I can't deal with anybody. I shut myself into my room and stay in bed with the covers over my head. That's what I did that night, and Mom didn't see anything amiss.

I was praying that she wouldn't decide to come up and check on me, maybe stay for a chat. I was counting on the fact that she knows better than to try to talk to me when I'm not well.

I didn't want to think about any large questions. I confined my worrying to the immediate problem at hand. How would I get another day off to have the sonogram? I couldn't come up with anything brilliant. The only solution I had was to "get sick" again that morning.

I kept my mind busy with the instructions about not eating any food and drinking nine glasses of water prior to coming in. I concentrated on the sonogram and tried not to think of other things.

———————— 𝄢 ————————

The only way I can describe my state of mind after the sonogram is "calm panicking." Inside, I was one big frightened scream. Out-side, I was the same old Michele.

The one thought I didn't waver from—probably the only clear thought in my mind—was that no one was going to know. I was going to get through this somehow—how, I had no idea—without anyone's ever finding out.

Sure, I could have told my mom. She would have ranted and raved for a while, then she'd have calmed down and been her usual competent self. She wouldn't throw me out of the house and she wouldn't faint. What she would do is handle everything; all I'd have to do is follow where she led.

I can't say exactly why I was so hell-bent on keeping it from her. Perhaps in part because she'd had enough problems in her life. And I was always the good one, the one who never gave anybody trouble. Part of it was pride; I couldn't bear to destroy that image. And part of it was concern for her; I knew how deeply it would hurt her.

She'd raised me to be a good Catholic and a good person. She didn't raise me to be a teenage unwed mother.

Things like this happened to other people, not to us.

But it *was* happening to me and I couldn't stand to see the look on Mom's face if she found out. I didn't want her to have to deal with this. It was my problem, not hers; my burden to bear.

I went right up to my room after the sonogram and stayed there. John came home from night school. I said, "Hi, don't bother me, I don't feel well." That sounded like the Michele he knew and loved. He went into the den and watched television.

I still had no real thought that I was going to have a baby. All I could think was, I'm pregnant and I'm more scared than I've ever been in my life.

And dumb as this may sound, as long as there were still test results to be gotten, it wasn't over yet, was it? There was still hope. Until somebody looks you in the eye and tells you to your face it's hopeless, then there's still hope.

That last shred of hope was destroyed the next day when Dr. Bergman called me at the office with the test results. He used the phony name we'd agreed on. I was so glad he thought of that, because I hadn't. I didn't think he was slick. I thought he was caring and sensitive and competent.

"The sonogram shows that you are twenty-seven weeks pregnant," Dr. Bergman said.

I couldn't take it in. "What does that mean in months? Tell me what it means in months."

"Six months. You're going into your third trimester."

That was the end of hope. There were no more tests, no more results to get. I felt the strength drain out of my body. I couldn't hear anything over the pounding in my ears.

"Michele, are you there?"

"Yes. I'm here."

He wanted me to come to his office the next day. We would talk more then.

He had calculated my due date. It was May 7, Kevin's birthday. Kevin's baby would be born on the same day he was. Usually when that happens it's an occasion for double celebrations and fun-filled family parties. Not this time.

This time they didn't keep me waiting in the anteroom. I was taken right into Dr. Bergman's office. Dr. Bergman was even warmer and more concerned than he was last time. I still had no idea what I was going to do about the baby, but now it seemed I didn't have to decide.

Dr. Bergman never asked if I wanted to give the baby up for adoption. I never volunteered that I wanted to give it up. He simply took it for granted that that was what was going to happen. And suddenly, as I sat there listening to him outline the plans he had made for me, adoption seemed like the perfect solution—the only solution, and it never occurred to me I hadn't been asked if I wanted to give up the baby or not.

Dr. Bergman knew an excellent adoption lawyer. He would put me in touch with him. I wouldn't have to do a thing; the lawyer would handle all the details. He would find the adoptive parents. The adoptive parents would pay for all my medical bills and expenses relating to the birth. I had paid for the sonogram, but my bill with Dr. Bergman had been left open because I was going to return in a day or two after the test. Now he didn't want any money from me, so I never actually paid him anything at all.

No other alternatives were discussed or even brought up. He never so much as hinted at the possibility that I might keep the baby, or suggested that there were other, more orthodox avenues such as an adoption agency, specifically a Catholic one, for I had told him that the baby's father and I were both Catholics and I wanted the child raised by a Catholic family. Actually, had he given me the choice of a private adoption such as he was arranging or an agency adoption, I would still have gone with him. I thought— mistakenly—that an agency adoption would be more public, that I would be required to list myself somewhere where my identity could easily be found out. That I didn't want. Also, I knew of two separate instances of people adopting privately, one of them in my own family, and both of them very blessed.

I made only two requests of Dr. Bergman: that the adoptive parents be Catholic and that they be a married couple. No cohabitants, no people living together without a commitment. That was important; the child had to go to a married couple. Those were the only two things I asked, the only conditions, if you will, that I made.

Dr. Bergman said the lawyer was very experienced; adoption was his specialty. My wishes would be complied with. The lawyer would find a nice, educated Catholic couple for the baby.

Dr. Bergman had already spoken to him, and he was willing to take my case.

A great burden was lifted off me, and I was almost shaky with relief. I wasn't alone anymore. This man—this wonderful man—was taking care of me. I thought he was just about the nicest person I had ever met. He was my knight in shining armor.

No, I didn't think that it was odd that Dr. Bergman had moved so fast. I was amazed that he had gone to so much trouble for me. He didn't know me; I wasn't a long-term patient. He'd never even seen me until four days ago. He must be one of those sainted people who are put on this earth to help others.

Dr. Bergman even had a place for me to stay until the baby was born. He'd arranged for me to move in with his office receptionist, Ginny Liebrader. Again, I would pay Ginny nothing. Any expenses would be taken care of by the adoptive couple.

On my way out he introduced me to her. He'd obviously spoken with her before. She knew all about the arrangement. Ginny was friendly and warm. "Hi, Michele. I hear you're going to stay with me for a while. I've got plenty of room. We'll be glad to have you."

"I don't know how to thank you. Both of you."

Dr. Bergman gave me a little pat on the shoulder. "Don't worry about it. This happens all the time. You're not the only one."

I tried again to express how I felt. Dr. Bergman didn't want to hear it. "We're glad to help," he said, and walked away. Ginny turned to me. "Move in whenever you want. And listen, Michele, try not to worry, okay? Like Dr. Bergman said, this happens all the time."

These people had to be the most caring people in the world!

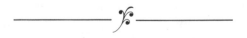

I left the office feeling warmed by Ginny's smile and Dr. Bergman's strength. My heart was eased for the first time in many months. Only now did I realize how much worry and tension I had been carrying alone.

My secret was safe. Ginny and Dr. Bergman had assured me it would all be handled in the strictest confidence. I had all the help I needed to get through this; I wouldn't have to tell anybody I knew.

What would I have done if Bergman hadn't taken things into this hands the way he did? I've asked myself that many times, and the answer I come up with may be strange, but it's the truth. I honestly think I would have gone off somewhere by myself and reappeared after the baby was born. How I would have moved out without anybody's knowing, where I would have gone, what I would have done with the baby, I don't know, but I do know that I would have done it, because I had to.

And Lisa would now be a happy, healthy nine-year-old.

The only person I was planning to tell was Kevin, but not over the phone. This was not the kind of news you break to someone over the telephone. The next day was the Friday before Valentine's Day weekend, and immediately after work Chuck and Maureen and I were driving down to Maryland to Kevin's college. There was going to be a big game, lots of parties—a fun college weekend.

I took my suitcase into work with me the next day. I had lucked out. They'd been doing inventory in the warehouse, counting and cataloguing pieces of long-stored metal on the shelves. It was dusty, grimy work and no one wanted to do it. I jumped at it. For me it was a lifesaver. My skirts and dresses were getting tight and this gave me the perfect excuse to wear jeans and a big shirt to work. The other good part was that I didn't have to be in the main office with my mother. I was trying to steer clear of her as much as I could, especially now that I had talked to Dr. Bergman and Ginny and everything was taken care of.

I was up on a forklift when I suddenly heard Mom yelling for us to get down from there. I hadn't even seen her come in.

A few minutes later we were all called into the office of the president of the company. Mom was tearing into him about having us doing work like that. It wasn't what we were hired for, we shouldn't be climbing those ladders, it was unsafe, blah, blah, blah. Mom said, "They're quitting. I'm quitting for all of them. They're going back to their regular jobs as of now!" The poor man nodded. He had no idea what he was up against when he'd unleashed the wrath of Anita Launders.

I had no idea what got into her. Later she told me that as she looked up at me, I reached up for something and she noticed that I was gaining weight. I didn't look heavier, exactly, just . . . rounded.

I couldn't wait for the weekend to start. I glanced at my watch. A quarter to five. Do the mail and that's it, we're gone. I was just finishing up the mail when Mom cornered me. We were standing in front of the Pitney Bowes machine.

"Michele, are you pregnant?" she asked.

I reacted with instant outrage. "How could you say a thing like that? What's the matter with you, of course I'm not pregnant!"

And I was out the door in a typical teenage huff . . . away to my weekend, during which I planned to break the news to Kevin that he was about to become a father.

Chapter 7

I spent the whole trip down rehearsing to myself what I would say to Kevin. He was the one person whom I had an obligation to tell and also the one person I could safely share this with.

"Kevin, I have something to tell you." No.

"Kevin, we have to talk." No.

"Kevin, we have something to talk about, something very serious." No good.

I couldn't make the scenario come out right in my mind.

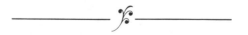

Kevin was thrilled to see me. He pulled me into a big hug. I was happy to be back in his arms.

Friday night there was a party in somebody's room in the dorm, directly across the hall from Kevin's room. Kevin and I were surrounded by college kids having a good time. We never got a minute alone, not alone enough for the kind of conversation I had in mind.

Everybody was drinking. I was nauseated, as I usually was those days. It was all I could do not to throw up. One sip of alcohol and I would have been a goner, but I didn't want anyone to suspect anything so I held a drink in my hand and pretended I was nursing it. Kevin and his friends kept moving from place to place, and every time we moved to a new bar or new party, I found a place to ditch my drink and accept a new one so nobody noticed I never tasted them.

I dragged myself through the evening, trying to blend in with the others. I was terrified that somebody would know, that they would somehow look at me and *know*.

Kevin lived in a coed dorm, girls on one floor, guys on another. All the female guests were officially listed as staying with the girls, but of course the couples paired off.

Kevin wanted to make love, but I put him off. I thought it was something pregnant women shouldn't do, that it might hurt the baby. I told him I didn't feel well. We fell asleep next to each other. Or at least he did. I just pretended to sleep.

I had this fantasy that I wouldn't have to tell him, that he himself would bring it up. "Michele, are you pregnant?"

It would have been so much easier.

I wanted to tell him. I didn't want to tell him.

I wanted him to find out. I didn't want him to find out.

I was keeping a secret, but I wanted him to know it. It doesn't make any sense, I know.

I was going to tell him. It was just a question of finding the right moment. I let Friday night go by. There was plenty of time. My main concern was not letting him know how sick I felt.

In the morning I snuck out quickly to the girls' bathroom and blessed whatever lack of funds had prevented them from putting one in each room. I kept from vomiting long enough to check each stall to make sure it was empty. All I needed was for some well-meaning girl to see me throw up and come at me with offers of comfort and Pepto-Bismol.

Chuck and Maureen were staying in a hotel nearby. We all met for breakfast. Just walking into the coffee shop, with the smells hanging in the air, made me sick. I told them that my stomach was a little upset and ordered something that didn't smell much, like cereal. But I thought I would throw up just watching the plates of bacon and eggs being set down on the table. Watching someone pour ketchup on his plate made me dizzy.

I was terribly emotional and that was another thing I had to watch. It was horrifying, as if some stranger had taken over my personality. If I weren't careful, I'd find myself bursting into tears for absolutely no reason. A fly landing on my shoulder could make me cry. I didn't know then that it's typical of pregnant women to feel that way, and in any case I didn't think of myself as a "pregnant woman." A pregnant woman was some married lady shopping for maternity clothes and being given baby showers. I was just me in a terrible situation.

One thing I can say is that I didn't feel sorry for myself. No thoughts of "Why did this happen to me, why am I in such deep trouble?" I would have felt that way perhaps before I met Dr. Bergman and Ginny. I wasn't alone anymore. I had a problem, but there were kind, competent people who were helping me. I kept thinking about how nice Ginny had been, how friendly and warm. I wasn't quite as panic-stricken and frightened and filled with dread as I had been.

I dragged through the day trying to force myself into the party atmosphere. We kept going from place to place, and everywhere we went I took myself off to a corner and sat there. Kevin asked me more than once what was the matter, but every time there were people around. I couldn't manage to say, "Could we step outside for a minute?" I just couldn't do it. So I said nothing, nothing was the matter.

Kevin was being very social, always in the middle of a crowd of laughing kids without a care in the world. It seemed as if he was very friendly with this one particular girl, but I told myself it was my imagination. My emotions were running hot and cold and east and north and west and south. Just because I was sitting like a bump on a log, I couldn't expect him to sit on the side with me. I didn't want to spoil his fun.

Months later Kevin told me that one of his friends asked him if I was pregnant. He said, "No. She would have told me."

Saturday night there was another big party. By then something had switched in my thinking. From the time I'd seen Dr. Bergman and he confirmed I was pregnant, I kept thinking of all the reasons to *tell* Kevin. Saturday evening I started to go the other way, thinking of all the reasons *not* to tell him.

I started thinking that maybe it would be best if he didn't know.

On the one hand, it was his baby. That was a strong reason to tell him. Also, he was my best friend, my love, my partner in life: another reason to share this with him.

But . . . he was enjoying school. Finally, he had found his niche. His injury had healed so he could play the sports he loved and in which he shone. He had made friends; he was having fun—he was having a ball! He was also doing well academically and would continue to do so . . . unless he found out some news that would throw him off his stride just before the midterms that were just then coming up. He wouldn't be able to concentrate. He might even flunk out.

Kevin had a career and a future ahead of him. By telling him I was pregnant, I could send it all down the drain.

I loved him. I didn't want to hurt him.

We had our whole lives to be together. Now that I had Dr. Bergman and Ginny, maybe it would be best if I didn't tell him at all. I could go to Ginny's for three months, come back, and Kevin and I would pick up where we left off. He would never have to know. I wouldn't destroy his wonderful college years.

I didn't know then how much of a ball he was having down there at college. . . .

Mom thinks I give my heart too intensely, that I'm loyal to people far beyond their loyalty to me, beyond what they deserve. She says that even if they're not doing right by me, I can't see it; I'm blind to their faults.

She could be right.

I left the party early and went back to Kevin's room.

If Kevin had followed me, or gone with me, that would have been the opportunity I was looking for. I would have told him then. I'd have had the perfect lead-in. "Kevin, I left the party early because I haven't been feeling well. I haven't been feeling well because . . ."

Kevin didn't follow me. He came back to the room later, and by then I was drifting in and out of sleep. I didn't have the energy even to attempt to wake up enough to have that conversation with him.

That was the turning point. I never did get a chance to talk to Kevin, and with each passing hour the desire to do so lessened. By Sunday morning Kevin and I were annoyed with each other. He was annoyed with me for being such a social lump and misread my behavior to mean that I was annoyed with him. I wasn't exactly annoyed with him, but I was unhappy and there's only so much you can cover up.

Not telling him was starting to look better and better.

But still I'd think: He has a right to know. It's his baby, too. And then I'd see again how happy he was at college, how well he fit in. I was sure that this news would disrupt his midterms at least and probably his college career. I really couldn't stand to do that to him. I'd be robbing him of his college years.

And realistically, what could he do? What difference could he make if he knew? He was in Maryland, I was in New York. What was the point of giving him some bad news he couldn't really do anything about? If he had asked, if he'd even come close to asking, if he'd commented at all about my weight or my queasiness or my preoccupation, I would have told him the truth.

And if I didn't have Ginny to go to and Dr. Bergman to take care of me, I really think I would have told Kevin anyway. Fantasies about going off on my own are one thing, but realistically I would have had to tell somebody and that person would—*should*—have been Kevin. But since I *had* met them and they were in my life, I didn't have to bring anyone else into it.

On Sunday morning someone knocked on Kevin's door. There was a phone call for me. I couldn't imagine who it could be.

I should have guessed. It was Mom. I still don't know how she got the dormitory phone number, but in thinking about it, I realize she could have looked it up on her phone bill.

She asked me again, "Michele, are you pregnant?"

This time I admitted it.

When my Mom gets panicked, she has a tendency to lose it, really lose it. It doesn't happen often; normally she is a reserved person. But when something really hits the fan, she gets hyper. She won't admit it, but she does. I put the phone away from my ear, she was screaming so loud.

There was no privacy, people were standing around. Kevin was at my elbow; I think Maureen was there, too. Everyone was concerned as to why she was calling. I said, "Mom, I can't talk now. Don't worry. There's no problem." And I hung up.

Mom called right back. I wouldn't take the call. I told whoever had answered the phone to say I wasn't there.

A little while later she called again.

This time I told her that I couldn't talk *then*. We'd talk about it when I got home. She went along with that.

I would have given anything not to go home. I knew Mom was just waiting for me to walk through that door. I didn't want to face her, but I also couldn't stay indefinitely in Kevin's dorm. I couldn't stay where I was and I didn't want to go where I was going. And through all this, I had to keep a reasonably happy demeanor and a semblance of a smile on my face.

What I really wanted was to find a hole right there in Emmitsburg, Maryland, away from Kevin, my mom, and everybody, crawl in, and stay there forever.

Kevin and I said good-bye. He thought we'd see each other soon. I knew I wouldn't see him again for a long time.

In the car going home I thought about the weekend. It had been as rotten as it was because of me. I was lying to Kevin, how could there not be tension between us?

I didn't know then that Kevin was lying to me, too.

Kevin decided that weekend to break up with me. I wasn't the cheerful, outgoing Michele he once knew. I couldn't seem to get into the spirit of his college life and there were plenty of girls who could. It was time he found somebody a little more fun, a little more happy-go-lucky.

It's a good thing I didn't know. The only thing that got me through the next few months was Kevin. Knowing that when all this was over we would be together gave me the courage to do the hard thing I had to do. The love that I had for him, the love I believed he felt for me . . . that's what sustained me. I don't think I will ever love anybody with that kind of purity, untouched by the slightest hint of doubt. Michele and Kevin, Kevin and Michele. I would close my eyes and see those names in different kinds of script, intertwined.

Chapter 8

I hung around Maureen's house for as long as I could when we got back to Rockville Centre. I knew that when I walked into my house, I would be walking into the "wrath of Kahn." Finally, I really had to go home.

Mom practically pulled me inside by the ear. I was glad she'd had some enforced waiting time before I got home. She asked me a thousand questions. Her voice was getting loud. Not angry, but emotional. I kept saying, "I've got everything under control. It's all taken care of."

Mom wanted to take me to a Planned Parenthood clinic. "I've made all my plans," I told her.

"We can get counseling—"

I cut her off. I didn't need counseling. My mind was made up.

She wanted me to go there for information.

I was really exasperated. What did I need information for when I had Dr. Bergman and Ginny?

Mom was rocked. Just rocked. I could see it.

She said, "You say you've been tested. How far along are you?"

"Almost seven months." (I shaded the truth a little with that "almost." I was actually just at the beginning of my seventh month.)

Mom didn't say anything for a minute. I could see she was shocked. Finally, she exploded, "You've known for months! There's a bomb ticking inside you. A time bomb! Why didn't you do any-thing about it?"

I didn't have an answer for her.

"Did you tell Kevin?" she asked.

"No. I wanted to—I intended to. But I didn't. I don't want anybody to know. I didn't want *you* to know."

There's a look on her face she gets when things are bad. I hated seeing that look. I was seeing it now.

"Mom, you don't have to worry about it! This is my problem, not yours. Anyway, it's all been worked out. I've taken care of everything."

Mom looked at me . . . her child—because that's what I was, just nineteen—sitting on the couch next to her. I could see she didn't trust me. She didn't think I had really taken care of everything properly. I told her I'd seen a gynecologist. I had a place to stay when I started showing—which was now, I guessed. And they do adoptions, too. They'll arrange the adoption.

Mom said, "Who are these people, this Dr. Bergman and Ginny?"

I told her they were the greatest people on earth.

Mom said, "Michele, maybe we should think a little more on this. Maybe there's another way to go."

I wouldn't hear of it. Why run around looking when you've already got the best?

"How did you find this doctor?" she wanted to know. "Where did you meet these wonderful people?"

I couldn't betray the friend who had had the abortion so I told Mom some cock-and-bull story I made up on the spot. I got him from some woman's sister, the sister of a girl who worked in the office who'd had a child and recommended Dr. Bergman highly.

My story didn't go over that well. I couldn't think of anything else. I wasn't going to tell her how I really got to him.

She said, "Michele, you don't know these people. They could be lying. Maybe you're not that far along. You don't know anything about it. You're a kid. I have more experience than you. I know something about picking a doctor—and having a child for that matter. You don't know anything."

"Mom! Would you please just relax!"

"At least be willing to go to another doctor to confirm the situ-ation."

"I'm not going to another doctor! Forget about it!"

Mom knows better than to argue with me when my mind's made up. I asked her if she would drive me over to Ginny's the next day.

Of course she would.

When I finally leveled with her and told her about the predica-ment I was in, she was with me all the way. She yelled a lot—nobody can carry on like my Mom—but she was there for me.

We started trying to figure out what to tell people. It was terribly important to me to keep this secret. We cooked up a story and it amazes me to this day that we got away with it. We told everyone that I had heard about this wonderful course and had suddenly decided to enroll. I was studying to be a wholesale travel packager, and since the course was being given all the way out in Suffolk County on the other end of Long Island, I would be staying with an aunt. Mom had read about just such a course in a Parents With-out Partners newsletter. The irony of that escaped me at the time.

I left it to Mom to tell Nana and Papa Jack. I couldn't intentionally bring myself to lie to my grandmother. I knew what they'd say, that they were proud of me and thrilled that I had this wonderful opportunity.

You don't know how low that made me feel.

I'd always been a person who was centered around my home. When I was a kid and we'd go someplace, I'd always ask where our house was, and only when I knew what direction it was in could I relax. That night would be the last I would spend in my own home for a long time. Right after work Mom was going to drive me to Ginny's house in Huntington.

I packed my things. Some clothes, not very much. Who knew what would fit? My TV. The comforter off my bed. I had no idea in what kind of surroundings I would find myself.

I didn't sleep much that night. I was apprehensive about going to a new place. I would be living with strangers. I had no idea what Ginny was like at home, what her household would be like.

I lay awake in bed, trying to think of what I would say to my friends. They had called wanting to know all about the wonderful weekend at Kevin's college. I didn't talk to them. I couldn't think of how to tell them I would be gone tomorrow, to take some course

I had never even mentioned until now. I hated lying to people. You know how it is when you lie, it's hard to remember what you said last time. I'd get my story mixed up and have to make up something else to cover it.

I was afraid to talk to anybody. Better to wait till I was at Ginny's and call from there. Try to sound excited and peppy and say it was a wonderful opportunity that came up all of a sudden, a chance I couldn't turn down. I was going to be a travel agent and get all those terrific free trips. Hurray for Michele! Doesn't she lead a charmed life!

Mom always said that I was a lucky person. Wherever we went, I came home with the door prize.

Kevin. What would I tell Kevin? The same thing, probably. The decision to keep him in the dark about the baby now seemed cast in concrete. The turning point was past. I wasn't ever going to let him know.

I couldn't wait till this was over and I was back in my own room with my normal life and my friends and most of all Kevin. I wouldn't be seeing him for three months or more. The tension between us during the weekend seemed fleeting; a momentary bad mood, a meaningless blip in the relationship. Neither one of us would remember it when we were back together again.

As much as I was apprehensive about going to Ginny's to live, I was grateful that I had her to go to. Maybe I was a lucky person after all. I wasn't sure I was in such great standing with God at the moment, but if he was hearing my prayers, Ginny and Dr. Bergman were certainly high on my list of people I was grateful for.

In the next room, I found out later, Mom was having a sleepless night herself. She told me she kept turning the same questions over and over in her mind: Who could these people possibly be? How had Michele gotten tied in with them? She didn't know them from the postman. Some vague story about a woman with female trouble. What the hell kind of way was that to get a doctor?

She had bad dreams that night—horrible dreams. She told me later:

> *Terrible thoughts went through my mind. I knew how Michele was about her friends. She always held her friends closer than her family. All I had to do was suggest the slightest criticism of a friend of hers and she'd be at my*

throat. Those strangers Michele had latched onto . . . were they going to be her new "friends"?

Maybe she didn't latch onto them. Maybe they latched onto her. You read about awful things in the paper. Baby-selling rings. Babies being kidnapped and sold. Maybe they were going to keep Michele and force her to carry to term and steal her baby.

I gave myself a mental shake. Those night-terror thoughts were just figments, induced by the tension and stress of the day. I told myself so over and over.

I really believed that. I thought my imagination was running away with me. I never dreamed that I was closer to the truth than I thought.

───────── ✌ ─────────

Even if Mom had told me what she was thinking that night, it wouldn't have changed anything. I, too, would have put it down to a hyperactive imagination. I knew these people were legiti-mate—more than legitimate, they were about the nicest people I ever met.

Mom was insisting on meeting Dr. Bergman before anything else happened. She wasn't letting me go anywhere until she met him and checked him out. At lunchtime we went over to his office. She'd already looked him up in a directory of physicians, and surprise, he was listed and his qualifications were listed alongside his name. Dr. Bergman had all the credentials.

I don't know what Mom was expecting, but she was pleased to find that Dr. Bergman had an established medical office in a medical building.

Says Mom, "His name was listed on the directory downstairs alongside the others. There certainly was nothing back-alley about him. Inside, his office was impeccable. Very modern, model equip-ment, two nurses in white outfits. Everything stiff-starched, pro-fessional."

Mom and I were immediately ushered into Dr. Bergman's private office. I saw Mom taking it all in; I knew she was thinking that it was in perfect taste. Mom told me it looked exactly like the office of the obstetrician who had delivered me and my brother.

Mom remembers that meeting well: "Dr. Bergman seemed like a calm, complacent kind of fellow. He told me he'd done tests on Michele, everything was perfect. She was in perfect health, the pregnancy was fine."

I think Mom surprised him with all the questions she threw at him. Mom wanted to know everything, all the particulars: How was he so sure I was six months gone? What tests exactly had he done? Could she have copies of them?

I just thought she was being . . . not difficult, really, just the way she was at PTA meetings. She tells me now that her horrors of the night before surfaced, even in that elegantly clinical setting. She was wondering if Bergman was really telling the truth. Maybe I wasn't that far gone and he was lying. I suppose she found it hard to accept that the daughter she lived with could be seven months pregnant without her knowing it.

In any case, Mom was really giving him the third degree. I tried to shush her, but she wouldn't be shushed. She held her gaze on him in a way that was challenging, and I could see he didn't like it. He didn't like being cross-questioned, and he caught what she was really suggesting, that he was possibly doing something wrong or improper.

Dr. Bergman was getting a little annoyed . . . but he kept his cool. He merely said that he'd handled this kind of thing many times in the past, involving young girls from upstanding families, and he'd never had any trouble.

Mom shot right back that in that case he wouldn't mind her taking me to our family doctor to be tested. I looked at her in surprise. We didn't have a family doctor. I almost said something, but I caught myself in time.

Mom kept her eyes on Dr. Bergman. Not that she didn't trust him, she continued, but she was a firm believer in getting a second opinion.

Dr. Bergman was starting to lose his temper. I hoped Mom would shut up before she made him really angry. I tried to make her cool it, but she wasn't paying any attention to me.

He said, "I do this all the time. Even kids from the college come to me."

I thought maybe his tone of voice, which was a little sharper now, would get to her. No. Mom still didn't see why she shouldn't take me to another doctor for a second opinion. "I just want to get all the information together and then make an informed decision," she told him.

He said, "The decision's already been made. Michele is my patient. It's up to her. She's over eighteen, she can make her own decisions now."

He was right. I'd turned nineteen the previous October. At least someone realized I was an adult.

Mom recalls:

> *I was caught up short. I remember thinking that I didn't count anymore. My opinion wasn't going to be listened to. Michele kept insisting that these people were so lovely, so caring, so interested in her. They were in charge, she didn't need me. I was hurt. I admit it. I was hurt that she didn't come to me first. She went to strangers for help but she didn't have enough faith and trust to go to her mother. I told myself kids always think their parents don't know anything about sex, that they themselves arrived in cartons like furniture.*
>
> *But I wasn't just hurt, I was very frightened for her.*

Mom didn't let up. She argued with him. Her voice got a little loud, then a little louder. I was starting to lose it, too. "Mom, you're going to mess everything up!"

"I'm not messing anything up. I just want another doctor to see you."

"Mom—please! Quiet down! You're embarrassing me."

"All I'm saying is I want another opinion. If he has nothing to hide, why can't I get another opinion?"

The nurse stuck her head in: They could hear us in the waiting room, we were disturbing the other patients. Mom didn't care. She would not be hushed.

"You've got lots of patients, I only have one daughter! I'm not a stranger, I'm her mother. I won't be treated like I'm a problem. Professional people should be willing to talk to a person's mother."

The nurse ushered us out of Dr. Bergman's office into another room, a little coffee room. I was near tears.

"Mom, these people are trying to help me. That's all they want to do, help me. They've got everything I need—even a lawyer to handle the adoption. If you don't let go of this crap about another doctor, you're going to blow this whole thing for me, and I'll never forgive you."

Mom was only looking for what was best for me. I told her this was best for me. I could see her waver, and give in. If I felt that strongly about it, she wasn't going to ruin it for me.

That night Mom drove me to Ginny's house. I hadn't eaten any supper because I didn't want to be sick in somebody else's house and mess up their bathroom. We waited till after dinnertime so we wouldn't intrude on their meal. I was more than a little nervous as we went up to her front door and knocked. Ginny opened it. She was just as she had been in the office: friendly, lively, warm. "Hi! Come on in."

I introduced Mom to her and we met Ginny's fifteen-year-old daughter, Nancy. Ginny offered Mom a cup of coffee while Nancy was helping me take my things upstairs to the room I would be staying in. Mom accepted readily. She sat down on the couch like someone who intended to stay awhile—and in fact, she stayed for hours. All her antennas were up. She was scanning Ginny as if she were radar and Ginny were a UFO.

I knew what Mom was doing. She was trying to find out everything she could about Ginny. I hoped it wasn't as obvious to them as it was to me.

If it was, Ginny was totally unfazed. She was so easy and pleasant. Ginny brought up what had happened earlier in the doctor's office, Mom's carrying on the way she had. Ginny told her, "You're getting yourself all upset for no reason. This is nothing out of the ordinary, kids get pregnant, they give the baby up, they find a place to stay, and it all works out fine. I don't know why you're so upset. It happens all the time. It's routine."

"Not to me, it's not routine," Mom said. "Maybe in the city—"

"No! Right here on Long Island."

"I had no idea."

"Because it's done behind closed doors. I'm telling you, it happens all the time, right here. Trust me."

She did make Mom feel better. A little bit, anyway. I could see it. But that didn't stop Mom from having a peek in every nook and cranny of the house. She went through the entire place. Every room. I'm sure Ginny noticed; Mom didn't make much of an effort to hide it. She couldn't care less if Ginny saw her poking around or not.

"Ask me what I was looking for, I don't know," says Mom. "What

I found was a regular home, a divorced woman with two children, a boy away at college and a girl at home. I think she got the house in the divorce. Okay, that was a story that was familiar to me. It turned out she even belonged to Parents Without Partners, an organization I was very active in. The membership secretary was a friend of mine. I made a mental note to ask her to look up Ginny's name. I did, but we couldn't find it. That didn't mean anything. She could have used her married name or another name entirely."

Mom was being nosy, asking question after question. You'd think she had a deep need to know how people laid out their laundry rooms and whether they bought the house with a finished basement or not. Ginny didn't seem to mind. She answered everything as if it were the most natural thing in the world.

Says Mom, "Ginny worked hard to put me at ease. She knew what I was doing—she could hardly miss it. I went through the place like a building inspector. If anything, she was overly friendly. When I left that night, I did feel better. Dr. Bergman had checked out, despite our little set-to in his office. And Ginny was very reassuring, very comforting.

"Still, it was hard to leave Michele in a stranger's home."

Once that door closed behind my mom, I felt more alone than I'd ever felt in my life.

Chapter 9

Ginny and Nancy were trying to make me feel at home, but it only made me feel worse, more of an outsider. I excused myself and went up to my room—the room I had been given. I didn't cry. Instead, I occupied myself unpacking, setting things out, trying to make this place feel like home. The room was small and the walls were half-paneled, with the upper half painted in some kind of rough-textured sand-paint. There was a bed, a dresser, a bureau, and a closet with sliding doors. I had my own TV, which I'd brought from home. I put my comforter on the bed, with my pillows. It helped a little, but not enough to make a difference. I still felt lonely and alone, out of my element, away from all that was dear and familiar.

I slept that night in strange bed, listening to all the creaks and noises I couldn't identify. This was not like being a houseguest in somebody's home. I didn't know these people from Calvin Coolidge. I felt as if I had to serve a prison sentence. I wasn't exactly in prison, but I couldn't go home, either. I had to be there a certain amount of time before I could begin living again.

The next morning I went downstairs feeling awkward. Nancy was getting ready for school, Ginny was getting ready for work. I didn't know their routine, who went into the shower first, how long they took; what time Nancy went to school, when Ginny went to the office. I didn't want to interfere with their morning rituals; everybody has his own way of doing things. I hung out in the kitchen nursing a cup of tea until they left. Then I showered and dressed.

And then I was alone. Everybody had someplace to go, something to do, except me. That in itself was depressing.

I walked through the house—not looking in drawers or anything, just trying to familiarize myself. I'd never seen it in daylight. I looked out the windows at the street. It was a nice day. I thought of going for a walk to look around the neighborhood, but was afraid to go outside. I didn't know whether or not Ginny had told the neighbors I was staying with her. What if she hadn't and they saw this strange person going in and out? They might call the cops. Then I realized Ginny hadn't given me a key yet—she was going to have one made that afternoon. I didn't want to leave the door open and maybe have the place burglarized, so I just stayed home and read.

Around lunchtime I made myself something to eat. You feel so funny in a stranger's house. You don't know if the eggs you took were the ones they were saving to bake a cake or something. I confined myself to things I was sure they wouldn't miss, like toast and jelly.

Even though I felt a little bleak, I preferred being alone. When Ginny and Nancy were there, I had to talk and be sociable, and I didn't know them well enough to know what they liked to talk about. I couldn't move around the house freely. I never knew if I was sitting in the chair one of them particularly liked to sit in. I wouldn't turn on the TV or the radio because what if they didn't want it on?

Mom came to visit about two days later. She took me out to dinner at a diner on Route 110. It was so good to see her. And she brought stuff from home, more of my own things to have around me.

After a few days I began to feel a little more at home in Ginny's house. Ginny and Nancy were really nice to me. When they had friends over, they introduced me as a friend of theirs who was staying with them for a while. They never mentioned that I wasn't married or anything like that, at least not in my hearing. I appreciated Ginny's trying to include me, but I wasn't interested in making friends. I couldn't stand to sit around chatting over coffee, so I'd exchange a few pleasantries, excuse myself, and go to my room. I spent most of my time there, in my little room upstairs, and Ginny didn't pressure me to join them if I didn't feel like it. It was amazing how tactful and sensitive and kind she was.

By the end of my first week at Ginny's I sprouted this little potbelly. Before I had been just a little rounded in front; now you could see it even on my hips. I felt the baby move for the first time. Lying in bed at night I became aware of the sensation, something rather porpoiselike turning over in my stomach. Perhaps only when I was safely away from those I knew was I free to be pregnant; perhaps only then did I give myself permission to feel the life growing inside me.

That weekend Ginny took me shopping for maternity clothes. I couldn't even try anything on. It just seemed wrong for me. A "pregnant lady" was somebody else, some radiant married woman. I was just Michele, with a body that felt increasingly strange, stuck in a situation I was trying to get through as best I could.

Ginny took me to a store that sold Indian clothes—loose things that wrap around the body. Looking at me, you really wouldn't know that I was anything but an ordinary nineteen-year-old girl who liked peasant-style clothing. I wore that stuff through my entire pregnancy. I got away with it because even by the end I didn't put on much weight.

I still felt sick to my stomach almost all the time. I've heard that that feeling is supposed to go away after the first few months. It never did in my case. I was nauseous all the way through. I could never tell when an attack might strike. Mornings were a good bet, but it could be anytime during the day if I came across the wrong smell. Sometimes I threw up immediately after eating. If my stomach was empty, I had the dry heaves. There didn't seem to be a rhyme or reason.

For the first time, lying in bed at night, it began to dawn on me that I was going to have a baby. There was a human being growing inside me. She seemed particularly active at night. I'd always slept on my stomach, and I was afraid that if I rolled over onto her, I'd hurt her somehow.

You may notice that I'm referring to the baby as "her." From the moment I started to think of what was inside me as a baby, I knew it was a girl. I never thought of her as "it" or "he." Don't ask me how I knew, or tell me that I couldn't have known. I did.

I realize now that since they can tell the sex of a fetus from the sonogram, Dr. Bergman may have known I was carrying a girl. He didn't tell me—but he may well have told Joel Steinberg and Hedda Nussbaum, who I now know were waiting for my child to be born, so they could, under the guise of arranging the adoption, steal her and keep her for their own.

I felt closer to the baby now. I wondered what she would look like, what color hair she would have. I prayed she would have ten fingers and ten toes and that she would be healthy. I prayed she would have a happy life and that I was doing the right thing. I prayed that if and when she found out what I had done, she wouldn't hate me.

I called my friends from Ginny's house and told them about taking the travel-agent course. They asked for my phone number; I said I'd keep in touch, but I didn't. It was just too hard. They'd ask questions that I didn't have the answers to. I had no idea what they would teach in such a course. I'd have to come up with more and more lies about the teachers, the other students, and I just wasn't able to do it.

I told Kevin the same story as everybody else, and he accepted it just like they did. I put a little shading on it, making it sound as if I were doing it because my mother wanted me to, she kind of forced me into it, it was easier to do it than to argue, and it was only for three months. It wasn't long, even if it felt like eternity. That's what Kevin said: "We're going to miss each other, but it's only for three months."

In the beginning Kevin and I spoke frequently. Then those calls tapered off, too. I didn't want to run up Ginny's phone bill with out-of-state calls, but mostly the strain of lying was too hard to keep up. Maybe I was concentrating so hard on how I sounded that I never heard anything in Kevin's voice to suggest he wasn't waiting as impatiently as me for the moment we could be together.

Eventually I was cut off from everybody. The only real solace I had was my mother's visits. She came regularly, twice a week, on Wednesday nights and Saturday afternoons, and I looked forward to them from one visit to the next.

Says Mom, "Michele hated being away from home; she was like a lost soul. But Ginny's daughter was around, there was activity in the house. The phone was always ringing, the washing machine was going. It was a true home with real people in it, not an institutional setting.

"I'd take Michele out for a bite, I'd ask her what she was doing, how things were going. Small talk. According to her, Ginny was very nice to her. Wherever Ginny took Nancy, she took Michele along, too."

Mom left me money each time she came to visit: twenty-five, fifty dollars, more if I needed something. I didn't need much. I only had two pairs of pants and a couple of tops. I didn't go anywhere; I didn't see anybody. Ginny was supplying me with room and board per the arrangement with Dr. Bergman or the lawyer or whomever she dealt with. I never paid her anything and she never so much as hinted at asking me for money.

I was bored being home by herself all day, so Ginny started taking me into Hempstead to work in Dr. Bergman's office now and then. Actually, it started with the blood tests. Every three weeks they sent me for a blood test. Ginny would take me with her in the morning and drop me off at the lab, Reese Health Labs in Hempstead, about five minutes from Bergman's office. It quickly became routine. The people there knew I was coming, Ginny would wait in the car while they drew my blood, then I'd get back in the car and we'd drive to the office. And then I'd just hang around; there wasn't much to go home to, anyway. So I'd do a little secretarial work, filing, general office chores, and eventually it evolved into a several-times-a-week thing. Ginny and the office nurse, Jackie—I don't remember her last name—were nice to me, welcoming and warm. They were the only friends I had in the world, true friends who were with me in my time of trouble.

Ginny didn't really care if I went to the office or not. The only thing she insisted I had to do was go to Dr. Bergman for checkups. The rest of the time she let me go my own way, and except for some hours each week in the office and the long walks I took by myself, I spent most of my time alone in my room.

Aside from my checkups, I didn't see much of Dr. Bergman. He spent most of his time in his office in the city, and I generally went to his Long Island office when it was closed, so I wouldn't have to deal with patients. That would be too much, answering questions about the happy event. Wasn't I thrilled, wasn't my husband over-joyed, did we want a boy or a girl?

Sometimes Ginny would find me just sitting, not doing anything, sunk in depression. Ginny would tell me that I shouldn't feel that I was doing anything wrong, that I had nothing to be ashamed of.

"You're not the first person in the world, and you certainly won't be the last," she'd tell me. The attorney handled cases like this all the time. They were good girls like myself. They went on to lead happy lives. I was doing the right thing.

With her own daughter, Ginny blew hot and cold. How much attention she paid to Nancy depended on what was going on in her own life. If she had a date or something to do that night, then Nancy was put on hold. If there was nothing going on, and Nancy wanted to talk, then she would listen.

Most of the time when Ginny and I talked the conversation centered around Ginny. Her personal life was really screwed up. She made no attempt to hide it; on the contrary, she loved to talk about it. I think she'd been married and divorced twice, I'm not really sure. I didn't pay much attention to the details, I just kept a polite, interested look on my face.

Living in Ginny's house, I found that she seemed to have two different personalities. In the office she'd dress conservatively, but on the outside she layered on the makeup and the jewelry and the doodads like some Long Island version of Joan Collins. Ginny looked like your average fortyish woman who'd had a couple of children; a little chunky, solid rather than fat. She'd get all gussied up, trying to look glamorous and young. She worked hard at it and sometimes she looked a little ridiculous.

Ginny was very man conscious, very involved in dating, in trying to hook up with somebody. Money meant a lot to her. She was always trying to get somebody to take her to the "right" places, which meant expensive places. There was one restaurant in Huntington she was forever trying to get somebody to take her to. She'd point it out as we drove by. It didn't look that special to me. I couldn't see why she was so desperate to get there, but to her it was everything.

Whenever she was getting ready for a first date with a new man, Ginny would prattle on about what kind of car he'd be driving, where he'd take her, what he would buy her, how much money he was going to wind up spending on her. I'd wonder, do people really plan out ahead that they're going to order the most expensive item on the menu? Don't they just order what they feel like having at the time? It didn't seem like fun to me, more like some kind of strange competition to extract the most amount of dollars in the least amount of time.

Then she'd come home afterward and complain about the date. There was always something wrong with the man: This one didn't have enough money; this one was boring. If they didn't take her to the "right" place on the first date, they were gone. No second chances. Ginny would be genuinely insulted. "Who does he think I am? How dare he take me to a cheap dive like that?"

The thought *almost* crossed my mind that it didn't jibe with someone who took a stranger into her home out of the goodness of her heart, but I just accepted that Ginny had two very different aspects to her personality.

Ginny was always complaining about not having enough money, and that made me feel bad. I began to feel guilty about every mouthful of food I ate, every tissue I used. I'd go out and buy sacks of groceries for the whole house with the money Mom gave me. And then Ginny would come home with a three-hundred-dollar outfit and complain that she didn't have money for the mortgage payment.

I don't know if she was really as poor as she claimed; I don't know the truth about anything relating to Ginny anymore.

Jackie was very different from Ginny; in fact they were almost opposites. Ginny was flighty and ditsy; Jackie was a very competent woman. Ginny, in her off-hours at least, put a lot of effort into making herself look sexy and alluring; Jackie had more substance. She had what I would call inner beauty. She was an attractive woman—at least I thought so—tall, thin, with dark, curly, shoulder-length hair. She spoke well and she made a good appearance. I liked Jackie very much. I actually looked forward to my visits to Bergman's office because she would be there; I enjoyed her company a great deal. I wouldn't say that Ginny and Jackie were close, but their relationship definitely was more than just coworkers.

I was at Jackie's house once; Ginny took me there. I needed to have blood drawn for a test. Ginny couldn't do it because she wasn't a nurse. Jackie's house surprised me. It didn't fit my image of her. I thought her home would be neater, less shabby and cluttered. Dirty dishes in the sink didn't jibe with my picture of her, but there they were.

Looking back, I think I idealized all these people. I was in the worst mess of my life and they were enabling me to get through it in the best possible manner, the way I wanted: with dignity and without causing hurt to anybody.

I spent a lot of time out walking by myself. I'd have silent conversations with the baby in my womb. I'd tell her how much I loved her. How much I wanted to keep her and see her grow up.

If I could do that, how happy I would be.

I'd think sometimes about keeping her, but I couldn't see a way to do it. I never so much as entertained a fantasy of Kevin and I marrying and raising the baby together. It was simply not an option. Kevin was eighteen, and years away from being able to support a family. I didn't want him dropping out of school to take a dead-end job; that would be the destruction of his future, the end of his hopes and aspirations.

And I myself felt totally and completely incapable of being a parent. If I tried somehow to raise her myself, she wouldn't have a father and she wouldn't have a mother to write home about either. Being a mother is something you do twenty-four hours a day. You have to be ready to give of yourself without reservation, as much as is needed. You have to be ready to put yourself second and another person first. I was young, but I wasn't dumb enough to think that love would conquer all. Love for the child, I had. What I didn't have was maturity. And I knew it.

It wouldn't be good for her and it would be horrible for Kevin. I've heard of movie stars refusing to name the father of their child. Maybe they could get away with that. I certainly couldn't. Everyone in Rockville Centre would know the baby was his. If it were just me, I could have handled it. But I couldn't stand to destroy Kevin's life, too—and his family's.

If he acknowledged her, it would be embarrassing at best. If he didn't, it would be worse. Would he pass us on the street, the baby and me, as we visited with Nana and Papa Jack, who lived down the block? My mind refused to conjure up the picture, it was so remote and insupportable.

Anyway, it was too late to change my mind. Nobody even knew I was pregnant. What would I do, suddenly show up with a baby in my arms? Every time people looked at her, they'd remember the circumstances of her birth. It would cast a shadow over her entire life.

That wasn't what I wanted for my baby. I wanted her start in life to be . . . perfection. I wanted her to have everything—starting with the most important, a mother *and* a father, and they had to be married. Anything else seemed second-best, not good enough.

Dr. Bergman knew my feelings from the start and he assured me there was no problem in complying with my wishes. I trusted him implicitly. A shadow of a doubt never entered my mind. I knew with absolute certainty that somewhere there was a married Catholic couple who would one day—quite soon now—get a call that their daughter was born.

I pictured their joy. I certainly didn't give my child up as an act of charity—my only interest was in doing what was best for my baby. But it was nice to think of the happiness I would be bringing to others.

Adoption seemed like a good thing to me. I had seen it firsthand only three years before; I was sixteen and it made a strong impression on me. I didn't know anything about Aunt Dianne and Uncle Hans's adopting a baby till after he was born. Nana broke the news—and I remember her joy and Papa Jack's. I remember their faces at the christening, pure joy shining from their eyes, everybody's eyes. I know everyone loves their children, but adopted children are never taken for granted. They are yearned for and worked for and anxiously awaited; and when they come, they're not just children, they're miracles, wondrous gifts, and you can see it in the eyes of everyone who looks at them.

My cousin Dillon is twelve now. He's special to our whole family. We all find it hard to get mad at him, even when he deserves it. He used to introduce himself by saying, "Hello, I'm Dillon, I'm adopted."

My aunt would say, "You know, you can leave off that last part. If it comes up, fine, but you don't have to announce it the moment you say hello." But Dillon wants to shout it from the rooftops.

That, to me, was how adopted children are treated.

There were times when I'd recoil. No! How could anybody give birth to a baby and give it up! And then I'd remember Dillon, and the other adopted children I knew. I'd remember how they were welcomed, the homes that were prepared for them, the love and attention that was showered on them, the special place they had in everyone's heart.

That's what I wanted for my baby.

Even so, I wavered. There were moments when I just couldn't bear to give her up. I'll run away. I'll just go. I won't do it.

And then I'd think of Nana. Nana was religious, proper, and she thought the sun rose and set on me. She'd swear an oath that I was a "good girl." How could I suddenly face her with a big stomach?

I figured that would be worse for her than her cancer. I figured it would just about kill her.

It turned out I was wrong about Nana; I think about that a lot these days. Nana didn't know about the baby until moments before the entire world found out, when I had to appear in open court and testify that I was her natural mother. By then Lisa was dead and I was fighting to claim her body.

If I'd known how Nana would react, I might have kept the baby. Despite everything, I might have kept her. And Lisa would now be a happy, laughing nine-year-old.

Chapter 10

I wept a lot, alone by myself where nobody could see me. During the night, when the baby kept me awake with her kicking, I passed the time picturing the nursery waiting for her in the home of her adoptive parents, that well-to-do married Catholic couple.

I could see it so clearly: soft plush carpeting underfoot, rainbows on the wall, painted clouds on the ceiling. In the movie *Kramer vs. Kramer*, which I had seen quite long ago, there was a boy's nursery in bright colors with a sky-blue ceiling and white painted clouds. For my daughter's nursery I changed the primary colors to pastels, the sky blue to pale blue. I tried different shades of pink for the background, choosing a shade so pale it was almost white, tinged with the faintest blush tone.

My fantasies at this point focused entirely on her in her room. I didn't take her out of there—that came later. Now I thought of her as a newborn and all the scenes I pictured took place in her nursery. I saw her being rocked in a rocking chair, snuggled by a doting mother. I saw her cooing and kicking on her changing table, reaching for a pretty mobile overhead.

The mother was never clear in my mind. My fantasy was always about the baby. I love baby clothes and I'd picture her closet with all those little dresses on tiny hangers, row after row, lined up in order from the smallest to the largest. I knew that at a christening people usually give you clothes all the way up to a year, so that's how I arranged them in her closet, from the tiniest little smocked dress with cherries embroidered on the collar like one I'd once seen, to her first birthday dress. I pictured her little stretchies folded neatly in a drawer.

I'd wonder about her name. What was it going to be? I didn't pick out names because I knew I wasn't going to be the one to name her.

Keeping the baby was wrong, but giving her away wasn't right either. It hurt like hell. I'd put my hands on my stomach and talk to her, silently, trying to explain to her why I was doing it. I was going to do this difficult and painful thing so she could have a happy life. I hoped that one day she would understand, and she should never, ever think I didn't love her, because it was my love for her that was enabling me to do this.

Never for a moment did I fear for my baby. I accepted without question that she would be placed with a couple who would shower blessings on her and cherish her with every breath they took. I guess that's the way it turns out most of the time.

Out of all the millions of people out there wanting a baby so badly, just waiting to give one a wonderful home, I had to get mixed up with Bergman and Steinberg! Even as I was mentally designing the baby's nursery that I would never see, the conspiracy had begun. There was no Catholic family; there would never even be an adoption. The couple who would steal my baby and raise her as their own were waiting even then in the wings.

Seven years later I would sit in a Manhattan courtroom and listen to Hedda Nussbaum testify under oath that she and Steinberg had "monitored" my pregnancy; they were aware of my every move, informed by Ginny and Dr. Bergman.

And worse, Ginny and Dr. Bergman knew all along that the baby was going to Steinberg and Nussbaum!

I believed them when they told me my wishes were being complied with. I felt nothing but gratitude to them: Dr. Bergman, who was so caring, who gave me all this medical care without charge; Jackie, who was so lovely to me; Ginny, who was opening her home to me; and the lawyer they had put me in touch with, who would find the perfect adoptive parents for my baby.

———————— ✶ ————————

Most evenings Ginny went out, and it was just Nancy and me. Nancy, a sweet girl, was excited about her upcoming sweet-sixteen party. We would talk about that a lot.

I remembered my own sweet-sixteen. Mom had made it in a place called Checkers in Rockville Centre that was popular at the time. We had games, favors, a DJ. It was a terrific party. I had a wonderful time.

It hurt to think about that. It had been only three years ago.

Once Nancy approached me, hesitantly. She wanted to ask me something. I told her she could ask me anything. She wanted to know about sex, what it was like the first time you had sex with a boy, how did you know when you were ready?

I told her to wait until she was married, or failing that to put it off as long as she could. If this happens to you when you're thirty, you'll be able to handle it better.

I told her I wished I had waited. I was certainly in no condition to preach. I didn't feel I was the best example for her.

She was curious about what it felt like to be pregnant. She'd put her hand on my stomach to feel the baby move. She was a very, very sweet girl.

And I . . . I was a stranger to myself, living in a time curiously unconnected to anything I had known. I was simply waiting for the days to pass until I could pick up my life again and go back to being a person whom I could recognize.

I had made a bargain and I would keep it. But I wanted it to be over.

I can't say I was sad every minute of the day, but I was never really happy. Mostly what I felt was depressed. Each night when I went to sleep, I'd think: I got through another day. One day less till I can go home.

I couldn't go home for Easter, obviously. Mom and I made up this story about my being in Florida, that I'd been given an assign-ment to arrange and take a trip for my course. One lie leads to another.

I missed everyone at home terribly. I could picture what they were doing every minute of the day. I would have given anything to be over there, cooking, eating, kidding around, hearing Papa Jack complain about the one vegetable dish on the face of the earth that wasn't on the table, which of course was the one he particularly wanted.

After I'd been at Ginny's for about a month, Mom went to Dr. Bergman's office. She'd been calling for reports on me, but she felt she was being sloughed off so she went in to see them and demand answers to her questions in person. After that she went there every few weeks. Jackie would tell her everything was fine; she would ask for specifics and they would tell her to stop worrying. I was never there when Mom was and I was only dimly aware of her contact with them. I knew she called now and then, but I had no idea that she actually went there. Mom didn't want to upset me by telling me of the friction between them, and I guess they didn't either. But bottom line, Mom felt they saw her as interfering, and in hindsight, she was right. Mom never really trusted them—she could never find what they were doing wrong, but she never really trusted them, and again, she was right. At the time I thought she was just being her usual, overprotective self.

I'd been having blood tests once a week since I got to Ginny's. I thought all pregnant women had weekly blood tests. I had no way of knowing otherwise. If Dr. Bergman was in his Manhattan office on the day of my blood test, I traveled in on the Long Island Rail Road. Now I ask myself if the test couldn't have been done a day earlier or later, but then it never occurred to me. If he was in Hempstead on the day of the test, then Ginny would drop me at the lab, wait for me, and drive me on into the office. I was going in to work at the office more and more, out of sheer boredom.

When I entered my eighth month, the tests were increased to twice a week. In my ninth month they were sending me three times a week. I asked why, and Dr. Bergman told me it was because I had diabetic tendencies and I was allergic to cats. I found the part about the cat allergy really strange because I love cats. I always had cats; Ginny had a cat that I played with all the time, and being around it didn't make me sneeze or wheeze or break out in a rash, nothing.

I've never been much of a sweet eater, but one day I walked into Dairy Barn, saw these macaroons—really awful, sticky-solid coconut confections—and I craved them like I never craved anything before. I used to buy them and sneak them into Ginny's house and hide them in my drawer. And that only happened after I was told to watch the sweets. The moment somebody tells you you can't have something, that's when you have to have it.

After a routine examination around the second or third week in April, as I entered my ninth month, Dr. Bergman said I needed to go to the hospital for a fetal-heart-monitor test. He didn't say why, but I wasn't worried. I thought it was routine, that all pregnant women had this.

I had to go into the city for the test, to New York Infirmary. Dr. Bergman did it himself. He hooked up electrodes to my stomach, and the baby's heartbeat registered on this long roll of paper, like a graph.

But when he wanted to do another one a week later, I did wonder why. I thought maybe the first one didn't take; someone forgot to plug the machine in or something.

I asked Ginny what was going on, and Jackie, too. They gave me vague answers, they kept saying everything was fine, it was all precautionary. They said that a lot: "precautionary." They just wanted to make sure, wanted to see that nothing would go wrong. At the time, I didn't realize that they were brushing my questions off. I thought I had been given all the answers I could need or expect. Now, if a doctor wants to do a test, I'd ask why, what does he expect to find, what exactly did he find—come to think of it, I'd sound exactly like my mother.

Dr. Bergman said everything was normal.

I told Mom what was going on—and by doing so, I lit a match that almost blew my plans sky-high. I wish it had.

Mom read up on diabetes and found out that it's not uncommon for women in late pregnancy to show signs of the disease. It's not serious and it goes away after the birth. She called Dr. Bergman's office, told them what she'd found out, and accused them of throwing a scare into me for no reason. She wanted to know what they were trying to pull.

Ginny, of course, told her she was out of her mind. They weren't pulling anything, they were just facing facts.

Mom was upset that they were worried about the baby and not about me. Says Mom:

> If something was wrong with my daughter, I wanted to know it. Ginny and Bergman kept telling me, baby, baby, baby. I asked, "Don't any of you care about my daughter? Doesn't she matter to you at all?"
>
> They told me they had things under control. I asked, "So what's with the blood tests and fetal heart monitor and the diabetes? You're getting Michele all upset—you're driving her crazy for no reason."
>
> I never did get any answers. I was just more or less told to butt out.
>
> Finally, I decided it was time to do something. I was going to take Michele to another doctor. If they were telling the truth, they should have no objection.
>
> Ginny said her only objection was that it wasn't necessary. She said that I was the one who was upsetting Michele by wanting to drag her around to other doctors.

They argued back and forth. Mom called them all day long. The first I knew about it was when Ginny came home that night absolutely fuming. She didn't tell me exactly what was going on, I got a kind of *Reader's Digest* version: "Your mother's a pain in the ass, she's blowing everything out of proportion, causing all this commotion, she's trying to tell us our business, she doesn't know what she's talking about . . ."

I wasn't happy to hear that. I needed these people.

Apparently, Mom kept up her barrage all the next day, and after work she drove over to Dr. Bergman's office. Ginny was home by then; he called her from the office. I overheard the conversation. Ginny was upset, and I knew Dr. Bergman and Jackie were, too.

Ginny hung up the phone. She looked at me. She never should

have said what she said next, and if she hadn't been so angry, she wouldn't have made the slip.

She was burning. "Whatever I'm getting out of this isn't worth the aggravation your mother is giving us," she yelled.

We still don't know—we may never know—what, if anything, Ginny was getting out of this.

But still, when she lost her temper and her control over her tongue, that's what she yelled at me.

"You better get your mother off our backs," she told me. "Because if you don't, you can forget the whole thing. You can pack your bags and get out of my house—now! Right now! Tonight!"

Dr. Bergman and Ginny and Jackie were powerful; I was not and Mom was not. She was just my mom and I was just me. Much as I felt these people liked me—and they had to, else why would they go to so much trouble for me?—I knew that their liking for me had its limits.

I was terrified of losing them.

I got on the phone to Mom—I was really screaming at her. "You're going to ruin everything! Just stay out of it! Stop bothering them! Everything is fine! Whatever you're doing, just stop it. Stop it!"

And she did. She didn't like it but she agreed.

Mom says, "I wanted to get Michele the hell out of there. But what can you do? I couldn't go against her wishes. I lay in bed at night and wondered if there was some way I could sneak into Ginny's house and steal Michele out of there. But you don't do things like that, do you?"

Mom felt they had brainwashed me. That they were using this diabetes scare as a way of keeping me under control. If they were, it succeeded, in that it made me feel wary of Mom and what she might do next, and even more closely allied with them.

Says Mom, "I just knew they were telling Michele that I was some kind of an ogre who was dying to mess up their wonderful plans, but they would help her withstand me."

And she's not far wrong. That's pretty much what they were saying. They were playing Mom and me against each other, but of course all I could see then was my terror of being abandoned.

Mom says, "Michele was positive they were looking after *her* and I could see they didn't give a damn about her and were only concerned with the baby she was carrying."

———————— ✄ ————————

At about the same time, mid-April, Dr. Bergman said it was time for me to meet with the adoption lawyer. I understood that in addition to finding the adoptive parents, the lawyer represented me in the adoption, and the couple would be represented by somebody else. Of course I wanted to meet him. Ginny arranged the mechanics of it, where and when it would be.

It was set for the next day, Saturday. I called Mom at at work to tell her; I wanted her there, of course.

I called her back a few minutes later. I forgot to tell her that the lawyer wanted five hundred dollars.

Mom said she would write him a check when she got there. No, no. Ginny told me it had to be cash.

That didn't arouse our suspicions at all. I could care less whether it was cash or a check. Mom, I guess, thought it was the way of the world. Some people want to be paid in cash; that's their business, not ours.

They said that it was "good faith" money. If they needed to be shown our "good faith," then fine, we would show them. Mom promised to bring it with her.

Six years later, when everything blew open about Steinberg and Lisa, Mom went back and looked through her old checkbooks. She's an accountant, remember, and she keeps her own books meticulously. She deposited her paycheck every Friday, but that week she doesn't show a deposit. She had cashed her check to get the money for Steinberg.

Chapter 11

The meeting was set for Saturday, April 18, about three weeks before the baby was due. We were to meet in a restaurant in Manhattan, on Fifth Avenue in Greenwich Village. Mom came by herself. Ginny and I were coming together in her car. Mom found a parking space one block away from the restaurant; she took that as a good omen.

The restaurant Steinberg chose was right around the corner from the apartment on West Tenth Street where Lisa would live for the brief six and a half years Joel Steinberg allowed her on this earth before beating the life out of her with his bare hands.

But then I didn't know that. Then, I saw Steinberg as my savior. I felt that the meeting was a test. If I didn't measure up, he wouldn't take my case. I had to please him. My baby's future depended on it.

That wasn't why he wanted the meeting. Steinberg never intended to place my baby for adoption—else why would he and Nussbaum "monitor" my pregnancy? He knew he was going to keep her and he wanted a firsthand look at the child's birth mother.

Ginny and I entered the restaurant together; Mom wasn't there yet but Steinberg was, at a table. Ginny introduced us.

Ginny would later testify that she had no recollection of such a meeting, did not drive me there, and wasn't present with us.

Mom came while the waiter was taking our orders. Nobody ate

but Steinberg. He ordered a hamburger and coleslaw. I was too tense to eat, and Mom was nervous, too. This meeting was important to us. I frankly was intimidated by him. I ordered a Coke, even though I couldn't drink it.

Steinberg was a large man. He took up more than his share of space and air. I noticed that first, then his eyes: intense, intelligent eyes with almost a piercing quality as if he saw everything and knew everything at a glance. Mom took note of his jacket: blue and gray and white in a rough tweed. "Understated elegance," she said later.

He ate his hamburger and coleslaw while he talked; I had the feeling it was a set speech, one he'd delivered before. Steinberg's table manners were not appealing. We were all crowded together; I was sitting between him and Ginny, with Mom across from me on Steinberg's other side. He kept leaning in toward me. The smell of the food, from the plate and from his breath, made me nauseous. Mom remembers more of what he said than I do. I was busy trying not to be sick.

She says:

> The lawyer—I can hardly bear to say his name—told us that yes, he handled adoptions, which, he indicated with some charm, Michele already knew. He had handled many adoptions in New York City and was very conversant with the applicable law. He'd handled more than three hundred adoptions on Long Island alone, with never a problem. He knew his way through the courts. He knew how to push things through—a necessary and admirable quality in a lawyer. I remember thinking, great, this man really knows what he's doing.
>
> I breathed a sigh of relief. Steinberg gave me the feeling that he was a man of sincerity and integrity. Some lawyers you see out of court and you hardly recognize them for the silver tongues they have in court. Not him. He was very glib, almost eloquent; businesslike, authoritative, sophisticated, and he seemed to exude power. He wasn't a man to be trifled with.

Personally, I didn't see all this sincerity and integrity. I didn't care for him; I didn't care for his table manners or his overbearing attitude. He did all the talking, throwing glances at Ginny as if to say, she knows, and Ginny would nod to confirm what he was saying.

Mom got the feeling that Ginny and Steinberg knew each other well; that they'd done this many, many times. There was no introduction between them, hardly even a "Hi, how are you." It was clear to me, too, that they hadn't just met, that they knew each other from before. They were comfortable together.

My mother said later that that was encouraging, too. They weren't just practicing on me.

Steinberg asked questions and took notes on a legal pad, although he already seemed to know a surprising amount about me. He asked about my health, childhood illnesses. Family history. Were there any hereditary illnesses on either side of the family? Any mental retardation? Congenital conditions likely to be passed on to the child? I answered no to everything.

"How about the baby's father?" he asked.

I didn't want to tell him Kevin's name. I told him Kevin had nothing to do with it; he didn't even know I was pregnant. Steinberg insisted. He said I must tell him, and that it would come under the heading of privileged communication with an attorney and would never come out.

I gave him Kevin's name and address.

Only two people ever got Kevin's last name out of me. I would reveal it to Judge Marie Lambert of the Surrogate's Court of the State of New York after Lisa's death, when I was fighting to claim her body for burial; the other was Joel Steinberg, to whom I told his name at this meeting. Judge Lambert had the power of law behind her. Steinberg had only the force of his personality.

Steinberg asked why I was giving up the baby for adoption. I told him I was single and too young to raise a child and so was Kevin. He nodded. It was a familiar story. He'd heard that one before.

I repeated that Kevin didn't know anything about this and I didn't want him—or anybody else—to find out. He nodded impatiently. I had already said that.

I was afraid of annoying him. I tried to keep my mouth shut as much as possible. I broached the subject of Kevin and I both being Catholic and my wanting the baby to be brought up in a Catholic home.

Steinberg said he knew that, he was well aware of that. He had exactly such a couple in mind. The proposed adoptive father was a well-to-do, accomplished attorney. They lived in Manhattan. The child would be raised in New York City. They were a professional couple. They weren't young, but their careers were well on track, very established, and there was no way for them to go but up.

Oh, how good that sounded. I could almost see them in front of me. Not faces, not specific people, but the kind of people they were. They were very much looking forward to having a baby, Steinberg said, and were prepared to give the child every advantage.

He didn't say much about the woman, didn't specify any particular career for her or say exactly what she did. I got the idea that she didn't have to work and would be happy to stay home and care for the baby. That sounded nice. A full-time mom to read stories and go to the park and bake brownies with.

I didn't ask him too many questions, which is my own fault. But it was the way he spoke. Things were insinuated, rather than spelled out. He didn't welcome interruptions. It was presumptuous to second-guess him; he knew what he was doing.

I didn't like Mr. Steinberg. I thought he was rude. But I wasn't there to like him, and the things I didn't like were all surface, not substance; they had no bearing on his doing the job that he was supposed to do. I had no reason to question his competence as an adoption attorney. He had been recommended—more than recommended, he had been *chosen*—by Dr. Bergman, whom I trusted implicitly. The fact that he knew so much about me was subliminally reassuring: Dr. Bergman had filled him in. He was an associate of Bergman and Ginny and Jackie, and that was more than good enough for me.

That meeting was the turning point that sealed Lisa's fate. If only I had sense enough to dig deeper, she might well be alive today. I don't trust people now. I don't trust myself to know when I'm being lied to, who is honest, who is not. I paid dearly—Lisa paid dearly —for my lack of sophistication.

From the moment I found out what Steinberg did to Lisa, I have never stopped berating myself. I was going to entrust this man with my baby's life! Why didn't I ask questions—and to hell with him if he didn't like them!

Mom says he was a consummate con artist. I say he is Lucifer himself. If Joel Steinberg is not the devil incarnate, then I don't know who is.

I asked him how we would go about this, what the process would be. Should we meet again in his office? He said, no, that wouldn't be necessary. He took a paper out of his briefcase and handed it to me to read. I don't know what it said—he took it away too fast. He held this legal-looking document in front of me for a second and said, "You'll sign something like this document—but not till after the baby's born." He put the document back in his briefcase. It could have been a closing on a building for all I saw of it.

Then he said, "There are costs, you know. Filing fees." He scribbled on the pad, adding under his breath. "Five hundred dollars. Five hundred dollars up front should handle it. Good-faith money."

It struck Mom as odd that he had to calculate it. We had been told the day before to bring five hundred dollars—then he'd called it good-faith money, not filing fees, but who cared. What was he adding up there? Mom told herself not to make waves.

Steinberg looked over at Ginny. "Do they have the money?"

I said, "Mom—did you bring the money?" I heard how nervous I sounded. I hoped nobody else did.

Of course Mom had the money.

Steinberg told Mom to pass him the money in a napkin. Did that strike me as strange? No, not in New York City where you don't flash money around.

Did I have any real misgivings? I wish to God I had.

I didn't know then what I know now: Women who give their babies up for adoption generally don't pay for anything, certainly not for "filing fees." Customarily, their medical bills and possibly even their upkeep during pregnancy are paid for by the adoptive parents, and this is perfectly legal. No gratuities are allowed to change hands. *That's* baby-selling.

But when you meet someone, especially someone who is going to be important to you, a thousand impressions flicker through your mind. There were tiny oddities, but on the whole, I felt he was more than impressive and we were in capable hands.

Later, it would come out that Steinberg wasn't even a lawyer. He had never passed the bar. I wasn't the only one he fooled; all the clients he represented, the judges he appeared before, and colleagues were taken in.

The meeting was over. Steinberg wiped his mouth, threw the napkin on the table, said his good-byes, and left. He didn't pay the check. I did.

He must have left thinking he was clever. He'd gotten the information he wanted, he'd gotten a look at me; he'd divulged nothing, not even where he lived. I had no way of contacting him, but then again I didn't need to. Dr. Bergman was our go-between.

The legal pad on which he took notes would eventually damn Steinberg. Almost seven years later he still had it, and it was found during a police search of his apartment after Lisa's death. By then they knew that Lisa was not Nussbaum's child, but they had no idea who her natural mother was. In bold letters at the top, written in Steinberg's hand, was the name "Michele Launders." The thorough notes Steinberg had taken led them directly to me.

I never told the police Kevin's last name. I didn't have to. They had it from Steinberg's notes.

Steinberg had left; Ginny was on her way out to the car. Mom and I were alone at the table for a moment.

"Suppose when the baby is born something is wrong with it," I asked her. "Suppose it has eye trouble like I had."

Mom leaned over and took my hand. "Michele, when I got you, when you came into my life and later on I found out you had trouble with your eye—you don't give somebody back because they're not perfect."

"But if something is the matter with the baby, they're not going to want it."

"It doesn't work that way. Once you have a little baby, even if there is something wrong with it, you don't give it back."

Mom told me later she didn't know if I was looking for a way out or for reassurance so I could stay in. I don't know myself.

After the meeting with Steinberg, adoption became more than just a word. It began to dawn on me that I was really going to give this baby away.

I thought more and more about the adoptive parents; the mother, mostly. The father was never clear in my mind, probably because I had no childhood memories of a father and except for what I read and saw, had no real sense of what a father did.

But I knew what a mother did. The woman I pictured had no clear face in my mind, but I could see her playing with the baby, rocking her, dressing her . . . kissing the little toes while putting her socks on.

I wished with all my heart that the woman could be me, that I would be the one to feel my baby's soft skin against my face, smell the sweet fragrance of baby shampoo and talcum powder, hold her against my chest and rock her to sleep, sing to her, whisper how much I loved her.

But I knew that wasn't to be, and I steeled myself against the ever-present ache in my chest and prayed for strength.

I think Ginny seemed to know when I was weakest about giving up the baby. I didn't really waver in the sense of backing out—I had already agreed to do it, and I honestly believed it was the best thing I could do for all concerned—but there were times when the thought of it became more than I could stand. And then Ginny would talk to me. She'd tell me again and again that I was doing the right thing—the only possible thing. "There are so many couples out there who long for a child and can't have one. Think of the good you're doing. Think of the joy you're bringing them. Don't be selfish, Michele. Don't ruin your life because of one mistake."

I knew she was right. That didn't make it any easier. Kevin gave me the strength I needed to get through each day, knowing he was waiting for me and that when this was over I would go to him.

I missed him so. During the day I wouldn't allow myself to think of Kevin too much; it became too painful. But while I could control my waking thoughts to a point, I couldn't control my dreams. Kevin was in my dreams each night and I couldn't keep him out. Every morning I would wake up and erect another wall that would dissipate with the coming of night and sleep.

It never once crossed my mind that Kevin wouldn't be waiting for me, that when I got home, he would have another girlfriend. To me, time had stopped when I went to Ginny's house and would start again when I got home.

Looking back, I see I was pretty naive to think that I would waltz back into Kevin's life after an absence of three months and nothing would have changed. Maybe it's a good thing, though. I don't honestly think I could have survived waiting to deliver a child I would never raise without the thought of Kevin to cling to, without the sure knowledge that when all this was over, Kevin and I would be together.

Chapter 12

*M*y due date neared, then passed. Ginny, Dr. Bergman, and Jackie all seemed concerned that something was wrong with the baby—nervous even, and their alarm frightened me. They kept telling me everything was okay, but I could see they were worried. In addition to the three-times-weekly blood tests, I had three fetal-heart-monitor tests during my pregnancy. The tests were longer, too. I'd be hooked up for an hour, an hour and a half, even more.

That's when they said that they weren't sure that the baby's heart was strong enough to survive the birth.

I don't remember feeling anything until that night, when I was alone in bed. I thought that it was something I had done, maybe those macaroons, and that I had hurt my baby. I told her I was sorry, and to hang on and be healthy and live.

I know now that ordinarily other pregnant women weren't tested as much as I was. While working in the office I found my file. It was far thicker than the others, and what made it so thick were the lab reports with the results of my blood tests. My file was eight or nine inches thick.

Why were they so worried? Perhaps all the tests were the right thing to do medically, but here's what I think. Bergman, Jackie, and Ginny all knew in advance that Steinberg would take custody of

my baby—a grand jury concluded that. Their report reads, "According to the obstetrician's receptionist [Ginny] and his nurse [Jackie],
it was always understood by them that the attorney and his com-
panion [Hedda Nussbaum] would be keeping the baby, and that
arrangement had been made even prior to the birth mother's meeting
with the attorney. The nurse initially denied receiving money from
the attorney for delivering the baby; however, after her recollection
was refreshed, she recalled being paid $100 for helping with another
adoption in which the obstetrician was involved."

In newspaper reports Steinberg was alleged to have made millions
in the illegal drug trade, and, although the police have not yet been
able to prove this, hundreds of thousands more in the black market
sale of babies for adoption. The police found large amounts of cash
in his home—many thousands of dollars, along with quantities of
cocaine and paraphernalia for the making and ingesting of illegal
drugs.

But Steinberg was notoriously tight with money. Apparently he
was famous for sticking people with his checks. His wallet, if he
had one, never saw the light of day. My upkeep and medical bills
had to be paid for by someone. Bergman knew that if I delivered
anything less than what doctors call a "good baby," a baby in perfect
health, Steinberg wouldn't cough up a dime.

And what about the five hundred dollars he extorted from me
under the guise of "filing fees"? Why inveigle five hundred dollars
out of Mom and me? Such a paltry sum, why bother?

I don't know.

Unless it was some weird exercise of power to see how far he
could push us, how much he could make us dance to his tune.

In fact, the police found a stack of unpaid hospital bills for Lisa's
delivery at his home. He never bothered to pay them. By then, he
had Lisa; what were they going to do, repossess her?

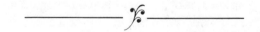

I got no preparation or information about labor, what it would be
like, what I should do. No one ever brought up the subject, not
Jackie or Ginny or Bergman or my mother. I never asked any questions. The only way I could get through this was by focusing on
each day as it came. If I let myself think about the future, about

the moment when I would hear my little girl's first cry . . . I would fall apart. So I didn't think about it, and when my labor started, I knew as much about giving birth as I did about astrophysics.

I was alone in the house when all this . . . liquid, this stuff, came pouring out of me. I vaguely knew about water breaking, something gleaned from half-overheard adult conversations in childhood, but nothing prepared me for this! My panties were soaked, my dress was wet. It was about six o'clock on a Wednesday night. Ginny had just started a new series of aerobics classes; Nancy was out at some after-school activity.

Jackie had called from the office before leaving for the day, and for the first time, for no particular reason, I asked for her home number before we hung up. I wasn't acting out of forethought, but it was lucky I did because not ten minutes after I hung up with her, my water broke.

The contractions started. I had never felt anything like this. I never even had period cramps to speak of. The suddenness of it amazed me. I had no warning at all. One minute I was fine, the next I was in labor. And I was terrified.

I called Jackie back immediately, hardly able to speak for my panic. Jackie told me to calm down. I tried to do what she said, but my fear was beyond control.

What was happening to me? What was going to happen next?

I was alone for about another forty-five minutes. Jackie had told me to lie on the couch. I tried to do that—I thought it was required—but my anxiety made me leap up time and again to pace around the room.

I tidied the room and tried to lie down again, but with the next contraction I sprang up, clutching my stomach.

The worst part was not knowing what would happen next, how bad would it get?

Ginny came home; Jackie had reached her or she came home on her own, I don't remember. She made some phone calls. It took her a while to track down Dr. Bergman and tell him I was in labor. I remember her trying him at different places, and I seem to remember that she beeped him and he called her back.

We didn't leave right away. I don't think we left the house for another hour or so; my sense of time at this point is cloudy. I just lay on the couch and tried not to give in to my terror. It was a losing battle. I was really scared.

About seven-thirty or eight o'clock, Ginny and Nancy and I drove into the city in Ginny's car. I assumed we were going to the hospital. I was lying down in the backseat, nearly hysterical. I kept thinking about babies born in the backseat of a cab on the way to the hospital; that's what I was afraid of. I had no idea how long this would take to happen.

I asked Ginny to call my mom. She said she or someone would.

Ginny parked the car and helped me out. We entered a long vestibule or hallway, with sets of French doors and a staircase to an upper floor. Dr. Bergman came out. It was his house. I didn't recognize the building; it was dark and I wasn't paying attention. Only later did I find out that this was the same building I went to for my blood tests. He lived in a triplex above the office.

I saw stairs and I automatically made for them. I thought that's where they wanted me to go. They stopped me—very purposefully. "No! Don't go up there!"

I was long beyond questioning anything they said. They sat me down on a little wooden bench. I bent over clutching my stomach. They kept telling me to take it easy, relax, things like that.

Dr. Bergman asked me a few questions. He didn't examine me. He may have been timing the contractions, I don't know. We weren't there long. I don't know why we were there at all.

I was shaking. I couldn't breathe, couldn't get air. The pain was getting worse—and I had no idea how bad it could get, what the next minute would bring. I didn't know if the baby would spring out of me or tear me or what. These people were all I had in the world. Anything they said to do, I was going to do.

I heard voices coming from upstairs. I know who it was: Joel Steinberg and Hedda Nussbaum. There's no objective evidence to support this, but I know in my heart who was up there. They'd been told I was in labor and were waiting there for the baby to be born. Probably drinking champagne.

If I'd gone up there and seen Steinberg, would anything have changed? I doubt it. Fool that I was, I would probably have thought the adoption lawyer always comes around when the baby is born.

After a while, Ginny took me back out to the car for the ride to the hospital. Nancy stayed behind at Dr. Bergman's house.

Mom was calling Ginny's home all that evening. We hadn't talked in a day or so and she was getting a little worried. The fact that I was overdue never left her mind, not to mention the scares about my health and the baby's health. Of course there was no answer at Ginny's house. At about eleven that night, Nancy called Mom. She said that I was in labor and that Ginny had taken me into the city. Nancy didn't know which hospital we were going to. This business of a Manhattan hospital was news to Mom. She'd assumed that since Dr. Bergman had a practice on Long Island, the delivery would be somewhere close by.

Mom remembers being a raving lunatic that night. Her baby all alone, having a baby of her own. She thought of just driving into the city, but that was crazy; she'd have to wait until morning. Mom smoked cigarettes and drank coffee and ironed. She remembers ironing a skirt of mine, over and over, till it was perfect, without a wrinkle or a crease.

At the hospital, Ginny helped me inside. They put me in a wheelchair and took me to an admitting office.

I answered some of the questions, but Ginny answered some of them, too, considerately, I thought. I was busy with my contractions and my panic.

I didn't find out what she had done until much later. My address on the record is given as "Care of Joel Steinberg, 14 West Tenth Street, New York City."

My birth date is wrong.

My social security number is wrong.

Ginny Liebrader is listed as my next of kin. Where it says "relationship," she is named as my sister.

I found all this out at the hastily convened special session of surrogate's court, at which I would fight for the right to bury the little girl I was now laboring to give birth to.

Before the Grand Jury called as a result of Lisa's murder to investigate adoption practices, Ginny testified that she had no recollection that she entered the hospital with me, merely dropped me off at the entrance and drove home.

According to her testimony, she practically threw me out of the car while it was still rolling. You wouldn't do that to a teenage girl who'd lived in your house for three months. You wouldn't do that to a stranger. You wouldn't drop a *dog* who was having puppies at the vet's, would you?

Certainly there is information on that form that did not come from me. I know my own birthday. I don't have any sisters. And how could I have given them Steinberg's home address? I had no idea where he lived until I read it in the paper following his arrest for Lisa's murder.

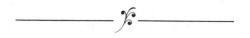

Ginny came with me as I was taken to my room. I only vaguely remember being undressed and put to bed; I remember Ginny's leaving shortly thereafter. I was left alone, to labor through the night.

I devised my own little systems of breathing and leaning to one side or another; I don't think it would have made much difference if they'd given me Lamaze classes or something. I did okay on my own. Your body really knows just what to do.

The contractions came closer together. It was much worse than it had been before. Maybe it was better I didn't have any preparation. I didn't know how bad it was going to get.

I wasn't completely alone; the nurses came in every now and then. I think they went out of their way to spend a few minutes with me. They were kind.

Bergman came once during the night. He examined me quickly. I could tell he was annoyed. The resident had misjudged my condition and told him I was further along than I actually was. He'd gotten Bergman out of bed for nothing.

The pain was bad. I kept begging for somebody to do something. After a few hours, they gave me a shot of Demerol, and maybe they gave me another a few hours after that; I'm not sure.

Sometime during that night they took prints of my thumb and forefinger. I didn't know they did it. I have no memory of it. Apparently this is routinely done with all women giving birth. Those fingerprints would later be instrumental in proving that I was the mother of the murdered child who was erroneously being called Lisa Steinberg.

The night passed somehow. I don't remember much of anything except pain, and a terrible loneliness.

I prayed that the little baby I was giving birth to would never find herself alone in a hospital laboring to deliver a child who would not be hers.

I was trying to hear what Dr. Bergman was telling me to do, but someone—an anesthesiologist I suppose—kept putting a mask over my face. I tried to shove the mask away. They kept saying, "Push! A real push! Hard!" I tried to tell them that I couldn't do it if that guy insisted on putting the mask over my face.

At eight-twelve in the morning on May 14, 1981, Lisa was born. Dr. Bergman said, "It's a girl."

I strained to see her. They were cutting the umbilical cord and my view was blocked.

Then they took her away. They didn't show her to me. I saw her for twenty seconds, maybe half a minute as the nurse carried her past my table. She was a beautiful, golden baby, not red and funny and wrinkled, but bathed in a golden glow, and oh, so beautiful that tears were running down my face. And then there were people between us. I couldn't see her anymore.

I would never see her again. That brief glimpse is all I would have of my little girl.

Chapter 13

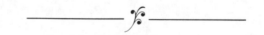 They brought me to a room shortly after the delivery. I lay in bed not really asleep, not really awake. I felt very, very empty.

———————— ✌ ————————

Early that morning, Mom called Ginny's house. "Michele is in New York Infirmary," Ginny told her. "No baby yet, but very soon." Mom immediately left for the city.

Mom recalls, "I remembered the moments when I first held my newborn children. Would they let Michele hold the baby? Probably not. It was probably better not to. I prayed she was okay, and the baby, too. I hoped it hadn't been too hard for her. They should have given her drugs. There's no point in suffering through the labor of a baby you're not going to keep."

Ginny had given Mom the address over the phone. Mom had expected a bustling big-city hospital. This was a quiet, little, private-type place, more like a sanitarium. It was a small, narrow, dark building, pretty cruddy looking, she thought. A nurse or receptionist sat behind a glass window. Mom gave her my name and was sent up to the third floor.

She thought the place looked spooky. The hallways were empty; no nurses, no orderlies, no doctors. No cleaning staff or aides. No visitors. Most of the rooms she passed looked vacant. Plaster was falling down in places.

Ginny had asked me during my pregnancy if I wanted to see the baby after it was born. We talked about it; she said it was up to me, but they advised against it. I thought it would be too painful for me, and we decided I wouldn't. Ginny said I was doing the right thing; it would be much better that way. She told me I wouldn't be put in the maternity ward so I wouldn't be around other mothers' babies. When Mom came to see me, I was sharing a room with an elderly woman. Mom says:

> *Michele looked awfully tiny in that bed, like a baby herself, especially next to this sixty-year-old woman.*
>
> *She looked tired; her movements were slow, but she basically looked okay. I asked her how things went. She said okay.*
>
> *She seemed sad, but back to herself again. Normal. Stomach flat. Seeing her heavily pregnant had never looked right to me. I always had the feeling she was wearing a costume or a disguise of some kind.*
>
> *We sat for a while, me holding Michele's hand. She dozed a little on and off. I could tell they had given her a sedative. She hadn't had natural childbirth like I had. What was the point? She wasn't going to bond to this child; she wasn't ever going to raise this child. Let it be as easy for her as it could.*
>
> *When she opened her eyes for a moment, I asked her if the labor was hard. She said yes, and that they'd given her a shot. She said she felt fine. She looked forlorn. Empty and forlorn.*

I was exhausted. Totally exhausted. Everything had been knocked out of me. I was awake, but I was disoriented.

Mom asked about the baby. I told her it was a girl.

"How is she?"

"Okay. Fine. They said she was healthy."

"Did you see her?"

"Only for a minute." A whisper: "She was beautiful."

It was a painful moment between us. Later, Mom told me what she was thinking: her first grandchild. She would've liked to see her, even if it was just a quick look. When Mom gave birth, they brought her babies to the room. She realized this case was different, and anyway, you have to abide by the rules of the hospital you're in.

She didn't have even a fleeting fantasy about taking the baby home with us. Even if she'd thought it, she wouldn't have said it aloud. She knew I was firm in my conviction and she didn't want to shake me. I seemed to know what I wanted to do, so Mom was backing me up. This was a deal I had made, she figured. I had paid a high cost for it. I was honoring it and she was honoring my decision. She knew I had to live with it; I had to do what was right in order to live inside *my* skin.

It wasn't even proper to bring up a thing like that.

Mom put her arms around me and said, "Shel, this is a milestone in your life. You've just given birth to a baby. You've had a baby! No matter what, that's a happy and wonderful thing. There will be other babies, and those will be happier times for you. But at those times you'll remember this one. Try to hold on to what's good about this, that she's healthy and beautiful and she's going to have a good life. Try to remember that, not the sad part. . . ."

We both cried a little. Mom tried to restrain herself. She felt she had to put up a front as if she had things under control, as if she could handle anything, even though she felt just as lost as I did.

It was time for Mom to go. They were discharging me the next day; Mom would come to pick me up.

Says Mom:

> I find it's almost impossible to talk about extraordinary things, to say them out loud. My daughter had just given birth to a daughter of her own, whom I will probably never see. My first grandchild will be raised by strangers. I will never sing her a lullaby. I will never cradle her in my arms. I will never share a secret, never giggle at a private joke, never beam from the second row of a school auditorium, never play the tooth fairy, never spend days searching for the perfect doll, never see the little face light with joy, never see the lips pursed to blow out birthday candles.
>
> Instead, Michele and I talked about which blouse I should

bring her and which jeans. But when I kissed her good-bye, I held her for an extralong moment.

On the way home, I thought of something Michele had said when she told me she was pregnant almost four months ago. "Don't worry," she had told me. She and Kevin had not "done it" many times. As if that made it better. I knew she was of age, but she was really just a baby at heart.

I was sad for what had happened to Michele so early in life, sorry that she had to be exposed to the seamy side of life without coming out of it with something. All she got was pain and suffering and a lost year of her life. She should have spent that year going to school, preparing for a career and to make a life for herself. But it had happened and it was over.

I felt a great sense of relief. We could get back to being a normal family, dealing with normal, everyday things. Believe me, I far prefer that. We're not Rockefellers or Kennedys. We're just ordinary people. We're not made for high drama.

Jackie came to see me that day, too. Jackie was calm, as always, and sympathetic. She brought me a present, a nightgown, because I didn't have anything of my own to wear. I hadn't packed a bag for the hospital because no one had told me to and I didn't think of it. All I had were the clothes I had been wearing. I was glad she came; I felt close to Jackie.

She asked me how the labor was. I said, okay. At times it got tough, at other times it was tolerable. I told Jackie I had changed my mind. I wanted to see the baby.

She said she would tell Dr. Bergman.

I wasn't going back on my word, I was still going to give up the baby. I just wanted to hold her for a few minutes. I wanted to feel her weight in my arms, to inhale her smell. I wanted to have something more than that single glimpse to remember her by.

I asked Ginny, too, about the baby. I didn't ask anybody else, such as the nurses, because I didn't know them. It was too embarrassing. I didn't know how to go about saying it. "I gave birth but

I'm giving up the baby, and I had agreed not to see it, but now I've changed my mind . . ."

But I know for a fact that I asked Jackie and Ginny.

They never did let me see her. I thought maybe they'd bring her to me, or take me to the nursery to see her. They didn't. The next morning, when it was time for me to leave, I still hadn't seen her and no one was around that I could ask.

Says Mom, "When I got there the next morning, Michele looked quite a bit stronger. But there was that same unnatural stillness, a kind of quiet sadness even though her face had a smile on it."

I dressed in the clothes Mom had brought. A nurse came in with a brown manila envelope that she put on the nightstand. I was supposed to drop it off at Dr. Bergman's office. I didn't know the nurse so I couldn't ask her about the baby.

Mom and I went down in the elevator to the lobby. The woman at reception barely looked up; she waved us away, toward the door. And we left.

It was good to get outdoors. Good to move and not feel weighted down and overblown. But I had gotten used to carrying the baby. I felt like something was missing, like when you're used to carrying a schoolbag, you feel unbalanced without it.

I wondered briefly where the baby was right now. Was she still in the hospital or was today going-home day for her, too? Tonight she'd sleep in her own crib, among the rainbows and the clouds.

That very day my perfect golden baby was released from the hospital to Jackie and Dr. Bergman, who personally took her over to the apartment of Joel Steinberg and Hedda Nussbaum.

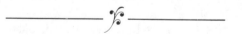

Nearly every street in Greenwich Village is one-way against you. Mom drove around and around until she could finally get parallel to Dr. Bergman's office. I had been to his office several times before for blood tests; I didn't connect it with the place I had been taken two nights before when I was in labor.

We were parked at a hydrant. Mom waited in the car while I went inside. I knew the receptionist from my previous visits and we chatted briefly. I gave her the envelope and my hospital bracelet, which Bergman had instructed me to turn in to them. I assumed that the envelope contained whatever forms or legal papers the lawyer had drawn up regarding the adoption.

I couldn't go home yet. My brother was there, and friends and neighbors. I still couldn't move freely; I walked slowly and I was still a little weak, so Mom drove me to Ginny's where I was going to stay for another night of rest.

But then I would see Kevin. Soon, I would see Kevin. I couldn't wait. That was all I could think about. I hadn't seen him since Valentine's Day. It seemed like years ago and yet just like yesterday.

Kevin and I both returned to Rockville Centre at about the same time. He for summer break, I from giving birth to our baby. John was there when Mom brought me back home. I walked past him —"Hi, John"—and directly to the phone. Kevin wasn't home so I left a message with his parents.

I went upstairs, took a bath, unpacked. I called Mary and then Maureen to say I was back. They had expected me a week earlier. I had told them the course I was taking was over around May 7, but then the baby was a week overdue, so I had to do some fast talking about a trip I had to arrange and underestimating the amount of time I would need. I know nothing about what a wholesale travel packager does, so this wasn't easy.

I called Kevin again that night. He still wasn't home, so I left another message for him to call me. I was surprised because I'd spoken to him about a week before and he knew I was coming home any day.

He didn't call the next morning, so I called him. His mother or father answered, I don't remember which. I was wondering if he had gotten my messages, but of course I couldn't say that, so I just said to tell him that I had called again.

I was sure there was a good reason why Kevin hadn't returned my calls yet, and any minute the phone would ring and it would be him telling me he was coming right over, he had missed me so much he couldn't wait to see me.

My life would start again when I was back with Kevin, and I lived for that moment—I had been living for that moment from the time I went to Ginny's house. I had taken the entire burden on myself. Kevin would never know the pain of having a child and giving her up. My reward was twofold: the knowledge that my baby would have a wonderful life, and that I would share the rest of mine with Kevin.

He didn't call me that day or the next. I knew he had to go home to sleep sometime. I was beginning to wonder what the hell was going on and I was getting upset.

Mary, Billy, and I were going to the park one evening, a few days after I got home. A whole bunch of people were going to be there, and I knew Kevin would, too.

He was. He was there when we got there, and within a matter of minutes after we arrived, he left. He said he had to go to the store for something. He never came back.

No hello. No, "Hi, Michele." Nothing.

I was stricken. I had no idea what was going on. I was confused and hurt, bewildered and insulted.

I didn't cry until I got home.

I called him again the next day, and the day after that. He didn't return any of my calls. Everyone knew what was going on. Nobody wanted to tell me.

I didn't find out for about a week and a half after I got home, and finally, it was two girls in my mom's office who told me; Patty and Antoinette, two girls I wasn't even particularly friendly with; semi-strangers. I had dropped into my mom's office, and I mentioned that I was calling Kevin and he hadn't returned any of my phone calls. Kevin's best friend, Chuck, worked there by then, so they knew Maureen and the others of my crowd through him.

They couldn't take it anymore. They realized nobody else was telling me and I was being played a fool.

Kevin was seeing another girl, someone from Rockville Centre. He had a new girlfriend.

I was devastated. I was destroyed.

I contained myself till I got home—I remember that trip home. Then I lay on the couch and just cried, I mean cried hysterically, loud, uncontrollable sobs. The pain I had been keeping inside me burst out like pus from a boil.

Mary came over, and I had to straighten up a little bit. I couldn't let anyone know that what had happened between Kevin and me was any more than just a broken romance. It was just another breakup. No one could know I had suffered a double loss, child and lover, almost simultaneously. I was completely bereft. If I had been empty inside before, now there was a great yawning hole where my heart had once been.

I had yet another secret to keep.

There was no point in being angry with my friends. They had wanted to tell me, but couldn't bring themselves to. I was so destroyed it hardly mattered.

What mattered most—what hurt—was Kevin, that he didn't have the guts, the simple courtesy, to come and tell me to my face that he didn't want to see me anymore. I could have handled that. Instead, he showed up at all the same places our crowd went to with another girl. And everyone knew except me.

All through the long months, through the labor and the recovery, I had drawn strength from one thought: Soon I would be in Kevin's arms, and that would take the hurt away.

And I had done it at least in part for *him!* I was protecting him!

The weeks after my baby was born were filled with sadness; a dead feeling that I carried with me all the time, even in my sleep.

Rockville Centre is a small town; there are only so many places you can go. Inevitably when I went out with my friends, we'd wind up in the same bar or restaurant with Kevin and his new girlfriend. He didn't have the guts to come over—but there was lots of eye contact. We'd stare at each other across the room. It became a strange game of chicken that no one was aware of except the two of us.

Kevin always lost. He would be the one to get up and leave. I wasn't going to give him the satisfaction of leaving. It seems so petty and foolish to me now, but that's what was going on.

One night, Kevin and I happened to go to the same bar. He was on one side of the circular bar, I was on the other. He was alone, without a date, and I guess that's why we were finally able to talk.

We looked at each other. Our eyes would meet, we'd hold the glance, then look away. I suppose he knew that sooner or later he was going to have to say something to me, and I guess he thought this was an opportune time. He came over. There were a few minutes of "Hi, how are you?" After that, Kevin couldn't find anything to say. He was clearly uncomfortable just being in the same room with me.

I suggested we go for a walk, just for something to do, and he agreed.

We walked for a while, then sat down in the deserted train station. Finally, I turned to him and said, "Kevin, what's going on? If you don't want to see me anymore, how come you couldn't tell me yourself? You could have had the decency to call me and tell me, not leave it to me to figure out. I'm not a mind reader and it's not a lot of fun to find things like that out from somebody else."

He apologized. I think. Kind of.

He didn't give me any reasons or explanations. He wasn't saying much of anything, just a lot of shrugging and silences.

I was getting angry.

I would have understood if he had said he didn't tell me because he felt bad about it or because he couldn't face me. But he wasn't saying any of those things. He was trying to make it sound as if it were my fault, that I was the one to blame. *I'd* gone off and disappeared for three months. *I* was the one who broke us up.

I was stunned. That really blew me away. I never expected anything like that.

Had he gotten tired of waiting? Was that why he was seeing other girls?

No, that wasn't it. He'd decided to break up with me a long time ago . . . on Valentine's Day weekend.

Valentine's Day weekend! Why?

Because I wasn't as much fun to be with anymore. I wasn't cheerful and lighthearted and I didn't get into the spirit of things. Who needs somebody moping around?

That was when I let him have it.

"You want to know why I was moping around on Valentine's Day? On Valentine's Day I was nearly six months pregnant and I didn't know what the hell I was going to do—that's why I wasn't a barrel of laughs.

"I just had a baby. Five weeks ago, Kevin. Our baby. Your baby. *That's* why I disappeared. Not because I wanted to. Not because I had better things to do than be with you. I was pregnant and I didn't want to mess up your life by telling you. I didn't want you to screw up on your stupid midterms.

"You want to know why I disappeared for three months? There wasn't any travel-agent course. I disappeared so you wouldn't have to know about it. And I didn't call you because I couldn't stand lying to you.

"I had your baby, Kevin, and I gave it up for adoption."

Chapter 14

I know it sounds spiteful. I hope I didn't tell him out of spite. I was in such pain, I was hurting so much, I guess I just wanted him to feel a small part of the pain I was feeling. I sure could have used Kevin's being with me all this time. But I kept him out of it. I went through it alone, to protect him.

Kevin didn't say much. He didn't seem stunned. He didn't seem anything in particular. Kevin is good at keeping things to himself.

He asked only one question: Was it a boy or a girl? He didn't ask why I gave her up. He didn't ask how I managed. He didn't ask if it was hard, if I had been lonely, if I needed anything now. Nothing.

He didn't ask me one question about the baby, other than her sex.

He never said he was sorry or expressed a word of sympathy. Kevin walked me home. The whole conversation hadn't taken more than a few minutes. I thought there would be something more coming from him, but there wasn't, and that was that.

I thought telling Kevin would make me feel better. It didn't. If anything, I felt worse.

I would never have guessed I would get such a nothing response to news like that. I don't know what I expected, but surely a little more response, a little more curiosity . . . a little more interest.

When Kevin and I ran into each other around town after that, we exchanged pleasant "Hi, how are you" 's and casual chatter. The subject of the baby was never brought up again. The next time we spoke about it was when I was forced by Judge Marie Lambert to call him from her chambers during the hearing at surrogate's court, when I was fighting to keep strangers from burying our daughter.

Shortly after my talk with Kevin in the train station, I went to Dr. Bergman for my six-week postnatal checkup. I had been dropping in at the office every now and then since I gave birth. I went over there a couple of weeks after I returned home: I'd been shopping and the office was a couple of blocks from the store, so on impulse I popped in. Ginny and Jackie were pleased to see me. They thought I was too thin; I told them I was eating, but they kept stuffing me with Oreo cookies anyway.

I asked about the baby. Ginny said, "Do you know that she had jaundice?"

How would I know that? This was the first contact I'd had with them since I left Ginny's house. They saw I was alarmed; Dr. Bergman was in the room and he and Jackie were quick to reassure me. The baby was fine now, the jaundice was over and done with. Though Dr. Bergman went on to explain that it was common, nothing out of the ordinary, I had no clear idea what jaundice was.

What about papers? Shouldn't I sign something?

No, nothing at the moment. They would let me know.

I dropped in a few more times after that. I felt distanced from my old friends. Ginny and Jackie and Dr. Bergman had been involved in such a powerful and traumatic part of my life, I felt closer to them than anybody I knew from before. Anytime I found myself in the neighborhood I'd use the excuse to stop by. I always asked after the baby, and about the adoption papers. I was concerned that everything be in order so she wouldn't have any problems later in life. I wanted every i dotted and every t crossed.

These things take time, they told me. It's all being taken care of. Everything is going perfectly, just the way it should. If they needed me to sign anything, they knew where to reach me.

I believed them. They were the experts. They were the professionals. Who was I to question them?

Then an odd thing happened. Slowly, my welcome grew less cordial. They acted surprised when I came, and with each visit they were less friendly, even a little cold. I was given to understand that they were busy, and I was keeping them from their work. I went one more time, about two weeks after my last checkup, and it was made pretty clear to me that they didn't expect to see my face around there anytime soon, so I stopped going.

They were my last link with my daughter.

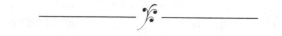

It was around that time that I started drinking.

Liquor is an anesthetic. I just didn't want to feel anymore.

I felt nothing.

I worked hard to feel nothing.

But I could never keep the baby out of my thoughts. She was always there. As I went about my daily life, while I was doing whatever I was doing, I was thinking about her.

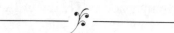

I went back to work shortly after Lisa's birth; less than two months after she was born I found a job in the claims department of a mortgage company. I held several jobs over the next few years, always in the general area of insurance adjusting. Each time I switched it was for the better. I did well at work and was rewarded with raises, promotions, benefits.

I stayed in the office till late, till nine, ten at night, and then I'd bring work home with me. I'd spread all my files out on the dining room table, put my head into my work, and not look up for hours. I took night courses in insurance, paid for by the company for which I worked, and that helped me to get on even more.

I was also active socially. In one firm my boss had his own plane and we'd fly to Connecticut for pizza. Friday nights he'd fly several of us from the company over to Atlantic City. I went boating with another of my friends; I spent weekends on Fire Island and in the beach resort towns of Long Island.

Mom says I reminded her of something Joseph Launders had once said to her. He had come home late, rather the worse for wear from drink, and he turned to her and said, "I bet you think I'm out there having a good time. You couldn't be more wrong."

I think there comes a point where you're not having a good time, the good time is having *you*. You're not in control anymore. And then it stops being fun.

Mom wasn't the only one who saw I was drinking too much. Other people would try to tell me, too. Mom felt that I was trying to blot out this memory that was not fading. Nothing I was doing was making it go away.

You can't just give a child up for adoption and expect it to be over. It just doesn't happen that way. For a period of three or four months after Lisa's birth, I drank heavily. Really heavily. Not enough to pass out, but enough to close the bars. I don't know exactly how much I drank, but I was there till last call, till the bars closed, then I went home. I won't say I was out every night during the week, but weekends and a couple of days in between were pretty definite.

After a while I got some kind of control over it. I didn't stop drinking; I stopped overdrinking so much. But still, at times I pretty regularly drank too much.

Mom and I didn't talk about the baby. That chapter was closed. But one day she said, "Michele, I hear about all these new programs where adopted children are looking up their natural parents. You'll see, one day your daughter will come knocking on the door. I can't say it's going to be a good thing or a bad thing. Maybe you won't want to know her; maybe she won't want to know you. But it's going to happen. You'll see her again. I'm sure of it."

That seemed to make her feel better, but it didn't console me much. I had thought of it, too, actually, but I wasn't so sure it would be a happy reunion. I prayed that when she did find me—if she did—she wouldn't hate me.

From the moment my baby was born, I never stopped thinking about her. I pictured her in her little nursery, and I celebrated every date in my mind. Now she's one week old, now a month. She must be smiling now . . . and cooing and gurgling and making sounds.

I looked in every baby stroller and carriage I passed, and I'd compare that child to mine. I didn't know what name she'd been given; I just thought of her as my baby. I'd see a child sitting up in a stroller, and I'd think not yet. She wouldn't be sitting up yet. Then a month later, I'd see another child and I'd think, I'll bet she's sitting up just like that now.

I pictured her gumming on a biscuit, poking at the space in her mouth where her first tooth was coming in. Every milestone a mother lives through in real life, I lived through in my imagination.

With one difference. I never pictured anything bad happening to her, not even a cold or the flu, not even sniffles.

Mothers who give their children up for adoption see only happy things. We don't see the heart-stopping falls from a swing, don't fight panic when the baby spikes a fever, have no dread of a sudden phone call from school or camp. We don't get up in the night to lean over a crib and brush a kiss on a child's forehead just to luxuriate in the now-cool skin. We are innocent of all that. We see only the joys; and how we long to be a part of them.

Summertime, and she's at the beach shaded by an umbrella, kicking her little feet in the air. Thanksgiving, and she's sitting in her high chair. Could you give a six-month-old a bit of turkey? Some sweet potatoes, surely.

At Christmas—her first Christmas—she was seven months old and I pictured her all dressed up in tiny little red velvet dress with a white collar embroidered with sprigs of holly. She'd have a bow in her hair.

By now she's crawling around, maybe even taking her first steps.

And now she's one year old; her first birthday party. I had a clear picture of that, very much like my parties as a child. I saw her sitting at a table full of kids, the adults standing behind them, proud and joyful. I could see the paper tablecloth, pink probably, with clowns or flowers or balloons. Then they'd bring out the cake, and how her eyes would light up. She couldn't blow out the candle herself yet, but they'd set the cake in front of her and help her blow it out and everyone would sing "Happy Birthday" to her.

Even though I never had a second's doubt that she was anything but happy and healthy and thriving, still I was eaten up by guilt for what I had done. I had a recurring dream that one day there'd be a knock at my door, and I'd open it to see a young woman standing there. "I'm your daughter," she'd say. "And I have one thing to ask you. Why did you do it? You carried me, you gave birth to me. Why did you give me away?

"Were you trying to get rid of me? Didn't you want me?"

Oh, how I wanted you, I would say. I wanted you so much. More than you will ever know; more than I can find the words to say.

"But you gave me away. Why did you do it? Why!"

How would I ever explain? How would I ever make her under-stand?

For your own sanity, you try to thrust aside those thoughts and concentrate on the good. The good was the lovely environment in which my child was being raised, the love and care she was getting, the happiness she was bringing to her new family. I never worried about that; I knew the people who had her loved and cherished her as their own.

But still, you could have woken me at any hour of the night and I'd be able to tell you exactly how old the baby was.

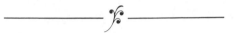

My life was work. That's why I lived at home so much longer than most people. I left in the morning to go to work and came home to sleep. Why should I pay a separate rent bill, a separate utilities bill? I moved out once, for about three months. I only lived a mile away, and I quickly realized how stupid it was, so I moved back home with Mom.

Mom was worried about me. "Michele was running like a deer," Mom says. "From work to the party to the next party to the next party to work. She'd stay at work till eleven o'clock and at home she worked, too. She kept going, going, going. I'd tell myself she was young. She could go like this for a while without burning out. But I was afraid when she was thirty, thirty-five or so, and the burnout came, it would be bad.

"All this was to push the memories down, to get so tired she could sleep without dreaming."

It worked sometimes. Other times it didn't.

With time, the anguish lessened, the pain of loss dulled. I guess I was trying to handle it as best I knew how, by moving fast, working, socializing, drinking. I dated lots of people, but they were mostly friends, not boyfriends, nobody special. I just didn't have the same feelings for anybody else that I had had for Kevin. They say your first love is the one you never get over, and as far as my life goes, that seems to be holding true. I probably still love Kevin a little. At least part of me does. And the funny thing is, I don't even like him anymore.

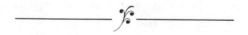

I'd put the events of the spring of 1981 out of my mind as much as I could. Sometimes I'd be reminded in odd ways. I was driving my friend Mary to a pub in Huntington to hear a DJ we knew. I took us there over the back roads. Mary was surprised. How did I know Huntington so well?

I didn't tell her the pub was three blocks from Ginny Liebrader's house, and I'd once lived there for three months while waiting to give birth to my baby.

Lisa never left my mind. By now she was in nursery school and I pictured her dancing with excitement on her first day, all dressed up in one of those cute outfits with a heart or a teddy bear on the front, so proud of her new Snoopy lunch box.

Maybe she had even started taking ballet lessons, like I did. How cute she would look in her tutu and tights.

Lisa did have ballet lessons. I have pictures of her in her costume, which were given to me by the police. I also have a videotape someone took at a school recital. It must have been another parent; the focus is on one of the other children. But Lisa is in it, too. She looks heartbreakingly beautiful. I look at the pictures and the tape and try to imagine how she was.

There were still times when I drank too much. I wasn't having blackouts exactly, but I'd wake up in the morning and not remember much of the party the night before. It was frightening. I didn't really get control of myself until I had an accident while driving under the influence. I could have cost a young girl her life.

I went out for a few drinks after work with a guy I knew through work. We argued; I have no idea what started it. He was drunk, and loud and obnoxious. He didn't like something I said so he reached over and punched me in the face. I guess he didn't know the owners of this place were friends of mine. To his surprise, he was escorted out of there without his feet touching the ground.

My friends offered to call a cab; I didn't let them. I was less than a quarter of a mile from my house; I could drive.

I was only three blocks away from home when I hit another car. The young girl at the wheel was unsure of the traffic pattern and had stopped in the middle of an intersection to figure it out. I guess I expected her to keep moving and I hit her. Thank God neither one of us was hurt, but the cars were pretty much totaled. Police in the neighborhood investigating another accident passed by, saw us, and stopped. I had liquor on my breath, so they took me into the station. I failed a Breathalyzer test.

The next day I went into work and told them what had happened. They suggested I contact a lawyer who handled legal matters for them: Joe Famighetti.

Mom and I went to see him. We were there for less than an hour, and I never did use him for the DWI. Joe is primarily a criminal lawyer. I didn't want to contest the charges. I had been driving; I had been drinking. The accident was completely my fault. I was just glad nobody had been hurt and I saw no point in tying up the courts with a trial.

I told Joe, "Whatever has to happen will happen. If I go to jail, I go to jail. I deserve whatever I get."

I pleaded guilty. It was my first offense. I got the mandatory six-months' suspension of my license and a three-hundred-fifty-dollar fine. The judge didn't see any need to place me on probation. I promised myself and everybody else I'd never find myself in that position again. And so far I haven't.

The good thing about that whole experience was that years later, when I found out the little girl the world knew as Lisa Steinberg was in fact the daughter I had given up at birth, I remembered Joe Famighetti. The police, the district attorney's office, the press, were all hounding me. Several lawyers had flatly refused to represent me. I don't know why I thought of Joe; I had only seen him for about forty-five minutes. But since Lisa's death Joe has been . . . what? A surrogate uncle, perhaps. I don't know what to call him, except to say that he has been a staunch friend and I trust him implicitly. I don't honestly think I could have survived what happened in November 1987 without him.

Chapter 15

❦In August 1984, I was spending the weekend at my friend Jim's beach house in Montauk, Long Island. My mother called me to say that my father, Joseph Launders, was very ill, dying in fact, and wanted to see us—my brother, John, and me—before he passed away.

I could feel the blood rush to my head. If I didn't get some fresh air, I would faint. I ran out of the house, which is up on stilts. I ran down the stairs and took off down the block. Jim came running after me. I yelled at him to leave me alone, I had some bad news and a decision to make. Jim said he knew all about it. Mom had called while I was out and told him.

"You knew and you didn't tell me!"

He was going to tell me that night as we drove back from Montauk.

I went crazy on him. Really out-of-control crazy. "You were going to tell me inside a car? Going sixty miles an hour?"

I took off down the street. Jim chased after me. Suddenly I changed direction and headed for the beach. Jim veered, too, and came after me. I called to him to leave me alone.

"I won't be with you; I'll stay behind you."

"I don't want a shadow, either."

Finally, he gave up and went back to the house. I stayed by myself on the beach for a while.

All those years my father hadn't wanted to see me, now he did? Frankly, Scarlett, I didn't give a damn.

But it was a deathbed wish. You have to put your own feelings aside in cases like that. Regardless of my feelings I couldn't turn my back on him.

Like he had turned his back on us.

I couldn't make up my mind what I was going to do.

Jim drove me home that night. We were out on the farthermost tip of Long Island, a ninety-mile drive from Rockville Centre. I wasn't very good company for Jim. I was anxious and apprehensive and I took out a lot of my emotion on him. I was about to meet a totally unknown person who was supposed to be my father. By the time we got home it was too late for me to go that night, and I was more than a little relieved.

Mom, Nana, and John had just come back from seeing him. Mom was off in a corner talking to Nana. She not only had to resolve her own emotions, she had to worry about Fred, the man she'd been seeing steadily for years. She didn't need me to press her with questions. I got the story from John.

Our father's relatives had tracked us down with some difficulty; Mom had made a point of hiding our whereabouts from his family. John was home when my cousin and my uncle first knocked on the door. Mom hadn't wanted to let them in. She'd acted pretty neurotic, and if Nana hadn't finally let them in, they might still be standing on our front porch. A lot of hurt had come my Mom's way from Joseph Launders, and she wanted nothing to do with him. She even suspected it might be a trick. He'd pulled things like that before, many years ago, having relatives call and tell her he was in trouble and asking her to rush off to some secluded address to rescue him.

But it wasn't a trick this time.

I still wasn't a hundred percent sure I wanted to go, but finally I agreed with John that we had to respect a dying man's wish. However, we also agreed that it would have been nice to have heard from him a little before that.

Search my mind as I would, I could summon up no memories of him. This was going to be my first and last impression of my father.

Apparently my father—I can't call him Dad—had moved out to

California the last few years of his life. He worked as an accountant, for a martial arts firm in Los Angeles, I believe. Then he came back here and lived in a single room occupancy. John found some papers of his after he died, that's how I know this. Somebody at the hospital handed John a legal-size envelope with papers in it—rent receipts, pay stubs—and we pieced together what information we could from that.

Mom didn't come in with us. She stayed in the hall outside his room. John and I went in alone. John had tried to prepare me for what I would see. "Don't expect to see a person in that bed," he had warned me.

Still, it was difficult to look at him. He was gaunt and withdrawn, drifting in and out; his eyes would open briefly, then he'd drift off again. He must've been pretty doped up with painkillers.

I searched his face looking for something familiar. I couldn't find it. I looked from him to John trying to see a resemblance. If there ever had been one, it was gone. His features had all sunk in. He was fifty-eight years old, but he looked ninety.

He had bone marrow cancer that had spread all over his body. He could not talk much at all and was in a lot of pain, even with the painkillers. I held his hand. So did John. When my father realized John and I were in the room, he motioned to us to move closer. He seemed to want to get a look at us. We stood around the side of the bed.

Mom walked in. I know she says she doesn't love him, but when she saw him in that state, it hit her. You could see her muscles tense up, could see the sadness of it register. She had loved him once even though she'd grown to hate him.

John talked a little. He was the only one. Our father couldn't speak. I couldn't think of anything to say.

John recalls, "The one thing I did say to him is that I didn't understand or condone what he did, but I did forgive him. I figured he did what he had to do. There really wasn't much else to say. He was hurting a lot, you could see that."

The only words my father said to me—the only words I ever remember hearing him say to me—were, "It's been a long time." That's what he said: "It's been a long time."

He died two days later.

I can't say that I miss him.

And even so, I know that my not having a father was a big factor in my giving up my daughter for adoption. I knew that some-where she was three years old and adored her daddy. I pictured him taking her places, the zoo, the circus, special outings for just Daddy and her.

I found out later that Joel Steinberg in fact had a habit of taking Lisa with him. Only the places he chose weren't the ones I had in mind. He took her with him to offices, to court, and even, it has been suggested, to meetings at which he made drug deals. I'm not sure he didn't use her to ferry drugs. She went with him on long trips to odd places.

I didn't know any of that then. I saw a laughing, happy child coming home with her face smeared with cotton candy, clutching balloons and souvenirs.

Mom had been seeing someone steadily for years. Fred was steady, solid, sensible, as different from my father as could be. On June 13, 1986, Mom and Fred were married by a judge at the Links Country Club in Rockville Centre, with their family around them, his and hers.

My daughter was five years and one month old, almost to the day. I tried not to picture her running around with the other young-sters, all excited by the fuss.

Mom and Fred moved to a condo in New Jersey and I finally moved into a place of my own. My childhood friend Mary and I shared the second floor of a house in Atlantic Beach on Long Island. Her boyfriend—now husband—Billy had the downstairs apart-ment, so we pretty much had the run of the place. In August I switched jobs again, for the fifth time in six years, each change a promotion, a step up.

Friday, October 23, 1987, I celebrated my twenty-sixth birthday. I went out with friends, and I ate and drank and laughed. Just hours later a car stopped at a tollbooth on the Thruway. The driver, a man, couldn't find the change for the toll. He got out of the car to search his pockets.

He was traveling alone with a little girl. The toll-taker noticed that the girl was crying—far too hard, not ordinary childish tears; she was sobbing convulsively. The toll-taker, noticing a bruise on the girl's forehead, asked the man what was wrong with the child.

"Nothing," he said, and hastily shoved some candy at the girl to quiet her. He found his change, paid the toll, and drove on.

Something wasn't right. The toll-taker thought the child might have been kidnapped. She took the action she had been trained to do—one of the few people around Lisa who did. She noted the license number of the car and called it in to the state police.

State troopers stopped the car a few miles down the highway. They questioned the driver. He was tall, glib, sure of himself, men-tioning several times that he was an attorney. The toll-taker had misunderstood. The child was fine. She was crying because of a "neck problem." She needed only a "massaging." He would see to it when he got home.

They asked for his telephone number and called his home. His "wife" confirmed his story.

They let him go.

The alert and caring toll-taker would later receive a medal and a thousand-dollar award for her good citizenship. By then it was too late for Lisa.

Others, too, in the last weeks of Lisa's life, noticed something amiss. A neighbor thought she looked "sad" and thought of calling the police, but didn't. A teacher noticed a black-and-blue mark. She reported it to a supervisor. The supervisor spoke to Steinberg, who explained it away: Her baby brother had hit her.

Once, when a neighbor commented on a bruise that Lisa had, Steinberg ran back to the apartment to get her brother, to show the man what a lively, strong boy he was, perfectly capable of bruising his sister in play.

And I, in my innocence, was picturing her carefully toting home from school a construction-paper Halloween pumpkin to be greatly admired and proudly and ceremoniously taped to the fridge, where it would stay until its eventual displacement by a crayon drawing of a turkey.

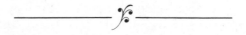

The whole city watched with horror as the story of Lisa Steinberg unfolded on November 2, as did I. A little girl in Greenwich Village had been beaten into a coma. They said her parents did it.

They showed her picture: a sweet-faced little girl.

I remember wondering how anyone, for any conceivable reason, could hit a child in anger, let alone hard enough to cause injury. I thought of the little girl for whom I'd baby-sat several summers

Mom, and my father,
Joseph Launders,
on their honeymoon
in Bermuda, 1955.

Me in the summer of 1962 at Long Beach, Long Island; I was nine months old.

Me and my big brother in the summer of 1963.

John and me in our apartment in Queens, N.Y.

John and me
outside of church
on Easter Sunday, 1964.

John and me with Nana
at her house in
Rockville Centre on
Easter Sunday, 1968.

Me, John, Mom,
Papa Jack and Nana
on Mother's Day, 1968.

Me, age eight.

Above right:
That's me, second from
the left, at summer camp
when I was nine.

My confirmation picture,
age twelve.

The family at Mom and Fred's wedding on June 13, 1986.
From the left: Fred's children, Bob, Dave and Jean;
Fred, Mom, me and John. *(Mary Conboy-Leck)*

Another wedding picture of Papa Jack, Nana, me, Fred, John,
Mom, and Fred's mother, Mary. *(Mary Conboy-Leck)*

A few precious pictures of
my daughter Lisa, which I
received after her death.

Mom and me at Gate of Heaven Cemetery.
(*New York Post*)

years ago. Sure, she was difficult at times, and yes, she tried everyone's patience. But hit her? No. Never.

On Wednesday, November 4, Lisa was declared brain-dead and
the life-support system was turned off the next day. Her "adoptive"
father, Joel Steinberg, was charged with attempted murder, assault,
and endangering the welfare of a child. His common-law wife, Hedda
Nussbaum, similarly charged, was taken to Elmhurst City Hospital
in Queens. I saw her on television. At first I thought she was his
mother. They said she was forty-five. She looked a hundred and
ten. Her face didn't look like a face, it looked like a cauliflower.
They said he beat her, too.

Steinberg's attorney said he was innocent of all charges, calling
him a "devoted father."

The district attorney's office announced that in all likelihood the
child would be declared dead in the morning. The charges would
then be upgraded to murder. I marveled that there were human
beings anywhere on the planet who could do such a thing.

The next morning, Thursday, I heard on the news that Lisa had
died, and I, like everyone else, felt a pang of sorrow for the child.
I never dreamed she was anything but a stranger. I mourned her as
a bystander, as would anyone hearing of a little girl fiercely and
brutally beaten until she died.

Even when it came out that Lisa was adopted, I didn't make the
connection.

That night Mom called me. "Are you watching television?"

"No, what's on, anything good?"

"Shel, I want you to think back to the time of Dr. Bergman and
Ginny. What year was that?"

"Why are you bothering about all that now, Mom?"

"Just tell me. What year was it?"

She kept bothering me about dates. I said, "Mom, would you stop
it! What brought this on all of a sudden? What's all this about?"

"This little girl—the Steinberg girl. They're showing a picture of
her. She looks just like you."

"That's crazy!"

"Shel, she looks just like you!"

"Mom, turn off the television and go to sleep."

I really thought Mom was off-the-wall. I didn't connect that poor murdered girl with my own baby until the police detective and the district attorney came to my home.

But I did turn on the television news. They kept repeating the news footage of Steinberg and Nussbaum being brought into the police station. Steinberg looked nothing like the man I had met. The man I had met was bigger, stronger; not in weight, in physique. He had looked as if he'd played football in college. This man on TV was disheveled and unshaven. He looked scrawny. They kept referring to him as Joel Barnett Steinberg. The addition of a middle name made it just dissimilar enough so it rang no bells. This man was agitated, full of tics and jerky eye movements. The man I met had been very much in control.

I had sat within a foot of Joel Steinberg for an hour, and I still didn't connect him with this man on television. I had told Mom to relax, turn off the TV, and go to sleep. And that's just what I did.

Maybe there are some things the mind just doesn't want to know. Says Mom:

> Despite what Michele had said, I stayed glued to the television set. She was right; it was ridiculous, it was crazy. But I couldn't stop watching. One report had it that he'd used the child to carry drugs. Another said something about sexual activity, child abuse. My stomach knotted.
>
> I got out the photo album and looked through pictures of Michele as a child. The resemblance was so strong. Michele had a way of pouting, a very specific pout. Lisa had that same kind of a pout on her face in one of the pictures they showed.
>
> I was letting my imagination run away with me. Michele had said it couldn't be her child.
>
> My mind told me one thing. But in my heart I could feel another. I guess I was the only one who knew at that point in time that Lisa was our baby.

A day later, on Friday night, I was lying on the couch with a blanket over me. I wasn't feeling well; not terribly sick, just under the weather. Mary and Billy were making dinner. We'd rented a couple of tapes and planned to spend the evening watching them.

There was a knock on the door, but no one came in. Our friends would have just walked in. I couldn't understand why they were waiting outside. I called, "Come in," and so did Billy, but they just knocked again. Billy went to the door.

I heard somebody say, "Does Michele Launders live here?" It was November, but we hadn't gotten around to taking down the screen door yet, and Billy was talking to them through the door. They seemed to want me. I thought, where are my manners? "Ask them in, Billy," I called from the couch.

Billy let them in; a man and a woman. Billy seemed a little wary, a little tense, but I didn't really register that then.

The visitors introduced themselves. George Schurz, a detective with the district attorney's squad, and Nancy Patterson of the district attorney's Crimes Against Children Squad. They asked if I was Michele Launders. I said I was.

They had a couple of questions for me.

"Go right ahead."

"It's kind of personal. Can your friends go someplace else?"

I have a perfectly sharp, vivid image in my mind of the moments before my life was shattered forever. The kitchen was the island kind, where you can see right into the living room. Mary was in the kitchen; she had a wooden spoon in her hand.

"What do you mean, go someplace else?" she said. "I'm in the middle of cooking dinner."

I thought it was funny, she sounded so offended. I wouldn't laugh again for a long time.

I said, "Mary, they seem serious. Do what they want."

Mary put down her spoon and she and Billy left, reluctantly. They told me later that as they went out the door, George Schurz told them not to go far. "She's going to need you," he told them. Billy and Mary stayed outside, trying to peek under the blinds of the bay window to get a glimpse of what these people were going to do to me. Mary thought it might be about parking tickets; maybe I'd left a bunch of them unpaid. Billy knew better. They don't send an assistant district attorney from another county to your house no matter how many outstanding parking tickets you have.

At least he'd been smart enough to catch that much. I hadn't. I saw before me some official-type people and I had no particular conjecture about what they were doing there. I figured it was some-what serious, but not earthshaking.

George Schurz asked me if I had given birth to a baby girl on May 14, 1981.

I said, "Yes."

And now my heart was in my mouth. I could feel the blood pounding in my ears. He asked if I'd followed the Steinberg case in the papers. I nodded.

He said, "We're reasonably certain that Lisa Steinberg was your baby."

Chapter 16

❧ Everything went blank. I couldn't hear. I couldn't speak. I looked at them, dumb, speechless.

They asked if I wanted a glass of water. I don't think I responded. When I finally found my voice, I asked permission to get up and get a cigarette from the dining room table. They exchanged a look of disbelief.

I was drowning, sinking down into a deep pit. They were talking. I didn't want to hear it. My mind was creating its own images. My baby hurt. My baby abused. My baby dead.

I asked the detective's permission to call my mother. I kept acting as if it were their home and I was the visitor.

When Mom answered the phone, I could not say the words; from my mind to my mouth, they just would not come out. I talked, but I wasn't saying anything. I didn't even realize I was babbling. Mom was getting scared.

"Michele, please! What's the matter?"

"Mom . . ."

"Michele! Tell me!"

I couldn't say the name Lisa. "Remember what we were talking about the other night? About that little girl . . . What you thought . . . it's true."

A long, long silence. Then: "How do you know?"
"There are people here, from the police. The DA's office."
Mom started to scream.

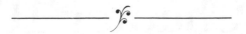

The detective kept trying to talk to me. He wanted me to sign a paper—I couldn't take in what it was about. They wanted me to come down to the station with them and sign something there. I was willing to go, but Mom started yelling at me over the phone that I wasn't to move, I wasn't to go anywhere. She was babbling on about them needing a warrant—she was totally panicked. She admits now she had no idea what she was talking about.

But she panicked me. Mom kept saying, "Don't sign anything. Don't say a word. We need an attorney. Tell those people to get the hell out."

When you need a lawyer, I make the association that you're guilty, that you've done something wrong. Mom's saying that made me feel even worse. It validated the guilt I had felt in my heart since May 14, 1981, when I had borne Lisa and given her away to strangers.

I was caught between two opposing voices. The detective wanted dates, places, people's names, and he kept telling me how important it was that I cooperate: "We really need you to do this. We need you to verify our information."

At the same time Mom kept telling me not to say a word. I'd say good-bye to her, get off the phone, and the moment we hung up, she'd call right back. "Don't talk to them, Michele, you hear me? Don't talk to them."

Fred got on the phone with me. He said, "Your mother is right, don't say anything, don't sign anything."

I said, "Fred, they're right here. What am I going to do, I have to talk to them."

I really didn't see why I shouldn't. I couldn't ask Mom—she was hysterical, she wasn't giving me logical responses.

I answered all their questions. I gave them Dr. Bergman's name, Jackie's name, Ginny's name. What hospital I gave birth in, everything.

Mom was calling back every few minutes screaming, "Don't say a word!"

I told her it was too late for that.

They told me there had been no official adoption papers, which I hadn't really known until that time. I knew I hadn't signed anything, but I figured it had been done some other way. That was the whole point about Steinberg. He presented himself as a man who knew his way around; if one way didn't work, he'd find another.

Detective Schurz was pressing me to sign his form. I'm sure they told me what the form was about, but nothing registered. I certainly was in no shape to read anything. I probably would have signed— I certainly *might* have signed—if Mom hadn't stopped me. On that I listened to her. I adamantly refused to sign anything. Detective Schurz and Assistant District Attorney Patterson finally gave up and left. They weren't happy.

Mary and Billy came back in. They were dying to know what was going on. It took me about ten minutes to tell them. I was pacing like a crazy person. I couldn't bring myself to say the words. Mary knew I had had a baby; Billy didn't. He almost went through the wall.

Neither one of them asked who the father was. They didn't have to. I asked Mary to call Kevin and tell him; there wasn't a way in the world I could make myself do that.

Billy asked if the detective had shown me his ID. I hadn't seen badges of any kind. I never thought to ask. Could it possibly be a mistake, a hoax, some crazy trick someone was playing? For all I knew they could have been totally phony.

The phone rang; Billy answered. Detective Schurz was calling from his car, taking one more shot at getting me to sign that form. I wouldn't get on the phone so he left a number. Billy called it— and there really was a Detective George Schurz with the police department.

They were who they said they were . . . and that meant that what they had told me was true. It wasn't a hoax or some crazy stunt somebody was pulling. Just as I had refused to admit I was pregnant until every bit of proof was in, now I clung to every last shred of hope that the dead child was not my baby.

I kept that hope alive right up until the time Hedda Nussbaum said my name on the witness stand. Long after I found out what had happened to Lisa, I still clung to the possibility that this was some terrible mistake and my daughter was alive and well in the home of the loving couple who'd adopted her and who doted on her every word. Only when I heard Hedda Nussbaum describe how she and Joel Steinberg had "monitored my pregnancy" did I let go of that last, slender glimmer of hope. When those words came out of her mouth, I knew that the child they had killed was mine.

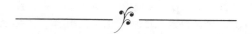

Mom and I had said our good-nights and left it that she would come over in the morning. Two minutes later she called back: "I'm coming to get you." Mom wanted me safe. She wanted me where she could see me and touch me. They lived a good hour-and-a-half drive away. I talked her out of coming that night. Mom agreed to wait until morning. A few minutes later the phone rang again: "I'm on my way. Get your stuff together, you're coming to stay with me."

Mom and Fred drove out to Long Island, listening to the radio all the way.

Mom remembers:

> The Steinberg case seemed to be on the news any minute of the night or day you turned it on. They were saying that the child was now dead, that she was in the morgue, and they couldn't bury her because nobody was claiming the body. They went on and on about what a shame it was, that nobody wanted to bury this poor child.
>
> When we got there, Michele was lying on the floor, crying hysterically. Mary and Billy were trying to get her up. She wouldn't move from the floor. We finally pulled her into a chair. She was like a floppy rag doll. Every time we got her up, she fell back down again.

There was no strength in me, no thought, no feeling, except a kind of drilling horror.

I'd given my baby away to the people who murdered her. I meant for her to have a beautiful, happy life. What kind of hell had she lived through? What kind of hell had I put her in?

Mom remembers:

Those times Michele wasn't crying, she stared straight ahead with a blank, vacant stare. I didn't want to know what she was seeing in front of her eyes. I was seeing the same thing.

I said, "Michele, we've got to get you away from here. They know you live here."

Michele's place felt so exposed, so vulnerable. Fred and I lived in a gated area where no unauthorized vehicles can get in. I know that wouldn't have protected us from the police, but it just felt safer having her with me at our house. I don't know why I was so afraid of the police; I was afraid of everybody. In a world where a baby could be cruelly murdered by those who purported to care for her, how could you know who to fear and who not?

She didn't answer me. She didn't respond at all. You couldn't tell if she heard or not.

I packed her up quickly. I didn't know what I was doing; I just threw things into large plastic garbage bags. As I worked, Michele was sobbing continuously. The only word you could make out was No! No! No! Just that word over and over. "No!" The rest was incoherent, but that word stood out clearly.

I had the car parked in the driveway facing out. We packed it so full you couldn't see out the rear window. We couldn't get Michele to walk. Together, Fred and I managed to get her into the car. All the way to New Jersey, Fred and I could hear Michele drawing jagged breaths in the backseat of the car.

I lay huddled on the seat, so many questions running through my mind, but most of all one great, overwhelming, compelling cry: Please let this not be true.

My sweet little girl, please let her be alive and well somewhere. Even now she is dreaming sweetly in her bed, surrounded by dolls and teddies. On a chair nearby her ruby velvet dress is waiting and her shiny black patent Mary Janes. She could hardly fall asleep for excitement. Tomorrow is Saturday and she will go to see the *Nutcracker Suite* at Lincoln Center. Her parents are sitting in the living room watching TV and wondering at the horror of those who maim and kill their children. Then they turn off the television and talk about tomorrow. Perhaps after the ballet they will take her for tea at the Plaza. She'll love that.

Lisa. They called her Lisa. Elizabeth is a name I have always liked. I had wanted it for my confirmation name, but for some reason Mom said, "Any name but Elizabeth."

So I didn't take it, but I'd always thought if I had a daughter, I'd name her Elizabeth and call her Lisa. I myself was supposed to be named Lisa but Mom felt that name belonged to a bright-haired child. It's amazing, isn't it, that the next generation saw a bright-haired Lisa?

Had I been allowed the privilege of choosing her name, I would probably have named her Lisa. I will never call her by the surname of those people, those killers, but from the first I found it easy to think of her as Lisa.

I slept for a couple of hours that night, I think. When I woke up, the house was silent; Mom and Fred were asleep.

I rattled around for a bit by myself. Mom came out of the bedroom first, Fred a while later. I wasn't crying continuously anymore; I was numb a lot of the time, until it would wash over me anew and I would feel the pain freshly.

I didn't want to see or talk to anyone. I went into the bedroom and stayed there. I drew the blinds and covered my head with the quilt. There was no escaping this thing, this horror that seemed to pulse in the very air around me.

I spent that weekend in the little spare bedroom hiding under the quilt. I wouldn't talk to anybody. Mom would come in and say, "Shel, would you like some tea?"

No answer. Nothing. Nothing. Nothing.

I had one thought in my head: I killed my baby. I killed her. My beautiful golden baby. I killed her.

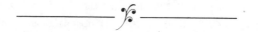

Mom says, "We kept the TV or the radio on all weekend. All they talked about was the fighting over Lisa's body, who was going to bury her. There was one announcement after another. This one wanted to bury her; this one wanted to do the funeral. This one wanted this,

this one wanted that. I tried to go in to tell Michele some of this; she didn't seem to hear. She was off some place of her own. She didn't even seem to know I was in the room."

Mom felt a lot of pressure to find the answer, to find the avenue to make things right.

On Saturday morning she went to the local shopping center with about twenty dollars in quarters. She sat at a pay phone outside Foodtown with stacks of change, calling around trying to find a lawyer. She wouldn't use her own phone; she was afraid the number would be traced, how and why she couldn't say, except that she had a general feeling of paranoia. The calls were interstate, from New Jersey to New York, so she needed lots of coins. It was Saturday so no one was in their offices, but she left messages for them.

Mom had one lead she was hopeful about, a lawyer who'd been highly recommended by a dear friend of hers who'd even given Mom his home number.

"Did you see the story that's going on television?" Mom asked him. "My daughter is the child's birth mother, we need help. We are in trouble. The police want us to do this and that. We don't know what the right thing is. We haven't had time to breathe or think."

The lawyer said to Mom, "You seem very upset. Is there any way I can speak to Michele directly?" Mom said, "The only way is for you to call us. I'm in a phone booth now. I don't want your number on my phone bill because they are tracking us down no matter where we go. We're safe for now, I don't know for how long. Maybe two days. As soon as the weekend's over, it's all going to break out again."

Mom gave him our number and went home. She dragged me out of the bedroom. She said I had to pull myself together enough to talk to this man. A few minutes later he called. We spoke briefly. I think his problem was he didn't believe what Mom had been telling him. It sounded too outlandish, too incredible. I confirmed everything she said—and doubled it. If he thought her story was crazy, I'm sure it was worse after talking to me.

He said the case sounded involved, complicated; he wanted to discuss it with his fellow attorneys. He would get back to us.

We thought we had him. Mom felt a lot better. We had been told he was a wonderful lawyer with wonderful contacts. Everybody in New York knew him.

I remember thinking that Joel Steinberg was a lawyer, too. A lawyer with wonderful New York contacts.

We waited all weekend for him to call. He never did. When Mom finally reached him on Monday morning, he said he was sorry, he couldn't represent me. He wouldn't touch us "with a ten-foot pole" is what he said. The other people he spoke to—I don't know who they were—told him they wouldn't touch this case, so he wouldn't either.

"So then what would you advise us to do?" Mom asked him.

"I would advise you and your daughter to get on a plane and go away for a month or two. Just disappear until all this blows over."

That sounded pretty good to me. For about five minutes, that sounded like a pretty good idea.

Several other attorneys refused to take our case. Apparently they were all considering the impact on their political futures, how it would look for them later on.

Another lawyer Mom spoke to told her to expect criminal charges against me, and that I should really be looking for a criminal lawyer.

That was something new. Was I going to jail? For what? What had I done? What were they going to prosecute me for? Heaven knows, I felt guilty, but not for breaking the law. I wish it were that simple.

Mom was really panicked. She was talking a mile a minute. Maybe we should go to Florida—no, we can't go to Florida, they'll be watching the trains. They'll be watching the planes. She and Fred were scheduled to go down to Florida the following Friday anyway. Now Mom was talking about sending me down with Fred on her ticket and she would follow later. What that would have helped, I don't know, but neither of us was thinking too clearly.

Through all this, George Schurz was keeping up the pressure about signing that piece of paper. I wouldn't talk to him. Mom took his calls. She remembers:

> It seemed like he called every few minutes all through that weekend. He kept saying that all they wanted from Michele was her signature stating that she was the natural mother of Lisa and she authorized the City of New York to bury her. Detective Schurz wanted me to use my influence with Michele to convince her to come into police headquarters in Manhattan and sign the paper. In one conversation he im-

plied that things would go a lot easier on her if she signed: Michele signs that piece of paper and they leave her alone.

I lost my temper and blew up at him. I told him Michele hadn't done one goddamn thing wrong. She had done everything right. I was with her the whole time, every step of the way. The professionals had screwed up, not her, so he didn't have to talk about going easy on her.

They weren't finding fault, he said, they just wanted the release. Lisa's body was in the morgue and they couldn't bury her until Michele signed that paper. They needed it to claim her body. They didn't care who buried her as long as somebody did.

Michele spent most of that weekend in her room with the shades drawn and the lights off. She lay in bed in the dark with the quilt over her head. Every now and then she came out or I dragged her out because I needed her. But I'd say twenty-two out of twenty-four hours she spent sobbing in her room.

If she wasn't visibly sobbing, she was sobbing inside. You looked at her and you knew that. She was one raw wound. Nothing would console her. I tried.

The TV or the radio was always on. The running battle over the body of my granddaughter continued. Who would bury Lisa? Who did Lisa belong to?

I didn't know what to do. I didn't know what Michele wanted to do; I don't think she did either. And if we knew what to do, we had no idea how to go about doing it.

Sunday evening, Fred and I were on the couch listening to the eleven-o'clock news. Suddenly Michele came out of her room and sat down on the sofa with us to listen.

I heard something that absolutely enraged me. The news was saying that the natural mother of Lisa had been contacted and that she had refused to have anything to do with the matter. She had washed her hands of the whole thing.

How wrong could they be? Where did they get the spurious information they presented as truth?

They were recapping the week's events: The police have still not found any record of adoption papers or filings, no proof that Lisa had ever been adopted.

Hedda Nussbaum is hospitalized under prison guard. The police are waiting until her physical condition improves before charging her with Lisa's murder. She was never indicted.

Joel Steinberg has been charged with murder.

They showed the footage again of Steinberg and Nussbaum being brought to the police station earlier in the week. I saw the same thing my mom did at the same moment. Mom blurted out, "I know that guy! Shel, look who it is! The lawyer! The guy from the res-taurant!"

The adoption lawyer! The one Bergman sent us to—the one Ginny took me to see! He looked so different, so much smaller than the man I had met.

The next thing I heard sent little hot-steel prickles stinging in my skull. Hedda Nussbaum was requesting that she and Steinberg be allowed to bury Lisa.

Lisa's killers wanted to bury her! Those who had turned her young life into a torment, who had sent her to her death before her seventh birthday—they wanted now to take her to her final rest?

No. No!

I reached over and grabbed Mom's hand. "Mom, we've got to go get her. We've got to get her away from them. We have to bury her. We're her family. She has nobody but us."

I never had a chance to hug my daughter. I never gave her all the kisses I wanted to give her. I never read her a story. I never rocked her to sleep. I didn't protect her or shelter her from grief.

There was no longer any comfort I could give her. All that was left for me to do was to place her in God's hands, to lay her to rest with dignity, with love.

And that, come hell or high water, I would do. I had been robbed of the lullabies and the bedtime stories. Nothing would stop me from accompanying my daughter to her final sleep.

Mom said, "Everyone's against you. The City, the Child Welfare, everybody. The pictures of the body being brought to the morgue —it was a wild mob scene. The press was insane. They were clawing at each other. They'll do the same to you. What can we do against all that, Michele?"

I said, "Whatever it takes, Mom. Whatever I have to do, I'm going to bury Lisa."

Chapter 17

I sat outside on the lawn that night, all night, as far from the house as I could get. It was twenty degrees and snowing. The snow was falling on my bare head. I didn't feel a thing; the chill in my heart was far worse.

I ached for my baby. I cried for hours, sobbing, screaming, yelling. I shrieked out my anguish, my horror at what they had done to my baby. No one could hear me over the wind.

They betrayed me! The same man who was supposed to give my baby to a kind and loving home killed her! He was supposed to find a home for her—he kept her! He made her young life a chamber of horrors, and finally he destroyed her.

And it was my fault! Forever, my fault, my error, my sin. I was her mother. I was supposed to shield her from harm. Instead I delivered her to Satan.

I would live with that for the rest of my days. And I would never, ever forgive myself. This was not in the realm of the forgivable.

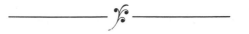

On Monday morning the detective called every fifteen minutes. I didn't want to talk to him, and by happenstance every time he called

I was out. Fred and Mom weren't lying when they told him I wasn't there. I simply couldn't stay in the house. I felt as if I were in a cage. There wasn't enough open space. I needed to be outdoors to breathe. I walked around the golf course; I must have walked for miles.

Schurz passed the word to me through Mom that he needed a decision from me. Nothing could happen with Lisa's burial until I decided something. This was news to me. I hadn't really gotten that out of what he had said on Friday night.

He had started then to go into who should bury Lisa. I remember his saying something about P.S. 41 in Greenwich Village wanting to bury her in the name of her schoolmates. My eyes had filled with tears and I held up my hand for him to stop. I couldn't hear any more.

He misinterpreted my gesture. George Schurz told me much later that he left my apartment convinced that I wanted nothing to do with Lisa.

It wasn't that at all. There was only so much I could take in at one time.

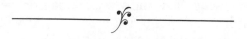

Mom took Schurz's calls. First he said he was coming out to New Jersey to get me to sign the form, then he wanted her to bring me in to police headquarters in Manhattan.

Finally Mom made a deal with Schurz that we would all meet at my house in Atlantic Beach. Mom said she would look over his paper and see if she thought I should sign it. If it was okay, she would advise me to sign, and after that it would be up to me. Mom wouldn't pressure me or try to talk me into it.

But Schurz had to come alone. She didn't want a crowd of detectives and police and who knows what harassing me.

Mom was pretty much on her own in making these arrangements. She says:

> Michele was either out of the house or closeted in the bedroom. She didn't want company. Every now and then she'd have a lucid moment and you had to grab them to talk to her, but most of the time she was just unreachable, locked

in her grief. I pitied her for the demons that were after her.
Judging from the images in my own mind, I could just imag-
ine what she saw every time she closed her eyes.

But still, we needed to act. Time was working against us.
Something had to be done about the child's burial. Every
newscast brought word of someone else who wanted to bury
Lisa. We wanted to do the right thing, but I had no idea
what the right thing was. We needed to find a lawyer, and
we needed to find one fast.

Suddenly, for no reason I can give, a name sprang into my mind. I
said, "Mom, what about Joe Famighetti?" His name just popped into
my mind, as if someone had put it there. We had seen him so briefly
and so long ago, Mom didn't even know who I was talking about.

Mom made the call to him. I was in no shape to talk to anybody.
She was put through to him right away. I couldn't believe we got him
on the phone. It was so smooth, as if Providence were directing the
whole thing. Maybe God *was* watching over us because unwittingly
we were doing the right thing. From the time we got Joe on, things
started happening, doors were opening, ways were showing up that
we would never have comprehended on our own.

Mom tried to sound businesslike when she spoke with him. She
introduced herself and said, "You might not remember me. My daughter and I were in to see you about an auto accident a couple of years
ago," and then she went on to tell him the same thing she had told
the other lawyers. She pleaded with him: We were in trouble; we
needed help.

Joe kept telling her to calm down. "I'm here. I'm listening. Calm
down."

He told Mom to call him in the morning. He didn't think anything
would happen overnight or during the evening. But if we needed him,
he was available.

Just knowing that there was another human being between us and
everything that was going on around us was comforting.

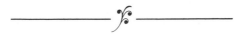

Late Monday afternoon Mom and I drove to Atlantic Beach for our
meeting with Detective Schurz. My roommate, Mary, told us when

we got there that she was so paranoid from what the press was doing with the story that she slammed the door in the face of a boy who said he was from the *Daily News*, and only afterward did she realize that he was selling subscriptions.

I was still in a very bad state. I'd be calm for a little while, then it would hit me afresh and I'd burst out into new tears. My body was limp; I felt out of time and space; I didn't know where I was; I didn't care.

Mom says, "Shel started crying hard when we got to her house. I guess it reminded her of being told about it. While Mary and I were trying to get her into a chair and to stop crying, there was a knock on the door. I opened the door. I hadn't met him before; he told me who he was: Detective George Schurz, Manhattan DA's office."

Mom asked if he had any identification. He showed her his ID. It seemed all right so she invited him in.

He turned and signaled to the car parked in front of the house. Two men got out and came toward the house.

Mom said, "What's going on? We agreed that you would come alone."

He couldn't help it, he said. He'd tried to come alone. Just as he was leaving, these people had jumped in the back of the car and he couldn't stop them because they were his superiors.

Mom told him that if he couldn't keep deals he shouldn't make them. Our bargain was off. He was not a man of honor and he couldn't be trusted.

"Please, don't take this attitude," he said. "We want to get this thing nailed down."

An unfortunate choice of words.

He went on: "The little girl is in the morgue. We can't bury her without her mother's permission."

Mom said, "We don't know that Michele is the mother. I want a blood test."

Mom turned and walked back inside. He followed her in. She let his two buddies in, too, even though she was angry. "I was afraid not to," she says. "They were the law."

The two other men turned out to be Bruno Cappellini and Tom Purcell from the Human Resources Administration of the City of New York.

I had retreated into my bedroom. Mary and Mom came in and dragged me out. They finally managed to get me to sit at the dining room table. The others pulled up chairs, too, and we all sat around the table.

The men explained again what the form was about. The words *daughter, morgue, funeral*, seemed like knives.

I knew nothing except pain. I felt nothing but pain.

Mom got me back into my seat. The three officials started leaning on me to sign their paper. One of them held a pen in front of me. I stared down at the paper, but I couldn't read it. The words blurred in front of my eyes.

It couldn't be my baby he killed. They're crazy. It wasn't my baby, it was somebody else's. Not mine.

My baby! They wanted me to give her away to somebody else to bury.

I couldn't have moved my hand to the pen under pain of death.

My beautiful golden baby. I had sent her to her death as surely as if I had strapped her into the electric chair and pulled the switch. Stupid fool! While I was dreaming of museum visits and pink party dresses and tea at the Plaza, those two had been beating her, they brutalized her until they beat the very life out of her. What kind of person batters a child to death with his bare fists? What kind of people had I sent my baby to?

My baby . . . ?

No! No! No!

It's a lie. They're crazy. They're wrong. It's a mistake.

Mom said to Schurz, "Look, she's in no condition to sign anything. I don't think she can even write her name. You violated our bargain. I don't know who the hell these other two guys are. We're going to get blood tests and we're not signing anything until we talk to our lawyer."

Cappellini said, "What lawyer? Between four o'clock and seven o'clock you got a lawyer?"

Mom said, "Yes, we've got a lawyer. His name is Joe . . ." And she blanked.

Mom says:

> I couldn't for the life of me think of his name. I looked at Michele. She said, "Famighetti."

I went for the phone book. "I'm going to call him right now."

Michele said, "His number is seven four two—" and Bruno Cappellini finished it for her!

"Do you know him?" I asked.

It turned out Joe Famighetti was the attorney for several police organizations including the New York State Police and the Nassau County Police Benevolent Association. His name carried weight. I called Joe, right then and there.

Mom was pretty upset. Joe told her to calm down. "Just tell the detectives that you've retained me to represent you and you're not doing anything until we all meet and resolve this," he told her.

Joe says, "I didn't know then that other attorneys had turned down the case, but I never had a problem taking it from the inception."

Joe immediately took charge. He says of that night:

I told her to put Bruno Cappellini, who was the public administrator, on the phone. I said, "Michele Launders is my client, I'm not going to permit you to talk to her any further." I'm a criminal lawyer, that's what I do best: Don't talk to my client!

Cappellini says, "We've got some urgent problems we have to resolve."

Michele and her mom are coming to my office, I told him. "They know the way. Follow them there."

We all arrived at Joe's office at once, naturally, and it was kind of a bedlam, with the three men all talking at once and Mom pretty hysterical and me not too well off myself. Joe stepped right into the middle of it. The first thing he did was to separate the two parties. He was great: "You go here. You go there. I'll get to you when I get to you." He sent the three men, Detective Schurz, Cappellini, and Purcell, to the law library and Mom and me to an office on another floor. He was pretty tough with them. He's a criminal attorney, not a tea-party giver.

Joe spoke to the men, then came and sat down with us. I was spilled into his chair like some kind of Gumby doll. If I had been told to raise my left arm, I would have raised it and not let it down until somebody told me to. Joe saw that. Thank God he was the type of person who would recognize the state I was in and allow for it. He directed most of his questions to Mom, and she filled him in.

Mom showed him a picture of me as a child next to a newspaper clipping of Lisa. That, along with the information he'd gotten from Detective Schurz and the others, was enough to convince him that the child was definitely mine. George Schurz told Joe the same thing: He knew I was her mother even before he walked into my house. He had seen me through the window and the resemblance was startling.

I sat there, saying nothing, barely attending to what was going on.

They were saying I was that poor little girl's mother. No! My baby was alive. My baby was happy. My baby was with people who couldn't look at her without smiling, who bragged constantly to their friends and relatives about the latest brilliant thing she had done.

What time was it? About nine? Right now she was drifting off to sleep in her bed, cuddling a stuffed animal. Her mom, the lady I had given her to, was moving quietly around the room, laying out her clothes for school tomorrow. A tape of lullabies was playing on the child's tape recorder she'd gotten for her sixth birthday five and a half months before.

Joe says of that meeting:

> *Michele had put a difficult period of time behind her. She had maintained a secret, the secrecy of this pregnancy and the existence of this child. She had in good faith placed the child in an adoptive home, a home she felt was that of a professional, sophisticated, religious family. That's what she had been led to believe.*
>
> *She wasn't very coherent, but she did convey to me that she had envisioned this child's life of being one of visits to museums, concerts, like that. And now it had all collapsed. That whole dream. The feeling of having done the right thing was gone.*
>
> *I realized quickly that what was operating most for Michele was that she felt a great sense of responsibility for this child. She felt that she had failed her, that she was responsible for the child's death. She kept saying she had killed her. That was really what she was carrying around with her.*

Michele cried on and off. Anita was wringing her hands most of the time. She was doing a little of the typical mother's "I told you so, if you'd done it my way, this wouldn't have happened, I never trusted those people," and so on.

I gathered that Michele had been taken in by Ginny Liebrader, Dr. Michael Bergman, and perhaps his nurse, Jackie. She had felt they were really trying to help her, while Mom had been going, "Oh, no, I know these people aren't right."

It appeared to me that Anita had been upset by Michele's pregnancy since Michele was only nineteen at the time, and it would be pretty tough for an unwed mother with a child to make her way through life. Michele knew that. She knew she had done "wrong," that she had failed the values she had been taught. She was looking for a way out, and there, at the very same time, were Liebrader and Bergman telling her, "How do you expect to provide for a child, don't forget you're so young, you have your whole life ahead of you," blah, blah, blah.

Michele had two major concerns. One was that her grandmother would find out about this, her grandmother whom she adored and who she felt would be very hurt by this information's coming out. The old woman was really sick at this time and all Michele kept saying was, "This is going to kill my grandmother."

Joe was right. Nana had started to show the effects of her long battle with cancer. When she had the mastectomy, the doctors had been quite optimistic that the cancer was in a dormant stage, even though it had spread to the lymph nodes and they weren't able to catch it all.

She'd had a few more good years, but by late spring of 1987, Nana's health had deteriorated. The cancer was spreading quickly. By summer we were told that there was not a lot of time left. And I was sure that the news of what I had done would hasten her death.

Joe said, "Don't let that worry you, because she's going to know anyway, and last time I looked, grandmas were once nineteen years old themselves, and they know better than you that these things happen."

Joe remembers another thing that was operating on me. He says:

> *It had to do with the fact that Michele was the natural
> mother of this child, and she felt an incredible responsibility
> to do the right thing by her. She thought she'd done that by
> placing her with a family she thought would be good for her.
> Now that trust had been betrayed and she had to resume
> responsibility to that child even to the point of taking over
> the burial.*
>
> *Michele was worried and frightened about what would
> happen to her, with the press coming after her and her life
> being . . . more than disrupted, ruined really. And the shame
> and having everyone know. But those two concerns, her
> grandmother and her child, they were paramount.*

Until Joe explained it to me that evening in his office, I never
understood that by signing the form they were all after me to
sign—Detective Schurz, Nancy Patterson, Bruno Cappellini, and
Tom Purcell—I would be releasing Lisa's body for *someone else* to
bury. I thought—if I had a coherent thought at all—that the form
would allow *me* to bury her. If I'd known what it really said, I
would never even have discussed signing it.

I still couldn't believe this happened. How did things go so wrong
for my baby?

Joe laid out all the possibilities of what might happen if I did or
didn't step forward, and he left it up to me to decide. Joe told me
not to make any decision that night. "Don't let yourself be pushed
or rushed by these guys downstairs; they aren't going to do anything
to you one way or the other. If indeed the city is going to bury the
child, they still have to have a court proceeding and that's going to
take time."

Joe thought we'd have at least two days. We'd be in court by
Wednesday, at the earliest, he estimated.

Says Joe, "I was still underestimating the speed at which events
would occur. I did not realize the powerful pull that child in the
morgue would exert on everyone."

We were at Joe's office two or three hours. He kept moving
between the two rooms, us and them. It must have been eleven
o'clock when they finally left and we were free to go, too. We made
arrangements to meet Joe the following day in Manhattan. More

correctly, Mom made the arrangements. I was still in a state somewhere between sleepwalking and hysteria.

By the time we got home to Mom's place in New Jersey, it was
long past midnight. Three days had gone by since we'd heard the
news. Three days in which nobody had slept and nobody had eaten.

We didn't sleep that night either. I was pacing around upstairs
in the bedroom. Mom was downstairs in the kitchen. She says of
that night:

> I put a big pot of coffee on. I got out a fresh pack of cig-
> arettes. I sat in the kitchen and I'm working all this out
> in my mind. I'm thinking, I'm thinking . . .
>
> I'd always told my children I'd be there for them no matter
> what. Shel needs me now. Get back under control. Force
> yourself. Being out of control is no good. It won't help any-
> body.
>
> Who has the right to bury Lisa?
>
> If it's us, where are we going to bury her? She can't be
> buried in Catholic ground. She hasn't been baptized.
>
> I suddenly recalled something from my long-ago religious
> training: There's more than one way to be baptized. There
> are several ways . . . three ways. Water. We know that. Fire.
> That's the second one. What's the third one? What's the
> third one?
>
> I couldn't think of it. I thought and thought and I couldn't
> bring it out. I woke Fred up. "Fred, what's the three ways
> you can be baptized?"
>
> He could only think of two also. He couldn't think of the
> third one either.
>
> I later called Joe Famighetti. He contacted his partner
> Tony Cornachio. They couldn't think of the third thing
> either. For heaven's sake, we're all supposed to be Catholics,
> and a sorry lot we are, too.
>
> I remembered I had the deed to my family's cemetery plot
> somewhere in Mother's papers. In the middle of the night I
> started ripping the place apart until I found the deed to the
> family plots. On it it said, "Trustees of St. Patrick's Cathedral."
>
> St. Patrick's owns that cemetery out in Westchester. Or
> they did many years ago when the plot was purchased. Did

they still? And if they did, gee . . . maybe there's a way. At least I know who to ask.

At six in the morning, my husband came out. I was sitting on the couch with a local phone book on my lap. I said, "Fred, let's get dressed and go down to our local church. I've got to find out what's the third way you can be baptized."

The TV was on. There was only one topic in the news— that's how it seemed to me. Lisa. Lisa. Lisa.

Fred glanced at the TV and said, "You're going to go to a little country church to talk about this? They're not equipped to handle something of this order."

He went back into the bedroom. I sat there and thought. We've always been good Catholics. Not exceptionally good maybe, in comparison to some. All right, so we don't go to church every Sunday or take Communion every day like some do. But we do go to church. We try to help our fellow man. We live our religion. My aunt was a mother superior. My grandmother used to give each young priest who took vows a diamond to set on his chalice. There are stained-glass windows in a church somewhere in Brooklyn bearing our family name.

And now we're in trouble. Shouldn't we be able to turn to them? I looked at the deed to the family plot. Owned by St. Patrick's Cathedral . . .

At about seven, Fred came out again. I said, "Let me bounce an idea off you before I go try it on Shel."

Michele was in her room with the quilt pulled over her head. At five-thirty I had looked in on her. She wasn't asleep; I knew she heard me. I said her name softly. She didn't answer. I walked out. There was little else I could do, except what I was doing, trying to help her with action, not sympathy.

"Fred, what if I take this deed and my daughter and go to St. Patrick's Cathedral and ask them what's the third way a person can be baptized and will it work for Lisa?"

Fred thought for a minute. Then he said, "That's it. Go ahead."

I went in to Michele. I spoke to the head I couldn't see because it was buried under the quilt. "Michele, I've got an idea. Don't say no right away. Think about it. Fred agrees with me it's a good thing to do, but it's got to be your decision."

I repeated what I had just told Fred. I added, "This is the only way I can figure out to give Lisa a proper Catholic funeral. You want to do it, and I want to help you. I admit we've got no clout. The other side has all the big guns. We've got to take it step by step: First of all, can we get the right to bury her? And if we do, can we use these deeds and bury her in our family plot? Can we bury her in a Catholic cemetery at all? There are lots of questions, Shel. I can't promise you anything except I'll try to get some answers."

Then I said, "Don't say a word now. I'll go make you a cup of tea and come back in fifteen minutes. Don't answer me now."

About ten minutes later I walked out into the kitchen and said, "Yes." Just that one word: "Yes."

Mom put her arms around me. I whispered, "Let's do it. Let's bring Lisa home."

Chapter 18

✤ **I**t was still raining when we got to New York. We hadn't said much on the trip. I'd opened my mouth, and Mom said to me, "Shel, don't talk. Just pray. Pray we're doing the right thing. I've never done anything like this in my whole life. I'm using every bit of experience I've ever had. Your experience doesn't count. You don't have enough. Nothing you've tried has worked. A few things I've tried have worked. So just pray. Don't talk to me. Pray."

What could I say? She was right.

Mom was in an advanced state of paranoia. I've never seen her so frightened. I stopped to buy an umbrella from a street vendor. Mom started yelling at me. She didn't want me out on the street a minute longer than necessary. She was going on about hit men, contracts being put out on me, they were going to kill me like they killed Lisa. I didn't know what she was saying, but it was driving me crazy.

We walked inside the imposing front entrance of St. Patrick's. No one was around who looked like someone giving directions. There was a little . . . gift shop, I suppose you'd call it, off to one side. Mom went in there and said we had to speak to a priest. The saleswoman was showing something to two tourists. She told us we'd have to go outside and around the block.

Now Mom went really off-the-wall. "Forget the rosary keepsake!" she yelled. "We're in deep trouble. We need to see a priest."

The woman looked up—kindly, not sharply, but clearly surprised. "I told you—go back out on Fifth Avenue and turn right."

"You're not listening! We're in trouble! Isn't there a tunnel or something we can go through?"

"Mom! I can walk around the block."

Mom wasn't budging. She badgered the saleswoman. "Look, lady, when the priests finish Mass they disappear behind the altar. I know there's a tunnel to the priest house. I want to use that tunnel!"

The tourists were turning to look at her. I said, "Thank you," to the woman and pulled Mom away.

I walked near the curb. She said, "No, walk near the building." I walked near the building; she said, "No, walk near the curb."

We found the right door. Mom told the receptionist that her daughter needed to speak with a priest about burying her infant daughter. "She doesn't know how to go about it. She needs advice."

They didn't keep us waiting. They showed us into a little room and a priest came right away. I don't know whether it was because of what Mom had told them or because we looked pretty distraught.

Father O'Brien looked like a little Irish elf. He was a real movie priest; the brogue, the kind, humorous face, the whole thing. "Yes, ladies, may I help you?"

Neither Mom nor I was very coherent. The priest seemed to think that it was an ordinary funeral, that someone in our family had died and he was being asked to help plan it. Mom kept waving the deeds to the graves in his face and asking if they were in order. The priest was confused. The documents weren't the problem.

I explained that the child had been given up for adoption at her birth six and a half years ago.

No problem. Let the adoptive parents bury her, the priest advised us.

Mom leaned forward in her chair. "She didn't just die. It turns out maybe she was murdered."

The priest looked at her. He still didn't see why we didn't let the adoptive parents bury her. He said, "Maybe the best thing for you to do is nothing. Let the people who adopted her handle her funeral."

I cried out, "No!"

Mom glanced at me. She tried to explain to the priest. "It seems the baby was never really adopted." He looked bewildered. I don't blame him. "She was supposed to go to a Catholic home, but she didn't. He kept her. The man who was supposed to arrange the adoption—the lawyer—kept her for himself. She was raised Jewish. Father, there are three ways to be baptized, water, fire—what's the third way?"

This at least he could answer. "Intent."

Mom sighed and sank back against the back of her chair. "Intent," she murmured. "Of course. I was trying so hard to think of it. A family full of Catholics and none of us could come up with it."

He was really a kind man, but he wasn't getting the picture. Mom said, "Father, have you been watching television? The news on television?"

"Yes."

"Perhaps you've heard about what's going on downtown, with the lawyer who killed the little girl."

"A little bit."

It was starting to come across to him.

"That's who we're talking about. That little girl Lisa is my daughter's daughter."

Now he got it. The priest's face was grim. He got up from his chair and said he had to talk to someone.

He came back soon with another priest, a big, tall man. We went over the story for him again. And again. He also couldn't get it on the first shot.

The tall priest left to confer with somebody else.

Father O'Brien called somebody on the phone. He spoke softly and we couldn't hear what he was saying.

The tall priest came back. He asked me questions. I answered as honestly and as best I could: I had assumed from the beginning that Lisa was going to a Catholic home and would be baptized by her adoptive family. The same way I had felt it was not my right to name her, I had felt it was not my right to baptize her.

If I'd known Lisa was going to a non-Catholic home, I couldn't say a hundred percent for sure that I would have stopped the adoption, but I would certainly have made sure she was baptized first.

They made several more phone calls. Mom asked whom they were talking to. One of them said, "The vicar-general."

My nerves were raw. I exploded, "Who the hell is the vicar-general?" Only maybe I didn't say hell to a priest.

Mom was more diplomatic. "I've been a Catholic for many years. I don't believe I've ever heard that title. What exactly does a vicar-general do?"

"The vicar-general speaks to the cardinal," came the reply.

That shut us both up. It appeared our case was being taken to the highest authority, Cardinal O'Connor himself.

The tall priest came back into the room with a smile for us and an affirmative nod for Father O'Brien.

"I spoke to the vicar-general," he told the father. "It's fine. They can go ahead."

The Church had ruled, formally and officially, that a child under seven is not held accountable for her own or other people's actions. Since I, her mother, had the full intention to baptize her, she was in effect considered to have been baptized and could be buried in Catholic ground, with Catholic ritual, as if the ceremony had in fact taken place.

They had gone out on a limb for us—for Lisa.

The tall priest turned to us. He said, "We as the religious will have to defend this theologically. But that is none of your problem. We will have to contend with it."

He looked directly at me. "You go out and bury your little girl."

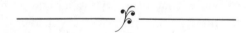

Lisa had lived her whole short life in Manhattan, in Greenwich Village. It wouldn't be fair to take the funeral away from the people she had known and who had known her. I thought especially of her school friends. I'm no psychologist, but I knew enough to know that children have to mourn a loss, and the worst thing you can do is deprive them of the chance.

I wanted to give the little ones a chance to say good-bye.

I wanted everyone to have that chance. I wanted every living soul who had known Lisa to be able to come to bid her farewell, if they so chose.

I wanted the funeral to be a joint Jewish/Catholic service, to honor the religion Lisa had been raised in as well as the one she had been born into. If ever there was a time to come together, to forget boundaries and differences, it was at the funeral of the little girl Elizabeth, known as Lisa. From the first I planned to bring Lisa home to our cemetery in Westchester. The final good-byes would be for us alone. I could afford to share those in the city with strangers. We had to find a funeral home that would allow us to have this kind of joint service.

Father O'Brien's anteroom was crowded with people waiting to see him, but still he placed himself and his office at our disposal. Mom and I didn't know Greenwich Village at all. We started looking in the phone book for funeral homes. I wouldn't have one that would only allow a Jewish service, and I wouldn't have one that would only allow a Catholic service. Some wouldn't allow a rabbi and some wouldn't allow a priest.

Father O'Brien made a few calls and put us in touch with Redden's Funeral Home. It was in the heart of Greenwich Village. Perfect! The children wouldn't have to go far. They agreed to the kind of service we wanted. They also refused payment, although we would have been happy to pay. Many people and organizations wanted to share in laying Lisa to rest, but Redden's Funeral Home was the first one I knew of.

My mother was going to call the cemetery and buy another plot, but now we had to leave. We were late for our meeting with Joe Famighetti.

On the way downtown to meet Joe, Mom and I shared a great sense of relief, as well as gratitude for the way the Church had come through for us. Despite what Mom had originally thought, that we were ordinary people, powerless people without special connections or wealth or influence, our case had gone all the way up to Cardinal O'Connor himself. He had taken our side and was prepared to defend it, even to the Pope if need be.

Our spirits were much eased. We were free to bury Lisa. All impediments had been removed. Or so we thought.

I'm going to let Joe Famighetti pick up the story from here, since I was in the dark about events while they were happening, and so for the most part was Mom. Joe says:

> *Things kept moving faster than I expected, I guess because of the press, which was playing the story tremendously. I had told Michele on Monday that she had at least forty-eight hours before anything happened, and almost as those words were coming out of my mouth, the public administrator filed a petition to claim the child's body for the city. The case*

automatically went before Judge Marie Lambert because she was the surrogate in charge of all matters relating to deceased people, including the burial of this child. If we were going to intervene, it had to be done immediately.

I still expected to have some time to play with. It didn't happen that way. The next day, Tuesday, Bruno Cappellini of the Human Resources Administration called to tell me that Judge Lambert, the Manhattan surrogate, wanted us to be present in her chambers that afternoon at two P.M.

He asked what Michele was going to do. They all wanted to know. I promised that when we met in surrogate's court I would have some indication from Michele as to which direction she wanted to go and would be prepared to inform them at that time.

In the twelve or fifteen hours since that first phone call from Michele and Anita, I had gathered quite a lot more information about the case. The police detectives had executed a search warrant of Joel Steinberg's home. In his apartment they found unpaid hospital bills relating to the birth of Lisa. They got the hospital records and that was how they tracked down Michele. Interesting. If he had paid those bills, would they have found her? I suppose eventually they would, but it would have taken time. The first thing you'd have to do is find the hospital. You'd never know which hospital the child was born in if you didn't have a lead from those bills in the apartment.

We believe that there was a conspiracy among the entire clan of these people and it was spelled out in those hospital records. They purposely misspelled Michele's name. They gave her a wrong date of birth, a wrong social security number. Her address was wrong—no way could she have given her address as care of Joel Steinberg. She didn't even know where he lived. This was not a lack of accuracy on their part. It was deliberate. They didn't want her to be traced.

Of course they were covering their tracks from an ordinary search. They weren't expecting anything like this. Those little tricks couldn't stand up against the Manhattan district attorney's squad, which is recognized as one of the finest investigative units in the world. They ran Michele's social security number through the computers fifteen different ways from Sunday; the same with her date of birth. It took them a few days, but find her they did.

Lisa was taken to the hospital on November second. She died on the fifth. They were probably in the apartment by the third or fourth and they had Michele by the sixth.

One of my sources told me that Lisa was just one of fifty or so children that Steinberg had bartered or sold. They were investigating him on charges of baby-selling and suspected that one of his prime sources for birth mothers was his good friend Michael Bergman.

Ginny's function, at least according to our theory of the case, was to keep Michele under control and not permit her to back out of the deal to give up the child. In a weak moment, when she snapped at Michele something like "They don't pay me enough to put up with this," that indicated to me that she was getting something for her efforts. People just don't do this for nothing. I think she was probably rewarded handsomely.

There was a theory, I don't know if it's true, that Lisa was indeed sold to a set of parents in New Jersey, and that the price was fifty thousand dollars and the guy came up with fifteen thousand and for whatever reason never paid the balance, so Steinberg took the baby back. . . . I didn't tell Michele this until setting down my thoughts for this book—she's really fragile and I don't tell her things that will upset her that she isn't immediately required to know. . . . Apparently Steinberg employed some longshoremen to go out to Jersey and recover the child. But by the time they got her back she was six, seven months old and her value in the marketplace was debased. He didn't know what to do with her, he took her home and Hedda fell in love with her, so they kept her.

The other story is that it was a straight deal from the beginning, that it was going to be Joel and Hedda's child because Hedda really wanted a child and Steinberg needed to do something to stabilize her because she was going off-the-wall.

Now, Steinberg was not only Bergman's friend, he was his lawyer, the lawyer for the medical office, the business. So did Ginny know Steinberg had the child? I certainly think she did. And, if that's true, all the time Michele was asking about the baby, Ginny must have been lying. She had to have known that the child hadn't been adopted according to Michele's wishes, according to what had been agreed upon. Don't forget, Steinberg lived around the corner from Bergman's office/home. Steinberg was there all the time. All that talking Ginny did while Michele was living with her, about the professional couple Steinberg had picked out—that was a lie, too. Unless you believe that other story about the couple in New Jersey. We still don't have all the answers here. It'll be years before we do.

My thought was to hire two guys I know to do some investigating in the case. The next morning, Tuesday, I called John Riede and told him to get Charlie Bardong and be at Forlini's at one o'clock. I wanted them at my meeting with Michele and her mom.

It was a horrible day. The rains were torrential. My partner and I took the train in because we figured traffic would be terrible and we couldn't get a cab from the subway, so we ended up having to walk three or four blocks. We got to the restaurant soaking wet. Michele and Anita weren't there yet. Everything was late that day. John and Charlie came in about a quarter to two and we sat down and went through the case with them. In the middle of that, I got paged from my office; it was Bruno Cappellini. He says, "Where are you? You're supposed to be in court at two, it's getting close to three."

I said, I'm close by, I'm in the city, I'm waiting for my client. I think she's been held up by the weather. He said —pretty sharply—"Well, the judge is getting anxious to see you."

I said, Fine. As soon as I have her, and I get some idea from her what direction she wants to go in, I'll be there.

Bruno said, "There's about a hundred reporters over here waiting for you."

I couldn't believe it. Even knowing what kind of publicity the case was generating, I still felt he was probably exaggerating a little bit. I hung up the phone and walked back to the table, and Michele and Anita were just arriving.

We got there late, about three-thirty. Joe was there with three other guys, his partner and two we didn't know. Mom was taken aback: "Who *are* these people?"

They turned out to be the detectives Joe had hired as "body-guards"—a word he never used to me. All I needed to hear was that I required bodyguards! He told me they were there to work on the case.

Mom and I sat down. The two new guys, the detectives, kept questioning me about how I met Joe. So I had to tell these total strangers about my DWI. It turned out that John Riede had retired from the police force two weeks before and knew George Schurz well. They didn't want any suspicion that George Schurz had sent me to Joe, that was why they were asking those questions.

We now talked about whether there was any way at all for me to claim the child and still remain anonymous.

Joe said, "Michele, I don't think that's going to happen."

He had extracted a promise from the DA to keep my identity a secret until such time as I chose to disclose it, provided the judge went along with it. But Joe told me not to think for a minute that I could come through this without my identity's being known. He said it was just not in the cards; it wasn't going to happen. The funny thing is, Kevin managed it. The press searched all over to find him, and they never found out who he was.

Joe asked for my decision. I told him that I was going to come forward and do what I had to do to claim Lisa. I was her mother; I would bury her, no one else, and whatever happened to me would happen. I would take whatever consequences I had to take.

Up until then, Joe hadn't told me that there was a surrogate's court hearing that afternoon, nor that I would have to appear, and certainly not that I'd have to make my way through packs of re-porters and television crews to do so. Joe understood from the first how much I could take at any given moment, and he always told me just enough to get me through the next thing. I was in no condition to hear any more.

Joe remembers:

> *Michele was walking a fine edge. I was afraid that at any moment she would collapse completely. But now that she'd come to a decision, I had to prepare her a little more.*
> *I explained to her that the public administrator of the*

County of New York is charged with burying all unclaimed bodies. Bruno Cappellini, the current public administrator, was petitioning the court to release Lisa's body to the City for burial, and if no parties with legal standing came forward, the judge would grant the petition.

However, we were going to come forward. The judge would hear all parties and then render a decision.

I made Michele understand that what she was about to do was irrevocable. Once she made it known that she was the natural mother of the child Lisa, her life as she had known it would effectively be over. And she would have a long, tough piece of road to get through before things got reasonably good again. There's something about having your name widely known; it takes a long time to wear off, if it ever does.

I was willing to accept that, for myself.

Nana had no idea I'd ever had a baby. She was literally on her deathbed. I was honestly afraid this news would kill her. They'd moved a big hospital bed into the living room, and she was for all intents and purposes bedridden. I don't remember whether she was still able to get up to go to the bathroom, but if so, that was all she did.

But she was able to watch television. Papa Jack was a great one for the TV news. I could see the scene in front of my eyes, as I had seen it hundreds of times. At six o'clock sharp he'd say, "Agnes, want to see the news?" He'd turn on the TV, and he'd see ... What? I had no clear idea of what would be on, except I knew they would talk about me.

And Nana would find out that she'd been a great-grandmother for six and a half years.

And that I'd robbed her of the chance ever to see her great-granddaughter. And that through my actions the baby I bore was now dead.

I was consumed with guilt. Somehow I'd managed to do harm to all the people I loved most in the world. If I could have taken their pain on myself, I would have jumped at the chance to do it. That would actually have been easy. Knowing that they suffered and being unable to take away their pain was far worse.

But apparently there was no way for me to claim Lisa's body

without Nana's finding out. The only thing I could do was keep her from finding out from the television. I would have to tell her first.

Joe knew the owner at Forlini's. He asked him to let Mom and me make a call from his private office in the back. Mom dialed the phone. I was crying so hard I couldn't speak. Mom got on the phone first. She said hi, hello, and all that. Then she said, "Michele would like to speak with you."

Mom handed me the phone. I couldn't get any words out. I kept gasping and crying, and when I could finally speak, I said, "I'm sorry, Nana, I'm so sorry," over and over.

I could tell I was scaring her, so I pulled myself together enough to tell her the story, between sobs and gasps for breath.

I said, "Nana, I had a child years ago. I gave her away to be adopted. But they didn't do what they were supposed to. The at-torney didn't do an adoption. He kept her . . . and he killed her. She's dead, Nana! I kept it a secret for so long—I didn't want to hurt you. I didn't want you to know. But now I have to go to court and say I'm her mother. They won't let me bury her unless I do that. I have to get her back—we have to bury her properly and get her to heaven. I'm so sorry, Nana."

I'll never forget what came next. I don't know what I expected Nana to say, but her words came as a complete surprise to me.

Nana said, "Why are you sorry? You did nothing wrong. You go get that baby and you bury her next to me. I'll be in heaven soon, I'll take care of her."

And Nana gave me her blessing.

I thought that by concealing my pregnancy I was protecting Nana from something she couldn't handle. It turned out I was wrong. Nana had courage to spare for both of us. It was Nana's strength that I carried with me into that courtroom to do battle over the body of my dead child. I wore her blessing like armor.

Now I was ready. I would do whatever I had to—even face the devil himself—so that Lisa could lie next to my grandmother for all eternity.

Chapter 19

    My phone call to Nana only lasted about twenty minutes, but when I came back to the table, it was as if a great weight were lifted from my shoulders. My face was tearstained, but I was composed, although the tears came again when I told Joe and the others about the conversation. I just couldn't get over the depth of Nana's understanding and the love she had for me, and for my little girl, whom neither of us had ever seen. With practically her last wish, she gave me forgiveness and acceptance and I was just swept away by her.

Joe and his partner left to go to surrogate's court. I told them I still had hope that while my name would be public, I might escape without being photographed. Mom and I stayed behind in the restaurant with the bodyguards, John and Charlie. The people at Forlini's were great. The place was popular with the courthouse press as well as the lawyers, so they put us in a back room just in case.

There was no television or radio on near where we were, so I had no idea of what was happening. For some reason everyone was trying to feed me. I guess it's just an instinct in times of crisis. Again, I'll let Joe tell what happened next:

> *I'll never forget that moment, stepping out of the car in front of the courthouse. Bruno had said a hundred people.*

I thought realistically maybe thirty. There must have been two hundred and fifty people there. It was sheer pande-monium. I said to myself, if Michele walks into this, she's going to be thrown completely for a loop. She's not going to be able to handle it.

Judge Lambert called all the parties to the case together in her chambers. Technically, we were all there in response to a motion by Bruno Cappellini, public administrator of the County of New York, asking that Lisa Steinberg's body be released to the Department of Human Resources of the City for burial. Bruno Cappellini was there himself, along with his deputy, Tom Purcell. Nancy Patterson, the woman who had been at Michele's house with Detective Schurz on Friday night, appeared for the Manhattan district attorney's office.

Joel Steinberg was represented by Robert Kalina.

Hedda Nussbaum and her parents were represented by Barry Scheck.

And I was there of course, on Michele's behalf.

We went through the whole case. I was trying to negotiate with Judge Lambert to keep Michele's privacy to whatever extent I could, and at the same time release enough infor-mation so we could go forward with the case.

I presented the material I had been provided by the district attorney's office in support of our claim that Michele was Lisa's natural mother—medical records and so on. It was not an easy matter to resolve. There were several opposing parties and they were all passionate about it. No one forgot for a minute that this was about a little girl lying in the morgue.

The afternoon news broadcasts were dominated by live reports from the courthouse. The press had succeeded in finding out Michele's name, although some of them were erroneously calling her "Michele Saunders" on the air.

Joe kept me in total ignorance of what was going on, and it's a good thing, too. As far as I knew, Joe was doing whatever he was doing and we were waiting for him to finish. Joe called a lot, but he never answered my questions. He was too rushed and busy; he always needed to get answers from me urgently. And, I realize now, he was shielding me. He was purposely avoiding answering my questions.

Joe asked about my meeting with Steinberg, the money that I paid him. He hadn't known any of that. He asked about Ginny, Dr. Bergman, Jackie, the part they'd played in it.

Says Joe:

> *On one of my calls to the restaurant, I made them put Charlie on the phone. I said to him, "Charlie, don't let her drink too much. I don't want her coming to court fritzed." I had no particular reason to think that Michele might drink too much, only the feeling that anyone in her shoes might want to knock a few back.*
>
> *Charlie said, "No, she's fine. She's doing good."*
>
> *He sounded proud of her. Michele does that to people.*

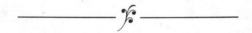

In between calls from Joe, Mom and I talked about the funeral, planning how we would do it, and about Nana, how fantastically she had taken it, how wonderful she was.

I still didn't quite get that I would have to appear personally in court. I thought Joe would do it himself and that I would maybe sign something, so I was able to stay relatively calm.

Joe remembers what went on that afternoon and evening:

> *Judge Lambert was . . . I tell you, she was wonderful. She was not hearing anything from anybody other than the fact that this case was going to be resolved, here and now, and that the child was not going to be left to lie around some morgue, but buried in a respectful way. That was what she wanted to see happen and nobody was leaving there until she did.*
>
> *The various attorneys jockeyed for position all afternoon. At six forty-five P.M. we went on the record with a preliminary hearing in judge's chambers.*
>
> *Judge Lambert got the attorneys to agree on behalf of all the parties that there would be no appeal to her decision, out of respect for the child and the need to see her buried*

as soon as possible. She got everybody to agree to keep the entire proceedings in confidence, except for the final decision. The press had asked to be present. Various counsel, myself among them, objected, and Judge Lambert therefore barred them for the time being.

We all knew it wouldn't be forever. Lambert's gag order lasted only through the dinner break. By then it became clear that certain parties were going to breach it anyway, so it was pointless to try to exclude the press.

Long before then, I knew it was over as far as keeping Michele's identity a secret. I finally said to her over the phone, "What are we playing games for? I know how frightened you are, but if this is what you want to do, you're going to have to face whatever comes. Your grandmother knows, let's do it. Just come on over here and do it."

Michele instantly said, "Okay."

And that was that. That's the way Michele is. She makes a decision, and when she does, she goes forward and she's fine. Nothing stops her.

By now it's seven, eight at night. The judge didn't care. She called a dinner break and ordered everybody back to court afterward for a special session of surrogate's court. It was highly unusual, completely extraordinary. Judge Lambert was going to try the case then and there. No preparation time, no nothing. She was going to resolve it that night and nobody was going home until she did.

When Joe came back to the restaurant during the break, that's when I saw a change in him. That's when he started to get serious. I think that until then he hadn't fully gotten the picture of what had happened to me. Now that he knew, he was going to get Lisa for me or die trying.

Judge Lambert sent a car for us. Joe sort of mentioned that there were a couple of reporters there, nothing too major, nothing I couldn't handle. He said, "The press can be barred from a courtroom, but they can't be prevented from massing *outside* the courtroom."

We were taken inside through a side entrance and up a freight elevator to a room on another floor, not the one the courtroom was on, which was where the press was camped out. They had no idea

I was in the building, and I still didn't know about the television broadcasts or the mob scene that was waiting for me outside the courtroom.

That accomplished, Joe took me aside. I looked at his face and I guessed it was time to take the gloves off. He told me that in order for me to win the right to bury Lisa, we would have to establish that I was in fact her mother. In order to do that I had to get up in open court and testify as to what had happened.

There was no other way.

This child who could with justice claim that nobody cared enough to save her from a horrifying life and a lonely, violent death had a plenitude of people ready to make her funeral.

The City of New York, the rabbi from the local temple, the public school she attended, all wanted to bury her.

Steinberg's elderly mother wanted to "play a role."

No.

William and Emma Nussbaum, Hedda's parents, wanted to bury Lisa on Hedda's behalf. I couldn't see that either. They had done nothing for her in life. They had never reached out a helping hand to a child they claimed to think of as their granddaughter. They hadn't seen her in four years. No.

Steinberg and Nussbaum wanted to bury her themselves. I would not see Lisa put to rest in a cemetery where Steinberg himself might lie one day. That was an unspeakable outrage. No.

Hedda Nussbaum had written some words she wanted read at the funeral. No.

I had done so little for my daughter. I was as guilty as anyone—more even than most, for I myself had delivered her into Steinberg's hands. But this one last service I would do for her. I and no one else.

Joe said, "Michele, last chance. What's it going to be? What are you going to do?"

"Lisa was my child," I told him. "I'm going to do whatever it takes to bury her properly."

Joe was happy that I made that decision, and he told me so.

Says Joe, "I felt that whatever Michele did during these few days and weeks would be with her forever, and I didn't think she could handle it unless she did it this way. She didn't really have the option to walk away from this. And she didn't ever really consider walking away. She was frightened, but once she realized there was nobody for this child but her, she realized that she had to come forward and take whatever happened to her."

Joe took a call and quickly turned back to me. It was time to go downstairs. They were ready to convene.

I said, "Gee, I kind of hoped everyone would come up here and we'd all sit down together in this little room."

I make jokes when I'm frightened. And I was very frightened.

The courtroom was just one floor away. You could hear the voices from the elevator shaft. "Here she comes!"

In that last half an hour Joe had tried to tell me what to expect when I got off the elevator, but I don't think you can describe it till you've been there. Nobody and nothing could have prepared me for that.

The doors opened. A flood of lights. A solid wall of bodies. People pushing, shoving, yelling, hundreds of people, all trying to get *at* me. Cameras pointing, lights aimed in my face, exploding flashbulbs.

"Are you Lisa's natural mother?"

"Where have you been till now?"

"Why didn't you come forward before?"

"Why did you give the baby up?"

"Are you sorry now that you gave the baby up?"

"How do you feel? Do you feel guilty?"

"What do you think of Joel Steinberg?"

"How do you feel about Hedda Nussbaum?"

Joe had warned me not to say a word. *Not one word.* And I didn't. I put my head down and kept walking. I was crying, but I don't think the others saw it.

The judge's paralegal was on one side of me, Joe on the other. Mom was behind me. They simply marched me right through the press right into the judge's chambers. I saw nothing but a blur.

Inside the judge's chambers, we stood around for a while, trying to get our bearings. I tried to blink away the afterimages of thousands of flashbulbs. It felt as if they'd taken a hundred pictures every five seconds.

Joe was busy dealing with what was going on. Mom and I waited. I was nervous, yes. Frightened, yes. But I had no doubt in my mind that I was going to do what I had to do.

It was ten minutes to ten at night when the court convened in special session to determine who would bury my little girl.

Joe was inside; I wasn't, since I was to be a witness, so again I'll let him pick up the story:

The first thing that happened, Judge Lambert lifted her gag order. Since it was clear that the press would have the story anyhow, it was pointless. All parties agreed to allow the press in the courtroom during the hearing. Cameras, how-ever, were excluded.

Judge Lambert quickly reviewed what had transpired in the interim. She had made every effort to find out if the Steinbergs had in fact adopted Lisa. In her capacity as judge of the surrogate court she not only handled all deaths oc-curring in Manhattan, but all adoptions as well. Whenever a family appeared before her to finalize an adoption, Judge Lambert used to give the child a lollipop afterward. It was her way of sharing in and marking a happy occasion. That afternoon, Judge Lambert had her adoption clerk search the records. Further, she'd spoken with the chief administrative judge of New York and had him check his records, trying to find out if Lisa had been one of the children Judge Lambert had sent out of her courtroom with her tearful and joyous parents, clutching a lollipop.

They construed Lisa's name every possible way they could: Elizabeth Nussbaum, Lisa Nussbaum, Elizabeth Steinberg, Lisa Steinberg, Lisa Steinberg-Nussbaum. Nothing was found, under any possible permutation of the name. No record of a child adopted or given up by the natural mother.

They did have the hospital records of Michele's delivery at New York Infirmary–Beekman Downtown Hospital. The baby she bore on May 14, 1981, left the hospital two days later, released to the care of Joel Steinberg.

The child was turned over to him by Dr. Bergman.

No birth certificate for the child had as yet been found. The only documentation that had been found was a certif-icate commemorating her traditional Jewish naming cere-mony in a temple in Teaneck, New Jersey. It was found in the Steinberg/Nussbaum apartment on West Tenth Street as a result of a search by the district attorney's office.

No adoption papers were found.

Judge Lambert challenged both Steinberg's and Nuss-baum's lawyers to produce adoption papers if there were any. Nussbaum's lawyer said her knowledge of the adoption was "vague," but she was under the impression that there were documents somewhere pertaining to Lisa. Whether they were adoption papers or not, she didn't know.

Steinberg's lawyer said that Steinberg had adoption papers somewhere. Steinberg did not have the papers with him at present, since he was currently incarcerated at Riker's Island; where they were exactly, the lawyer didn't know.

Judge Lambert gave the lawyer every chance to find out from Steinberg where these papers were. If he wanted to go ask him, we'd be happy to wait. Arrangements were made for a further search of Steinberg's apartment, although the judge pointed out that it had already been searched, so a second one was likely to be fruitless.

Michele was the first witness called.

Now she wasn't keeping her head down anymore. She sat upright, head up, ready for what was coming.

I couldn't believe what was happening to me. I was fighting to bury my baby, and the people who killed her were trying to deny me that right. They were saying that there had been a legal adoption, and that I was not the natural mother.

They didn't know how I prayed that were true.

But I knew in my heart it wasn't. The evidence was too strong, too incontrovertible.

Now it no longer mattered to me what anybody said. I didn't care what anybody thought. I was there for a purpose. I was going to accomplish it. Nothing and nobody was going to stop me.

Joe took me through the story, establishing who I was, my age, and that when I found myself pregnant, I went to Dr. Bergman for obstetrical care. That Bergman arranged for me to stay with Ginny. That Bergman led me to Steinberg. That I paid him five hundred dollars. That he told me I'd sign papers after the baby was born. That I gave my baby up thinking she was going to a married Catholic couple. That I never heard from Steinberg or saw my baby again.

The fact that Joel Steinberg was the lawyer I went to for the adoption was a bombshell. No one realized that yet.

I fully understood their shock. I remember how stunned Mom and I were when they said on television he was a criminal lawyer.

Joe formally showed me a copy of the New York *Daily News* of that past Tuesday—only one week ago. There was a photo of Joel Steinberg and Hedda Nussbaum being brought into the police station. Joe asked me if I could identify one of the four people as the lawyer I had met in the restaurant that April day six and a half years ago.

I said yes and as instructed, drew a circle around his face.

My birth date is given as 1959. I was born in 1961. I couldn't have given my birth date wrong, no matter what my state. I know my social security number. I did *not* know Steinberg's address and certainly did not give it as my home.

Those questions must have been answered by Ginny.

She is listed as my next of kin—my sister. I have no sisters. She must have listed herself that way.

Joe had me sign my name several times. My signature was compared to the one on the hospital admitting form I had signed on May 13, 1981. He showed them around so everyone could see they were the same.

The sketch artist was sitting right next to me, and in the interminable silences while the legal process went on, I could hear the scritch-scratching sound of charcoal on paper. Throughout the evening the door at the back kept opening and closing as reporters dashed out, went on the air, and returned.

I was only minimally conscious of anything except the reason I was there.

Mom held a picture of Lisa throughout the proceedings. She prayed silently that things would go our way. A grandmother praying for the chance to bury her granddaughter. It shouldn't be that way, but it was all we had.

Joe finished up by asking me about my visits to Dr. Bergman's office after I had the baby. I wasn't allowed to say what Ginny and Jackie told me when I asked about the baby and the adoption papers. Steinberg's lawyer objected on the grounds that it was hearsay.

The judge took over and asked me a few questions. She asked if Ginny was alive. I answered that I didn't know, although I have since found out that she is. I've been told that she's selling cable television time out on Long Island.

The judge asked if Dr. Bergman was alive. Just the night before I had found out from George Schurz, the detective, that he was dead. Detective Schurz had been asking me questions about Bergman that I couldn't answer. I told him to ask Bergman. That's when he told me Bergman was dead.

About three months after Lisa was born, Bergman married his

office nurse, Jackie. Soon afterward he had a series of heart attacks and strokes, finally dying of heart disease while still a young man in his forties.

He was never really well after what he did to Lisa, and he died a month before her. Maybe there is such a thing as divine retribution. I believe there is.

And if in fact they had been selling babies, if in fact they had anything to do with Joel Steinberg's keeping my daughter and murdering her, I wish Jackie no joy in her widowhood. Bergman, I am sure, is suffering at the hands of One who metes out the ultimate justice.

Joe closed by asking me, "Michele, why are you here today?"

I answered simply and truthfully, "I don't feel it's right to have my child, as it so has been presented to me, be buried near, close to, or by the people that did kill her."

Mom remembers:

> The thought of Lisa's killers burying her repulsed Michele so, you could almost visibly see her courage rise and the adrenaline flow in her veins. I couldn't measure the moment, but I could feel its effect on Michele.
>
> Michele looked completely different than she had in the last few days. She looked quite calm, quite dignified. She was drawing on tremendous reserves of inner strength.
>
> And I knew why. She was doing it for her daughter.
>
> A mother working on behalf of her child has unlimited strength. She can move mountains; she can do whatever she has to. Michele put all thought of self behind her. She was out to do what had to be done for her baby. The tragedy was that was all that was left for her to do.

We took a recess. The judge let me wait in her chambers, away from the eyes of the press.

I resented the press. I felt they were the enemy. They wanted me to talk to them. My attitude was I didn't *want* to talk to them, and I wasn't talking to anybody I didn't want to talk to.

Inside, Joe said to me, "Michele, get this through your head once and for all. The choice is not between speaking to the press or not speaking to them. It's a question of *when* you will speak to them."

Joe has a way of getting around my Irish stubborn streak. He talks plain good sense and keeps on doing it until I give in. He strongly advised that I make myself available to the press on a onetime basis. "Answer their questions for a set period of time, and that'll be it. They'll leave you alone."

Joe wanted me to talk to them that night. I told him that was out of the question. I just couldn't. He accepted that. Instead he released an announcement to the press that I would hold a press conference the following day, Wednesday, at twelve noon.

It seemed so bizarre. Press conferences were for rock stars and heads of state. I couldn't imagine what I had to say that would interest these people. But it didn't look as if it were up to me. I went along with it partly because I had no choice, but also because Joe pointed out it would be a good way to let everyone know about Lisa's funeral. The whole purpose of having her funeral in Manhattan, in Greenwich Village, was so everyone who wanted to be there could come, and this way everyone who would want to go would find out when and where it would be.

When we returned, the judge herself took over questioning. She asked me if I remembered being fingerprinted in the hospital. I didn't, but apparently it's done routinely when a woman gives birth. They sent for a fingerprint expert, who was to fingerprint me right then and there. The judge was great. She didn't care that it was late. She didn't care what time it was. She didn't care that the next day was a holiday and people were disappearing. She was going to get this settled that night, and whomever she needed to haul into court to do it, she was going to haul into court.

Chapter 20

*J*oel Steinberg's lawyer was the first to cross-examine me. I can't help it; the distaste I felt for Steinberg—a small part of what I felt for Steinberg—rubbed off on his lawyer. I know about every person's being entitled to counsel, but I still wouldn't have represented Joel Steinberg and I felt contempt for the man who did. He went over the April meeting; I told him the same thing I told the court and everybody else. He asked if I put Joel Steinberg's name on the hospital records as my address. I said, "I certainly did not." I had been asked my address and I gave my actual address, Mom's house, where I lived. How Steinberg's address got there I couldn't say, unless it came from Ginny.

He badgered me about not having Lisa's birth certificate. The judge really took him on about that one. She said, "If we have to get a birth certificate, we will hold up the decision until we get a birth certificate. . . .We're going to sit here until we get the birth certificate."

Mr. Kalina backed down. He said he just wanted to know if I had one, yes or no. I said no, and that was that.

Hedda Nussbaum's lawyer, too, cross-examined me. Barry Scheck tried to use this opportunity to get his client off the hook. He asked me if I'd seen pictures of Hedda Nussbaum, if I knew how injured she was. I had. I did. He tried to get me to say I felt sorry for her.

I didn't. She had a responsibility to do something for the child. She had a responsibility to get Lisa out of there. I had no sorrow or pity to waste on her.

Barry Scheck also suggested that I couldn't understand the tor-ment of a battered woman. I told him he was wrong; my mother was a battered woman. She got herself out and her kids out. She saved my brother and she saved me.

The fingerprint experts arrived, and we broke for a few minutes while I was fingerprinted.

The judge said she wanted to talk with the baby's father. My blood thinned in my veins; I hadn't expected that.

Judge Lambert was nice about it. She got the lawyers to stipulate that since the child's father is an Irish Catholic, that his family has no knowledge of the fact that he had a child or of what happened to that child, therefore she would talk to him privately on the phone, alone except for the stenographer. Minutes would be taken and then she would, privately and not for publication, tell the lawyers who the natural father is. Kevin would not have to testify in open court.

But I had to identify his voice for them.

Mary had called him on Friday night as I'd asked, but he was away for the weekend. She got him at his office on Monday and broke the news to him. Later, he told me that he'd stopped off for a couple of beers on the way home on Tuesday evening and saw on the bar television everything that was going on in surrogate's court. Kevin immediately left the bar and went home, which is why he was there when Judge Lambert made me call him. Tony Cor-nachio, Joe's partner, actually dialed the number. He asked for Kevin; when Kevin got on the phone, Tony passed the phone to me.

I said, "Kevin, this is Michele. I'm sorry I have to do this, but . . ." That was about as awkward and uncomfortable as I have ever felt in my life.

Judge Lambert was waiting right next to me for me to say, yes, this is him. Which is what I did. The judge formally asked me to listen to Kevin's voice and state under oath who he was. They gave him a code name, "Mr. A," for the record.

I testified that he was indeed Mr. A, and that Mr. A was the child's father. I was then requested to leave the room. No one but the judge and the stenographer were to hear Kevin's testimony. His name and address were to be kept secret. I can't say I didn't envy him—I did. But I was glad for him. I would do my damnedest to keep him out of it if I could.

I stayed in the anteroom. Judge Lambert was in her chambers with the door closed.

Then we all went back into open court.

Judge Lambert read a statement into the record about what had transpired. She had asked Kevin if he had objected when I told him I had put the child up for adoption, and if he objected to my application to bury the child. He said no to both questions. She asked him if he relinquished all rights he might have to bury the child. He said yes.

That was it. Kevin's part was over.

Steinberg's attorney, Robert Kalina, had been demanding that he be able to go and search Steinberg's apartment personally to see if they could find these adoption papers Steinberg kept saying he had. At this point Judge Lambert announced that, despite the hour and the fact that the following day was a legal holiday, Veterans Day, she had arranged for Kalina to go with the DA to search the apartment, and we were all going to wait there while they did it.

Kalina backed down again. If the place had been searched once and no adoption papers found, maybe there weren't any adoption papers. Okay, maybe there wasn't an adoption.

But he still claimed for the people he referred to as "Mr. and Mrs. Steinberg" the right to bury Lisa on the grounds that they had custody of her.

Steal a child, kill her, and call that having custody? Not to me.

In case anyone should feel that Steinberg's rights weren't completely protected, Judge Lambert offered to go to Riker's Island personally to take his testimony.

Everybody in that courtroom knew she meant it.

Kalina backed down again.

The fingerprint expert testified that my prints matched those of the Michele Launders who gave birth at New York Infirmary–Beekman Downtown Hospital on May 14, 1981.

The judge asked if anybody had any further witnesses. Nobody did. Just as the judge was about to declare the proceeding over, Kalina brought up again the unorthodox way Judge Lambert had handled the hearing, interviewing an unsworn witness by telephone. Again, the judge offered to call him back and swear him in.

No, no, Kalina wasn't looking to waste anybody's time. He was merely recounting what was presented in court. He wasn't asking the judge to call Kevin back.

Judge Lambert asked each attorney in turn if he had anything else. Nobody did. She said she would have a decision for us in just a few minutes.

It was over. I'd soon know if I would be the one to bury Lisa or not.

Judge Lambert came back and read her decision out loud, directly into the record.

She ruled that there was never an adoption, and that "Michele Launders is the mother of the child Elizabeth, also known as Lisa Steinberg, also known as Elizabeth Lisa Nussbaum."

She ruled that I had the right to the body of Lisa and directed the medical examiner to release the body to me or my agent.

I would bury her, no one else.

"It was well past midnight, near two in the morning, when Judge Lambert read her finding declaring that Michele was the natural mother of Lisa, and that she could bury her," Joe remembers. "Michele cried a little, but she was happy, I think. She felt a deep responsibility and she was happy that she was given the opportunity to fulfill it."

We had convinced the Church and we had convinced the law. Everything that had stood in our way was conquered. I could give my baby the decent and dignified burial she deserved.

With the judge's decision, the child's name was permanently restored under the law. She was not and never had been Lisa Steinberg. She would be buried under her rightful name, Lisa Launders.

That much I had done for her.

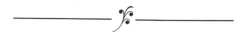

It was impossible even to move out of the courthouse. Reporters, photographers, all kinds of press, were pushing, shoving, separating me from the people I was with. They were actually elbowing my mother away from me. I didn't know where anybody else was—I couldn't see past the curtain of flashing strobe lights. I seemed to be the center of it all. They were all after me. It was a dizzying, frightening, unnerving feeling.

Somehow, with the help of John and Charlie, Mom and I made

it to the front door. It was a horrible night—raining, snowing. The press were like wolves, shoving, pushing, shouting questions at me. I hadn't slept. I hadn't eaten. The shock. The emotion. It was all spinning around in my brain. Lisa. My grandmother. My mother. Kevin. There was so much coming at me, all at once.

I raised my hand to my hair—and flashbulbs exploded, just from that small gesture that I had made. I'd never thought this would happen to me. I was disoriented. All I wanted to do was get out of there.

Not home. I didn't want to go home—I still saw the detective sitting at my table when he told me—but I wanted to be someplace else, away from all of this.

The judge had said that the same car that brought me would be parked directly out front. Between the TV lights, the flashbulbs, and the freezing rain, I was nearly blind. I spotted a station wagon. It looked like the right one. I headed for it.

As I was about to get into the backseat—I practically had one leg inside—this King Kong arm came out of nowhere and literally lifted me up off my feet: "Michele, you're not going in there!"

The arm belonged to John Reide. The car I was about to get into belonged to the *New York Post*.

We all jammed into a small car and went over to Forlini's. We were leading a pack of press like hounds to a fox. This long caravan of cars and vans trailed us. They weren't about to disappear, either.

We managed to get inside, and those lovely people who owned Forlini's simply shut the door behind us and tried to keep the press out. The press screamed "discrimination, public place," and all that. They couldn't keep them out forever, so they took us into a back room. That, they maintained, was not a public place; they could decide who ate there, and who ate there was us and not the press.

Okay, we were inside, but we were trapped there. We were under siege. The press could outlast us; they could change shifts. They were just biding their time, knowing that I couldn't stay in the back room at Forlini's forever.

The court had not released my address. They didn't know where I lived. They were waiting to follow me home.

That thought was absolutely terrifying.

One of the waitresses even offered to switch clothes with me, since we were both dark haired and about the same height. She was sweet—all the people of Forlini's were wonderful—but the whole situation made me angry. I didn't want to skulk around like a criminal. I didn't want to keep all these good people from their beds. It brought out all the Irish in me—and there's plenty to bring out.

I said, "I'm tired, I'm exhausted, I'm filthy. I'm just going to get up and walk out."

"And where will you go?" Joe wanted to know.

I had no place to go. And I had no way of getting there. That was not a nice thought.

I didn't want to go back to my house. Mom's place in New Jersey was too far away. We had to be out on Long Island for the press conference at Joe's office by noon. The only thing to do was find a hotel or motel room somewhere on Long Island. Because of the lateness of the hour and the weather, they couldn't even find a hotel room for us. The closest place was in Plainview, which is pretty far out on Long Island.

Joe, John, and Charlie worked out a plan to get Mom and me out of there and into hiding. I don't remember the details and I'm not sure I ever knew them. I just followed instructions. They put me in one car, Mom in another. I scrunched down behind the front seat so I couldn't be seen. My car drove a block or two, then pulled up alongside another car while a third car blocked the cars that were following us. I jumped out into the second car. We did that a couple of times until Mom and I wound up in the same car, headed for the Long Island Expressway.

And the caravan of reporters and photographers was right behind us.

The next hour or so is still unbelievable to me. It was the kind of wild chase you see in the movies. I was in the backseat of this car with my mother. Joe was in the car behind us with his partner Tony and Tony's brother, who had come to pick them up. They'd come in that morning on the train, never dreaming this thing would turn into The Day That Wouldn't End. Our driver was this doll named George. George was Hispanic. His English was heavily accented. We're driving through Long Island at breakneck speed, going through red lights, breaking every law on the books, and the press is still after us. There was this line of cars—we could see them behind us—zooming in and out of traffic with us. George had a radio. In every town we passed, George radioed the local police and asked them for help. As soon as they found out who we were—I guess we were a hot media event—they wanted no part of us. George was yelling into his radio, "There are people driving like maniacs, running red lights, everything." But by that time we were approaching the next town and they said, "Tell *them* about it."

So George muttered, "I'll take care of this." He talked a lot in Spanish on the radio, then he turned to us. "Hang on, ladies, we're going for a ride."

Now I can laugh, but then it wasn't funny. I started to feel as if I were living in some strange movie and nothing was real. Which was a nice thought. If nothing were real, my baby was alive, asleep somewhere cuddling a stuffed animal. George was talking Spanish on the radio the whole time. I looked out the window. We were in Port Washington. George zoomed us into a parking lot. The press followed us, seven, eight, ten cars.

We zoomed out. Suddenly these other cars appeared out of no-where: one blocked the exit, one blocked the entrance. George's buddies.

We sailed on to the Long Island Expressway. Our "tail" was trapped in the parking lot, undoubtedly cursing colorfully. I'd like to thank George sometime. He was a great guy.

Finally, at about four-fifteen in the morning, we staggered into the Holiday Inn in Plainview. Joe checked us in, stayed until he was sure we were all right, then he finally went home. That's one of the reasons I love him. He could have spent that night with his wife and kids safely tucked into his own bed instead of chasing around Long Island with me.

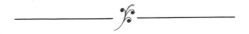

Inside our room, I just fell across the bed with my clothes on. Mom lay in the other one. We were each pretending we were asleep. I know I didn't sleep more than a few minutes at a time, and I don't think Mom did either.

There was no point in even trying to sleep. I wouldn't rest until my baby was out of the morgue and properly laid to rest.

I hoped—I prayed—that afterward I would find peace. I wasn't sure I ever would.

I was so tired. I hadn't thought of sleep all night. You don't think of sleeping until you have a place to sleep. I hadn't slept since the previous Thursday night. Friday, Saturday, Sunday, Monday, Tuesday. Five nights without sleep. I was exhausted but my body couldn't relax enough to sleep.

Finally it was morning. Mom and I went through the motions of waking up. We had nothing, no change of clothes, not even a toothbrush. Just what was in our handbags and pockets. We ordered something from room service for breakfast. Neither of us ate.

It got late enough for Mom to call her office to tell them she wouldn't be in.

I called my boss. "Jeffrey, I'm not coming in today. Don't ask me why. I don't know if I'll be in tomorrow. I don't know if I'll be in next week or next month."

"What is it? Is it drugs? Alcohol?"

"No. I can't tell you the reason. You just have to trust me. I'm not even thinking about work right now."

Mom and I both looked like hell. We needed a change of clothes, at the very least. We couldn't go to either of our homes. We went to Macy's in Roosevelt Field, a large Long Island shopping center. That day was November 11, Veterans Day, a day off for most people and a day of huge sales. The stores were packed. I could hardly stand, let alone push through the crowds of shoppers. People were grabbing and tearing at the stuff. I've been known to shop a sale or two myself, but now it looked grotesque, bizarre. I felt dizzy and hot. I thought I was going to pass out.

I was afraid people would recognize me from the papers and television. Mom said, "Michele, trust me on this. From all my experience these people are so wrapped up in what they're doing you could walk in stitch-stark naked and nobody would notice."

I kept my head down most of the time.

Mom was moving me around like a puppet. We stopped at a drugstore and bought hair spray and toothpaste and things like that. Mom kept saying, "Shel, you're doing great."

Until we got out of the car near Joe's building.

Reporters were coming from all directions. A news truck was in front of the building. Another reporter was posted at the only pay phone on the block, keeping it tied up while he had a full view of the entrance. I'm sure he thought he was clever.

I wanted to keep Mom out of it. I told her to walk a block behind me so she wouldn't have to deal with it.

She said, "Shel, walk calmly down the street with me like two ladies with nothing on their minds but lunch. You can get away with murder if you don't look guilty or anxious."

We walked right past the one on the pay phone who thought he was such a wise guy. The people on the truck were paying us no attention. Not a head was turning. We were within a few feet of the door when Billy pulled up in his red roadster or whatever he was driving that year. Mary got out. She saw me and ran across the street, arms open wide, screaming, "Michele! Michele!"

I saw the press and I saw Mary and Billy getting out of their car. I knew what was over there and what was over here, and what was over here was my friends. I chose my friends.

I went to Mary and we hugged in the middle of the street. The photographers, of course, now knew who I was. They had me pegged.

Mary came into the bathroom with me while I freshened up and changed clothes. We talked over everything that had happened. Now I was settled in upstairs, nice and comfortable. I didn't want to face those people down there. I had no idea what they would ask me, but it sure wasn't going to be as comfy as I was up here.

Joe thought that was amusing. He took me by the arm and led me inside. Whatever was going to happen would happen.

We sat down in front of the microphones. They threw questions at me. I answered everything truthfully. Why had I given up Lisa for adoption? I was nineteen, unmarried, and there were things I thought she deserved that I couldn't provide for her at the time.

They didn't ask any questions about Kevin. I was surprised until I found out that Joe had arranged up front that no questions be asked about the father. Joe knew how I felt about protecting Kevin. I just couldn't see why he should have to go through all this and have his life messed up the way mine was. It wouldn't help anything, would it?

The press conference lasted ten minutes. People told me later that I sounded okay and did well. I'm surprised I made sense at all. Later, when Mary asked me what they had asked, I couldn't tell her. I had no idea.

But it was done. The secret I had kept for so long, that I had sacrificed so much for to keep, was not only out, it had been broadcast on television and radio. My most personal thoughts and actions were public knowledge, for everyone to comment on and talk about. Strangers would know my name and my face.

I would, for the rest of my life, be the person whom this had happened to. I had said from the moment I set out on this course that if this was the price I had to pay to bury my child, I would pay it.

Chapter 21

After the press conference, we sat in Joe's office for a while; Joe had a lot of things to go over with me. For one thing, the media was blitzing his office with requests for appearances and interviews with me. He started to read the list. *Donahue, Today, Good Morning America, Geraldo*—I cut him off. I wanted no part of the media attention. I just wanted it all to go away and let me do what I had to do.

Joe told me that there were offers coming in from all over from people wanting to pay for the funeral. I told Joe to decline it all, with thanks. We would pay for Lisa's burial ourselves.

Joe kept casting worried glances at me. I was holding myself together by a thin thread. He wasn't sure I'd come through this in one piece. Unbeknownst to me, he was making some arrangements of his own.

Joe says, "With the kind of attention Michele was drawing, and the crowd we expected at the funeral the next day, you cannot be sure that someone won't jump out intending to do something crazy. I arranged for three big guys to be there to take care of Michele. No one did ever try to hurt her or do something crazy, but that's hindsight. Going in, you never know. We had been getting threatening letters and phone calls and stuff. I worried about some fanatic who might try to do her in."

I understood that Hedda Nussbaum had written a few words she wanted read at the funeral. No chance. I could not then and cannot today understand how she had the nerve to express concern for Lisa after her death when she obviously ignored what was going on while the child was alive.

She had so many options, could have done so many things. Put Lisa in a cab and send her to the grandparents. To her aunt, Nussbaum's sister. To a neighbor, a friend, a high-school chum. Anywhere, just get her the hell out. Instead, she was busy worrying about herself and her lover.

Nussbaum had been charged along with Steinberg, and when Lisa died, the charges against her were upgraded to murder as well. Yesterday, the day of the surrogate's court hearing, Manhattan district attorney Robert Morgenthau had announced that his office would defer indicting Hedda Nussbaum for thirty days to give her time to recover.

In the end Nussbaum was not indicted in Lisa's death. She agreed to testify against Steinberg, and just before his trial the charges against her were dismissed. I think that is wrong. I thought so then, and I still do today.

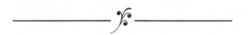

Mom took me home with her to New Jersey that night. Mary and Billy came with us. The phone was ringing off the hook. Friends were calling from all over. Uncles, aunts. My brother called from California. Mom told me Fred's daughter had been sitting in front of the television for days crying over Lisa, without knowing she was my daughter.

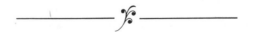

Finally the house settled down, but I don't think anyone slept. Everyone spent that night thinking about Lisa, the little girl none of us had ever seen whom we were going to bury in the morning.

The morning of the funeral I showered and dressed. I put on my black suit. I moved like a robot, as if I were on automatic pilot. People pointed me in a direction and there I went. There was stuff out for breakfast. I couldn't eat. George, our driver, came to pick us up. He sat down and we gave him breakfast.

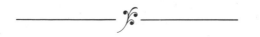

When we got to the funeral home, they took me inside, past the crowds, to a little office. Joe kept putting pieces of paper in front of me for me to sign, and I signed where he showed me. To this day I have no idea what they were.

I had wanted to put something in the casket, a piece of jewelry or a locket. The people from the funeral home were about to open the casket for me; they asked Mom to go get me. Joe overheard and caught Mom's arm. "Michele is on no account to open the casket," he told Mom. "Keep her busy, keep her distracted. Don't let her do it."

Says Joe:

> *I had seen the autopsy report. I have never shown that to Michele, nor do I intend to. It was horrifying for a stranger to read, let alone the mother.*
>
> *The original identification at the morgue had been made by William Nussbaum, who listed himself as "friend/grandfather," an odd thing in itself. He declared he had not seen the child since 1983 but was making the identification from a recent photo. Friend or grandfather or both, I don't envy him the responsibility of looking at that body.*

I never did put anything in the casket.

I remember walking up stairs jammed with people, and it was like the parting of the Red Sea. They just shrank back to the sides so I could pass. People were clawing at me, pulling at me.

"Bless you. We're with you."

"I was beaten, too. I was abused."

"Lisa, poor angel, we cried for her with you."

"Our prayers are with you."

All spoke directly from their hearts, one soul to another.

I heard them, but I was completely off somewhere else. They tried to put things in my hands: letters, notes, drawings. The men Joe had hired to be with me took them for me.

I didn't look at anybody. I just kept walking. I saw friends of mine—Jim was there, my boss Jeff was there. I couldn't speak, not even to thank them for coming.

Someone led me to a chair in the front row. I looked up and saw the casket for the first time. Thank God I was near my seat. My knees gave way and I all but collapsed into it.

Mom's recollection is better than mine: "The people in the room, their were faces lined, haggard. You could see the sorrow on their faces. They came to show support, to be with Lisa in death, even if they couldn't be with her in life."

The service was beautiful. The priest spoke. The rabbi spoke; he gave Lisa a Jewish blessing. Rabbi Math was the same man who had been in surrogate's court offering to bury Lisa. He spoke eloquently of the fragility of life, how fragile it is for all of us.

I was weeping quietly.

Mom prayed: "Lisa, I want you to know that we care about you, and we always will. We were silent, but in no way did we agree with what happened to you. Please know that. We want you to know that. Lisa, darling, hang on. Nana will be there soon to take care of you. In the meantime you won't be alone. You'll be with your great-grandpa, who you never knew in this world. You'll never be alone anymore."

Says Mom, "It occurred to me that Joseph Launders was buried in Gate of Heaven, too, in our family plot. In no way, shape, or form could I see him tending to this child, his granddaughter, in heaven or anywhere else."

From the cemetery we drove back into the city, to Forlini's. The people at Forlini's gave us a beautiful dinner. It's more or less the custom after a Catholic family returns from a burial that there is a kind of party or feast. The mood lightens and you presumably focus on the good parts of the person's life.

I was not in the mood for any kind of party. I think that's the craziest thing you can put anybody through.

I felt out of place. Everybody was going along with the traditional lightening of spirit. I couldn't join in with them. They weren't feeling what I was feeling.

Mom tried to show me the newspapers. She said they were treating me nicely, admiringly even. I didn't care. I didn't want to see them.

Someone turned on the television at Forlini's, and when the news came on, everyone went to the bar to watch. I didn't want any part of it. There I was in the middle of this long table in a booth all by myself. I tried to join them at one point. I got about three-quarters of the way there, but the moment I heard the voice of the newscaster talking about the funeral, I couldn't do it. I turned around and went back to the table. I didn't need to relive it again. I was reliving it in my mind all the time. It was very, very vivid to me. I didn't need television footage to remind me.

I just wanted to go home. My home. Mom wanted me to go back to New Jersey with her, but I just couldn't. I had to be in my own place. When I finally got there, I curled up in a chair in my living room, and finally, for the first time in a week, I slept.

The tension that had been with me for a solid week all went out of me at once. But the guilt was still there, and as time went on, it got worse rather than better.

Kevin called the next morning. He wanted to come over. Mary and Billy weren't altogether wild about him at this point. Mary was upset that when she had called to alert him before my press conference, his main response was concern for what would happen to him. Which I think is a very normal initial response.

Billy and Mary had supported me ever since they found out. Kevin didn't come; he never even called. They resented Kevin for not reaching out a hand to help me. After all, part of the burden I was shouldering was his. They didn't necessarily feel that he had to step forward publicly, but they did think he should be at my side in private.

They both thought I shouldn't see him.

"Are you sure you want him to come over?" Billy asked.

"Yes," I told him, "I'm sure."

There was no doubt in my mind. We'd hardly ever discussed what had happened, and never in any detail. He hadn't asked and I hadn't volunteered. Kevin needed some questions answered, too. I thought he deserved at least to know as much as I knew about what had happened to our daughter.

And I needed him. I was hurting a great deal. I couldn't stand to share my pain with anybody . . . except Kevin. He was my partner in this. It had happened to him as much as it had happened to me.

The moment he walked into my room, I burst into tears. All the emotion of the past week erupted from me in violent sobs.

Kevin didn't cry. He didn't say much of anything.

I found out later that when he drove up to the house, the only light he saw was downstairs. I was sitting upstairs in the dark. He went down there first and spent about forty minutes with Mary and Billy before coming up to me. Mary told him I needed him to be strong, that I was upset and emotional and on the verge of coming unglued and that he had to restrain himself for my benefit.

She was wrong. I didn't need Kevin to be strong. I needed him to cry with me. I needed him to weep over the death of our daughter. He and I were the only two people in the world who could say "Lisa was our daughter and now she is dead."

I was hysterical, screaming and sobbing. Kevin didn't shed a tear. Was he that cold? I wondered. Didn't he have one tear to shed for his baby?

I didn't know then that he was following Mary's advice. When I found out about their conversation a few days later, it didn't make me feel any better. I was still upset that Kevin had shared his grief with them and not me. He had cried with them and never showed his feelings with me. Why did I want Kevin's emotion so? I don't know. Except perhaps that I was Lisa's mother, he was Lisa's father, and just as I'd wanted her to be loved by two parents in life, I wanted her mourned by two parents in death.

That night, when I calmed down a little and stopped crying enough for conversation, I took out some of the letters and mass cards that had been left at the funeral home. Kevin looked at them, but without a lot of interest. I don't think that Kevin shared my bereavement. I don't think he feels that he lost a daughter. I have to say that strangers mourned Lisa more than Kevin did.

Even though I'd had Mary call to warn him, Kevin never got up the courage to tell his parents. His mother found out by seeing me on TV. They didn't have to ask who Lisa's father was. Kevin's father had offered to go to the funeral with him if he wanted to go. Kevin didn't.

I've finally had to admit to myself that part of the reason Kevin came over that night was because he was nervous that I would disclose his name to the press. I reassured him that nobody would find out from me who he was, and I've kept my promise.

Mary and Billy made it clear they were unhappy that I saw Kevin again. I knew they would be. They judged him far more harshly than I did, and still do. It's not Kevin's fault that he doesn't want to be involved now. I never gave him the opportunity back then when Lisa was born even to know I was pregnant. I never gave him the chance to be involved, so it's kind of my fault he doesn't want to, isn't it? At least partly? I know deep down that it wouldn't have changed anything if I had told him. I'm ninety-nine percent sure of that.

But from that night, after Lisa's funeral, Kevin and I picked up our relationship. We started seeing each other again. I was happy to be back with him and I have to admit, I still loved him.

Chapter 22

The morning after the funeral I was alone for the first time in a week. No people around, no decisions to make, no pressure to be somewhere or to do something.

I was finally able to sit down and mourn Lisa.

I thought of the life she had. The life I had given her. It turned out to be pretty miserable. I went over in my head everything that had happened. That first meeting with Steinberg played over and over in my mind. Why didn't I sense that he was crazy? Why didn't I sense that he had the capacity to kill a child?

There were so many turning points. If I'd gone to a different doctor . . . If I had asked more questions . . . If I'd changed my mind at the last second—Lisa would be alive.

I craved details of her life . . . I hungered for them. What had she been like? Was she happy? I know that sounds funny, given the conditions they found her in, the filth, but was she ever happy? Or did I condemn her to a life of nothing but sadness and abuse.

I wanted to know about her death. I wanted to know what in hell had happened in that house! One thing's for sure, the pastel nursery with the clouds and rainbows never existed—not even close.

My daughter lived in hell. And I put her there.

Along with sorrow and guilt, I was consumed with hatred for

Joel Steinberg. I still am. I think he's the devil incarnate. I've never known anybody before that I wished pain on, cancer, torture. I wish it on Steinberg. I want him to suffer. It's not a pleasant feeling.

I hate him, and despise *her*. I despise that woman.

Prominent women jumped to her defense. Who came to Lisa's defense? Nussbaum was compared to Karen Straw, a battered wife who killed her husband in self-defense.

Excuse me, doesn't anybody see the difference?

I'm often asked if I feel compassion for Hedda Nussbaum. The answer is no! Why should I feel sorry for her? She could have gotten out! She *should* have gotten out! For the sake of the children. She called them her children, why didn't she do something for them? I don't care what kind of sex games she was playing with Steinberg. I don't care what kind of sick fantasies she had. I don't care what kind of drugs she took. She had a choice, Lisa didn't.

They both killed Lisa, no matter who dealt her that fatal blow. They killed my baby, my Lisa . . . my beautiful Lisa.

She was only mine for twenty seconds. Twenty seconds while a nurse carried her out of the room. I sent Lisa to her death. And for that, I will never forgive myself.

In the weeks after Lisa's funeral, I tried to spend as much time at Nana and Papa Jack's house as I could, both to be with Nana and to give Papa Jack a chance to get out of the house.

Nana's body was weakening, she eventually lost control of her bodily functions, but her mind was never touched. It was as clear as ever.

Nana and I talked a lot those last few weeks. She knew how depressed I was. She kept trying to get me to focus on the future. I would put this tragedy behind me. I would make a life for myself, I would go on to have more children.

She was trying to help me heal, to give me one last blessing. This one I could not accept. My guilt is too evident, too powerful. I don't think I will ever be able to let go.

And I don't think I'll ever have another child. I had one child. I failed her. I'm not going to risk having any more.

In the days and weeks before Christmas, people left toys and cards at Lisa's grave. I found them there when I went to visit. One of the notes that had been left for me said, "Your little girl must be very happy in Heaven to know that her mommy came through for her."

Small comfort. Sure, I was there after she was dead. Where was I when she was alive?

Toward the end of January, I decided to stay the whole week at Nana's house. For no particular reason. I can't tell you we saw the end coming any more than we did before. Nana had been in a bad way for some time. I moved into Nana's room, since she was downstairs in the living room, which had been turned into a hospital room.

Saturday night we all watched some television. At one-thirty I got up to go to the bathroom, and while I was up, I went into the living room to check on Nana. Sometimes the oxygen slipped off and I would replace it. She was fine.

Papa Jack got up before I did Sunday morning. He came into my room, shaking. "Shel, Shel . . . I think Mom's gone."

He couldn't bring himself to go near enough to make sure. I jumped up and ran into the living room.

He was right. Sometime between one-thirty and seven in the morning, Nana had died.

I don't know exactly what happens when you breathe your last, but she looked peaceful to me. Very, very peaceful. I'll always remember it that way. The bed sheets were still tucked in. There really wasn't much of a change from the last time I had seen her. She didn't look very different. She was in the same position. She hadn't struggled. She hadn't been gasping for air or kicking or anything. She just went naturally and peacefully.

I'm glad she looked the same. I'll be eternally grateful that she doesn't seem to have suffered. I don't have a horrible picture of her to carry in my mind.

The monsignor used to come every Wednesday to give Nana Communion. When he couldn't make it, he would send a woman named Anne in his place.

Papa Jack called and told her Nana was gone.

Anne and Nana had grown close. Anne had told us that Nana was having trouble letting go. Her strong spirit was keeping her alive long after the doctors had predicted she would die. She was wasting away physically, her body was going, but her mind was alive. That's hard.

I called Mom and told her. She started screaming over the phone. I said, "I'm sorry, Mom."

We were both crying.

No matter how much the doctors tried to prepare us, no matter what the evidence of our own eyes, we couldn't believe Nana was really going to die. When it did happen, we were all taken by surprise.

We buried Nana as we had planned, in our family plot next to her first husband, alongside the new grave where Lisa lay.

I mourned Nana, but not as much as I would have done under other circumstances. I missed her, but I knew she had a job to do. There was a little girl in heaven who needed her much more than we did. We'd had a family to love and care for us. She'd had nobody.

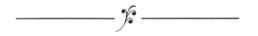

I felt completely empty inside. Half of me had died when I gave Lisa away; the other half died when I found out what had happened to her. I went through the motions of living. Inside was an empty shell, nothing and less than nothing.

Everybody kept telling me I should get on with my life. I tried. I looked for a job, but it was hard. People recognized me. Sometimes they couldn't put their finger on who I was right away, but they knew I was involved with something notorious. I tried working in a doctor's office, but I couldn't keep any kind of a job where I'd have contact with the public. They were too distracted by who I was. Just being in the room I seemed to cause a fuss. It wasn't fair to my employer and it certainly wasn't easy on me.

It's not easy to make a life for yourself when you are consumed by guilt and eaten up by hatred.

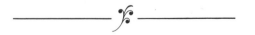

The two things I've hated all my life are having my picture taken and speaking in public. I've always been a private person and not a good public speaker. I never was one for the spotlight. Even as a kid, I was always the one in the background. I was good at orchestrating things for others, but I never wanted to be in the limelight myself. There are few pictures of me prior to November 1987. In one day all that changed. Reporters and photographers were after me all the time. I wouldn't talk to any of them. That didn't stop them from taking my picture. Holidays, Mother's Day, Lisa's birthday; they knew when I'd be at the grave, and they were there.

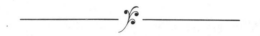

Mom wasn't too thrilled about my seeing Kevin again; neither were my friends. Kevin and I had easily fallen back into the old rhythms, even though our relationship perhaps wasn't as intense as it had been seven years before. We were both adults now, not high-school kids. We saw each other on weekends, not almost constantly as we had before. We did the same kinds of things; we went to concerts and movies; we went bowling. Kevin and I would talk sometimes about what happened, the baby and everything. I was the one who brought it up.

One weekend when Kevin was out of town, I went over to his parents' house. "Kevin's not here," they said.

"I know that," I told them. "I didn't come to speak to Kevin. I came to speak with you."

They were surprised, but they let me in and we wound up having a nice conversation. I tried to explain to them what had led me to give up Lisa, to make them understand that I was looking for everybody's benefit and I never meant this to happen. I meant no harm to anybody; just the opposite. I had been trying to avoid hurting anybody by taking the burden of secrecy on myself.

They understood, they really did.

They were bewildered by what had happened. They had a lot of questions. I answered them as best I could. I was able to give them more detail than they'd gotten from anybody thus far. I went through the whole thing, step by step. Finding out I was pregnant, meeting Dr. Bergman. They agreed that Kevin was in no position to take responsibility for a child—that was never in question. They said I had done the right thing, which made me feel pleased.

I told them I would continue to keep Kevin's identity secret. I was going to have to bear a lot of grief anyway. Why should I involve somebody else? What difference would it make if Kevin came forward? None. We knew who Lisa's father was. That was enough. His picture on the front page of the newspaper wouldn't serve any purpose that we could see.

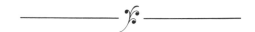

I tried to throw myself into work the way I had when I gave up Lisa for adoption. It didn't work. I had no desire to do what I was supposed to do. I didn't care if somebody was buying a house or not. I was completely unmotivated by anything. I couldn't make myself care enough to hold down a job.

Mary and I had a spat, mostly due to the fact that I was impossible to live with. The truth was no one could have lived with me. I couldn't live with myself. I left that place and moved in with my mom and Fred in New Jersey, but I still paid rent because I had signed a lease.

Sometimes Mom and I would talk about Lisa. There were so many questions. Some we still don't have the answers to, and maybe never will. One day we took a drive into the city. We went to Dr. Bergman's office—and that's when it clicked for the first time that his home, where I'd been taken on the night I gave birth, was in the same building as his office.

We went to the restaurant where we met Steinberg and just stood outside. Then we drove to 14 West Tenth Street, the house where Steinberg had lived and Lisa had died.

Much as Mom and Fred love me, I couldn't stay with them indefinitely. I found a place of my own near Rockville Centre where Papa Jack is and moved in. I had no job. I used up whatever little savings I had and then started borrowing from Mom.

In the months—nearly a year—between Lisa's death and Joel Steinberg's murder trial, I grasped at some semblance of normal life.

Is it any surprise that it eluded me?

Nearly every day it seemed, I picked up the paper to see a picture of "Mitchell Steinberg," now renamed Travis Christian Smigiel and reclaimed by his natural mother, Nicole Smigiel. After Lisa's funeral,

Nicole came forward publicly as the boy's mother. Little more than a week later, she was awarded custody of Travis. Nicole and her parents, with great fanfare, welcomed the child back to their home.

"Everybody, this is my baby, Travis Christian," Nicole announced to the gathered relatives and the camera. He was dressed in an adorable yellow outfit. There was a banner over the fireplace that read "Welcome home, Travis."

The press besieged the Smigiels, too, camping out in front of their house. The Smigiels didn't have the aversion to publicity that I had; they went along with it. The Smigiels held open house for the press; they gave press conferences on the front lawn. They appeared on talk shows. I couldn't pick up a newspaper without seeing them. It was, See Travis celebrate Thanksgiving; See Travis at Christmas, See Travis go to church; See Travis with his new sneakers.

I honestly did share in their joy, but it was painful for me. They had their baby back home with them; I had nothing but a nightmare. Nicole got a second chance—and I had to see it every time I turned on the television. Watching her hold Travis, laugh at his antics, express her gratitude for having him back . . . it hurt like hell.

Nicole sent me a letter of condolence: "Dear Michele, I pray for you and your little angel, because without her I would not have *my* little angel. You are forever in my heart. With deepest feelings, Nicole."

It was on the front page of the *New York Post* days before it arrived in my mailbox. Her attorney released it to the press. I actually heard it on the television news before I got it in the mail.

But she was right. There is a bond that will tie us together forever. That bond is Travis. He and Lisa shared seventeen months in hell. Lisa saved his life with the sacrifice of her own. For that alone, he will always be special to me.

I wanted to see Travis. I toyed with the idea for a long time, never quite sure I could carry it off. It took me eight months to get up the courage, but one day I was simply overcome with the urge to see him and I decided today was the day. I didn't call ahead, I just drove to the Smigiel home in Massapequa Park, Long Island, and rang the bell.

Nicole opened the door. Her mouth dropped open when she saw me. "Oh, my God!" she said. "Come on in."

Not only did I go in, I stayed for hours. I've been close to the Smegiels ever since then, particularly to Graceann, Nicole's mother.

And I watch Travis grow up. Travis is almost four now, and like Lisa is an unusually handsome and intelligent child. What luck these Steinbergs had! To "adopt" two children separately and have each turn out to be such a spectacular child! And what they did to them!

On weekends, on her birthday, just any day I felt like it, I drove out to Gate of Heaven Cemetery to sit at Lisa's grave. Sometimes, on my way in or out, strangers would ask me if I knew the way to "Little Lisa's" grave. I'd smile and say, "Come on, I'll take you there," and then they'd recognize me and realize who I am.

Most often I'd be alone. I'd cry myself out, then just sit awhile. Lisa's grave is not a lonely place. It's a nice place to sit. It always looks new, freshly tended. There are fresh flowers, left by strangers. Throughout the year people leave stuffed animals, balloons. At Easter I found bunnies, at Halloween pumpkins.

There were always notes and letters. People left them in Ziplock bags. Sometimes the notes are from expectant couples. They say that if the baby is a girl, they will name her Lisa.

In the midst of their daily lives people found the time to think of the little girl who died before the age of seven at the hand of the man who called himself her father.

Her pain was over now. I could find no respite from my own.

Chapter 23

I turned twenty-seven that October 23. I found little cause for celebration. Two days later, on October 25, 1988, eleven and a half months after her death, Joel Steinberg went on trial for the murder of his "adoptive" daughter Lisa.

From the moment I found out about Lisa I had been fired with a consuming hatred for Steinberg. All I wanted was five minutes alone in a room with him. . . . Now, I would come face-to-face with my daughter's killer.

Not only did I plan to attend the opening of the trial, I was going to sit through every minute of it.

Everyone I knew thought I was crazy. They all tried to talk me out of it, Mom, John, Papa Jack, Joe. I wouldn't listen to anybody. It was just something I had to do. I had no choice. I had to be there.

As the date drew nearer, the tension inside me rose. I was all knotted inside with a combination of emotions I couldn't untangle: fear of the unknown—I didn't know what to expect, how I would react, how I would feel. Consuming, burning hatred for Steinberg and Nussbaum. Pity for my daughter. Regret. Guilt. Anger—at whom, I don't know. Myself. Fate. God.

I prayed for control, I prayed I would not behave badly and disgrace my daughter's memory.

I hadn't been a regular churchgoer for a while, not for years really. I have a relationship with God, He is a presence in my life, but I don't necessarily mind the p's and q's of observance. However, the first morning of the trial, I drove from Baldwin where I was living to Rockville Centre so I could stop into my childhood church, St. Agnes. Not for long, just to say a prayer. Then I got on the Long Island Rail Road for the train ride into the city. I hadn't eaten in days. I simply couldn't, and I was also afraid of the involuntary urge to vomit.

With the trial approaching, the press had come after me with a vengeance. The day before I'd given an interview to a reporter who worked for the *Daily News*. I'd promised her months ago that if I did give an interview, I'd give it to her. I thought that by giving one interview, the others would leave me alone. They would simply copy the information that was in her article and not bother me.

When I called her, she was stunned; she'd forgotten about my promise and never for a moment thought I would keep my word. I met with her in Joe's office. I didn't like the fact that she brought a photographer—she hadn't mentioned that—but I'd promised her an interview so I gave it to her.

As I sat on the train on my way into the trial, every commuter seemed to have a copy of the *Daily News* with my picture staring out from it large as life.

I got to the criminal courthouse early, even before it opened to the public. By arrangement I was allowed in through an employees' entrance. I was inside without the press's even realizing I was there. As I entered the courtroom, my knees were shaking.

I was apprehensive, but not of the press. It was *him* I worried about. Lisa's murderer. How would I react when I saw him?

I was seated in the front row of spectators, directly behind the defense table where Joel Steinberg would sit. The mind plays funny tricks. As they led me to my seat, I was reminded of a wedding where the usher leads you to the groom's side or the bride's side, and all I kept thinking was, I'm on the wrong side.

A door on the side wall near the front of the courtroom suddenly opened. Joel Steinberg was led out by guards. Apparently that door led to a holding cell just off the courtroom. You didn't even see a door till you knew it was there. That first time I wasn't expecting anybody to come from that direction.

Our eyes met the instant he walked out. He was ten feet away

from me. I had to hold myself back from going after him. I wanted
to tear him apart with my bare hands.

I could do nothing.

The judge had warned that he would allow me to stay in the
courtroom as long as I didn't engage in unseemly behavior or emotional outbursts. I held myself under rigid control, so tense my
muscles ached.

I didn't want them to remove me from the courtroom. I wanted
to be there for Lisa. Everybody else was there because they had to
be. It was their job or they were curious, or in the case of Steinberg,
because he was overpowered. No one was there just for Lisa. Except
me. I couldn't let them throw me out.

He moved to his seat in front of me. I was close enough to see
the pores of Steinberg's skin and the hair on the back of his neck.
He could probably feel my breath on his neck. They had assigned
me that seat in order to prevent the press from turning around and
seeing my face, but it served my purposes just fine.

I wanted him to know I was there, bearing witness, and that as
long as I lived, there would be someone who would remember what
he had done and hate him for it.

I didn't manage to get through the prosecution's opening statement without shedding tears, but I sat quietly and tried to be as
inconspicuous as I could. Peter Casolaro, the prosecutor, opened by
stating what was the essence of the case: that Steinberg had been
given the baby by me and had brought her into his home as a parent,
but instead of nurturing and loving her, he killed her.

He described the living conditions in that house. Until then I
didn't know that Lisa did not have a room of her own, a dresser of
her own, or even a bed! She had slept on the living room couch.
How stupid I had been with my visions of pastel nurseries and
rainbows and clouds.

I had dreamed of plaid dresses with white collars, bright hair
ribbons and shiny patent-leather Mary Janes. They had dressed her
in clothes that were filthy and ill fitting.

I suppose the prosecution had to begin the presentation of its case
with the police officers and paramedics describing what they found
when they were called to the Steinberg apartment, but it was difficult for me to listen to.

When they first went in, it was very, very dark. All the bulbs
were either missing or burned out. The paramedics asked if they

could get more light—they were trying to resuscitate Lisa and they were working by flashlight.

That's when Steinberg asked if it was really important.

He didn't want them to see what the light would reveal, that Lisa was naked and dirty and severely beaten. The paramedics described the bruises on Lisa's body, the conditions under which she'd lived, the filth, the neglect.

I found out for the first time that Lisa was left to lie naked on the bathroom floor for twelve hours before the paramedics had been called.

And that if either Steinberg or Nussbaum had put aside their pride, or whatever stupidity it was that drove them, and called for help sooner, Lisa would have lived.

I felt as if . . . as if my heart were torn open.

You hear something like that, you think you've heard the worst; nothing can be more painful than this. The next day you go in there and you hear something even worse. The press kept asking me what was the hardest part of the trial. I'll tell you now, it all was.

Sometimes, despite all the warnings I'd had, tears would run down my face and I would cry, but very quietly.

The paramedics testified that Steinberg had been cool and calm in the ambulance. He had never touched or kissed the girl he claimed was his daughter.

They had never seen a parent behave that way.

The emergency-room nurse testified that Steinberg seemed unconcerned as they battled over the lifeless body of his "daughter." When they told him that Lisa had severe brain damage and was probably brain-dead, he asked, "Have you found anything else wrong with her?"

The nurse testified that she suspected child abuse and advised the doctor to notify the Bureau of Child Welfare. She said it loudly enough for Steinberg to hear. She *wanted* him to overhear. She wanted him to know that somebody was on to him.

What did he do then? Steinberg walked over to the stretcher on which Lisa lay unconscious, stood over her for a few seconds, patted her head—and swiftly left the hospital.

The testimony went up the medical hierarchy; paramedics to nurses to doctors. Every word, every sentence, opened a fresh wound in my heart. These were the people I had delivered my daughter to. I had given her into the hands of this man.

The neurosurgical resident came out and told Steinberg that he thought Lisa would live, but she had suffered irreversible brain damage.

Steinberg replied, "What you're saying is she won't be an Olympic athlete, right?"

It was clear he disgusted these people. He repulsed me. A reporter caught me off guard one evening on my way out of the courtroom. He asked me what I thought of Steinberg. I shot back that I didn't think he was human.

The witnesses told about the medical procedures Lisa was put through in a vain attempt to save her life. Steinberg's lawyer, Ira London, went through those in great detail because one of the defense's contentions was that the bruises on Lisa's body resulted from the medical procedures performed by the paramedics and/or the hospital staff. I was almost overcome listening to them describe the hole they drilled in her skull, the smell, the tubes and respirators they hooked up to her.

They went through every bruise on her body, describing its size, color, and age.

I thought I would scream.

In the breaks I'd go to the ladies' room, sob in hysterics, and always compose myself in time to return to the courtroom. At lunchtime I left the building for some air—I couldn't breathe inside—and then was instantly sorry, because the press besieged me. Stay inside and suffocate or venture out and face the mob.

Because of the suspicion of child abuse, the hospital photographer was called to photograph the bruises on Lisa's body. He took pictures of her legs, her back, her chest, her head. Those pictures—large color blowups—were introduced in evidence. They were shown to the jury and passed to the defense table while whoever was testifying talked about her injuries.

Whenever Steinberg had the pictures in his hands, he always conveniently held them up so I would get a clear view of my daughter's battered corpse. He did that on purpose, I know he did. Ostensibly he was holding them so he and Ira London could examine them simultaneously, but he always positioned the photos between their two bodies and leaned away so as not to block my view.

I, Lisa's mother, and he, Lisa's murderer, engaged in staring contests as he entered and left the courtroom, contests that Steinberg would lose, since he was forced by the proceedings to face forward. I would not have lost in any case. There was little I could do except to glare my hatred at this man, but that, in my daughter's name, I could do.

I wanted Steinberg to know that nothing they could do to him would be bad enough. And that if I had my chance, I would kill him myself.

We would hold each other's gaze for ten seconds, twenty seconds. He would always be the one to look away. This went on for about a week and a half. After that, he stopped trying and would look past me, over my head, ostentatiously scanning the courtroom. He was very interested in who was there.

Early on he tried to have me barred from the trial on the grounds that Lisa's grieving natural mother sitting in the courtroom might influence the jury against him. But I think the real reason was that I made him nervous. The judge refused to bar me, on condition that I make absolutely no public outbursts. I was warned that if I felt I was going to lose control, I should just get up and leave. Any display of emotion in the courtroom and they would remove me and keep me out.

Having failed to remove me from the courtroom, Steinberg tried, also unsuccessfully, to have me moved from the front row. My sitting there, inches away, was too much for him.

I'm glad.

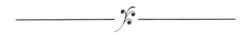

I missed only two afternoons of testimony. I stayed through the morning while the defense's expert pathologist from Minnesota testified, but I didn't come back that afternoon. He was getting into the question of the degree of force used to kill Lisa. I'd been through that. I didn't need to hear again that the blow that killed her had the force of a fall from a three-story building.

I also left early during the testimony of Amanda Wilhelm, a sixteen-year-old girl who lived on the same block as Lisa and whose younger sister played with her. Listening to someone who'd actually been a child with Lisa was harder somehow. Her testimony was more directly, poignantly childlike. I hung on and hung on—I'd been warned in no uncertain terms about making a spectacle of myself—and I managed to hold out until the DA said "no further questions." Then I got up and walked out of the courtroom. Bolted, actually.

I didn't come back for the cross-examination of the girl. Amanda had visibly been frightened; it was clearly a big ordeal for her. I couldn't take seeing Ira London put her through cross-examination. I didn't want to sit and watch somebody else's child suffer.

It seemed that there was no possible permutation of suffering that Lisa did not go through. There was even testimony of sexual abuse, of pornographic videos made of Lisa and a little boy. Even though those charges proved to be probably unfounded, it was hard to sit in the courtroom and listen to the torture inflicted on my baby. At times tears ran down my face, and I make no apology for that.

Oddly, the only time I saw any particular expression on Steinberg's face was when he turned toward Nussbaum as she was describing Travis, whom she called Mitchell. She was explaining why they had to tie him up, how active he was, how they had a rabbit cage and a fish tank and Travis would poke his hands into the fish tank and crawl inside the rabbit cage. As she spoke, Steinberg had a look of fond recollection on his face, a big smile.

It hit me hard. These people tied their curious toddler up so they could go into the next room and smoke cocaine unhindered! And he was nostalgic about it.

On the first anniversary of Lisa's death there was no court session because one of the jurors had an illness in the family. That night there was a candlelight vigil in her memory, in which I participated.

I stayed in my apartment alone during the trial. I couldn't bear to have anyone around. Each night I'd go home and sift through the piles of mail. I got hundreds, thousands, of letters, mass cards, notes of sympathy, all from strangers.

A small percentage of it was hate mail. They called me a prostitute and worse. They said I would burn in hell alongside Steinberg and Nussbaum. After I read a few of those I pretty much lost it, and Joe started screening my mail.

But I didn't need letters from strangers to remind me of my guilt. Lisa's sad eyes in the photo taken at a Halloween party mere days before her death were reproach enough to rob me of sleep.

I slept for no more than an hour at a time during the trial, sometimes only minutes, before I'd wake, screaming, in the cold sweat of nightmare. I ate almost nothing, knowing that whatever I ate I would vomit.

I vomited anyway, dry, painful heaves.

I'd come home from the trial and I would trash my apartment. Just throw things. Break things. Dishes. Vases. Some silk flowers I had around I tore into shreds. It started to get expensive. I tried to stick to pillows.

I started drinking heavily again. Many nights I got drunk in an attempt to block out the pain. It didn't help.

Each morning, I got up, dressed, and rode the train back into the city, to relive my daughter's agony.

And to come, for the first time, to know my daughter. I hadn't seen her since birth; all I would ever know of her was what I learned in the trial. I listened while witness after witness described how special she was, how graceful and smart and gifted. They told how articulate she was, how grown-up and ladylike she acted.

My child was a treasure any parent would be grateful to have. And I would never know her.

Lisa Launders came from a line of strong women. I claim nothing special for myself, but her grandmother and her great-grandmother—Mom and Nana—certainly are women you can emulate. It was that very strength that led to her undoing. Witness after witness testified that she was not only unusually beautiful, but outgoing, cheerful, precociously verbal, enchanting. Steinberg and Nussbaum used the child's strength against her. Had Lisa shown up at school whimpering, cringing, wetting her pants, inquiries would have been made. Lisa never did that. She never gave herself—or her "parents"—away.

To the contrary. To look at Lisa was to be sure she led exactly the kind of life I had wished for her. She chatted of art lessons, drew pictures, loved to dance. She seemed for all the world like a child who was cuddled in a mother's lap for a bedtime story while Daddy smiled nearby. Had she given a hint of what went on in that house, she might have lived.

Was it harder to listen to a picture of Lisa happy? It varied from day to day depending on my frame of mind of the moment. The truth is, there was nothing about this that didn't fill me with horror. Some people said that should have made me feel better. It made me feel worse. It made what happened all the more senseless. Steinberg robbed me of her twice; once when he kept her and then again when he killed her.

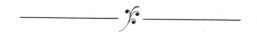

And I lost Kevin again, during the trial, and this time it's final. Even though we weren't as love struck as we had been when we were teenagers, still I thought he cared about me and still it hurt when two weeks into Steinberg's murder trial, I walked into a restaurant and saw Kevin with another girl.

I don't know why it hurt so much. I should've been getting used to it by now.

Chapter 24

$\mathcal{F}$ **I** sat in my place in the court-
room and listened to the stories about Lisa, the details of her life I
had hungered for.

At night, released from the need to control myself, I cried bitter
tears for the brave and magnificent soul that I had, however inadvertently, delivered into the hands of her killers.

I still say "killers," even though charges against Nussbaum had
been dropped in the first week of the trial on the grounds that she,
too, had been battered, physically and psychologically, and on the
condition that she testify against the man who was her great love.
For the sake of his pride she had allowed Lisa to die, for it is
incontrovertible that had Lisa received medical attention earlier,
had the flow of blood seeping into her brain been quenched, she
might well have lived.

She knew Steinberg well enough so that when he brought her
the comatose, half-naked body of her child, she suspected he might
have forced huge amounts of water so vigorously into her mouth
and nose that he had drowned her.

Did she call a doctor? Did she run next door for help? Did she
scream with anguish?

No. She helped Steinberg lay the unconscious child *facedown* on
the cold bathroom floor. Not on a blanket. Not on a bath mat or

towel. Not on her lap. Just the child's naked body on the stone-cold tiles.

And then she walked out. She sat down to do paperwork. She wanted to keep busy. To take her mind off the dying child in the next room.

Merciful God, she is like no mother I have ever known.

The district attorney may feel she is innocent, but I don't. I hold her completely culpable. Battered-women's syndrome—forget about it. This was no poverty-stricken woman with no place to go. She was an editor. She had parents, a sister. You can explain to me about battered-women's syndrome from now until the day I die, I'll never understand it. Let other people "understand" Hedda Nussbaum. Not me!

Maybe I don't wish to understand it. Some things I just cannot tolerate. I can't imagine anybody's looking at a child and wanting to hit her for any reason whatsoever.

I had a brief moment of sympathy for Nussbaum when I read about all those operations she had to have to repair the damage he did to her. Maybe I did feel a little compassion for her, but it evaporated as soon as she came walking through those doors into the courtroom and I saw her for the first time.

She became real—my daughter's "mommy." My daughter's murderer! Whatever compassion I might have had for her got wiped out that second. It was gone!

Hedda Nussbaum looked at me. Steinberg looked at her, then he'd follow her eyes to me. Frequently, he would turn around to look directly at me. The whole time Hedda was on the stand there was this weird, three-way thing going on. It was like a triangle, some wacko triangle I didn't want any part of. It just sickened me.

The testimony that had gone before was bad enough, but with Hedda it got really bizarre. The trances Steinberg claimed Hedda and Lisa fell into or were trying to put *him* into . . . all that garbage about his not letting Hedda eat and making her sleep in a bathtub. Not letting her go to the toilet. Beating her up, again and again. What kind of a woman is she? I was horrified to think two innocent babies were in that house watching these two weirdos play out their sex fantasies.

And they're all saying: Hedda, are you comfortable, do you want anything, a recess, a drink of water?

Enough of that!

She only became a prosecution witness to keep from standing trial. She couldn't save those kids but she sure knew how to save her own skin. She belongs in jail right along with Steinberg. Put them in the same cell, let them live out their fantasies. Let them enjoy each other. They can kill each other for all I care!

Instead, she's being put up in a hotel, getting room service, eating T-bone steaks, being escorted here and there—living like a queen and my tax dollars are paying for it! Why? She murdered my daughter as much as if she raised the fist that killed her! She had a year in a hospital to heal her wounds. My daughter has nothing but a grave!

I sat there, listening to Hedda talk . . . and all those images I had of Lisa . . . everything I held on to for six and a half years was gone. Everything I believed, everything I held sacred . . . was just finished. Destroyed. Everything was turned upside down.

Oh, my baby . . . This wasn't the way I meant it to be!

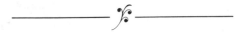

On weekends during the trial, I went to the cemetery to sit at Lisa's grave and beg her forgiveness. I wept and wondered what kind of a God could let this happen.

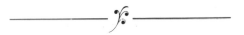

During the three months of the trial I tried not to look at the jury or even think about them. Nobody was going to accuse me of jury tampering. I didn't want to so much as catch the eye of a juror. I didn't want to get within ten feet of them. That bastard was not getting a mistrial because of me. I wasn't going through this a second time. Arriving in the morning or returning from lunch, we all pretty much got there at the same time. If I arrived at a bank of elevators at the same time as a member of the jury, I waited for the next car. I would not go up with them. I didn't even want to be in their vicinity, not even if there were other people around.

Once, I was already in the elevator when Jeremiah Cole, the jury foreman, entered. Steve, the bodyguard Joe Famighetti had gotten me, asked him a question—just making conversation: "Has anybody told you look like a young Barry Goldwater?"

I moved to the other end of the car—how far away can you get in an elevator? After Cole got out, I blew up at Steve. "Are you crazy? I don't care if you just said it's raining out, don't do that!"

The defense seemed to consist of a smorgasbord of theories, pick any one you liked. They contended that Lisa's fatal injuries might have been caused by the Emergency Medical Service workers or by the hospital staff in trying to resuscitate her. Or perhaps she had an obscure childhood disease called Reye's syndrome. Medical experts disposed of both those theories quite conclusively in my opinion.

Then came the question of whether or not Steinberg was insane. He refused to submit to prosecution psychiatrists for examination, so he couldn't claim insanity. Perhaps my favorite defense tactic was the one in which they claimed that Hedda Nussbaum was lying because she herself dealt Lisa the fatal blow, *but* if perchance the jury believed her testimony and felt that Steinberg was the killer, then his client was insane. "If she's correct, he's insane," the lawyer said.

The press speculated constantly as to whether or not Steinberg would take the stand in his own defense. I knew he wouldn't. Nancy Patterson of the DA's office had been filling me in during my lunchtime bouts with hysteria in the ladies' room. She tried to prepare me for what was going to happen next. She told me Steinberg wouldn't dare testify. That would open the way for cross-examination regarding his other criminal activities, drug-dealing, possible baby-selling.

The defense rested, quite suddenly. It seemed to me they had run out of even the most farfetched explanations of what happened to Lisa other than the obvious one, that Joel Steinberg had killed her.

I was absolutely certain the verdict would be first-degree murder. I thought the jury would stay out maybe an hour, maybe an hour and a half. Long enough to have a cup of coffee and a sandwich, just to make it look good.

They stayed out for eight long, and to me, incomprehensible days. Just when I thought it was finally over, the torment stretched on.

I was always on call, for they never knew when the verdict might come in. First I walked the halls. Then the DA got us a conference room with a VCR and some tapes. Who could watch a movie?

Four times we were called back to the courtroom, Steinberg being brought in from his holding cell. Each time the tension blistered. And each time it was a false alarm. The jury merely wanted testimony read back.

I couldn't understand what their problem was. Just declare the man guilty, sentence him to spend the rest of his life in jail, and go home.

I was in a restaurant across the street from the courthouse when they called me to the phone. Nancy Patterson told me the jury was in. They had a verdict. No more false alarms. This time it was for real.

I wanted to scream. I felt as if my body were going into convulsions. I was crying before I even got to the building. I remember running through a playground to get to the courthouse. Just as I reached the steps, Nancy Patterson came running out to meet me, to warn me that the press was mobbing the place. I didn't give a hang about the press. I didn't care about anything—except that they were finally going to send Steinberg to jail for life.

I raced to the courtroom. Everyone was waiting for me. They had pleaded with the judge to hold up the proceedings until I got there. I took my seat, bending down to hide my face. I couldn't stop crying. I don't think anybody could have.

The jury was brought in. I kept my head down to hide my tears; I had it so ingrained in me that I had to behave myself.

Anyway, if I'd met someone's eyes—especially *his*—I think I would have lost control completely.

The first charge was murder in the second degree. The jury foreman said not guilty.

I just died. I felt such emptiness. As if whatever little bit of my heart were left had been ripped out of me.

Now I was afraid to hear the next charge. Please, God, don't for some crazy reason let this man off! The court clerk read the second charge: "In the matter of the death of Lisa Steinberg, Joel Barnett Steinberg is charged with manslaughter in the first degree. How do you find the defendant Joel Barnett Steinberg?"

The jury foreman said, "Guilty."

Everyone was happy with that. I wasn't. I was miserable. My

whole body started to shake. If my life depended upon it, I couldn't have stopped the shaking. One juror was crying. It took me a while to realize it. I thought I was seeing my own tears.

I felt Steinberg had gotten away with murder.

They explained to me that the prosecution hadn't done badly in convicting Steinberg of a murder that, after all, nobody had seen. There were no witnesses to what happened that night. Only Hedda and Joel. And poor baby Travis. For the record, while I'm absolutely certain that Hedda did abuse Lisa, I'm also certain that she didn't strike the blows that killed her. That was Steinberg.

There was unquestionably a murder. A charge of murder would have been the right verdict in this case. I was astounded that they didn't get it because to me, anybody who would strike a child with the force that Steinberg struck Lisa, that's depravity.

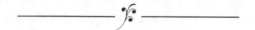

As far as the other participants go, Bergman obviously is beyond the law. A grand jury that was convened to reexamine our adoption laws—a good thing that came out of great evil as far as I'm concerned—failed to indict anyone else in Lisa's death. Their report said, "All others who actively participated in the illegal 'placing out' of the baby girl in 1981, escaped being charged with even the misdemeanor penalty . . . because the two-year statute of limitations had long since expired."

Of Hedda Nussbaum it is often said that she will have to find her own punishment in life. That's not good enough for me.

But at least it was over, and Lisa could rest. The very next morning, I went out to her grave.

Chapter 25

*ve never told anybody, but this is what I was thinking all during the trial, this is what made me go there every day: I felt that Lisa couldn't rest until this was over, and if I weren't there, she'd have to go through it alone. I gave her so little, my baby. At least I could give her that much. To be with her in whatever way I could, to help her through this last ordeal. She suffered so much in life. At least I wouldn't be leaving her alone at the end.

For the rest of my life I'm never going to escape the fact that if I'd done things differently, Lisa would be alive. Ultimately, I'm responsible. I'm the one who handed her over to the people who abused her, tortured her, and finally killed her. I'm going to have to try to find a way to live with that.

I had been angry with Kevin—"furious" is probably a better word. But I called him that night after I came back from the cemetery. I needed somebody to talk to, and he seemed like the right person, considering he was her father.

I called from Papa Jack's house. I stopped in there on my way home. Kevin came over—he lived down the block—and we went out for a drink. We tried to talk about what had happened—at least I did. He didn't have anything to say. Trying to get a response from him was like trying to get blood from a rock. It couldn't be done.

I wound up crying, tears of anger and frustration and hurt. The last thing I said to him was "I hope you can live with the fact that you didn't do a goddamned thing for your daughter."

I slammed the door in his face.

I used to think that Kevin only appeared to be distant and cold, that underneath he was covering his real emotion. He wasn't. There was nothing there. There never was anything there. Never.

He only went to the cemetery once that I know of. It was a Wednesday during the trial. He called me suddenly and said he wanted to see Lisa's grave. He wanted me to come with him. I don't think he would have gone alone.

He was quiet on the way up. The day was pleasant and I enjoyed the trip; it felt like coming home to me.

He held me for a long time—that's all he did, hold me. For Kevin, I guess he was displaying a lot of emotion. As much as Kevin can.

The footstone was there, the stone we had paid for together. The headstone for the family plot bore the name McGrane; I had asked for and received permission to put up a special footstone to mark Lisa's grave. But then it took a couple of months to get around to doing it. I kept stalling. I finally went with Mom to the place where you buy gravestones. The guy had a dog; I remember playing a lot with his dog, throwing sticks for that dumb dog. It was all an excuse not to do what I had to do. I can't imagine anything more final than picking a stone for a grave. It took me about three hours to make a simple decision. Mom and the stonecutter are discussing different kinds of granite, I'm playing ball with the dog.

Then we had to decide on the words to put on her stone.

I spoke to Kevin about it. I asked if I could put his name. He said no, he didn't want anything about him on it.

I didn't want to take that for an answer. I gave him a little more time to think about it. In the meantime, I was thinking about the rest of it. I had decided on "God's Little Angel, Elizabeth 'Lisa' Launders," but I wanted my name on it, and Kevin's if he'd let me.

I called Kevin about a week and a half later, and this time he agreed that his name—his first name only—could appear on Lisa's footstone.

I put Kevin's name first, which I think was very nice of me. Mom

even asked if I was sure I wanted it that way, all things considered.
I said yes.

They say that the hardest tragedy to bear is the loss of a child.
How much more so when you never had the chance to hold that
child in your arms, to love her and comfort her and cherish her?
And even more so when through no fault of yours, your child is
sentenced to a life of torture and a needless, senseless, lonely death.
People who lose a child through accident or illness at least have
memories. I have only a few pictures, some secondhand anecdotes,
and a grave to visit.

Someone told me that when Hedda Nussbaum visited the grave,
she commented that the footstone was small. Then she broke down
in tears, crying, "What's the point, Lisa's not here."

I hope she doesn't think Lisa's with *her.*

As far as Joel Steinberg goes, Judge Rothwax sentenced him to
the maximum. He is to serve from eight and a third to twenty-five
years. The judge recommended against parole.

I would have liked to see him spend the rest of his life in jail.

As the primary victim, I was invited to meet with the sentencing
board prior to the sentence's being pronounced. I requested two
things: maximum sentence to be served, with no time off, and that
Steinberg be placed in the general prison population. Even criminals
don't care for child-killers.

I've never in my whole life really wished pain on someone. Cancer.
Torture. Agony. Wishing harm on somebody is totally against my
religion. They say forgiveness is divine. You're supposed to find it
in your heart to forgive. Well, I haven't gotten that far yet. And
if he's waiting for my forgiveness, Joel Steinberg will have a long
wait. Till eternity, and after, because there never will be such a
time.

I don't know what exactly I expected when I came forward publicly
as Lisa's mother, but to my great surprise the reaction of the public
and the press has been, from the first, positive, even favorable. The
press at times tried to paint me as a brave person, someone of unusual
courage, someone to be admired. Nothing could be further from the
truth. I'm the most ordinary person you could ever hope to meet. I

still can't believe some of the things that happened to me. I was frightened most of the time, and in great anguish all the time. I just kept putting one foot in front of the other, trying each day to do what needed to be done, and to do it with as much dignity as I could manage.

I got hundreds of letters, a great outpouring of support and sympathy. People wrote me to express their sorrow over Lisa's death, and to say that they prayed for her soul and for strength for me. Many of them wrote that they had cried for Lisa and wanted to share their grief.

To all of you, I am grateful.

Some spoke of Lisa as "our child" and wrote that she belonged to us all. They were right. In the end, an entire city claimed Lisa. In the end, she belonged to everyone.

"She has touched the hearts of all without ever knowing it," a letter said. "May her soul rest in peace."

Amen.

I got letters from birth mothers who had gone on to have several other children, while never for a moment forgetting the one they had given up. They understood that adoption itself was not at fault. Lisa had not been adopted, she had been abducted.

One woman wrote, "I just feel so awful that this could happen when you were trying to do such a beautiful thing. It was so brave of you to give birth to her and put her up for adoption. There are so many good, deserving couples wanting to adopt, and not enough babies to fill the need. You did the right thing. I'm sure I speak for many people who want to say how much they support you through this difficult time. You can be sure that the reaction to this tragedy will prevent abuses in the future, and so some good will come of it."

That is my hope.

That is one of the main reasons I'm writing this book. I want people to *know!* I want the laws changed so this can never happen again. I want teachers trained to recognize child abuse and better channels set up to report it.

Immediately after the funeral, Joe's office was besieged with phone calls and letters from every newspaper, magazine, and television show you can name. Phil Donahue, *Good Morning America*—you name it, they all wanted me to appear for interviews. At the time I told Joe not even to bring it up to me.

Maybe now the time has come. Maybe it's time to shout and scream and make enough noise so we will be heard. They say that Lisa fell through the cracks in the system. If I can be an advocate for all the other children still living who are in danger of falling through those cracks—so be it.

One thing I don't want to see is our laws changed in a way that would diminish a woman's right to control her own body. I was then—and still am—pro-choice. At the time I came forward, I was widely quoted as saying that if I had wanted Lisa killed, I would have had an abortion. That is untrue. I never made that statement. I couldn't have. It goes against everything I believe. That I didn't choose to have an abortion is my right. I would never deny another woman the freedom to choose on her own. Any sensible person knows that it is disastrous to bring unwanted children into this world. They wind up being small sacrifices to an egotistical philosophy.

I would like to work toward the founding of homes where unwed pregnant women could come to wait out their pregnancies and then, without pressure and with the benefit of counseling, give their child up for adoption or not, as they decide. I've gotten letters that have moved me to tears from adoptive parents who say that not a day goes by that they don't thank God for the gift they have been given and pray for the birth mother who found the wisdom and the courage to give her child to others to raise when they could not.

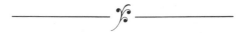

"Michele, I hope this thought will help you," one letter said. "You have a little Angel in Heaven that will be watching over you always and praying for you. She is at peace and happy with God. Hopefully all her sufferings won't be in vain and society will recognize and help other children who are being abused."

I often read through the letters. It's amazing how astute they are, how knowingly the writers guessed at my emotions. A woman wrote, "I pray that God gives you the strength and wisdom not to perpetuate this tragedy by blaming yourself. You did the best that you could do, and we would all do many things differently in hindsight."

I do blame myself. But perhaps a little less with each passing month and year. I hope so, because I do know that until I shake off this burden of guilt, or at least make it manageable, the ruin of my life, too, must be added to the tally against Joel Steinberg.

One of the notes I got said that until I forgive myself, Lisa will not be completely at rest. I hope that's not true, because I have a way to go before I can do that.

Something happened in October of last year that made me understand how important it is that I come to grips with what happened. Through Joe I'm suing Joel Steinberg and Hedda Nussbaum, the estate of Michael Bergman, Jackie Cohn Bergman, Ginny Liebrader, the New York City Police Department, the Board of Education, the Department of Human Resources, and others, on behalf of Lisa and myself.

The first step was to have me declared administrator of my daughter's estate. The judge who heard the case, Eugene Nardelli of the State Supreme Court in Manhattan, ruled that I was not entitled to sue for damages on the grounds that *I had abandoned Lisa by giving her up for adoption.*

Mom broke me the news of the judge's decision over the phone.

I screamed, just let out a wild scream. I ran out without even bothering to hang up the phone.

I couldn't listen to any more. I couldn't take any more.

I ran out of the house, down to the ocean where I always go when I'm troubled. I walked around for a while. I called Graceann and tried to tell her what had happened. I couldn't get the words out; I was mumbling and raving. When she finally understood, she said, "Michele, are you sure?"

I just sobbed into the phone. Graceann said, "Michele, where are you?"

She came and got me. We went to a neighborhood restaurant and just sat there, talking. Finally, it was about eight-thirty, nine o'clock. I knew Mom would be looking for me. We went back to my house, and of course Mom was there, pretty frantic. We went back to the restaurant and talked some more. That is, they talked; I was mostly silent.

I was thinking about Lisa. Every day it seems you read about women leaving their newborn babies in garbage cans, in airplane rest rooms, in vacant lots. Judge Nardelli had put me in that category.

Something began to change in my thinking. I *had* done everything right. I had gone to an obstetrician who had recommended a lawyer.

They were professionals. I abided by their advice. Any money they asked for I paid them.

Never was it my intention to abandon Lisa.

The judge slandered me and every other woman who makes a plan for her child and surrenders it for adoption.

Adoption is the third option. There is abortion. One can also keep a child one is unprepared to raise, the way the so-called pro-lifers urge. And one can give it up for adoption. If they take away that third option, what have we left? Either more abortions or more unloved and unwanted children growing up to murder and steal and deal in the latest lethal designer drug.

I will stand by any woman who chooses to have an abortion—and not just in cases of rape or incest.

I will stand behind any woman who chooses to keep her baby. There is no such thing as an illegitimate child.

And I will stand behind any woman who makes a plan for her baby that involves giving it up for adoption. I will never consider adoption to be abandonment. I have personally seen the joy that it brings to all concerned. Despite what happened to me, I have the good sense to know that.

The important thing is that the girl or woman be helped to make an informed choice without pressure. I can't imagine the feelings of a woman finally nerving herself up to have an abortion—never a decision made pleasantly or easily—and having to face down a group of screaming lunatics outside the clinic. Or worse; women's clinics have been bombed, and I think that's an outrage. I know people have a right to demonstrate, to voice their opinion, but not when they interfere with the basic rights of others. There's no right more basic than control of your own body.

We have to stop those who want to take this control away from us. And we are not alone.

A few days after the Judge Nardelli's decision, people gathered on the courthouse steps in a miserable rainstorm to protest his de-cision. And I am going to appeal. This cannot be allowed to stand, and I am finally beginning to understand that it is up to us to determine whether we will be victims or not.

I had a choice, too. I could let the judge's decision be the final straw in my total destruction—and I could easily have gone that way, let me tell you. I found my healing at Lisa's grave.

November 4 is the day they declared Lisa brain-dead and on the fifth, they turned off her respirator. That's the date I keep as the anniversary of her death and I visit her grave. I had been in Pennsylvania for my aunt's wedding, and I drove the whole three hours back to Westchester sobbing in the car. When I got to the cemetery, of course my pal the photographer from the *New York Post* was there waiting for me.

I stood at her gravesite, and after a few minutes I went over to him and said, "Enough. Enough with the pictures."

He said, "What, no tears this time?"

I thought, no, there aren't. You weren't here two weeks ago after the judge's decision. You weren't up here when I sat for an hour and a half. That's when you would have seen tears.

That was the day when I came to peace. I had a long talk with Lisa in my mind. I tried for a long time to explain to her that nobody in this world loves her more than I do and I did *not* abandon her.

And suddenly I realized that she knew that.

Lisa knows what I did or didn't do. The only one I have to answer to is her.

When I came to understand that, a great weight lifted off my shoulders. I got a sign from her—nothing overt, nothing anybody could see, just a feeling inside myself.

Lisa gave me the go-sign. She said, "It's okay. You can go forward. You can live."

When that photographer goaded me with a snicker on his face, my first reaction was to be hurt. And then a smile came on my face. I just turned and walked away from him.

He can't hurt me anymore. Nobody can hurt me anymore.

I can be at her grave quietly now, without crying.

"Lisa is in the best playground of all. God's playground." Someone wrote that in one of the notes I found on her grave and I think it's true. In my mind she's nine years old and I imagine her skipping rope and playing hopscotch and doing all the things nine-year-olds do. I know I'm not actually seeing her, but the picture is so real in my mind that I watch her and smile.

I never heard her laugh in life, but sometimes as I sit at her grave, I think I hear a child's happy laugh. I don't turn my head. I know it's Lisa.